CW01035046

Christ Unab

Christ Unabridged

Knowing and Loving the Son of Man

Edited by

George Westhaver
and
Rebekah Vince

scm press

© Editor and Contributors 2020

Published in 2020 by SCM Press
Editorial office
3rd Floor, Invicta House,
108–114 Golden Lane,
London EC1Y 0TG, UK
www.scmpress.co.uk

SCM Press is an imprint of Hymns Ancient & Modern Ltd
(a registered charity)

Hymns Ancient & Modern® is a registered trademark of
Hymns Ancient & Modern Ltd
13A Hellesdon Park Road, Norwich,
Norfolk NR6 5DR, UK

All rights reserved. No part of this publication may be reproduced,
stored in a retrieval system, or transmitted,
in any form or by any means, electronic, mechanical,
photocopying or otherwise, without the prior permission of
the publisher, SCM Press.

Scripture quotations are from the New Revised Standard Version Bible: Anglicized
Edition, copyright © 1989, 1995 National Council of the Churches of Christ in
the United States of America. Used by permission. All rights reserved worldwide.

The cover image, 'Dream of the Virgin', by Simone dei Crocifissi (1330–1399)
is used by kind permission of The Society of Antiquaries of London ©.

The Authors has asserted their right under the Copyright,
Designs and Patents Act 1988
to be identified as the Author of this Work

British Library Cataloguing in Publication data

A catalogue record for this book is available
from the British Library

ISBN 978 0 334 05828 1

Typeset by Manila Typesetting Company
Printed and bound by CPI Group (UK) Ltd

Contents

List of Contributors

Lewis Ayres, Professor of Catholic and Historical Theology at Durham University, and Professorial Fellow at the Institute for Religion and Critical Inquiry of the Australian Catholic University in Melbourne.

John Behr, Fr Georges Florovsky Distinguished Professor of Patristics at St Vladimir's Seminary, New York, and Metropolitan Kallistos Chair of Orthodox Theology, Vrije Universiteit, Amsterdam.

Anthony Burton, Rector of the Church of the Incarnation, Dallas, and sometime Bishop of Saskatchewan, Canada.

David Curry, Rector of Christ Church, and Chaplain and Teacher at King's-Edgehill School, Windsor, Nova Scotia.

Paul Dominiak, Vice Principal of Westcott House, Cambridge.

Simon Francis Gaine, O.P., Fellow of Blackfriars, Oxford, and Regent of the English Dominicans.

Malcolm Guite, Poet, writer, and Chaplain of Girton College, Cambridge.

Carol Harrison, Lady Margaret Professor of Divinity and Canon of Christ Church, Oxford.

Andrew Louth, Professor Emeritus of Patristic and Byzantine Studies in the Department of Theology and Religion at Durham University, and Rector of the Orthodox Parish of St Cuthbert and St Bede, Durham.

Ian McFarland, Robert W. Woodruff Professor of Theology at Emory University, Atlanta, Georgia, sometime Regius Professor of Divinity in the University of Cambridge.

Oliver O'Donovan, Professor Emeritus in Christian Ethics and Practical Theology at the School of Divinity in the University of Edinburgh, and sometime Regius Professor of Moral and Pastoral Theology and Canon of Christ Church, Oxford.

Polycarpus Augin Aydin, Metropolitan and Patriarchal Vicar for the Archdiocese of the Netherlands of the Syriac Orthodox Church.

Lydia Schumacher, Reader in Historical and Philosophical Theology at King's College London, and Director of the European Research Council Project on Early Franciscan Thought.

Robin Ward, Principal of St Stephen's House, Oxford.

Kallistos Ware, Assistant Bishop in the Greek Orthodox Archdiocese of Thyateira and Great Britain, sometime Spalding Lecturer of Eastern Orthodox Studies at the University of Oxford and Fellow of Pembroke College, Oxford.

George Westhaver, Principal of Pusey House, Oxford.

Rowan Williams, Master of Magdalene College, Cambridge, sometime Archbishop of Canterbury and Lady Margaret Professor of Divinity, Oxford.

N. T. Wright, Professor of New Testament and Early Christianity at the University of St Andrews, and Senior Research Fellow at Wycliffe Hall, Oxford, sometime Bishop of Durham, Dean of Lichfield, and Canon of Westminster.

Johannes Zachhuber, Professor of Historical and Systematic Theology, Fellow and Tutor in Theology at Trinity College, Oxford.

Acknowledgements

This volume draws together and develops the papers presented at the conference 'Totus Christus: Knowing and Loving the Son of Man', 9–11 July 2018 at Pusey House, Oxford. In other words, behind this book lies the labour of those who helped to fund, organize and assist the running of the conference. Petter Kringberg produced publicity and service booklets, as well as coordinating the large team of volunteers who cheerfully assisted with different tasks and jobs each day. Ryan Cox kept the House in order and running smoothly. The librarian Anna James welcomed visitors and booksellers to the library and to the House, and once again provided the *pains au chocolat* at breakfast. The steward Karen Westhaver ensured that our guests had a place to stay. Louis Harris helped with recording the lectures. We are especially grateful for the support and gracious cooperation of St Cross College, with whom Pusey House shares both buildings and a common life. The hard work of Flori Olteanu and the catering team at St Cross produced the refreshments and the fine meals that sustained us during three of the hottest days of the summer. The sacristan Richard Keeble enabled us to offer edifying worship by coordinating the serving teams at the liturgies. The Master of the Music Matthew Reese, the choir, and all the angels attending upon us, beautified and elevated the worship. We are also most grateful to Archpriest Stephen Platt, Rector of the Parish of St Nicholas the Wonderworker, and to Fr Ian Graham, parish priest of the Greek Orthodox community of the Holy Trinity, for leading Vespers one evening at the conference.

Finally, the book came to fruition only with the support and encouragement of David Shervington and Mary Matthews at SCM, and all who worked with them, including Rachel Geddes and Kate Hughes. We are grateful to Francis Young for again producing the index for this volume. We would also like to thank David Harris for his work on designing the book cover, and the Society of Antiquaries, London, for permission to use the image 'Dream of the Virgin' by Simone dei Crocifissi (1330–99), an image that evokes at least some of the many registers of the *Totus Christus* explored in this book.

We are especially grateful to the following sponsors whose support made the conference and the ensuing volume possible:

The Fellowship of St Alban and St Sergius
The Anglican Association
The Prayer Book Society
The Anglican and Eastern Churches Association
The St Theosevia Centre for Christian Spirituality
Lady Peel Legacy Trust
The John Bishop Charitable Trust

To God be the Glory.

Introduction

Christ Unabridged

Good Measure[1]

Luke 6.38: Give, and it will be given to you. A good measure, pressed down, shaken together, running over, will be put into your lap; for the measure you give will be the measure you get back.

More than good measure, measure of all things
Pleroma overflowing to our need,
Fullness of glory, all that glory brings,
Unguessed-at blessing, springing from each seed,
Even the things within the world you make
Give more than all they have for they are more
Than all they are. Gifts given for the sake
Of love keep giving; draw us to the core,
Where love and giving come from: the rich source
That wells within the fullness of the world,
The reservoir, the never spent resource,
Poured out in wounded love, until it spilled
Even from your body on the cross;
The heart's blood of our maker shed for us.

1 Originally published in Malcolm Guite, *Parable and Paradox* (Norwich: Canterbury Press, 2016).

I

One Mystery in Many Forms

GEORGE WESTHAVER

The Christian faith has only one object, which is the mystery of Christ dead and risen. But this unique mystery subsists under different forms: it is prefigured in the Old Testament, it is accomplished historically in the earthly life of Christ, it is contained in a mystery in the sacraments, it is lived mystically in souls, it is accomplished socially in the Church, it is consummated eschatologically in the heavenly kingdom. Thus the Christian has at his disposal several registers, a multi-dimensional symbolism, to express this unique reality. (Jean Daniélou)[1]

In this beautiful evocation of the Christian faith, Jean Daniélou invites us to delight in the different forms of the mystery of Christ dead and risen. It is a mystery complex and rich enough for unceasing speculation and praise, and at the same time supremely simple, personal and intimate. We apprehend and know this mystery not from a distance, but by responding with love and faith. This volume draws together the papers presented at a conference in July 2018 at Pusey House, Oxford: 'Totus Christus: Knowing and Loving the Son of Man'. The authors who contemplate and examine the different forms of this mystery in these pages demonstrate that, far from being exhaustive, Daniélou's words can only gesture towards a unique reality characterized by divine excess, a glory that indwells and overflows the divine and creaturely forms – ecclesial, liturgical, sacramental, biblical and theological – by which we know and grasp it. The chapters both present the rich complexity of the mystery of the whole Christ and describe the knowing and loving that are a response and an apprehension of the mystery, a dwelling in and with Christ Jesus in the bosom of the Father, as a creature among creatures, and the author and perfecter of all faith and all praise.

The book is in five parts, which arrange the chapters both historically and thematically. Each part is introduced and beautified with a poem by Malcolm Guite. These poetic invocations of the Incarnation – what Guite calls 'the supreme act of divine poesis' – assist us to ascend and descend with the theological angels 'from heaven to Earth, from Earth to heaven', to adopt a Shakespearean phrase that Guite examines in detail in his chapter.

This Introduction offers short summaries of each part to provide an overview of the whole volume and to show why the chapters belong together, suggesting also how common themes and ideas help to amplify our appreciation of the mystery of Christ. Hopefully, these summaries will also enable readers to discover the richness of the presentations for themselves, to find their way deeper into the mystery.

Part 1 – Christ the True Temple, True Sabbath and True Human Being

In Chapter 2, 'Son of Man and New Creation', Tom Wright argues that the way that the earliest followers of Jesus would have understood the title 'Son of Man' was shaped especially by the prophecy in Daniel 7, which describes 'one like a son of man' who is 'coming on the clouds' to the Ancient of Days. The narratives of creation, and of God's battle with the forces of chaos in Genesis, Exodus and the Psalms, also shaped the reception of both the title 'Son of Man' and Daniel's prophecy in 'the Jewish world of Jesus' day'. While modern readers might be tempted to write off the significance of such symbolic narratives as reflecting an outdated and primitive worldview, Wright challenges the reader to consider if we 'late-flowering Epicureans' are not rather blinded by empirical assumptions and a sensibility that banishes God or spiritual powers from the world.

In the conceptual world shaped by Genesis and Exodus, and by the expectation that God would bring together heaven and earth, 'the Temple was where heaven and earth overlapped, pointing forward to the day when they would be joined together for ever', while 'the Sabbath was the regular day when the Age to Come appeared in the midst of the Present Age'. In this context, Wright argues, the presentation of 'one like a son of man' to the Ancient of Days, 'there to receive kingly authority', pictures not the '*second coming*' of the Son of Man, but 'his *vindication and exaltation*'; '[t]he movement is upward, not downward'. This prophecy of 'the Messiah's exaltation and enthronement' also promises the conquest of the chaotic powers of evil and the vindication of God's suffering, righteous people by the one who 'stands in for "Israel as a whole"'. For followers of Jesus, his death and resurrection revealed him to be 'the one who all along was equal with the Creator' and 'the place where, and the means by which, heaven and earth were coming together'. In this Son of Man, 'the new day' arrives toward which the 'symbols' of the Temple and the Sabbath 'had been pointing'.

In Chapter 3, John Behr's description of 'the figure of the Son of Man' in the Gospel of John illuminates and complements Wright's account while at the same time adding new elements to the picture. Behr's presentation revolves around Jesus' enigmatic reply to Nathanael in John 1.51, 'Truly, truly, I say to you, you will see heaven opened, and the angels of God ascending and descending upon the Son of Man.' Like Wright, Behr emphasizes that the Son of Man is one in whom heaven and earth come together, 'an intermediary, a figure who embraces both heaven and earth, in himself'. Also complementing Wright's presentation, Behr argues that the Gospel of John describes the work of Christ as 'a carefully framed account of Jesus' construction of the true Temple of God, which he himself is and which climaxes when he is crucified'. The same event also fulfils the promise of the Sabbath; when Christ rests in the tomb 'God ceases from his work, for his project is completed'. This project, 'to create a human being in his image and likeness' or, in the words of Isaiah, 'to make the human being forever', continues in the Church, who is 'the true "mother of the living"', and she who perfects what 'the figure of the "woman"' in John's Gospel promises. Behr argues that in Christ we have 'the completion or perfecting, the appearance or unveiling, of God's project announced from the beginning'.

Part 2 – Christ the Word and Wisdom of God in Human Form

The chapters in the next section ponder how we can know God or speak of God who cannot be contained by human thought or comprehensively expressed by human words. At the same time, in asking how we can know God, or how divine knowledge can be communicated in human form, the authors reveal more about the kind of wisdom and life that we find in God, and more about how the divine Word is lived or spoken in us.

In Chapter 4, Ian McFarland considers what we can learn about our knowledge of God and Christian life from St Paul's enigmatic comment that we no longer know Christ 'from a human point of view', or 'according to the flesh' (2 Cor. 5.16). McFarland points out that there is more here than simply a statement of the theologically obvious, that having been raised from the dead, the life which Christ lives is not a normal human life. To get a clearer view of the question, he widens the lens to ask how we can know or perceive God at all: 'as the transcendent cause of all that is, the one who is not reducible to any item in the universe, but equally related to all as its immediate cause, God's presence in the world is inherently hidden'. Having surveyed this landscape, McFarland uses the Chalcedonian description of the two natures of the Lord Jesus Christ united in one hypostasis 'without confusion or change' as a means of considering how in the Incarnation the invisible God emerges from hiddenness 'to encounter the creature as creature'. While Jesus shares a complete human nature, what makes him different is his hypostasis, 'his identity, or *who* he is'. Unique among human beings, his divine hypostasis, his identity as the eternal Word, 'pre-exists' his humanity. This focus on the significance of the divine hypostasis orders McFarland's consideration of the transformation that the human nature of the man Christ Jesus undergoes in the resurrection and the ascension. He argues that while Jesus continues to live or subsist 'humanly', he does so 'outside the realm of space and time', or not according to the flesh, not according to the 'web of secondary causes' that orders the world as we know it. This also establishes 'a new possibility for human existence', so that all those who are children of God receive their life directly from God. This is what it means to be forgiven, 'that one's identity is not determined by one's past actions'. What St Paul says of Christ is true of all Christians: 'our humanity is no longer to be understood *kata sarka*, according to the possibilities of created cause and effect within space and time'. Not knowing Christ from a human point of view is not a loss, but rather an invitation to know in a way that exceeds the capacity of human nature, to know that an individual may remain entirely human while becoming, by grace, 'entirely God in soul and body'.

In Chapter 5, 'Sound and Silence in Augustine's Christological Interpretation of Scripture', Carol Harrison reformulates McFarland's question about how we can know the invisible God who is hidden in the world to ask how we can speak about God or utter sounds about God who abides hidden in divine silence: 'how *does* sound, how do words . . . communicate what is unknowable and ineffable'? Whereas we may think of silence as an absence or an emptiness, for Augustine, 'silence is in fact the fullness of God's eternal and immutable substance'. Considering a recently discovered sermon alongside the *Confessions*, Harrison asks 'how we move from words spoken in time' – from McFarland's phenomenal world and its network of secondary causes – 'to the eternal Word; from the mutable to the immutable . . . from sound to silence'. She shows that this movement 'is achieved in and through the temporal, mutable sound of the divine Mediator, the Word incarnate'. It is part of the paradox of mediating the fullness of divine substance with earthbound sounds that the 'most successful words or sounds' are those that are 'open-ended, allusive and indeterminate'. By considering the different ways in which the Word is presented in Scripture, Augustine's reflections on language and speech become a discussion of ecclesiology and Christology, of 'the three natures of the Word of God (his eternal Godhead, his incarnate Godhead and manhood, and his union with the body of the Church)'. Harrison argues that sound is another form of the Incarnation – 'Sound is like the flesh of the incarnate Christ', it is 'sacramental', 'the form that silence takes'. An appreciation of the sacramental character of language and sound also shapes our appreciation of the whole Christ who is communicated and given in sacramental signs and forms.

In Chapter 6, 'How Could the Earthly Jesus Have Taught Divine Truth?', one of two contributions in this volume which supplement papers from the 2018 conference, Simon Gaine, O.P., considers the problem of communicating divine knowledge in a human way with the help of Thomas Aquinas and the Thomist tradition. Focusing on Jesus as the 'Revealer' of 'the truth about God', he argues that it is not enough simply to assert that 'Christ can teach us humanly about divine things because his divine knowledge is the source of this teaching'. Even if one grants that Christ enjoyed the beatific vision, 'the highest participation of a created intellect in God's knowledge', this does not give an adequate account of how such knowledge, which is 'transcendently disproportionate to the workings of the finite human mind', could nonetheless 'be expressed or articulated by the finite mind'. Without this capacity, while Jesus the man might have been in full possession of divine knowledge, he could not have communicated this knowledge in a way that would be intelligible apart from a series of epistemological miracles. Gaine offers three possibilities that would explain how Christ might 'render his ineffable knowledge "effable" or speakable'. He proposes a kind of analogical thinking in reverse which, rather than apprehending or abstracting ideas or concepts from sense data, instead extracts or distils discursive thought or sensible images from the beatific vision. He argues that what is known '*in* the inexpressible vision of God' – 'God's effects' rather than his essence – might be translated by 'similitudes or finite ideas', which could then be communicated accessibly and effectively. In this way, Gaine's argument both helps us to appreciate the work of 'Christ the teacher', who 'teaches us about divine things *humanly*', and invites us to consider that what is communicated and given are not just ideas, but a participation in the knowledge by which God knows himself.

Part 3 – Christ the Centre Indwelling and Perfecting All Things

The chapters in this section consider how the Son of God reconciles all created things in himself, how 'the universal' indwells 'every particular'. By becoming a creature, the Son of God who speaks divine truth in a human manner also communicates divine life in particular or earthly forms in the sacraments of the Church.

In Chapter 7, 'The Centre of Everywhere', Lydia Schumacher directs our gaze to the Franciscan Summa, the 'Summa Halensis', named for Alexander of Hales (1185–1245) and completed more than 20 years before Thomas Aquinas (1225–1274) began his much better-known work. According to the *Summa Halensis*, all creatures express an 'idea' that already exists perfectly in God. In Trinitarian terms, it is the Son who receives these 'ideas' from the Father and then instantiates them, or 'carries them out', in the Holy Spirit. The Son is 'Archetype' and 'Exemplar' as well as 'the centre of everything because the basis for every being comes from him'. While on the one hand, 'there is no commensurability between the finite and the infinite', on the other, there is a kind of similarity between the Son and human beings made in his image. While the Son contains the 'ideas' for all creatures in himself, the human being is able to 'contemplate a mental likeness' of these creatures, and this thinking is a kind of intellectual power to unite and to 'encompass all created things'. The human being's special role as a microcosm of the whole universe is the basis of the Summa's argument that, even without the fall, Christ would probably have become incarnate in order to bring all created things to perfection by uniting them through humanity to

7

God. Schumacher concludes: 'God's primary intention in becoming incarnate was to establish his place as the centre of everything by joining himself to the one being, the human being, to whom all beings are ordered and through whom he can be joined to all beings, thereby achieving their completion and perfection.' To contemplate the whole Christ is to contemplate the origin and perfection of all creatures in 'the universal' who becomes 'every particular', who reconciles 'all creatures to himself once and for all', and who gives to humanity the vocation to order and guide all created things toward 'the meaning and significance they have in him'.

The following three chapters consider the way in which the divine Son, the centre of everything, both enlivens and unites his body the Church, and orders all creation to himself through the divine and creaturely gifts of the sacraments. In Chapter 8, 'Christ in the Eucharist', Andrew Louth takes us back to Augustine who serves as a particular inspiration for the theologians considered in the remaining chapters of this section. Louth argues that for Augustine the idea of the 'totus Christus' means not just a loose association, not merely that the Church and Christ are 'bound up together', but that 'We become Christ, *Christus*, himself'. The Christian's voice and song is the voice and song of Christ, and the love of Christ is 'the lifeblood of the Church'. Louth argues that Augustine works out his understanding of an 'ontological identity between Christ's head and Christ's members' especially in relation to the Eucharist where we find together 'the One who offers and the One who is offered'; 'For we have become his own body and by his mercy what we receive, that we are'. Louth emphasizes that while this is an objective reality, it is not a static one; 'the Liturgy, the Eucharist is an *action*, an action performed by Christ'. In gathering us together with himself in that offering, and in gifting himself to us, Christ also makes us to be gifts to one another: 'every person who comes back from the holy chalice is Christ'. To receive and know the whole Christ in this way is not just to be joined together externally, but to live from within a shared and graced existence that we have only as Christ together.

In Chapter 9, Paul Dominiak illustrates how 'an Augustinian sensibility of the *totus Christus*, the whole Christ' is worked out in the theology of the English reformer and divine Richard Hooker. Dominiak argues that what Hooker says about the government of the Church in his *Laws of Ecclesiastical Polity* emerges from 'a greater vision of the Church as the ecclesial reception of the divine life through its participation in the whole of Christ'. Hooker puts 'the Athanasian *dictum* in Elizabethan language, "God became human that humans might be made divine"'. Dominiak's treatment of Hooker also highlights an argument we have encountered in the chapters by Wright, Behr and Schumacher, that by re-creating the human being and becoming a creature among creatures, God seeks to complete and perfect the whole creation. Or, in Hooker's words, 'the participation of God himselfe' is not just for those 'incorporated into Christ' by baptism, but rather this returning and rest in God is 'the purpose of creation', what all created things 'covet more or lesse'.

Speaking more specifically of the Church, Dominiak displays Hooker's Augustinian sensibility by showing how Hooker develops themes examined by Harrison and Louth. For Hooker, the union with the 'verie mother of our new birth' is both the result of the 'generative force' of the sacraments and also a sharing in the one voice of Christ, 'his speaking into us and our being heard in him'. The participation which Dominiak describes is both liturgical and ethical. The 'generative force' of the sacraments is matched by an interior or ethical kind of transformation, a 'transubstantiation' of the members of the body of Christ. The worship of the Church is a 'liturgical training' that shapes 'holie desires'. These desires are not merely transient affections, but a real participation in the love of Christ: 'Hooker's account of worship constructs the Church as a school of virtue preparing for the fullness of beatific union given gratuitously through God's grace and participation in the ascended and glorified Christ'.

In Chapter 10, 'Reasoning upon the Essentials', the second that supplements the papers presented at the 2018 'Totus Christus' conference, David Curry examines what it means to be 'partakers of the divine nature' with the help of Lancelot Andrewes (1555–1626) and the less well-known John Bramhall (1594–1653), Archbishop of Armagh. Curry helps us to appreciate how 'we participate in what is believed' by considering T. S. Eliot's reflections on 'the necessary relation between form and content', and on the harmony between 'intellect and sensibility' which he found in Andrewes. In Curry's argument, the necessary relation between form and content lies behind the determination of Bramhall and Andrewes to focus on the 'fundamentals or essentials of Faith' and their presentation of 'the harmonious interplay of Word and sacrament'.

Curry argues that, for Bramhall and Andrewes, the relationship between the sacramental signs and the spiritual reality that they make present and confer is worked out by a careful application of the four key words in the Council of Chalcedon's description of how the human and divine natures are united in Christ: 'truly, perfectly, indivisibly, distinctly'. Considering how the sacraments order our participation in Christ according to this 'Chalcedonian paradigm', Andrewes describes 'a kind of hypostatical union of the sign and the thing signified, so united together as are the two natures in Christ'. Curry draws on the work of Robert Crouse to argue that the 'Chalcedonian sacramentalism' found in Andrewes and Bramhall, and in Hooker before them, shapes 'the Anglican conception of the nature of a sacrament'. According to this 'Christological paradigm', the sacraments are 'a mixture or conjunction of the natural and the supernatural, the divine word and the natural element, of the finite and the infinite, of the outward sign and the inward grace'. It is this union of the human and divine in the sacraments, understood in terms of the unity and distinctions of the

Chalcedonian definition, which orders our participation in Christ so that 'grace does not destroy nature but perfects it'. Curry argues that this exposition of necessary unity of form and content expresses 'the harmony of intellect and sensibility' which Eliot found in Andrewes, a harmony that orders how we know and love both Christ and all things which are held together in him. In Andrewes's words, 'for as there is a recapitulation of all in Heaven and earth in Christ, so there is a recapitulation of all in Christ in the holy Sacrament'.

In Chapter 11, Robin Ward concludes this section with a description of the 'chronic vigour' of the seventeenth-century French School, which has 'proved itself able to refresh the Church', and whose distinctive and original approach to Christology has a continuing relevance for contemporary approaches to liturgy, doctrine and ethics. His treatment is also a display of Christ at the centre of all things, the Word in the bosom of the Father and the creature who perfectly offers the praise of the whole created order to the Creator. Ward points to the three figures who shaped the school: Pierre de Bérulle (1575–1629), 'founder of the French Oratory and Cardinal'; Charles de Condren (1588–1641), 'the mystic of the school'; and Jean-Jacques Olier (1608–1657), the 'extraordinary' parish priest of St Sulpice, Paris, and founder of the Sulpician congregation. Ward focuses especially on the work of Bérulle, 'the Apostle of the Incarnate Word' and the 'affective theologian of the doctrine of the mysteries of Christ's incarnate life'. In Bérulle's words, the mysteries of the life of the incarnate Christ 'are past with regard to execution, but present with regard to their virtue'. Bérulle's Christology, Ward argues, emphasizes 'the role of the incarnate Christ as the perfect adorer of the Father'. This adoration is worked out practically in Bérulle's controversial 'vow of servitude', which sees 'the old Adam' renounced and 'in its place the divinized humanity of the Word is adopted', in what might be described as an ethical partaking of the divine nature. This focus on adoration is also the foundation of 'Bérulle's intense and distinctive Marianism' and of 'the importance of the Blessed Virgin as the "first altar" on which divine praise is paid'. Among the possible implications for contemporary questions, Ward notes that 'in an environment in which liturgical worship is reduced to an ever more unattractive pedagogic and didactic grind, restoration of adoration as the end of cult is a fundamental driver of reform and renewal'. Complementing Schumacher's ethics of creation, Ward argues that Bérulle's emphasis on 'the servitude of Christ to the most abject deprivations of our nature' inspires and offers 'a rich solidarity for the dispossessed and powerless with the work of the Redeemer'.

Part 4 – Christ the Universal Paradigm and Local Habitation

This volume as a whole considers the problem of mediation in various ways: how divine silence may be spoken, how God who is Spirit may take the form of a temple, or how God is manifest in the flesh in the Church and in the sacraments. This part places German Christology alongside both the Oxford Movement and the poetic imagination of Shakespeare and Coleridge in order to help us to see how it is that we discover the richness or fullness of the whole Christ not in blending the divine and human, the universal and particular, the eternal and historical, but in the movement between these poles, 'the angels of God ascending and descending upon the Son of Man' (John 1.51).

In Chapter 12, Johannes Zachhuber challenges the widespread view that nineteenth-century German theologians present not a 'whole' Christ, but 'a partial Christ, a Christ stripped of his divinity and reduced to a merely human figure, the so-called historical Jesus'. F. W. J. Schelling expressed the common sense of his day when he described Christianity as 'inseparable from history'. Yet, because the Incarnation describes the 'coming together of God and world, the infinite and the finite', history is not merely a closed 'natural order of causality', but is also open to 'the spiritual order of freedom'. Zachhuber argues that one can find two different approaches to history at work, which shape roughly two schools of Christology. One group, particularly influenced by Schelling, conceived of history 'as a process', 'by necessity supra-individual', which subsumed the role of individuals into 'bigger trends, patterns and developments'. In this view, Christ is not first or fundamentally 'an individual, historical person' but 'the principle of the union of the infinite and the finite', a union that is enacted not only in Jesus of Nazareth, but in 'the historical succession of individual persons'. F. C. Baur found support for seeing 'Christ's humanity as somehow both particular and universal' in Patristic reflections on Jesus as 'the suffering servant', 'the true Israel' and the new Adam.

The second approach emphasizes the way in which individuals and 'individual events and occurrences' are more fundamental than patterns or trends. Exemplifying this approach, Friedrich Schleiermacher described individuals as 'flashes of activity inserted into otherwise inert nature', and Christ as 'the ideal, paradigmatic human being' because he is 'the brightest flash issuing forth from humanity's universal nature'. Building on this approach, Isaak August Dorner emphasized 'Christ's human individuality and historical particularity'. Dorner found in Irenaeus and in his understanding of recapitulation the view that Jesus Christ, in all his historical particularity, represents 'all human beings in and through his personality'. Zachhuber concludes that while nineteenth-century German theology 'could lead to an inadequately reductionist picture of Jesus Christ', the theologians he considers also emphasize 'the need to treat the quest for the "whole Christ" as an open-ended reflection on the one person that stands at the very centre of the Christian faith rather than a doctrine that has, at some point, once and for all been settled'.

In Chapter 13, George Westhaver considers the all-embracing and comprehensive approach to the Incarnation offered by the leaders of the

Oxford Movement. While, as Zachhuber shows, E. B. Pusey criticized 'Rationalist' tendencies in German theology, Pusey's ideas also support Zachhuber's insistence that there is more to nineteenth-century German Christology than historical reductionism. Pusey's argument, that 'the gift of the Christian life is nothing less than "union with that mystery, whereby we are made partakers of the Incarnation"', could be seen as a version of the view of Schelling and Baur that the humanity taken on by the Word is not only that of Jesus of Nazareth, but also that of the 'succession of individual persons' who are, in Pusey's words, 'In-Godded, Deitate'. Moreover, Newman's argument, that the historical existence of Christ does not simply belong to a distant past, but rather that Christ is the paradigmatic individual who *mystically reiterates* in each of us all the acts of His earthly life', may be compared to Dorner's assertion that Christ recapitulates in himself 'all particular individualities'. In this view, Christ 'unabridged' incorporates the whole diverse body into himself precisely in and through the particularity of his earthly life and in all the 'flashes' of light in the histories and prophecies that have their ultimate source in him.

Considering the Oxford Movement alongside Iain McGilchrist's *The Master and his Emissary*, Westhaver argues that Pusey and Newman sought to cultivate an incarnational or sacramental sensibility, a kind of sanctified perception, as a way of apprehending the highest kind of knowledge through biblical types or symbols and poetic images. McGilchrist's description of a way of seeing that 'needs both to rest on the object and pass through the plane of focus' exemplifies this approach. The Tractarian emphasis on never leaving behind the 'apophatic moment', and on the necessary tension intrinsic to communicating what is inexhaustible, points to another connection with Zachhuber's conclusions. Living the mystery of the Incarnation requires that we avoid resolving the distinctions between the particular humanity and universal divinity of Christ. We apprehend the mystery better if we are able to live in between what we know and do not know, in the 'little whiles' in between the goings away and returns of Christ (John 16.16–19), which are not just prophecies of the resurrection and the ascension, but realities mystically reiterated and lived in the Church and in every Christian soul.

In Chapter 14, 'Christ and the Poetic Imagination', Malcolm Guite offers a compelling portrayal of 'the Incarnation as the supreme act of divine poesis'. Coleridge's search for a 'symbolic language' to express 'hidden truth' provides a nineteenth-century anchor in a presentation which begins with Shakespeare's *Midsummer Night's Dream* and passes via Seamus Heaney to C. S. Lewis's poetic reconciliation of reason and imagination. Guite argues that the description of 'The poet's eye, in fine frenzy rolling', and glancing 'from heaven to Earth, from Earth to heaven', offers Shakespeare's 'best account of the poetic imagination as a truth-bearing faculty'. The product of this movement from earth to heaven, from Heaney's 'soggy peat' to the 'not yet visible', is the poetic fruit that the imagination 'bodies forth'. In giving shape to the 'unknownness' that is apprehended without being fully comprehended, imagination makes a place 'which is habitable', 'something that invites you into it, that has doors and windows'. Theologically, Shakespeare gives a poetic 'riff' on the Prologue to John's Gospel: 'the divine Logos which would otherwise be an apprehension or an abstraction in the human mind, is literally "bodied forth", literally given "a local habitation and a name"'. Christ is both 'a kind of window or doorway into heaven' and a place where ideas, individuals and imaginative symbols can live side by side and together.

Coleridge offers a theoretical framework for Shakespeare's poetry, describing the imagination as 'a repetition in the finite mind of the eternal act of creation in the infinite I AM'. Coleridge implies, according to Guite, that to perceive is 'in some sense to co-create what the Logos himself is saying', a description evocative of Zachhuber's account of the universal taking on flesh in individual perception. On the other hand, the imagination enables us to move from the particular to the universal, 'through *comprehending* the earthly towards *apprehending* the heavenly'. In other words, it is the earthy or 'peaty' particularities of Heaney's poem 'Digging', which transforms 'the slant of the spade as it goes into the earth' into the 'the slant of the pen', that bodies forth what 'clear' reason apprehends in her commerce with 'celestial light'. Guite describes the task of theologians and poets as fashioning an incarnational shape or home that thought can inhabit: 'whether their "glance" starts at heaven or whether it starts with earth, they are concerned to bridge the two, to make the connection and to make the shapes that make a habitation for insight'.

Part 5 – Christ the Saviour Irreducible and Complete

The chapters in this section consider how Christ saves us – how we are incorporated into the sacred humanity of Christ, how we apprehend the character of this redemption in worship or in theological reflection, and how faith in Christ reorients our lives. What Christ has accomplished for and in us both generates speculation and disciplines a humble attentiveness to Christ which does not allow us to reduce his saving work to a principle or a system.

In Chapter 15, 'The Work of a Theologian in the Body of Christ', Lewis Ayres argues that 'We are saved through the unity of the Word with the human nature that he took as his own.' He probes how a theologian is called to examine this 'complex set of relationships', but without reducing it to 'a simple pattern or concept'. All flesh, even the sacred humanity of the Word, resists reduction to theories and concepts: 'the stark imagery of flesh on flesh, flesh in flesh, and flesh consumed by flesh' cannot be left behind. The interplay of this fleshy givenness and theoretical speculation also suggests another tension which illuminates the theologian's task, the tension 'between the faith of the unlearned Christian, the faith into which we are all baptized, and the speculations of those with appropriate intellectual gifts who feel the draw to explore the riches of our faith'.

Ayres presents the theologian's task 'under two basic headings, those of "handing on" and "speculating" – *traditio* and *speculatio*'. On the one hand, because our relationship to God is as members of a body – 'as Christians we are *in* the events of Christ's incarnate life – the complex images and terminologies which constitute that relationship must be handed on without being reduced to abstract concepts'. This is 'the faith delivered in catechesis', what is handed on, *traditio*. On the other hand, this 'fount of images and narratives *generates* particular avenues of thought that cut across those that may have been common currency in a particular culture or in a particular life'; what is handed on invites speculation, *speculatio*. Ayres evokes the '*ressourcement* project' to argue that the Church's tradition is best conceived not as an inert deposit, 'a historical succession of opinions', but rather as a gift made up of 'the succession of God's "visitations"'. Speculation is the human response in faith and love which these visitations elicit and which is at the same time a 'divine activity'. The theologian's task also includes the negative one of discerning 'where and how theological thinking is pressed into a retuning', into disrupting rather than expressing the divine–human harmony. Ayres does not resolve this tension, but he describes how to live in it creatively, both aware of pitfalls and open to new 'movements of faith and love drawn from our human freedom by God's grace'.

In Chapter 16, Kallistos Ware also asks how Christ saves us, presenting the 'divine act' of our salvation in the form of six models. Like Ayres, he emphasizes that the images and symbols which invite us to 'enter more deeply into the living mystery of Christ's saving work' resist being resolved or reduced to a single system: 'If we consult the New Testament, what we find is not a single way of understanding the saving work of Christ, not one exclusive and systematic theory, but a series of different images and symbols set side by side.' Ware interrogates the models of salvation according to a series of questions, asking if the images 'envisage a change in God or in us', if they 'separate Christ from the Father' or 'isolate the Cross from the Incarnation and the Resurrection', and finally, if they 'presuppose an objective or a subjective understanding of Christ's saving work'. He considers, first, Christ as 'Teacher', 'as the one who reveals to us the saving truth, who illuminates us and disperses the darkness of ignorance from our minds'. The second model he proposes is that of Christ as 'Ransom', laying down his own life on the cross to secure the liberation of humanity. Reflecting on the third model, that of 'Sacrifice', he argues that the essence of sacrifice is not death but life, that the life of the victim 'may be released and offered to God'. The key to sacrifice is 'voluntary self-offering, inspired by love – love to the uttermost, love without limits'. This view leads him to criticize the 'satisfaction' model of Anselm of Canterbury as reflecting instead 'the principles of the medieval feudal society', a description which some might find incomplete or harsh. The fourth model, 'Victory', is also an expression of love, not a coercive victory, but rather 'the victory of suffering love, of inexhaustible and unchanging love'. He probes this idea further in the next model, which he traces to Peter Abelard, that of 'Example': 'Christ's love, revealed most intensely on the cross, acts as a spiritual magnet, drawing us all to him'. Ware argues that this love is not 'merely a subjective feeling', but rather 'an objective power in the universe', a 'transfiguring force' which we offer and unleash when we love one another. The sixth model, 'Exchange', enables us to appreciate how divine love breaks down distinctions between objective and subjective, presenting salvation 'in terms of *theosis* or "deification"'. The love to which Christ the Example calls us is not a moral effort, but 'a genuine participation in the divine life'.

Amplifying and supplementing Ware's presentation, Polycarpus Augin Aydin shows in Chapter 17 how liturgy both expresses and teaches the saving and transforming work of Christ. Aydin examines how Christ is portrayed in the three anaphoras, or eucharistic liturgies, of the Syrian Church: the anaphoras named for St James, 'the brother of our Lord', for St Dionysius Bar Salibi, the twelfth-century Metropolitan of Amid (now Diyarbakir, Turkey), and for Sixtus, the third-century Bishop of Rome. The Syriac anaphoras imprint vivid symbols which communicate how Christ accomplishes the work of salvation. Christ is the 'Good Doctor' who, in the words of St Ephrem, 'comes to heal the wounds of Adam, and to provide a garment of glory for his nakedness'. Ephrem also describes Christ as 'Divine Fire' in the womb of the Blessed Virgin Mary, in the water of baptism and in the 'holy *Qurbono*', the holy offering of the eucharistic elements: 'In Your Bread there is hidden the Spirit which is not consumed, in Your Wine there dwells the Fire that is not drunk'. These same elements are the medicine of life administered by the 'Heavenly Physician' and the 'Merciful Judge', the one who may 'consume and burn up' or may 'purify and sanctify'. The divine fire is also suggestive of the love of the 'heavenly bridegroom' which is the food of the wedding banquet. In this marriage, the soul is the bride and the body is the bridal chamber. By putting on the robe of humility, 'The Son has made beautiful the servant's deformity, and he has become a god, just as he had desired'. In the liturgy, Aydin argues, doctrines are 'lived' rather than simply taught, images become reality, and the promise of '*theosis*', which was restored for humanity through the coming of Christ, is 'expressed, celebrated, and transmitted'.

In Chapter 18, 'Christ the Categorical Imperative', Oliver O'Donovan also begins by asking how Christ saves us. He distinguishes between 'the highroad of soteriology', how God in Christ redeems humankind, and 'the less-travelled road of Christian ethics', which considers 'how our lives are reoriented by faith in Christ, to live and act as those whom Christ has saved'. O'Donovan proceeds to examine Hans Urs von Balthasar's short text, *Nine Propositions on Christian Ethics* (1974). For Immanuel Kant, the categorical imperative expressed the idea that one ought to act so that 'the maxim' or principle expressed in one's action could be a universal law. In such a framework, Christ offers humanity at best 'a supreme exemplification of a moral truth'. In opposition to this view, O'Donovan argues that for Balthasar, Christ's life has a 'moral force' not in offering 'an instantiation', not as a uniquely attractive and compelling example, but as 'a historical achievement'. The norm which Kant sought cannot be 'a principle', but the person who fulfils 'the whole content of the "Ought"'. O'Donovan's description of Christ as 'the generative principle' of moral action fits with Ware's argument that the example of Christ is not only a moral exhortation but a participation in divine love, or, in Dominiak's presentation of Hooker, an example which is 'a school of virtue', one not so much taught as 'given gratuitously through God's grace and participation in the ascended and glorified Christ'.

From the standpoint of the completion of morality which is present in Christ, Balthasar looks 'backwards' to the morality of the Old Covenant and to the call of God to Abraham, and back again to 'elements of pagan morality'. Balthasar is critical of attempts to establish ethics on the basis of another kind of moral example, on 'the natural possibilities of physical existence'. Here Balthasar's criticism of 'a priori moral principles' includes Aquinas's natural law as well as Kant's categorical imperative: 'neither personal nor social morality can have a self-authenticating "natural" standing'. This is the context of Balthasar's criticism of post-Christian ethics, of both 'an unfree collectivism and an egocentric liberalism', and of the prescriptive claims of the supposedly 'value-free' human sciences, 'comprehensive' but 'without love'.

O'Donovan argues that Balthasar's contribution to the question of how 'practical reason can be "evangelical", shaped by good news', is in 'integrating the categories of ethics into Christology'. Christ is the one in whom 'everything is done already'. The goal of practical reason is to 'participate in that achievement', not to discover a principle but 'a concrete life actually lived and shared with disciples'.

Conclusion – Knowing and Loving the Son of Man

Summing up and considering the ideas and arguments put forward in this volume, Rowan Williams notes that the focus on Christology leads back to the questions explored at the 2016 Pusey House conference on Trinitarian theology, 'A Transforming Vision': 'Where are we? Where do we live, where do we stand, as Christian believers?'[2] In the first chapter of the Gospel according to St John, the apostles ask Jesus, 'Rabbi, where do you live?' Serious grappling with the mystery wrapped up in this question leads us to ask about the place the Son occupies in relation to the Father, and also about the place where we stand or live in relation to the Son. Williams suggests that the 'Word made flesh Jesus' is both 'the one who lives in that eternal place where God's own image actively reflects back to God's own superabundant love and glory' and also 'the place in which the world, all that is made, is to be found'. Williams's chapter is all the more remarkable in that it offers not the fruit of days or weeks of pondering and looking back, but his reflections at the end of the third day of a packed schedule. Drawing together key themes that unite the chapters in this volume, he concludes that 'the "place" we are called to occupy' is one that will take our whole lives to make sense of, 'that place which is the Word's place in the bosom of the Father, the place where the whole world finds itself naturally and supernaturally, where the whole world is pulled together, remade, re-created'. The knowledge that finds a way to this place is a knowledge shaped by sacrificial love; it is those who stoop down 'to where Christ is' who come to 'know and love the Son of Man most effectively and most truly'.

The conference in 2018 concluded on 11 July, the Feast of St Benedict of Nursia, 'the Father of Western Monasticism'. In the sermon given at the service of Evensong that concluded the conference, Anthony Burton recalled the hard-won stability and Christlike character that emerged from Benedict's tumultuous life. Benedict offered the fruits of his struggle in the Rule which shaped and guided Western Monasticism, seeking to inculcate 'an ordered spiritual life, *ora et labora*, in which first things are put first'. Burton considered what we can learn from the efforts of both Benedict and his biographer, Gregory the Great, to reconcile lives of active service with contemplation and prayer. As contemporary interest in the 'Benedict options' available to us today makes clear, the kind of spiritual life that Benedict nurtured does not give up on the world, but rather leads us to ask how 'Christian communities might, in the providence of God, play a role in the renewal of Western culture'. Here Burton reminds us, in a powerful phrase, that Benedict and Gregory 'disdained to be discouraged'. The Venerable Bede recalls the principle that Gregory himself offered in the 'Epistle' prefixed to his Commentary or *Moralia* on the Book of Job: 'amid the incessant battering of worldly cares', Gregory and Benedict strove to be 'fastened, as by the cable of an anchor, to the peaceful shore of prayer'. Burton's conclusion sums up our hopes in organizing the 2018 *Totus Christus* conference and in offering this collection for publication: 'In the midst of our own busy lives, may we likewise remain anchored to that peaceful shore, as we press forward in the great work of renewal in our own generation.'

O Lord Jesus Christ,
Thou Word of God and Son of Man, Creator and Redeemer,
possess our mind and conscience, our heart and imagination,
by Thine indwelling Spirit;
that we, and all people,
may find and rest in that Love which is Thy very Self.

Notes

1 Jean Daniélou, 'Le Symbolisme des rites baptismaux', *Dieu vivant* 1 (1945), pp. 17–43 (p. 17).
2 See Rowan Williams, 'Conclusion: Knowing and Loving the Triune God', in *A Transforming Vision: Knowing and Loving the Triune God* (London: SCM Press, 2018), pp. 232–3.

PART I

Christ the True Temple, True Sabbath and True Human Being

Strange Surprise[1]

None of this need have happened, all of this,
These unexpected gifts, this overflow
Of things we know, and things we'll never know,
None of this had to be, but here it is,
The here-and-now in all its strange surprise;
A space to be ourselves in, and a grace
That spins us round and turns us to the source
Whence all these gifts and graces still arise.

And now the one through whom all this was made,
Whom we ignore, on whom we turn our back,
Whom we denied, insulted and betrayed,
Gathers and offers for us all we lack,
Voices on our behalf creation's praise,
And calls us to become the song he plays.

[1] Originally published in Malcolm Guite, *After Prayer* (Norwich: Canterbury Press, 2019).

Son of Man and New Creation:
The Biblical Roots of Trinitarian Theology

N. T. WRIGHT

Introduction

The conference on Christology that Pusey House hosted in July 2018 was remarkable for many reasons, but for me as a biblical specialist it stood out because I was the only professional exegete within a glittering array of historical and systematic theologians. I speculated at the time whether I might turn out to be the exegetical fly in the theological ointment or the biblical Daniel in the theologians' den. Daniel is obviously relevant, since the phrase 'Son of Man' in the conference title is inevitably linked to the vision in Daniel 7. But my lonely position invited two preliminary reflections before we get to the text.

Exegesis and theology have been going their separate ways. They no longer share a common table; they hardly even recognize one another in the street. The systematician might comment that exegesis has dug itself into a series of smaller and messier holes from which no clear meaning ever emerges; and that, since Athanasius, Aquinas and the rest all read their Bibles and prayed for the Spirit's guidance, we should assume they knew what they were talking about and take it from there. Scholarly oral tradition recalls that Paul Tillich once remarked to C. H. Dodd that the systematician can't be expected to sit there waiting for some useful nugget of exegesis to come down the hall from the biblical specialists. One might wait a long time. The exegete will respond that systematic and historical theology appear to be playing an inhouse game in which the large concepts invented by later generations are endlessly rearranged with scant reference to the first-century historical reality to which they ostensibly refer. Anyway (both sides will comment) there's no time to say more, because academics these days need to get on with the next project in the field and don't usually have time, or get any extra praise, for speculative cross-disciplinary interaction.

The phrase 'Son of Man', at the heart of this volume, is a case in point, and leads to my second introductory remark. Generations used to be taught – perhaps still are – that 'son of God' and 'son of Man' indicated Jesus' 'divinity' and 'humanity' respectively. This has worked its way into popular discourse. When journalists ask a bishop if Jesus really was 'the son of God', they want the prelate either to affirm or deny an almost Docetic belief in Jesus' 'divinity'. When the Christmas carol declares that Jesus 'loves to be, and call himself, "the Son of Man"', it means, uncomplicatedly, that Jesus is 'one of us', a human among humans. But this was not what those phrases meant in the Jewish world of Jesus' day – a world increasingly opaque once apocalyptic messianism had been abandoned following the failure of the Bar Kokhba revolt, and a world still more opaque, for quite different reasons, in the increasingly Epicurean cosmology of the Enlightenment and the movements of critical thought within it.[1]

It was within the latter framework that Adolf Harnack famously sketched an early Christianity in which the simple timeless gospel of Jesus was muddled up by Hellenistic philosophy, which invented strange things like the Trinity, unknown in the early period. The fact that Harnack was wrong in most respects makes it harder to argue the point that still needs to be made, to which this chapter will contribute: that there was indeed a turn from the first-century Jewish context to the world of the third and subsequent centuries, but that the classic doctrines of the high Patristic period, particularly Trinity and Christology, were clearly expressed by the earliest Jesus-followers, albeit in an idiom, and within a conceptual framework, that was all but ignored once its original Jewish context had disappeared in the disasters of 70 and 135. The question would then be: do the subsequent retrievals of the doctrines, within the very different idioms and conceptual worlds of the fourth and fifth centuries, successfully display all that the early texts were saying? Or are we forced to concede, like Henry Chadwick in his article on Chalcedon, that, though we affirm Chalcedon itself, something of what the New Testament was saying seems to have slipped through its fingers?[2]

I assume that even the non-exegetes will know the remarkable turn of the tide in the last generation towards an 'early high Christology'. The old picture of an early 'human Jesus' who gradually 'became' more 'divine' as the Church moved away from its roots in Jewish monotheism, is still popular, not least among those for whom Geza Vermes had said what they wanted to hear and so didn't bother to read anything else.[3] But the work of Larry Hurtado and Richard Bauckham, and most recently of Richard Hays on the four Gospels, has shown this up as a historically unwarranted fiction, happily embraced, though for quite different reasons, by many liberal Protestants and many Jewish scholars.[4] In fact – and this will be the heart of my own proposal in this chapter – the more we understand the first-century Jewish world, particularly its key narratives and symbols, the more we see how the early high Christology of Paul and all four Gospels, not to mention Hebrews and Revelation, belongs within that world – as an explosive new reality, to be sure, but a reality that makes the sense it makes precisely within that world.

The narrative world of the first-century Jews is on display in the various retrievals of the obvious text, Daniel 7, to which I now turn.

Daniel 7 and the first-century Jewish hope

Daniel 7 poses several historical puzzles, but some of them are irrelevant for the first century. We do not need to know the pre-history, angelic or otherwise, of the phrase 'one like a son of man'.[5] What matters is how the text was read in the first century. Here we have five converging pieces of evidence.

The first is the text of Daniel itself, as a whole.[6] The book is clearly about the Creator God vindicating his suffering, righteous people. The stories of Daniel and his friends in chapters 1, 3 and 6 and of divine judgement on arrogant pagans in chapters 4 and 5 give grounding to the visions of chapters 2 and 7. These then set the tone for the further visions of chapters 8 and 10, the prayer of chapter 9 and the promise of final deliverance in chapter 12. The different genres contribute to the common theme: the one God will establish his reign over the wicked nations, and the faithful, vindicated after suffering, will share this divine rule. That is how first-century readers would understand chapter 7: when violent pagan arrogance reaches its height, God will rescue his people and exalt them to share his newly inaugurated worldwide regime.

> The kingdom and dominion and the greatness of the kingdom under the whole heaven shall be given to the people of the holy ones of the Most High; their kingdom shall be an everlasting kingdom, and all dominions shall serve and obey them. (Dan. 7.27)

That is what the text itself insists is meant by 'one like a son of man' 'coming on the clouds' to the Ancient of Days. It means both vindication and installation into a position of authority. It resonates, in fact, with the way in which Daniel is regularly promoted to positions of high authority in Babylon.[7]

Two notes about this reading of Daniel itself. The symbolism of the four monsters coming up out of the sea and the exaltation of 'one like a son of man' would be obvious to first-century Jews. The narrative is familiar from Psalm 2, with the warring nations confronted by God's exaltation of the king; or, indeed, from the book of Exodus (with Pharaoh's troops overthrown in the sea and Israel rescued) or the Wisdom of Solomon 1 – 5. Daniel 2 presents substantially the same scenario: the multi-metalled idolatrous statue is demolished by the Stone. Psalm 46 repeats the point: the nations are in uproar, the kingdoms totter; but God utters his voice and the earth melts; the Lord of hosts is with us, the God of Jacob is our refuge. In a sense, this is Israel's only story, the theme that generated many variations, finding expression in symbol, liturgy and political action.

The second note follows from this: what to the modern world has appeared as 'apocalyptic', a strange dark world of dualistic fantasy distinct from older prophecy, was nothing of the sort.[8] Expressing the horrible this-worldly realities of brutal empires through the well-known metaphor of the beasts from the sea was a way of aligning political realities with the ancient cosmology reflected in Genesis 1 – the waters of chaos overcome by the good creation – and the parallel soteriology of Exodus, both evoking earlier ancient Near Eastern mythology. Daniel 7 was a way of saying that the vicious imperial rule of the post-Babylonian empires was the accumulated violence of the chaos to which the Creator's answer would be a great act of new creation. Genesis 1 and 2 would be recapitulated at last, with the human one sovereign over the monsters. The vision of 'one like a son of man' means what it means, in the first century, within this well-known and widely shared narrative.

So far, the reading of 'one like a son of man' in Daniel 7 could be simply incorporative: Israel, the righteous sufferers, will be vindicated like the humans over the animals. The other four points, though, indicate from different angles that many Jews in the period were reading it in terms of the coming king, the Messiah. There was no single, unified 'messianic expectation' at the time.[9] Many Jews hoped for a coming king, drawing variously on scriptural prophecies, but their visions did not always agree, and many were unsure or sceptical. Nevertheless, Daniel's 'one like a son of man' was certainly interpreted by some as Israel's representative, the coming Messiah.

The second of the converging pieces of evidence is found in the second 'Similitude' of Enoch (1 Enoch 45—57). This is still controversial, not least because of textual and dating difficulties. These are irrelevant for our purposes. What matters is that the author is clearly reading Daniel 7 messianically.

Much more important, third, is the vision of the eagle and the lion in 4 Ezra chapters 11 and 12. The eagle is transparently Rome; the lion, equally obviously, is Judah's Messiah. The interpreting angel explains that 'the eagle that you saw coming up from the sea is the fourth kingdom that appeared in the vision to your brother Daniel. But it was not explained to him as I now explain to you' (12.11–12). The Messiah will judge the wicked nations but have mercy on the remnant of God's people (12.31–34). This vision, dateable to the generation after AD 70, shows both that Daniel 7 was being read as exemplifying the narrative I sketched above (the sovereign God overcoming wicked chaos and giving authority to a human being) and that it was focused on a coming Messiah.

Fourth, the most important evidence is that of Josephus. What most of all drove his contemporaries to revolt in AD 66, he says in the *Jewish War*, was an oracle in their Scriptures which prophesied that at that time a world ruler would arise from their country.[10] Josephus does not give the reference. But when he discusses Daniel in the *Jewish Antiquities* (10.267) it becomes clear. In the *War* passage, he reinterprets the oracle: it was, he says, a prophecy about Vespasian, who went from besieging Jerusalem to be emperor in Rome. Josephus was of course living on an imperial pension at the time. For the same reason, he radically tones down his interpretation of Daniel. When expounding chapter 2, he skips over the obviously messianic 'stone'; and then, after a detailed description of chapters 3 to 6, he jumps over the crucial chapter 7 altogether and goes straight on to 8. He knows only too well what chapter 7 was about. He then insists, however, that Daniel is unique among the prophets, in that he not only prophesied what would happen but put a specific time on it. This can only be a reference to Daniel 9, where the time of 'exile', when Israel was ruled by the pagans, would last not for 70 years, as in Jeremiah, but 'seventy weeks of years', in other words, 490 years, a sabbatical of sabbaticals. We know that many Jews in the first century were indeed calculating that 490 years, mostly arriving at some time in what we call the first century AD.[11] Josephus thus, despite his cautious approach, bears witness to a first-century reading of the book in terms of a prophecy about a coming worldwide ruler arising from Judaea 'at that time'. The 'one like a son of man' would be brought to sit alongside the 'Ancient of Days', and the dark, chaotic power of pagan empire would be condemned at last.

This reading is confirmed, finally, by the controversy at the Bar Kokhba revolt in 132. Rabbi Akiva, supporting Bar Kokhba, used Daniel 7, which speaks of 'thrones' being placed in heaven before the 'one like a son of man' arrives there: 'One for the Ancient of Days,' he explains, and 'one for David'.[12] This confirms three points. First, Daniel 7 was still being read messianically. Second, the apocalyptic genre was understood to refer to political or revolutionary events, investing them with theological significance. Third, here at least Daniel is presumed to teach that the coming messiah, a successful revolutionary leader, will *share the very throne of Israel's God* – a point deemed blasphemous by some of Akiva's contemporaries, perhaps not least because it sounded suspiciously like some of the things the Jesus-followers had been saying.

All this, I suggest, gives us a sense of exegetical, theological and political possibilities inherent in a reference to the 'one like a son of man' in Daniel 7. The idea of this figure being 'human' in the sense of being 'one of us' is irrelevant. That isn't the question on the table. First-century Jews had rather few books, but the main ones they had – Torah, prophets and writings – were extremely well known, studied, prayed and sung. The echoes awoken by Daniel 7, as a whole and in its parts, would resonate with the large narratives of both creation and exodus. The one God wins the victory over the waters of chaos and over the political monsters that gain their power from that dark force.

But in Scripture the story doesn't stop there. In Exodus 15, in Psalm 2, and not least in Isaiah 52, this goes with the launching of God's kingdom, the establishment of the Temple, and particularly the personal and visible return of Israel's God to that restored Temple. This complex of vast interlocking themes, I have argued elsewhere, was not only well understood but also, in various forms, taken for granted as part of the overall biblically resourced hope: not that humans in general, or Israel in particular, would be rescued from this present world to live somewhere else, but that Israel's God would finally come to dwell amidst his people and, through that indwelling, would rescue and transform the whole creation, suffusing it with his glorious presence.[13]

All the lines converge at this point. Central to the royal vocation, from the Psalms and Isaiah to Qumran, the Psalms of Solomon and beyond, is the task of defeating the enemy, building or cleansing the Temple, and so preparing the way for the return of the glorious divine presence.[14] Equally central is the task of doing justice and mercy, especially on behalf of the poor, the widow and the orphan, so that, as in Psalm 72, the glorious divine presence may fill the whole earth. The two go together. Imagery from the creation story (chaos waters overcome by God's creation, and the human authority within it) is applied to what we call political realities; equally, the order and structure of the Tabernacle and Temple are seen to reflect, and to reflect upon, creation itself, and thereby to point ahead to creation's ultimate renewal and filling with divine presence. Tabernacle and Temple were seen – at least by the editors of the Pentateuch – as small working models of the whole creation, signs of the ultimate divine intention. Architecture and decoration alike spoke of the larger cosmos; the High Priest, going into the shrine once a year, stood in for Adam in the original garden-temple. The Temple was thus an *eschatological symbol*, a forward-looking signpost for what the Creator God intended to do for the whole creation. Israel's vocation was to be the guardian, not simply of a building, but of the promise signified by that building: that there would be a new creation, a time when heaven and earth would come together at last so that the earth would be filled with the knowledge and/or the glory of God as the waters cover the sea. This glorious divine return, as I have argued elsewhere, is the hidden clue to early Christology and Pneumatology.

All this forms the implicit echo-chamber within which an allusion to Daniel 7, and to the 'one like a son of man', would make sense in the first century. But there is one further element before we move to the Synoptic tradition. This is the Sabbath. As Jewish scholars have long pointed out, the Sabbath was to time what the Temple was to space. If the Temple was where heaven and earth overlapped, pointing forward to the day when they would be joined together for ever, the Sabbath was the regular day when the Age to Come appeared in the midst of the Present Age. Thus in Jesus' Jewish world there were twin symbolic themes, taken for granted then but largely opaque to modern scholarship: the Temple, signifying the joining of heaven and earth; the Sabbath, signifying the advance appearing of the Age to Come.

All this thrives in the first-century Jewish worldview. It lives in symbol and story, and is easily retrieved when facing challenge or innovation. And that's what happens when the Synoptic Jesus speaks of the 'son of man'.

'Son of Man' in the Synoptic Gospels

Three introductory remarks on the 'son of man' in the Synoptic Gospels. First, Geza Vermes was correct to point out that the phrase 'son of man' could simply mean 'someone like me', an oblique self-reference.[15] But Vermes was reacting against an older assumption that 'son of man' meant 'Messiah' in an unnuanced sense of 'a divine redeemer figure', so he screened out Daniel 7, just as he screened out the significance of Jesus' action in the Temple. Once scholarship had moved on with Ben Meyer and Ed Sanders, making Jesus' temple-action and associated sayings central rather than marginal to the tradition, it became natural, and far more credible historically, to situate Jesus within the more complex and multilayered first-century world.[16] Vermes' Jesus was basically a Jewish version of Bultmann's dehistoricized existentialist sage.

Second, many scholars have assumed that the three categories of 'son of man' sayings – authority, suffering and future 'coming' – are incompatible, so that Jesus couldn't have said them all.[17] Debate has then been derailed by the stand-off between 'conservative' scholars, deeming the sayings all genuine for the sake of their inerrant Bible, and 'liberal' scholars, wanting many of them to be inauthentic for the sake of their errant one. Both 'conservatives' and 'liberals', though, read the 'coming on the clouds' sayings as referring to the second coming, the latter insisting that it didn't happen and the former that it still would. But when we bear in mind the larger Jewish contexts of meaning – in a way quite foreign to those earlier debates – then everything looks different.

In particular (my third introductory remark on 'son of man' in the Synoptic Gospels), the context of Daniel 7, and its retrieval by 4 Ezra and the loud silence of Josephus on the subject, indicates that the 'coming' of the Son of Man is not his *second coming* but rather his *vindication and exaltation*. In Daniel 7, the 'one like a son of man' comes on the clouds to be presented to the Ancient of Days, there to receive kingly authority. The movement is upward, not downward. Nor must we imagine this 'coming' in terms of a literalistic three-decker universe. Three-decker language was serving the Jewish vision, common in other cultures as well, that the domains of gods and humans might overlap, the focal point of overlap being of course a temple – a temple with an image.

This is certainly how the 'coming of the son of man' was taken among Jesus' first followers. In 1 Corinthians 15, claiming to build on very early common tradition, Paul pulls together Psalms 2, 8 and 110, weaving in echoes of Daniel 7, to say that Israel's Messiah *is already reigning*. He has already inaugurated the Age to Come and is now working to bring all things into subjection.[18] Paul doesn't use the phrase 'son of man', but the whole chapter is framed within explicit exegesis of Genesis 1–3, Adam and the Messiah, with Psalm 8 vital to its climax.

A further word about this now-and-not-yet inaugurated eschatology; some have recently suggested that this is a modern way of getting off the hook of an apparently unfulfilled promise.[19] The world didn't end, and nobody came to earth riding on a cloud. This is simply unhistorical. When Simeon ben Kosiba was hailed as Messiah in 132, that inaugurated a three-year rule over a small independent kingdom. The coins say Year One, restarting the calendar like the French Revolutionaries would centuries later. The kingdom had begun. But that was only the start. They still had to defeat Rome and rebuild the Temple. The Age to Come was *anticipated*, as with the Sabbath itself. That's how kingdom-claims worked in the Jewish world of the time.

So when Jesus responds to Caiaphas' question about messiahship, he is not saying that the High Priest will see him, Jesus, or anyone else flying downwards on a cloud. That would both literalize the apocalyptic metaphor and reverse the direction of travel. He is asserting, rather, that Caiaphas *will see Jesus vindicated* through events that will carry the message that he really was the Messiah, that he really did have authority over the Temple, and that he was indeed replacing the Temple as the place where, and the means by which, heaven and earth were coming together. Matthew and Luke, perhaps clarifying Mark, insist that Jesus is talking about a more or less immediate vindication. 'From now on', *ap'arti* in Matthew (26.64) and *apo tou nyn* in Luke (22.69), the Son of Man will fulfil both Psalm 110 and Daniel 7: seated at the right hand of Power, coming on the clouds of heaven. Psalm 110, perhaps the most frequently alluded to biblical text in the New Testament, carries here the extra meaning that Jesus is claiming a priestly status that, as the Letter to the Hebrews would later draw out, was effortlessly superior to the Levitical or indeed Aaronic line. No wonder Caiaphas shouted, 'Blasphemy'.

Matthew insists on this again later. The risen Jesus claims, in Matthew 28.18, that 'all authority in heaven and on earth has been given to me' – another clear echo of Daniel 7. This global rule had been offered him by the dark enemy in chapter 4, in return for a switch of allegiance.[20] Now it is granted by the one God instead, as the result of Jesus' obedient suffering. This sovereignty is the foundation, here as in Paul, for the mission of the Church. The enslaving enemy has been defeated, and the true king enthroned. The Church's mission is not to offer people a new religious experience, or to invite them to escape earth and attain heaven instead. It is rather about enlisting people in the present time for the work of the kingdom, against the still-future day when heaven and earth will be one. That future day is of course reaffirmed in the tradition, but not, in my judgement, either in the saying to Caiaphas or in the similar saying in Mark 13 and parallels. There, the emphasis falls on the vindication of the son of man in the coming events of resurrection, ascension and the fall of Jerusalem, the city and the Temple that had refused the gospel way of peace. Rather, the future 'coming' or 'return' of Jesus will be to complete the work 'on earth as in heaven', to effect the cosmic transformation promised in Romans 8 and the equivalent personal transformation promised in Philippians 3.[21] All this would take us into many fascinating areas for which there is no space here.

We can now fill in the picture with the other 'son of man' gospel sayings. Once we read the 'coming' sayings seen in terms of 'vindication', it is relatively easy to see both the 'authority' and the 'suffering' sayings within the same implicit narrative. Jesus claims authority to forgive sins as part of his kingdom-inaugurating public career.[22] This is the Jubilee, the seventy-weeks moment, when 'the time is fulfilled' so that 'the kingdom is at hand': the real return from exile, which is itself the forgiveness of Israel's sins, is taking place, *and Israel's God is now returning in person to judge and save.*

How does this work out? Not straightforwardly in our terms. Christology has often been short-circuited in the modern period, with even the word *Christos* being treated as a 'divine' title, and once more with conservatives insisting that this divine meaning was present to Jesus and liberals insisting that it wasn't and couldn't have been. This merely throws dust in the eyes.

What matters, once again, is the narrative and the symbols that encode it. When we go back to Daniel 7, the 'one like a son of man' is clearly interpreted as 'the people of the saints of the most high'. When this is reapplied in the first century by 4 Ezra and Josephus (and probably earlier in the *Similitudes*), the corporate figure has become an individual. Here are the roots of Paul's incorporative messianic theology: *the Messiah represents Israel within the divine purposes.* The authority which in Daniel 7 is vested in the saints is now vested in Jesus, because God has done for him, in raising him from the dead, what in Israel's traditions was to happen to all the righteous at the end of time. Jesus' resurrection is the key to inaugurated eschatology, as indeed to more or less everything else.

The 'authority' sayings are associated in particular with the Sabbath.[23] Here is a classic interpretative riddle. Generations were taught that Jesus broke the Sabbath because it was a piece of restrictive Jewish legalism while he believed in freedom, in grace not law. That is an irrelevant anachronism. Jesus acted as he did on the Sabbath, and justified his actions in that way, because *the time was fulfilled*; the 70 weeks of years were up; the kingdom was breaking in then and there. The Sabbaths had been forward-looking signposts to the Coming Age, when heaven and earth would be joined as always intended. They were now upstaged.[24] You don't put up a sign saying 'this way to Oxford' in the High Street of the city. And if the Son of Man has authority over the Sabbath, he also claims authority over the Temple. Both Matthew and John, describing Jesus' dramatic temple-action, echo Psalm 8. Matthew has Jesus quoting 'out of the mouths of babes and sucklings you have drawn perfect praise'; John, echoing the authority of the son of man in the Psalm, has Jesus casting out *ta probata kai tas boas* (the sheep and the oxen). It looks as though, in very early tradition, Jesus' temple-action was associated with his status as the implicitly royal 'son of man' of Psalm 8. This picks up the older idea that the 'image' in Genesis 1 was itself a royal motif, now democratized to include all humans, but still available for specifically royal use.[25]

For Jesus thus to claim authority over both Temple and Sabbath was to say, in symbol as well as word, that the new day was dawning towards which both symbols had been pointing. Forward-looking symbols become redundant when the reality arrives. 'Something greater than the Temple is here' (Matt. 12.6); and the humans for whom the Sabbath was made can now enjoy the reality of which it spoke. Jesus, in fact, went about redefining 'kingdom of God' itself, around what he was doing and saying. *This is what it looks like*, he was saying, *when God becomes king as promised!* And central to that redefinition was suffering. Jesus took the theme of suffering – of exile, of martyrdom, of the persecution of the prophets – and, in making it his own, he redefined it. No longer would it simply be the dark pathway *through which* the righteous would walk to attain the new day. Now, the suffering would be *the means by which* the eventual redemption would be won. This is where, of course, Jesus invoked Isaiah.

As with 'the son of man' itself, the 'suffering servant' has been off limits to many scholars. This was partly in reaction to the over-concentration on the passage by one strand of exegesis, and by the limiting of that exegesis to a particular theory of atonement. But when we step back from those older discussions, the conclusion is clear. In the 2018 St Andrews conference on the atonement in Jewish and early Christian thought, it was remarkable how often Isaiah 53 turned up as the key allusion in Jewish texts of the Second Temple period, irrespective of Christian interpretation. Different groups, of course, read that chapter differently.[26] Some, like 2 Maccabees, took it as a prophecy about the redemptive quality of the martyrs' deaths – but not as in any sense messianic. Some, as with the later Isaiah Targum, saw it as a messianic prophecy, but turned the 'suffering' references the other way round so that they became, as in Psalm 110, the suffering the Messiah would inflict on God's enemies. It looks as though Jesus himself made the creative exegetical and vocational move to hold these together, so that the Messiah himself would become the ultimate redemptive martyr; and to hold together with that, too, the entire narrative of the 'one like a son of man', so that Isaiah 40–55 as a whole, and the book of Daniel as a whole, would come true together in the same way. Isaiah spoke of the personal return of Israel's God to Zion, with the 'servant'-poems woven into the larger pattern to reveal the means by which this redemptive return would be accomplished. 'Who would have believed', asks the prophet at the start of chapter 53, 'that he was the Arm of the Lord?' The Servant embodies the promised divine return. The result, in chapter 54, is covenant renewal. This leads, in chapter 55, to the renewal of creation itself. Several psalms make the same point.

This is picked up in the opening of Mark's Gospel. The two biblical passages with which he begins, Malachi 3 and Isaiah 40, are not about an Elijah-figure preparing the way for Israel's Messiah; they are about preparing the way for Israel's God.[27] Mark 1 is full of allusions to both creation and exodus: Jesus comes out of the water, with the Spirit like a dove descending upon him, and the voice proclaims his identity and vocation in terms of Psalm 2 and Isaiah 42. After his sojourn in the wilderness, he announces that the time is fulfilled and God's kingdom is at hand.

Mark's redefinition of what it will look like when God comes back emerges from Jesus' own redefinition of the kingdom. It will involve healing and celebration; it will involve victory, not over Rome, but over the dark power that has lent its weight to Rome and also, tragically, to Israel's misguided leaders and revolutionaries. It will involve the destruction of the present Temple and the establishment of something else which will do the job towards which the Temple had been pointing. It will involve the arrival of the Age to Come in such a way that the Sabbath will no longer be needed as a forward signpost. All this and more Jesus declares in hints and riddles, with the parables teasing people towards a larger and shockingly redrawn picture of how the Scriptures were to be fulfilled.

At its heart is the redrawn vision of power itself. What will it look like, Jesus is asking, when God becomes king? James and John assume it will be a normal kingdom, with men to the monarch's right and left to enforce his decrees.[28] No, says Jesus, that's how the rulers of the world do it, but we're going to do it the other way. Someone who wants to be great must be your servant; anyone who wants to be first must be slave of all, *because* the son of man didn't come to be served but to serve, and to give his life a ransom for many. That last line has been wrenched out of context to serve abstract theories of atonement, but part of the point is that to begin with the cross was at the heart of the redefinition of power, because the cross was the ultimate means through which God's kingdom would be established. All the evangelists insist upon this point, with Jesus crucified as 'king of the Jews'. Later theology has found it hard to hold together kingdom and cross. The two have drifted apart in exegesis, in theology and in church agendas. But for the Gospels there is no split, just as Isaiah 53 and Daniel 7 are fused together, as they cry out to be, into a single kingdom-bringing narrative, the story of the personal return and redemptive accomplishment of Israel's God.

The three strands of Synoptic 'son of man' sayings – authority, suffering, vindication – likewise fit together into a fresh but perfectly recognizable construal of the many-stranded first-century Jewish narrative. Jesus really did believe that the events he was precipitating would be the point around which world history, cosmic history, would turn. He did not of course believe in the coming literal 'end of the world'. That is nineteenth-century German mythology projected back, with breath-taking anachronism, onto the first century.[29] He was a Jew, living from within the Scriptures in which the Creator God had promised to dwell on the earth. He was heir to the promises that spoke darkly about how that would be accomplished despite the failure and exile of the promise-bearing people. Paul understood this already, but it's clear he didn't invent it. The four Gospels reflect all this in

31

their different ways. But they, too, go on to make new points from it. They are not inventing it from scratch. Once we do our best to locate our reflection on Jesus and early Christianity within the larger first-century Jewish symbolic, narratival and conceptual world, all sorts of fresh options open up: new highways in the desert . . .

From exegesis to theology

The options open up for theology as well as exegesis. By starting with 'son of man' in Daniel and the Gospels, we have reached a vantage point for some wider reflections. Perhaps the most important is that, in some readings of Daniel 7 in the period, the 'one like a son of man' is *both* the literary figure who stands in for 'Israel as a whole' *and* the messianic embodiment of that Israel-shaped vocation – *and also* the one who then shares the very throne of the one God himself. We see how all this can be held together in passages like John 1 or Colossians 1, which invoke Genesis 1 so as to let the Messiah appear as the true image, the ultimate human being, while being also the one 'through whom all things were made'. It looks as though the first Jesus-followers, trying to understand just who it was they had known as friend and master, reached for the text that spoke of humans being made to reflect the stewarding power of the Creator into his world and the worship of the world back to the Creator. The image stands at the heart of the ultimate Temple which is creation itself. And, as in other passages like Hebrews 1, 1 Corinthians 8 and Philippians 2, the human who is now exalted is identified with the one who all along was equal with the Creator. The phrase 'son of man' does not of itself indicate Jesus' divine identity, but the narrative which it evokes generates the world in which that makes sense.

The earlier critical assumption, then, was wrong. Many of us were told as students that the idea of incarnation itself was a category mistake. The first followers of Jesus begged to differ, not because they were primitive while we were modern, but because they were Jewish while we were late-flowering Epicureans for whom any commerce between heaven and earth would be off limits. Instead, John 1, Colossians 1, Philippians 2 and other passages are saying that Genesis 1, with humans called to be image-bearers, is itself, like Temple and Sabbath, a forward-looking signpost: God made humans in his own image, to reflect his personal presence into the world, so that in due time he might himself become human in order to embody his own intention. That long-range plan was not thwarted by the vocational failure of the humans. Rather, it called forth a fresh dimension of the same generous love through which creation came to be in the first place. God called Abraham and his family to be the means of redeeming the world, so that in due time he might himself become the world's redeemer by embodying in himself the dark vocation of Israel, a vocation initially enacted in the slavery and redemption of Egypt and Exodus and reaching its climax in cross and resurrection. These purposes were then expressed in the symbols of Temple and Sabbath, with the image-bearing humans always central, and the royal and priestly vocations occupying a kind of liminal space, poised between the purposes of heaven and the paradoxes of earth. The New Testament then represents the astonished celebration and exploration of exactly this, with Jesus as himself the Royal Priest who simultaneously embodies *both* Israel's returning God *and* Israel's own act of utter self-offering worship, and reveals that those two vocations are not two but one. He is the image of the invisible God; no one has seen God, but the only-begotten God has unveiled him, explained him, made him known. I have long been of the opinion that, if Christology would begin here, many other questions would appear in a fresh light.

Where then does the Spirit come into the picture? The authority that Jesus claims as 'son of man' in the Gospels is exercised in the power of the Spirit which anointed him at his baptism, and this provides one clue. The purpose of it all, of the whole biblical narrative, is not to save humans away from the world but for the living God to flood all creation with his presence, effecting the new creation spoken of in Isaiah and the Psalms. Jesus' healings are then to be seen, as he pointed out to John the Baptist, in terms of the new-creation prophecies of Isaiah 35. The healing, world-renewing Spirit is then the one through whom the Creator God will in the end be 'all in all' (1 Cor. 15.28), not in a kind of eschatological pantheism but in a fusion of heaven and earth. Each will be truly itself while being perfectly united with the other, an image for which, as in John 2 or Ephesians 5, marriage is both metaphor and metonymy. In one passage after another – and not in writing only, since Paul at least saw the practical work of the Church in these terms – the Spirit is at work in the present to fill Jesus' followers with new and transforming life as itself a sign and anticipation of what is intended for the entire cosmos at the end. The present equipping of the Church with the Spirit's varied gifts in Ephesians 4 is to the end of the eventual 'filling of all things' that results from the Messiah's exaltation and enthronement. It is, in other words, the outworking of the Daniel 7 moment, the time when the risen Jesus fulfilled Psalm 110 and obtained executive authority over the whole world.

Of course, that executive authority, like Jesus' authority in his public career, was always to be fulfilled by the same kind of power, the new power of suffering and healing love. That is why the Sermon on the Mount is what it is. The regular objection, that things still don't look as though Jesus is in charge, is the equivalent of the objections people raised to Jesus himself when they asked for signs. Jesus gave them the sign of Jonah, launching the new creation in his own risen body, not only thereby possessing authority to renew the creation but embodying and modelling that new creation in himself. This is where the vindication of the son of man joins up with the larger prophetic narrative: Daniel 7, pointing back to Genesis 1 and 2, points on to the rescue and renewal of creation itself.

The Spirit that is thereby let loose – since Jesus has overcome in his death the dark powers that had held the world captive – is spoken of by Paul, within 25 years of Jesus' death and resurrection, in terms reminiscent of the pillar of cloud and fire that accompanied the Israelites in the wilderness. For Paul to refer to the personal presence of the divine glory as the appropriate image for the indwelling Spirit was to state as high a pneumatology as could be, though it took the Fathers centuries to catch up. In Galatians, which I take to be the very first New Testament writing, Paul declares that after their former idolatry the converts had 'come to know God, or rather to be known by God'.[30] And the God he is referring to in the previous verses is the God of redemption, the God of the Exodus, the God who sent the Son and the God who sent the Spirit of the Son.[31] There is the choice, starkly presented in (I think) the late 40s AD. Either you have this threefold God or you have paganism.

And that is why, though I love the Church's great traditions and revere her great teachers, I cannot escape the sense that the Jewish roots of Christology and Trinitarian theology, long pruned to below ground level by the sceptical agendas which have called themselves 'historical criticism', are actually full of sap, ready to sprout, blossom and flower once more. By all means let us translate them into new idioms, as the Spirit leads us, to address new contexts. But let us be sure that it is these that we are translating. Even if we were to take the phrase 'son of man' in its misleading popular sense, this much ought to be clear: we are followers of the first-century Jew called Jesus, and we need to think into his world. This means taking the risk of history, if we are to understand him in his own terms and those of his first followers. But if we then take the phrase 'son of man' seriously in that first-century context, as I have sketched in this chapter, then we are invoking the larger narratives of Daniel 7, and of Genesis, Exodus and the Psalms which that passage itself invokes, as well as the symbols of Temple and Sabbath which form the symbolic matrix for first-century interpretation. And, once we are there, we will find striking possibilities both for systematic theology, not least Trinity and Christology, and also for the practical mission of the Church. Perhaps those vocations are part of what is really involved in 'knowing and loving the Son of Man'.

Notes

1 On the radical change in the second-temple worldview following the Bar Kokhba revolt, see N. T. Wright, *The New Testament and the People of God* (London: SPCK, 1992), pp. 161–6, 199f. On the resurgence of Epicureanism in the modern period, see N. T. Wright, *History and Eschatology: Jesus and the Promise of Natural Theology* (Waco, TX: Baylor University Press, 2019).

2 Henry Chadwick, 'The Chalcedonian Definition', in *Selected Writings*, ed. by William G. Rusch (Grand Rapids, MI: Eerdmans, 2017), pp. 101–14.

3 See, for example, Géza Vermes, *Jesus the Jew* (London: Collins, 1973) and many subsequent works.

4 See, for example, Larry Hurtado, *Lord Jesus Christ: Devotion to Jesus in Earliest Christianity* (Grand Rapids, MI: Eerdmans, 2003), and several other works; Richard J. Bauckham, *Jesus and the God of Israel: 'God Crucified' and Other Studies on the New Testament's Christology of Divine Identity* (Grand Rapids, MI: Eerdmans, 2009), and other works; Richard B. Hays, *Echoes of Scripture in the Gospels* (Waco, TX: Baylor University Press, 2017).

5 On which, see the full treatment by John J. Collins, *Daniel* (Hermeneia Commentaries) (Minneapolis: Fortress Press, 1993), ad loc.

6 See Wright, *The New Testament and the People of God*, pp. 291–7; and N. T. Wright, *Jesus and the Victory of God* (London: SPCK, 1996), pp. 513–19.

7 See Daniel 2.48; 5.29; 6.28.

8 On the much-misunderstood term 'apocalyptic', see particularly N. T. Wright, *Paul and his Recent Interpreters* (London: SPCK, 2015), Part II; and Wright, *History and Eschatology*, ch. 4.

9 See recently, for example, Matthew V. Novenson, *Christ Among the Messiahs* (Oxford: Oxford University Press, 2015).

10 Josephus, *Jewish War*, 6.312–15. See the discussions in Wright, *The New Testament and the People of God*, pp. 312–14 and in N. T. Wright, *Paul and the Faithfulness of God* (London: SPCK, 2013), pp. 117, 130, 142, 293, 1065.

11 See the texts cited and discussed in Wright, *The New Testament and the People of God*, as above.

12 On all this see the now classic study of Alan F. Segal, *Two Powers in Heaven: Early Rabbinic Reports about Christianity and Gnosticism* (Leiden: Brill, 1977).

13 See Wright, *History and Eschatology*, ch. 5.

14 On the 'royal' vocation see, for example, Wright, *Jesus and the Victory of God*, pp. 481–6; Wright, *Paul and the Faithfulness of God*, pp. 817–25.

15 See the refs. in Wright, *Jesus and the Victory of God*, p. 517.

16 See Ben F. Meyer, *The Aims of Jesus* (London: SCM Press, 1979); E. P. Sanders, *Jesus and Judaism* (London: SCM Press, 1985).

17 See the discussion in Wright, *Jesus and the Victory of God*, pp. 510–19; and, for a thorough recent survey, Larry Hurtado, *Who Is This Son of Man? The Latest Scholarship on a Puzzling Expression of the Historical Jesus* (London: T & T Clark, 2012).

18 For this point and what follows, see N. T. Wright, 'Hope Deferred? Against the Dogma of Delay', *Early Christianity*, 9.1 (2018), pp. 37–82; and the further discussion in Wright, *History and Eschatology*, chs. 2, 4.

19 See, for example, David W. Congdon, *Rudolf Bultmann: A Companion to his Theology* (Eugene, OR: Cascade Books, 2015), pp. 10f.

20 Matthew 4.9; more clearly in Luke 4.6.

21 On both of which, see N. T. Wright, *Surprised by Hope* (London: SPCK, 2007).

22 See, for example, Mark 2.10. For the 'suffering' sayings, see, for example, Mark 10.45.

23 See, for example, Mark 2.28.

24 See N. T. Wright, *Scripture and the Authority of God* (2nd edn; London: SPCK, 2011), ch. 9; Wright, *History and Eschatology*, ch. 5.

25 See N. T. Wright, 'Son of Man – Lord of the Temple? Gospel Echoes of Psalm 8 and the Ongoing Christological Challenge', in *The Earliest Perceptions of Jesus in Context: Essays in Honour of John Nolland on his 70th Birthday*, ed. by Aaron White, David Wenham and Craig A. Evans (London: Bloomsbury/T & T Clark, 2018), pp. 77–96.

26 See the discussion of different interpretations of Isaiah 53 in Wright, *Jesus and the Victory of God*, pp. 588–91.

27 Mark 1.2–3, quoting Malachi 3.1; Isaiah 40.3.

28 Mark 10.35–45.

29 See Wright, 'Hope Deferred'; and Wright, *History and Eschatology*, chs. 2, 4.

30 Galatians 4.9.

31 Galatians 4.4–7; more fully in Romans 8.18–30.

3

The Son of Man in the Gospel of John[1]

JOHN BEHR

The figure of the Son of Man in the Gospel of John is one of the most enigmatic, perplexing and debated aspects of the Theologian's Gospel. The term 'son of man' of course is, in itself, simply a Semitic idiom, *barnasha*, used to refer to a human being, and can, in certain contexts, be used in an oblique manner to refer to the speaker himself. This is true of many of the 'son of man' sayings in the Synoptics. But through association with the enigmatic figure of 'one like a son of man' in Daniel (7.13), the figure denoted by the expression (now capitalized) 'Son of Man' comes to have apocalyptic associations. Aspects of the description of the Son of Man in Daniel are already evident in the Synoptics: in the predictions which speak of the Son of Man as 'sitting on his glorious throne' (Matt. 19.28), coming 'in clouds with great power and glory' (Mark 13.26), 'seated at the right hand of the power of God' (Mark 14.62; Luke 22.69), and all the tribulations that will occur at his fearful coming (Matt. 24.27–51; Luke 17.24–30).

But what is affirmed in the last mention of 'the Son of Man' from Christ's own lips in the Synoptics – that 'hereafter, you will see the Son of Man seated at the right hand of power' (Matt. 26.64) – is promised already at the beginning of the Gospel of John, in Jesus' enigmatic reply to Nathanael: after a string of titles applied to Christ ('the Lamb who takes away the sin of the world', 'Messiah/Christ', 'Son of God', and 'King of Israel' 1.35–49), the title 'Son of Man' is introduced in an apocalyptic fashion:

> You [ὄψῃ, singular] will see greater things than these . . . Truly, truly, I say to you, you [ὑμῖν, ὄψεσθε, plural] will see heaven opened, and the angels of God ascending and descending upon the Son of Man. (John 1.50–51)[2]

Not only does the apocalyptic Son of Man step on to the pages of the Gospel of John in this most dramatic manner, but there are features associated with the Son of Man in John that are specific to John, and striking. In particular, the Son of Man is said, in John 3.13, to ascend and descend (or is it descend and ascend?), and he acts upon earth in the present: he offers his flesh for consumption (6.51–53) and asks the man given sight if he believes in the Son of Man (9.35).

With the narrative of the Gospel prefaced by the Prologue, and many centuries of theological reflection thereafter, it is easy to read John's language of descending and ascending in terms of the Word, a heavenly figure, becoming incarnate on earth and then returning to the Father, an account of a descending and ascending Saviour, which Bultmann claimed was drawn from various Gnostic redeemer myths. But this is *not* what we are presented with in the Gospel. As John Ashton points out, 'in the body of the Gospel when John combines the notions of descent and ascent it is in relation to the Son of Man, not the Logos'.[3] Indeed the Logos, as a heavenly figure, does not appear in the rest of the Gospel nor is Jesus identified there by this title.[4] Moreover, regarding the title 'Son of Man', with whom the language of ascending and descending is associated, John Ashton also points out that far from what we might expect – that 'Son of Man' would refer to Christ as human and 'Son of God' to Christ as divine – the identification is paradoxically the reverse: '"Son of God", originally at any rate, indicates a human being, the Messiah; whereas "Son of Man" points to a figure whose true home is in heaven'.[5]

There are eight passages in which the term 'Son of Man' occurs in the Gospel of John: (1) 1.51; (2) 3.13, 14; (3) 5.26–27; (4) 6.27, 53, 62; (5) 8.28; (6) 9.35; (7) 12.23, 34; and (8) 13.31. Five of these are relatively straightforward: two pertain to judgement, which has been given to the Son 'because he is a Son of Man' (5.26–7), and similarly 9.35, where Jesus asks the man with his sight restored if he believes in the Son of Man, and then obliquely identifies himself as such, though, importantly (as we will see) not as an object of sight but of hearing (9.37), and three passages pertain to the Passion (8.28; 12.23; 13.31).[6] John 3.13–14 also speaks of the ascending and descending Son of Man, but is more involved.

[13] Both no one has ascended into heaven except he who has descended, the Son of Man,
[14] and, as Moses lifted up [ὕψωσεν] the snake in the wilderness, in this way [οὕτως] must be lifted up [ὑψωθῆναι δεῖ] the Son of Man,
[15] that whoever believes in him may have eternal life.
[16] In this way [οὕτως] God loved the world: that he gave the unique Son,
that whoever believes in him should not perish but have everlasting life.

John Ashton argues that the perfect tense of 'has ascended' naturally implies that by the time of his discussion with Nicodemus, Jesus has already ascended into heaven and also descended from there as the Son of Man *in that order*, that is, that Jesus has already ascended into heaven, perhaps at the Transfiguration (though not mentioned by John), and descended as the Son of Man, to later ascend the cross and return to the Father.[7] But rather than speculating about events that are not mentioned, the apparently confusing nature of the verse is best explained by the merging of times or melding of horizons that characterizes the Gospel of John. That such a fusion of temporal horizons is at work here is made abundantly clear in verse 11: 'Truly, truly, I say to you, we speak of what we know, and bear witness to what we have seen; but you do not receive our testimony.' 'I say' changes to 'we say', where the 'we' clearly includes John and his readers, engaged in dialogue with the teachers of Israel. Regarding verse 13, J. Louis Martyn comments:

> The Son of Man ascends to heaven on the cross, but in some sense he returns to earth in the person of the Paraclete and can therefore enter into conversation with 'Nicodemus' as he who *has ascended* to heaven (3:13). The Paraclete makes Jesus present on earth as the Son of Man who binds together heaven and earth.[8]

Jesus is present in this discussion with Nicodemus as the one who has ascended to heaven through the cross. Moreover, 3.13 is so intimately tied to verses 14–16 that it cannot be taken separately: verse 13, as does verse 14, begins with a modest *kai* (both/and; which is almost invariably left out of translation and consideration), and both end with 'the Son of Man'; and the step from Moses to the Son of Man is then connected, through the repeated 'in this way', to God's love: 3.13 and 14 are set in parallel, with the purpose given in verse 15 and traced back to God himself in verse 16.

Let us now turn to John 6, where Jesus asks the question 'Then what if you were to see the Son of Man ascending to where he was before?' (6.62). There is, in this chapter, no mention of the Son of Man 'descending', but there are instead plenty of references to the bread that 'descends' from the heavens (6.33, 50, 58), to Jesus as the one who has himself 'descended from heaven' (6.38, 42) and to Jesus as the 'bread which descended from heaven' (6.41, 51) – seven mentions of 'descending' before the single description of the Son of Man ascending (6.62). The descending of the bread from heaven, I argue elsewhere, is tied to Christ's ascent of the cross, to become the bread which we consume, 'chewing' his flesh, in meditating upon the Scriptures, consuming his flesh and becoming his body through following him in martyrdom.[9]

And finally 9.35, where the blind man, whose sight was restored (or rather given to him) by Jesus, is asked by Jesus: 'Do you believe in the Son of Man?', and when asked who this is, Jesus replies: 'You have seen him and it is he who speaks to you'. There is no mention here of ascending/descending, but the transition from sight to hearing is suggestive and important, and we will return to it. To conclude this survey of the 'Son of Man' in the Gospel of John, it turns out that John 1.51, the passage where the Son of Man steps onto the pages of the Gospel of John, is thus the only passage which speaks of ascending and descending Son of Man with no obvious reference to the Passion.

John 1.51

In this verse, John alludes to Jacob's vision of the ladder with angels ascending and descending upon it (or him), but subtly changes its locus, from a place, Bethel – 'truly this is the house of God and this is the gate of heaven' (Gen. 28.17) – to a person, the Son of Man, as the sole locus of revelation. The key questions regarding this verse are, first, why does John describe this figure as the Son of Man, and, second, when ('hereafter you will see . . .') is the promised vision actually seen? Before we turn to these questions, there are two other peculiar features which need to be investigated. First, why do the angels ascend before descending? Surely they should descend from heaven before ascending? And, second, why do the angels move up and down not upon a ladder but upon a person?

The idea that the angels ascend and descend upon a person is facilitated by the ambiguity of the Hebrew, where the pronoun can be taken as referring to Jacob, unlike the LXX where the feminine pronoun must refer back to the ladder (Gen. 28.12). Various scholars have pointed to rabbinic discussion about this verse to find parallels for John 1.51, and to a text known as 'The Prayer of Joseph', preserved by Origen, in which the figure of Jacob is duplicated: he is both asleep on earth below and simultaneously portrayed in the throne of Glory above, while the angels, on the other hand, who must ascend and descend to see him in heaven and on earth, cannot be in both places simultaneously.[10] One further text which puts Israel/Jacob and Christ in a heavenly and earthly realm mirroring each other, previously not commented on, is Origen's conclusion, in *On First Principles*, about how the narrative of Scripture should be read. Paul's statement, 'Behold, Israel according to the flesh' (1 Cor. 10.18) implies, Origen argues, that 'there is an Israel according to the Spirit',[11] a distinction that Origen also finds in Paul's words, 'For it is not the children of the flesh that are the children of God, for not all who are descended from Israel belong to Israel' (Rom. 9.8, 6), and in the apostle's contrast between one who is 'a Jew openly' and one who is 'a Jew in secret' (Rom. 2.28–29). As such, Origen proposes that we should read Scripture in a double fashion, as parallel or corresponding narratives, in which, on the literal or physical level, Jacob is the head of the 'bodily Israelites' and is descended from those further back, while, on the spiritual level, Jacob, by means of a spiritual birth, traces his lineage back through Isaac and Abraham to Adam, whom, Origen says, is Christ.[12] Following Paul, Adam and Eve – the heads of all those descended from them – are paralleled by Christ and the Church – the heads of all those who live in God. Besides the reference to Christ, Origen's picture also differs from that of the rabbis in that for them it is Jacob's 'image' that is in heaven, whereas for Origen the earthly figures are 'types' of their spiritual counterparts. With a different end in view, and the heavens now opened, 'our citizenship', as the apostle says, 'is in the heavens and from it we await a Saviour, the Lord

Jesus Christ, who will change our lowly body to be like his glorious body' (Phil. 3.20–21).[13]

These rabbinic and early Christian readings of Scripture indicate very vividly a fundamental feature of apocalyptic thinking, that is, the idea of correspondences between heaven and earth (and between beginning and end). On this, John Ashton points out:

> For Enoch, and for apocalyptic writers generally, there are not two worlds but one: or rather the whole of reality is split into matching pairs (rather like the biological theory of DNA) in which one half, the lower, is the mirror-image (albeit in this case a distorting mirror) of the higher. That is why a revelation of what is above is not just relevant or related to what happens or is about to happen on earth: rather what happens on earth is a re-enactment in earthly terms of what has happened in heaven: a correspondence![14]

In the light of these considerations, the dramatic words of Jesus in John 1.51 seem not so out of place as it might have first seemed. From the rabbinic texts, then, there are parallels to the idea of angels ascending and descending upon a person, although, as these texts are later than John, it may well be that it was John himself who prompted the rabbis to suggest that the ambiguous pronoun of Genesis 28.12 could be taken as referring to Jacob rather than the ladder. And from Origen we have a wholesale picture in which all rational beings have descended in the foundation of the world as we know it, the world that labours in travail towards the unveiling of the sons of God, much like 'the woman' of John 16.20–22, suffering tribulation 'in this world' (cf. 16.33), until that tribulation is changed into joy when 'a human being is born into the world' (16.21).

Ashton suggests that in the rabbinic texts that speak of Jacob as being asleep on earth while his image is engraved on the heavenly throne, there is no concern to establish which is the 'real' Jacob: 'to put the question in this way may be to presuppose a dichotomy not envisaged by the writer, who is more concerned to establish the identity between the two figures than to arbitrate between them'.[15] The gist of this is certainly correct, but there remains the fact that the angels nevertheless have to ascend to see him above and descend to see him below. The Son of Man figure in John 1.51, on the other hand, although only appearing when the heavens are opened, is not some kind of divine man standing in the heavens now accessible to sight, or ready to be sent on a mission, to descend to earth. The language of mission is nowhere used by John to describe the Son of Man and his activities. The Son of Man, at least in 1.51, is not a divine emissary sent from above, but rather an intermediary, a figure who embraces both heaven and earth, in himself, the place, or rather the person, where heaven and earth meet together. If the angels ascend and descend upon him, it is because, to borrow a saying of Heraclitus, 'the way up and the way down is one and the same'.[16]

We can now turn to the two questions regarding John 1.51 we asked earlier: first, why does John describe the figure who appears when the heavens are opened as 'the Son of Man', and, second, when is this promised vision seen? Regarding the title itself, that it is introduced as the climax of an ascending series of titles across 1.35–49 (the Lamb of God, Messiah/Christ, Son of God, King of Israel) indicates that something more is yet to be seen; as noted earlier, four of the instances of the use of 'Son of Man' in John refer to the Passion (3.14; 8.28; 12.23, 34; 13.31). That the other titles are used across the Synoptics, in which the last mention of the 'Son of Man' from Christ's own lips is the promise that 'hereafter you will see the Son of Man seated at the right hand of Power', seems to indicate that John is picking up where the Synoptics left off (reinforced by the ἀπ᾽ἄρτι in 1.51 in some manuscripts) and providing an account of Jesus permeated from the beginning and thereafter with this high vision.

As to when the promised vision is seen, it is important to note that the promise to Nathanael alone in 1.50, 'you will see [ὄψῃ, singular] greater things than these', morphs into a promise made to many in 1.51, 'you will see [ὄψεσθε, plural] the heavens opened and the angels of God ascending and descending upon the Son of Man', which must, as Ashton asserts, be taken to include not only other disciples present at the scene, but all readers and hearers of the Gospel thereafter.[17] After the promise of 1.51, the next words are 'on the third day' (2.1; following the 'days' of 1.35 and 43). Although John does not use the terminology of 'the third day' in describing the resurrection of Christ (he is encountered, rather, on the first and eighth days, 20.1, 19, 26), anyone with a broader knowledge of the Christian gospel would have made this connection. It is moreover in the following scene at Cana that Jesus performs 'the first of his signs' and 'manifested his glory' (2.11). However, it would be wrong to take the promise as being fulfilled only here: the whole of the Gospel of John is a carefully framed account of Jesus' construction of the true Temple of God, which he himself is and which climaxes when he is crucified. So, in a sense, Benjamin Reynolds is right to conclude that the vision of the apocalyptic Son of Man 'encompasses all of Jesus' work, his revelation and glorification of the Father, which is ultimately fulfilled in the death, resurrection, and return to the Father in glory'.[18]

However, perhaps one can be more specific. If we are promised 'to see' the Son of Man, this, I would argue, is specifically fulfilled with Pilate's injunction, given unwittingly and with a typical Johannine double meaning, *to see*: 'Behold the human being' (19.5). Already in the nineteenth century Westcott suggested that 'the human being' in Pilate's statement was a reference to the Son of Man, and he was followed by Charles Dodd and Joseph Blank.[19] Much of recent scholarship on the Son of Man in John, however, has seen John's use of this title as deriving from apocalyptic texts referring to such an otherworldly figure, as Ashton does, while others have emphasized a continuity with the figure of the suffering Jesus in the Synoptic

Gospels. It is possible, however, that these two positions are not diametrically opposed. As Francis Moloney puts it:

> Throughout the Gospel the reader has been directed to look forward; in
> 13, 31 he has been told: 'Now is the Son of man glorified' and finally, in
> the ironic coronation and investiture of Jesus, it is Pilate who announces:
> 'Here he is – the Son of Man!' The absurd glorification through humilia
> tion has reached its high point.[20]

The way up and the way down, that of glorification and humiliation upon
the cross, are, once again, one and the same.

The human being

But there is more that we can say about this identification made by Pilate
of the human being. Following John in the second century are those whom
Lightfoot called 'the school of John', for they form a tight group in their
theology and paschal practice.[21] In fact, it seems that, initially, they were
the only ones to have an annual feast of Pascha.[22] They also have a very
distinctive use of the term 'human being'. For instance, Ignatius sees his
impending martyrdom as his birth into life as a human being and urges the
Christians at Rome not to try to dissuade him from following in the footsteps of Christ:

> Birth-pangs are upon me. Suffer me, my brethren; hinder me not from
> living, do not wish me to die. . . . Suffer me to receive the pure light; when
> I shall have arrived there, I shall be a human being (ἐκεῖ παραγενόμενος
> ἄνθρωπος ἔσομαι). Suffer me to follow the example of the passion of my
> God.[23]

Likewise, when Irenaeus asserts that 'the glory of God is a living human
being and the life of the human being is to see God',[24] he specifically has in
mind the martyr (for no one can see God and live).[25]

Ignatius and Irenaeus (and also Melito) certainly have a very distinctive
approach to what it is to be a living human being, that is, a martyr and
the glory of God. The glory of God was seen, according to John, by Isaiah
(12.41), the prophet who repeatedly refers to those things spoken about
from of old but only revealed in the end, especially the particular purpose
of God, 'to make the human being for ever' (Isa. 44.7). If we do indeed
go back to what is spoken about from of old, at the very beginning, in the
opening words of Genesis, we will find that the distinctive understanding of
'the human being' shared by the school of John is grounded in the way in
which Genesis is played upon by John himself, as he indicates already in the
opening words of his Gospel.

There is a striking, but little noticed, difference in the way that God's creative activity is described in the opening chapter of Scripture. It begins with God issuing commands: 'Let there be light . . . a firmament . . . let the earth bring forth living creatures' (Gen. 1.3–25). This divine 'fiat' – 'let it be' – is sufficient to bring all these creatures into existence: 'and it was so . . . and it was good'. But then, having declared all these things into existence by a word alone, setting the stage as it were, God, not with an imperative but with a subjunctive, announces: 'Let us make the human being [ποιήσωμεν ἄνθρωπον] in our image, after our likeness' (Gen. 1.26). This is the only thing about which God specifically deliberates; it is his divine purpose and resolve. With Scripture opening with this announcement of the particular project of God, we can now hear a further dimension to Christ's last word from the cross in the Gospel of John: τέτελεσται, it is finished, completed, perfected (19.30), confirmed, moreover, though unwittingly, by Pilate: 'Behold, the human being' (19.5, ἰδοὺ ὁ ἄνθρωπος)! The particular project of God, to create a human being in his image and likeness, is not accomplished simply by a divine fiat, then and there; it depends, rather, upon the fiat of Christ, and those like Ignatius who also, in Christ, give their own 'let it be'.

Discussion about the relation between the seven days of creation and John's presentation of Christ seems to go back to the earliest days, beginning perhaps even with John himself. Irenaeus and Victorinus of Pettau independently record a tradition that goes back to Papias and the elders in Asia who knew John, about the seven ages of Christ's life, affirming even that John informed them that Christ had reached the age of a teacher, that is, between 40 and 50 years old (*haer.* 2.22.4–5). According to Victorinus, in words which most likely go back to Papias, Christ 'consummates his humanity [*humanitatem . . . consummat*] in the number seven: birth, infancy, boyhood, youth, young-manhood, maturity, death'.[26] In modern times, attempts at correlating Genesis 1 with the Gospel of John have focused on the structure of John's narrative, seeing the seven days of creation played out over specific parts, such as 1.19–2.12, or chapters 1–5, or with the Gospel as a whole, or as correlated to the seven 'signs' worked by Jesus.[27] However, none of these modern suggestions have met with much approval, nor do they help in making the point argued here. It would of course be satisfying to see the days of creation plotted out along the course of John's Gospel, such that they culminate with Christ saying 'it is finished', and to have these marked out as clearly as the liturgical markers plotting the course of the narrative in John's Gospel. However, there are three points prior to the Passion which indicate an understanding of 'human being' that not only laid the basis for the way in which it is used by his 'school' but that it was used in this way by John himself.

The first of these occurs during the healing of the lame man in John 5, where it states that the healing waters were inaccessible to him because he has no 'human being' to immerse him in them (5.7). Christ directs him to 'rise' (5.8, ἔγειρε), and in the ensuing exchange about working on the

Sabbath, Christ asserts that 'my Father is working still [ἕως ἄρτι ἐργάζεται] and I am working' (5.17), leading the Jews to seek to kill him for making himself equal to God (5.18). As Jesus further expounds what this work is, he specifies that what the Father does, and the Son seeing this does likewise, is to 'raise [ἐγείρει] the dead and give them life' (5.21), so that one who hears the word of Christ and believes in him who sent him, 'has eternal life; he does not come into judgment, but has passed from death to life' (5.24), and this is so because 'just as the Father has life in himself, so he has granted the Son to have life in himself' (5.26). In these ways, then, the question about working on the Sabbath has been significantly increased in scope: the work in question is to bring life out of death, and so the 'sixth day' when 'God finished his works [συνετέλεσεν . . . τὰ ἔργα] that he had made and left off on the seventh day from all his works [ἀπὸ πάντων τῶν ἔργων] that he had made' (Gen. 2.2) refers to the 'hour' that is yet to come, when the work is 'finished' (19.30), and life comes about through death. Although crucified on the day of Preparation, the timing of the event, after the sixth hour (cf. 19.14), which, because of the multitude of lambs that needed to be slain, was reckoned to be 'towards the evening' as specified by Exodus 12.6, ties that day, on the Jewish pattern of reckoning days, to the Sabbath, which was not only the Sabbath but 'a great day' (19.31). The true Sabbath is Christ's rest in the tomb, celebrated in the feast of Pascha: God ceases from his work, for his project is completed.

The second instance occurs during the Feast of Tabernacles, when Jesus, referring back to the healing of the lame man the last time he was in Jerusalem (cf. 7.22), argues that if circumcision is permissible on the Sabbath, they should not be angry because 'on the Sabbath I made the whole human being sound' (7.23: ὅλον ἄνθρωπον ὑγιῆ ἐποίησα). This theme is continued, during the period of the same feast, but on the Sabbath (9.14), when Jesus heals the man born blind by spitting on the ground and smearing the mud where his eyes should have been. The whole lengthy account is skilfully divided into seven scenes, during the course of which Jesus is mentioned by name seven times. The question of his disciples that prompted this whole event, 'who sinned, this man or his parents, that he was born blind?' (9.2), though later taken in terms of theodicy, is answered by Jesus quite differently: he was born blind 'so that the works of God might be made manifest in him' (9.3). In the first interpretation of this passage we have by Irenaeus, he notes how Christ's words and the peculiar manner by which he heals the blind man parallels the way in which Genesis describes how God creates human beings. This leads Irenaeus to conclude that 'the work of God is fashioning the human being' (haer. 5.15.2: opera autem Dei plasmatio est hominis). Thus, the Sabbath on which this happens is once again not simply the Sabbath of the Pharisees, on which no human work is carried out, but the Sabbath of God himself, whose 'work' is 'fashioning the human being' in the stature of Christ himself, who is indicated by the number seven, not six, and is completed in the Passion when Christ is crucified after the sixth hour on the day of Preparation, that is, 'towards the evening', and then rests in the tomb on the Sabbath.

It is, as noted earlier, also important to note that when Jesus asks the man who now sees if he believes in the Son of Man, and the man asks who this is, Jesus replies: 'You have seen him and it is he who speaks to you' (9.37). Sight belongs to the past; being addressed vocally by the Son of Man is in the present. It is, after all, only after the crucifixion, and as the crucified one, that Jesus is called the Word of God: it is the one who sits on the white horse (Rev. 19.11), who is 'clad in a robe dipped in blood, and the name by which he is called is The Word of God' (Rev. 19.13: κέκληται τὸ ὄνομα αὐτοῦ ὁ λόγος τοῦ θεοῦ). A further parallel with the book of Revelation is when, after being instructed to write to the various churches, John says: 'I turned to see the voice that was speaking to me' (Rev. 1.12). John, just as the blind man, sees the voice speaking to him. It is also striking that Ignatius, too, by following Christ in martyrdom, hopes to become not only a living human being, born into life through his death, but also 'a word of God': if you are silent about me, he tells the Roman Christians, I too will be 'a word of God'.[28]

The third indicator, bringing together the beginning, middle and end of the Gospel, is the figure of the 'woman'. She appears at Cana, when Jesus' 'hour' was not yet (2.4), and, when the 'hour' had come, she is standing at the foot of the cross, where she is addressed by Jesus as 'woman' (19.26) and described as 'his mother' by the evangelist (19.15) but as 'the mother' when seen from the perspective of Jesus himself (19.26). The woman also appears in the words of consolation given by Christ to his disciples as his departure approaches:

Truly, truly, I say to you, you will weep and lament, but the world will rejoice; you will be sorrowful, but your sorrow will turn to joy. When the woman [ἡ γυνὴ] is in travail she has sorrow [λύπην] because her hour has come; but when she is delivered of the child [ὅταν δὲ γεννήσῃ τὸ παιδίον], she no longer remembers the tribulation [θλίψεως], for joy that a human being is born into the world [ἐγεννήθη ἄνθρωπος εἰς τὸν κόσμον]. So you have sorrow now, but I will see you again and your hearts will rejoice, and no one will take your joy from you. (John 16.20–22)

'The woman' whose 'hour has come' is the link between Cana and the Passion. This passage also contains a transition from the birth of a 'child' to that of a 'human being into the world', words which, as Judith Lieu points out, recall the 'human being coming into the world' mentioned in the Prologue (1.9, ἄνθρωπος ἐρχόμενον εἰς τὸν κόσμον).[29] Although the disciples' 'sorrow' at the departure of Christ is paralleled by the woman's 'sorrow' during her travail, with both also being turned into 'joy', the 'tribulation' of the woman is not simply paralleled by the disciples' anguish between the departure and return of Christ. In the world, they certainly have 'tribulation' (θλῖψιν), but Christ comforts them: 'be of good cheer, I have overcome the world' (16.33). As Lieu further notes, the perfect in 16.28 ('I have come into the world') 'is coterminous with the parallel perfect' in 16.33 ('I have overcome the world'), so that, as she puts it: 'this woman too mediates a beginning that is also an ending/an ending that is also a beginning in the merging of times and experiences that characterize these chapters'.[30] Lieu asks: 'So is this a birthing or a dying? . . . we meet birth here only when we encounter death. Indeed, the birth, which is not narrated in this Gospel, becomes through 16.21 a death, or is the death a birth?'[31] Perhaps the proper answer is both, and both together – as with Ignatius, born, through martyrdom, into life as a human being.

There are further parallels with Genesis at play in these words of comfort and the crucifixion scene. As Tertullian points out, with Adam being a figure of Christ, Adam's sleep foreshadows Christ's death, and so as Eve came forth from the side of the sleeping Adam, so too the Church, in the form of blood and water, comes forth from the side of Christ in mortal slumber.[32] Furthermore, 'the woman' (ἡ γυνή) in Genesis 3 is promised 'sorrow' (λύπη) in childbirth (Gen 3.16), just as is 'the woman' of John 16.20–21, and when Eve does give birth it is a 'human being' that she acquires 'from God' (Gen. 4.1, ἐκτησάμην ἄνθρωπον διὰ τοῦ θεοῦ), as it is also a 'human being' that is born in 16.21. However, although Adam calls 'the woman' 'Eve' (or 'Life' in the LXX), 'because she is the mother of the living' (Gen. 3.20), all her children in fact die, for which the word 'sorrow' (Gen. 3.16), rather than 'travail', is the appropriate term, as Lieu points out, applying as it does to mental anguish rather than physical or birth pain.

Thus the Church turns out to be the true 'mother of the living', 'our mother' (Gal. 4.26, re. Isa. 54.1), as Christ is the true human (and Adam but a 'type', a preliminary sketch, cf. Rom. 5.14). And she acquires as living human beings those who, following Christ, are born through martyric death, anticipated by baptism (cf. Rom. 6.3–11) and in partaking of the eucharistic cup (as in John 6). Again, this combination of Pauline and Johannine themes, seeing Genesis as speaking about Christ and his Church, seems to have originated, according to Anastasius of Sinai, in Asia Minor, in the circle of the elders who knew John and whose traditions Papias recorded.[33] God's purpose, spoken of old and reiterated by Isaiah, 'to make the human being forever' (Isa. 44.7), is thus completed when women and men give their own fiat to God's purpose, by following Christ, as Ignatius did, becoming witnesses, martyrs, no longer trying to secure their lives, but rather taking up the cross and living by dying: 'as dying, behold we live' (2 Cor. 6.9). 'Be my witnesses/martyrs: I too am a witness/martyr, says the Lord God, and the Servant whom I have chosen' (Isa. 43.10). The Gospel of the Theologian, thus, encompasses the beginning and end of all the work of God, as Christ's 'it is finished' brings to completion God's own purpose, the living human being, the glory of God.

So, to return to the question of when it is that the vision promised in John 1.50–1 occurs, the vision is not simply the appearance in this world of an otherworldly figure, but the completion or perfecting, the appearance or unveiling, of God's project announced from the beginning. What it means to see Christ in this way was seen by John, the only disciple – the beloved disciple – to stand at the foot of the cross while the woman gives birth to a human being. It is also seen *in John*, as Origen points out, reflecting on the words of Christ from the cross in the Gospel of John:

> We might dare say, then, that the Gospels are the firstfruits of all Scriptures, but that the firstfruits of the Gospels is that according to John, whose meaning no one can understand who has not leaned on Jesus' breast nor received Mary from Jesus to be his mother also. But he who would be another John must also become such as John, to be shown to be Jesus, so to speak. For if Mary had no son except Jesus, in accordance with those who hold a sound opinion of her, and Jesus says to his mother, 'Behold your son,' and not, 'Behold, this man also is your son,' he has said equally, 'Behold, this is Jesus whom you bore.' For indeed everyone who has been perfected 'no longer lives, but Christ lives in him,' and since 'Christ lives' in him, it is said of him to Mary, 'Behold your son,' the Christ.[34]

It is, moreover, a vision not limited to that specific occasion but also seen by those of John's 'school' in those who undergo martyrdom: when Blandina, for instance, was 'hung on a stake [ἐπὶ ξύλου]', her fellow Christians alongside her in the amphitheatre, 'seeing her hanging in the form of a cross . . . beheld with their outward eyes, through the sister, him who was crucified for them', providing encouragement to those who had lapsed, so that 'there was great joy for the Virgin Mother in receiving back alive those who she had miscarried as dead'.[35] The glory of God revealed in the Passion of Christ is beheld in the martyr, 'the living human being' who is, as Irenaeus puts it, the very 'glory of God' (*haer.* 4.20.7), and, indeed, the embodiment of Christ, the Son of Man.

Notes

1 Much of the material in this essay is drawn from my *John the Theologian and His Paschal Gospel: A Prologue to Theology* (Oxford: Oxford University Press, 2019).

2 As Benjamin Reynolds, *The Apocalyptic Son of Man in the Gospel of John*, Wissenschaftliche Untersuchungen zum Neuen Testament 2.249 (Tübingen: Mohr Siebeck, 2008), p. 100, notes, some early manuscripts (A Θ Ψ $f^{1.13}$ 33) and the Syriac versions have ἀπ'ἄρτι in John 1.51, suggesting that 'at least some early Christians may have made the connection between the final Son of Man saying in Mark and Matthew and the first Son of Man saying in John'.

3 John Ashton, 'The Johannine Son of Man: A New Proposal', *New Testament Studies*, 57 (2011), pp. 508–29 (p. 512).

4 There are of course numerous other ways in which Jesus' heavenly origin is made clear without using either the title 'Son of Man' or the language of ascending and descending: he is 'from above' (3.31), 'sent' from the Father (5.23–24) and so on.

5 John Ashton, *Understanding the Fourth Gospel*, new edn (Oxford: Oxford University Press, 2007 [1991]), p. 240.

6 It should also be noted that the three passages which speak of the Son of Man being 'lifted up' do not use the verb ἀναβαίνω, 'to ascend' (as in 1.51; 3.13; 6.62), but ὑψόω (3.14; 8.28; 12.34), undoubtedly derived from Isaiah 52.13: 'my servant shall understand and he shall be exalted and glorified exceedingly [ὑψωθήσεται καὶ δοξασθήσεται σφόδρα]'.

7 Ashton, 'Johannine Son of Man', pp. 519–20.

8 J. Louis Martyn, *History and Theology in the Fourth Gospel*, The New Testament Library, 3rd edn (Louisville, KY: Westminster John Knox, 2003 [1968]), p. 138.

9 Behr, *John the Theologian*, pp. 148–60.

10 See Jacob Neusner, *Genesis Rabbah: The Judaic Commentary to the Book of Genesis: A New American Translation*, 3 vols, Brown Judaic Studies 104, 105, 106 (Atlanta, GA: Scholars Press, 1985), 68.12.6; *Targum Neofiti I: Genesis*, ET Martin McNamara, The Aramaic Bible, The Targums, 1A (Collegeville, MN: Liturgical Press, 1992), 28:12; and Origen, *Commentary on John*, 2.189–90, ed. and trans. by R. E. Heine, FC 80 (Washington, DC: Catholic University of America, 1989), pp. 145–6; for these texts and discussion see Behr, *John the Theologian*, pp. 222–5.

11 Origen, *Origen: On First Principles*, ed. and trans. by John Behr, Oxford Early Christian Texts (Oxford: Oxford University Press, 2017), 4.3.6.

12 Origen, *Origen: On First Principles*, 4.3.7.

13 On this, see John Behr, introduction to *Origen: On First Principles*, pp. lxxx–lxxxviii, and Behr, *John the Theologian*, pp. 225–7.

14 Ashton, *Fourth Gospel*, p. 327.

15 Ashton *Fourth Gospel*, p. 247.

16 Heraclitus 61 (F38): ὁδὸς ἄνω κάτω μία καὶ ὡυτή.

17 Ashton, *Fourth Gospel*, p. 251.

18 Reynolds, *Apocalyptic Son of Man*, p. 103.

19 Cf. Brooke Foss Westcott, *The Gospel According to St John* (London: John Murray, 1882), p. 269; Charles Dodd, *The Interpretation of the Fourth Gospel* (Cambridge: Cambridge University Press, 1953), p. 437; Josef Blank, *Krisis: Untersuchungen zur johanneischen Christologie und Eschatologie* (Freiburg: Lambertus, 1964), p. 289, n. 60; and Josef Blank, 'Die Verhandlung vor Pilatus Joh 18,28–19,16, im Lichte johanneischer Theologie', *Biblische Zeitschrift* 3 (1959), pp. 60–81 (p. 75, n. 38).

20 Francis Moloney, *The Johannine Son of Man*, Biblioteca di Scienze Religiose, 14, 2nd edn (Rome: Libreria Ateno Salesiano, 1976), p. 207.

21 J. B. Lightfoot, *Essays on the Work Entitled Supernatural Religion* (London: Macmillan, 1889), esp. p. 217.

22 Behr, *John the Theologian*, pp. 77–92.

23 Ignatius of Antioch, *Letter to the Romans* 6; ed. and trans. by Alistair Stewart, PPS (Crestwood, NY: St. Vladimir's Seminary Press, 2013).

24 Irenaeus of Lyons, *Against the Heresies*. 4.20.7. *Haer.* 1–3 ed. and French trans. by A. Rousseau and L. Doutreleau, Sources chrétiennes 263–4, 293–4, 210–11 (Paris: Cerf, 1979, 1982, 1974); *Haer.* 4 ed. and French trans. by A. Rousseau, B. Hemmerdinger, L. Doutreleau and C. Mercier, Sources chrétiennes 100 (Paris: Cerf, 1965); *Haer.* 5 ed. and French trans. by A. Rousseau, L. Doutreleau and C. Mercier Sources chrétiennes 152–3 (Paris: Cerf, 1969); ET Ante-Nicene Fathers 1; *Haer.* 1, D. J. Unger, rev. J. J. Dillon, Ancient Christian Writers 55 (New York: Paulist Press, 1992); *Haer.* 2, Ancient Christian Writers 65 (New York: Paulist Press, 2012); *Haer.* 3, D. J. Unger, rev. Irenaeus M. C. Steenberg, Ancient Christian Writers 64 (New York: Newman Press, 2012), 4.20.7.

25 Cf. Irenaeus, *Against the Heresies*, 5.9.2; John Behr, *Irenaeus of Lyons: Identifying Christianity*, Christian Theology in Context (Oxford: Oxford University Press, 2013), pp. 198–203.

26 Victorinus, *On the Making of the World*, ed. and French trans. by M. Dulaey, Sources chrétiennes 423 (Paris: Cerf, 1997), 9. Cf. John Chapman, 'Papias on the Age of Our Lord', *Journal of Theological Studies* 9 (1907), pp. 42–51.

27 See Carlos Raúl Sosa Siliezar, *Creation Imagery in the Gospel of John*, Library of New Testament Studies 546 (London: Bloomsbury, 2015), pp. 123–49.

28 Ignatius of Antioch, *Letter to the Romans*, 2.1.

29 Judith Lieu, 'The Mother of the Son in the Fourth Gospel', *Journal of Biblical Literature*, 117.1 (1998), pp. 61–77 (p. 72).

30 Lieu, 'The Mother of the Son in the Fourth Gospel', p. 72.

31 Lieu, 'The Mother of the Son in the Fourth Gospel', p. 73.

32 Tertullian, *On the Soul*, ed. by Jan Hendrik Waszink (Amsterdam: Mülenhoff, 1947); ET Ante-Nicene Fathers 3, 43.10.

33 Anastasius of Sinai, *Hexaemeron*, 1.6.1; 7b.5.5; ed. and trans. by Clement A. Kuehn and John D. Baggarly, Orientalia Christiana Analecta 278 (Rome: Pontificio Isituto Orientale, 2007).

34 Origen, *Commentary on John*, 1.23.

35 Eusebius of Caesarea, *Historial ecclesiastica*, 5.1.41, 45; ed. and trans. by Kirsopp Lake, Loeb Classical Library, 2 vols (Cambridge, MA: Harvard University Press, 1989).

PART 2

Christ the Word and Wisdom of God in Human Form

The Naming of Jesus[1]

Luke 2.21: And when eight days were accomplished for the circumcising of the child, his name was called JESUS, which was so named of the angel before he was conceived in the womb.

I name you now, from whom all names derive
Who uttered forth the name of everything,
And in that naming made the world alive,
Sprung from the breath and essence of your being.
The very Word that gave us words to speak,
You drank in language with your mother's milk
And learned through touch before you learned to talk.
You wove our week-day world, and still one week
Within that world, you took your saving name,
A given name, the gift of that good angel,
Whose Gospel breathes in good news for us all.
We call your name that we might hear a call
That carries from your cradle to our graves
Yeshua, Living Jesus, Yahweh Saves.

1 Originally published in Malcolm Guite, *Parable and Paradox* (Norwich: Canterbury Press, 2016).

4

'From a Human Point of View': The Problem of Knowing Christ in Chalcedonian Perspective

IAN A. MCFARLAND

The problem

In February 1519, Martin Luther wrote the following to his friend, Georg Spalatin: 'Whoever wishes to deliberate or speculate soundly about God should disregard absolutely everything except the humanity of Christ.'[1] Although Luther is not typically seen as a champion of strict Chalcedonianism, I view his dictum as profoundly Chalcedonian in that it reflects the principle that in Christ the two natures of divinity and humanity are united 'without confusion or change', such that the Incarnation does nothing to modify the essential attributes of the divine nature – most especially its invisibility.[2] Thus, in opposition to Leo the Great's interpretation of the communion of the two natures in Christ to mean that the divine 'shines forth with miracles' while the human 'succumbs to injuries', Luther reminds us that the only nature that we see in Jesus – and thus the only one to which we can and therefore must attend – is human.[3] Insofar as this nature has been enhypostatized by the second person of the Trinity (so that Jesus may without qualification be identified as the eternal Word or Son of God), it is by attention to this instance of humanity that we come to know God, so that all talk about God must finally be tested against the humanity of this individual. The Incarnation, in short, means that God is most fully and truly known in Jesus, and thus humanly.

And yet the strict application of Luther's dictum – and of the Chalcedonianism I take it to represent – as a basis for reflection on Christian hope runs into problems when it is juxtaposed with a second quotation, which comes from Paul's second letter to the Corinthians: 'Even though we once knew Christ from a human point of view, we know him no longer in that way' (2 Cor. 5.16). If Luther insists that knowledge of God turns on our knowledge of Jesus' humanity, Paul's declaration seems to cast doubt on the ability to acquire such knowledge in the first place, for how can we, being human, possibly know the human Christ except 'from a human point of view'?

In trying to understand Paul's claim here, it is necessary to turn to the Greek of the passage, which reveals that the NRSV's 'from a human point of view' translates *kata sarka*, or 'according to the flesh'. This is a tricky phrase, as it can reasonably be taken as referring to the subjective as much as the objective dimensions of our knowledge of Christ – that is, to *how* we know as much as *what* we know – as the NRSV translation suggests. Yet, in contrast to the NRSV, I would like to stress the objective dimension, not least because the question of how we know anything is inseparable from its objective characteristics. Moreover, this emphasis seems to me justified by the passage itself, insofar as Paul is willing to grant that we may have once known Christ 'according to the flesh', even though we are no longer able to know him in that way. The most obvious interpretation of the contrast Paul has in mind here is with reference to the change in the objective character of Christ's existence: because he is now risen from the dead, we are no longer able to know him on the basis of encounter with the flesh-and-blood materiality that defined his earthly ministry prior to Good Friday. Insofar as Jesus has now 'ascended into heaven' and 'is seated at the right hand of the Father', he has transcended life in time and space, and so it seems to follow that our knowledge of him therefore no longer can or should be defined by the physical parameters of his fleshy existence. This line of interpretation seems further supported by the immediately preceding verses, where reference to Jesus' death and resurrection is quite explicit: 'For the love of Christ urges us on, because we are convinced that one has died for all; therefore all have died. And he died for all, so that those who live might live no longer for themselves, but for him who died and was raised for them' (2 Cor. 5.14–15). Life 'according to the flesh' has ceased to be relevant, because the flesh has died.

Yet closer attention to the text shows that things are not quite so simple, for the transformation in question is not restricted to the person of Christ. On the contrary, on the grounds that '*all* have died', Paul argues that 'From now on . . . we regard *no one* from a human point of view'; indeed, it is only *after* having made this more general point that he adds, 'even though we once knew Christ from a human point of view, we know him no longer in that way'. Paul's line of reasoning thus comes across as a bit puzzling. Most obviously, the claim that 'all have died' seems belied by the fact that many people – including Paul and his Corinthian correspondents – are still alive. Presumably, Paul intends the 'death' to which 'all' have succumbed to be understood in some extended sense (most likely with reference to baptism, in line with Rom. 6.3–6; cf. Col. 3.3), but by itself this explanation does not resolve the problem. One might suppose that Paul would argue as follows: just as Christ, having physically died, is no longer known 'according to the flesh', neither is anyone else, since they, too, have 'died' – but that is not what he does. He begins in verse 14 by reasoning from the example of

Christ (i.e. on the basis of the fact *Christ* has died, it is 'therefore' possible to say that '*all* have died'); but then in verse 16 he reverses direction of the argument, stating that because all have died, 'no one' is any longer to be regarded *kata sarka* – including Christ. The result is neatly chiastic (from Christ to 'all', and then from 'all' back to Christ), but the chain of inference is obscure.[4]

It might be thought nothing much hangs on this quirk of sequence. After all, the upshot of these verses seems clear enough: Christ's death and resurrection have somehow radically transformed the human condition, such that 'if anyone is in Christ, there is a new creation: everything old has passed away; see, everything has become new' (2 Cor. 5.17). But if that's all there is to it, why add – almost as an afterthought – the remark about no longer knowing Christ 'according to the flesh'? That somehow even ostensibly living human beings can be said to have 'died' in Christ and are therefore no longer to be viewed on the same terms as before certainly seems to merit an argument, but one might suppose that the claim that our view of Christ has been transformed by his having quite literally died and then been raised from the dead would go without saying.[5] What, then, is the point of Paul's saying it?

It may be that Paul's precise meaning in 2 Corinthians 5.14–16 eludes definitive resolution on purely grammatico-historical grounds; it nevertheless provides a stimulus for thinking through the implications of Christology for anthropology. For whatever else Paul is doing in this passage from 2 Corinthians, he is clearly trying to make some connection between the status of all human beings (or, at least, all the baptized) and that of Jesus, and the link has to do with Jesus' – and our – status as having died. Specifically, those who have died are no longer to be regarded *kata sarka* – but what does that mean? What I want to suggest is that while the significance of their humanity, body as well as soul, is not in any way diminished, it has been set on a new footing, the upshot of which is that while they continue to be (and therefore to be known as) human, the fact of Jesus' resurrection and ascension means that their humanity is no longer sustained in the same way as it is on the hither side of death.

Humanity considered according to the order of creation

To make sense of this contrast, let us consider first how we subsist apart from the effects of the Incarnation. Christians confess that God made all creatures from nothing and thus (since if all creatures are from nothing, there is nothing other than God that holds them in being) that all creatures exist at every moment of their existence solely by virtue of God's holding them in being and enabling them to be just the kind of creatures they are. As Thomas argued, this understanding of God's work of creation is the basis for the Christian confession of divine omnipresence: God is at no time absent or distant from any creature, since it is only by virtue of God's actively holding them in being that creatures can exist at all.[6]

Of course, God is not in creation in a local or spatial sense, as Augustine thought in his Manichaean period, when he imagined God's presence in the world to be like that of an infinite sea permeating an enormous sponge.[7] And herein lies the problem, for precisely as the transcendent cause of all that is, the one who is not reducible to any item in the universe, but equally related to all as its immediate cause, God's presence in the world is inherently hidden. God could only be visible if God were able to be identified as one object among others, even if an object (like Augustine's sea) of infinite extent. As Creator God is not other (not even 'wholly Other'), but (in the words of Nicholas of Cusa) precisely the 'Not other': that is, not relating to creatures as creatures necessarily relate to each other, by way of contrast (as *this* rather than *that*), but rather as one whose difference – precisely as the difference between the Creator *ex nihilo* and the creation thereby brought into being – has no genuine parallel in the phenomenal world.[8] We encounter and know things only as they are other, but if we know God, we do not know him in that way.

But if that is the case, then in what sense can we be said to know God at all? The answer would seem to be that we cannot. It is not simply that God cannot be perceived directly as one item alongside others in our inventory of middle-to-large-sized dry goods; God cannot even be perceived indirectly by reference to any perceptible effects on such dry goods of which he might reasonably be posited as the cause. Within creation, we are able to reason from visible effects to not-immediately-visible causes by processes of inference; but that is precisely because we are thereby moving from one *object* to another – here to there, then to now, this to that. But if God is not one object among others, but 'Not other', then there can be no reasoning from the phenomenal to God.[9] According to a Christian doctrine of creation, in other words, God's invisibility is not accidental, but intrinsic to the reality of who God is.

Again, this invisibility of God is a corollary of his omnipresence as Creator. That is, it is precisely as the immediate cause of everything (other than God) that exists, and who thereby holds all things in being at all times, that God is not visible *as* a cause.[10] That one who causes in the comprehensive sense that the Christian God is said to do should be invisible is suggested by the well-worn but it seems to me still fundamentally serviceable analogy of God's creation of the world with an author's creation of a novel: in the absence of some deliberate effort by the author, the story she creates entails no reference to her.[11] This is because the novel, like God's creation, is a self-contained world that includes its own immanent causal structures, ranging from the more or less predictable operations of processes governed by natural laws to the free decisions of rational agents, all themselves created by the novelist. The operation of these created, or secondary, causes is sufficiently expansive to provide a perfectly adequate account of the world in its various and diverse aspects, such that we do not explain events in a novel by appeal to the whim of the author, but by reference to the interaction of character and circumstance within the text. God's working in the world is likewise invisible insofar as the ability to refer to secondary causes makes reference to God otiose when seeking to account for phenomena.[12]

This relation between divine invisibility and God's work in originating and sustaining creation highlights a fundamental asymmetry in the Creator–creature relation: while creatures are always immediately present to (and thus known by) God, God is not naturally present to (and thus known by) creatures.[13] God relates to us directly, insofar as God can with perfect justice be named the cause of everything we are and do (even if those aspects of being and action are brought about by God through a network of secondary causes), in much the same way that an author is the immediate cause of everything that happens in a novel (without it being any less the case that Dickens, for example, 'causes' David Copperfield to acquire his personal characteristics by means of various physical and social factors, as well as through his own free decisions as enacted in relation to those factors). We are creatures of the divine Word 'without whom not one thing has come into being' (John 1.3), but while the Word's creative activity is absolutely unmediated and direct when considered from the side of the Word (in that the entirety of the created causal network within which we find ourselves is immediately dependent on the Word), from our side it is mediated and indirect, since we do not perceive the Word's creative activity directly, but only that network of secondary causes through which we are held in being.

The Incarnation in relation to the order of creation

This understanding of creation raises significant problems for the possibility of creaturely knowledge of God, in that the very transcendence that allows all creatures to be immediately present to God apparently precludes God being present to (and thus perceptible by) any creature: for this kind of mutual presence to be realized, either God would have to become an 'other' among others – that is, to assume a definite position in space and time – and in so doing cease to be the transcendent God; or creatures would have to become divine – and thereby cease to be finite creatures. As the infinite source of all that exists, the Creator God is not one existent among others (i.e. not one more item in a universal inventory) who can be identified by contrast with creatures, in the way that we distinguish creatures from one another through comparison and contrast. It follows that in order for God to be able to be present to creatures, God would have to change the mode by which God relates to creation – but it is not clear how God could do this without undermining God's own identity, and thereby the very conditions of creation's existing at all.

And yet Christians confess that at a certain point God did change the way that God relates to the created world, and that this change was effected by the divine Word taking flesh in Jesus of Nazareth. It is not that God thereby ceased to relate to the world through secondary causes, as before. The Chalcedonian insistence that the divine and human natures were united in Jesus 'without confusion or change' means that God did not for a moment cease to be God in taking flesh. Likewise, the confession that Jesus is fully human means that through the whole course of his earthly existence in first-century Palestine he was, with respect to his humanity, perfectly ordinary, depending on the same network of secondary causes that govern his metabolism, as well as his interactions with his physical and social environment, as anyone else.[14] This ordinariness was a feature recognized by his contemporaries; indeed, it was just what seemed to make Jesus' implicit and explicit claims to authority so puzzling (see, for example, Mark 6.3; John 1.46; 8.57). To be sure, Jesus did many remarkable things, but he himself claimed that this was due to the gift of God's Spirit (Matt. 12.28; cf. John 3.34), and in this sense the mechanics (if you will) of his teaching and miracles are no different than that of the prophets who preceded him or his disciples who would come after (see John 14.12).

So what happens with Jesus is not that the extant Creator–creature relationship is dissolved, but that it is augmented. Jesus is not different from the rest of us in his nature, or in the way his nature is related to the rest of creation (as far as that is concerned, he is, following Hebrews 2.17, like us 'in every respect'). Rather, and invoking another feature of the Chalcedonian definition, the difference lies in his 'hypostasis': that is, in his identity, or *who* he is. All human beings are hypostases in this Chalcedonian sense of the term – that is, every individual human is some*one* in addition to being some*thing* – but only in the case of Jesus is it that the someone in question is God; that is, only in his case does a human being have a divine hypostasis.[15] This means that while it is no more true of Jesus than of me or you that when he eats a piece of bread, for example, it is God as Creator who is the direct and immediate cause of that human action, only in the case of Jesus is it true that God is also the actor. That is, to say that Jesus is the Word made flesh is to say that when Jesus eats, talks or breathes, the one eating, talking and breathing is God. What Jesus does God does – and that is not true of any other human being.

Now, this feature of Jesus' existence carries with it certain further implications. All other human beings come into being as (human) hypostases together with their (human) natures. Thus, while it is possible to say that a person's hypostasis is that which defines her as the particular individual she is (so that the hypostasis is that by which a given instance of humanity is recognized as Mary rather than Peter or Dolores), nevertheless the hypostasis is not prior to the nature. Rather, it is just insofar as I am conceived as a human being (and so as the sort of being – a 'rational nature' in the words of Boethius – that subsists as a 'who') that I have (or, better, am) a human hypostasis. For this reason, it is possible to say that for human beings it is typically the case that their natures sustain their hypostases, meaning that human beings subsist as persons by virtue of their being human (again, because 'humanity' is the just kind of nature that in being individuated is also 'personalized').[16]

Because Jesus is the eternal Word, however, the relation between hypostasis and human nature is different in his case. Because his hypostasis is divine, it is not secondary to his human nature as your or my hypostasis is. Rather, because it eternally subsists as a hypostasis of the divine nature apart from taking flesh, it may be said to 'pre-exist' his humanity in a way that is not true of the hypostasis of any other human being.[17] Consequently, while the Word, too, lives his incarnate life in Roman Palestine by virtue of the physiological and psychosocial features of the human nature to which he has bound himself, the Word is not dependent on that nature in the same way as the hypostases of other human beings are. It is just the reverse: even though during the period between his birth and death Jesus lives his human life by means of the same processes of respiration, digestion and so forth characteristic of all human beings, because Jesus, as the Word, is God, in his case the ontological sequence is one in which hypostasis sustains the humanity.[18]

This feature of Jesus' ontology is what, in the language of the Fathers, distinguishes him from a *psilos anthropos*, or mere human being. And it also is what ensures that death, the cessation of the physiological processes that sustain his nature in time and space, affects him differently than it does other human beings. For every other human being, death claims hypostasis and nature together and irrevocably, because the hypostasis has no ontological basis other than the nature that sustains it.[19] But because Jesus is hypostatically the very Word of God, although the death of his human nature also entails the death of his divine hypostasis according to this assumed nature, nevertheless because his hypostasis is also inseparable from the immortal divine nature to which it is bound from all eternity, the process of death works itself out differently in his case.[20] Unlike the rest of us, Jesus, having died in his humanity, is also and necessarily raised again from the dead in that same humanity, 'because it was impossible for him' as the eternal Word 'to be held in [death's] power' (Acts 2.24). In other words, because this indestructible divine hypostasis has bound itself to a human nature, the divine life that is inseparable from the hypostasis sustains the human nature, too.

And yet, as risen from the dead, Jesus does not live on the same terms as he did before he died: resurrection is not resuscitation – the miraculous return of the dead to earthly life. People raised in this sense (see, for example, 2 Kings 4.32–35; Mark 35.42; Luke 7.11–15; John 11.41–44) will die again, but the risen Jesus lives in such a way that he 'will never die again; death no longer has dominion over him' (Rom. 6.9). The Scriptures do not give much helpful information about this new form of life. As I have already noted, according to Paul, it entails the acquisition of a 'spiritual' in place of our current 'psychic' (i.e. soul-animated) body (1 Cor. 15.44). But this information is of limited value, since we are not told what a 'spiritual body' is, beyond the fact that it is one sustained by the Spirit. Based on the resurrection narratives, it would seem that this sort of body has some sort of substantial reality (since John 21.4, 9–13, for example, has Jesus cooking and serving breakfast); at the same time, Jesus can pass through closed doors (John 20.19, 26) and instantly vanish from sight (Luke 24.30–31). There seems to me little point in trying to work out the biophysics of all this; the upshot, however, is evidently that a body animated by the Spirit lives in a manner that is qualitatively different than earthly life on the hither side of death: the Jesus who dined with his disciples on Maundy Thursday is the same one who met them again on Easter Sunday, but the fact that on the latter date 'death no longer has dominion over him' means that 'the life he lives', as risen from the dead, 'he lives to God' (Rom. 6.10).

This difference between the mode by which Jesus' life is sustained after his resurrection and during his 30 years in Roman Palestine can be described in Chalcedonian language in terms of a fundamental shift in the relation between nature and hypostasis. Then, as already noted, Jesus' hypostasis was sustained in its humanity through the same sorts of secondary causes that hold all creatures in being. Since such causes are subject to interruption in a way that renders creatures vulnerable to death and dissolution, the claim that 'death no longer has dominion over him' means that his humanity is no longer subject to the same vulnerability. While he remains human, with a human body that maintains at least some of the characteristics of his earthly body (viz. the ability to eat, walk, talk, move things about), the subsistence of that body is now independent of the causal chains that sustain creatures in time and space. This is manifest in his ability to spontaneously vanish and appear, but takes definitive form in the ascension, when he departs bodily from the sphere of bodies altogether to sit at the right hand of God.

Without delving too deeply into thorny metaphysical thickets, I think it is safe to say that the point of the ascension is that Jesus subsists humanly (i.e. as a psychosomatic whole rather than as an angel or other form of disembodied spirit) outside of the realm of time and space, and thus (again) independently of the web of secondary causes by which human beings subsist within the order of creation. For him to sit at God's right hand is thus for him to occupy a 'place' that is outside of space and time, and thereby to subsist as a creature directly before God. Of course, as the eternal Son, he always subsists directly before the Father in his divine nature (for he is God along with the Father), but as incarnate, and then risen and ascended, he now lives before the Father according to his human nature as well. Importantly, however, he does not do this by the power of his human nature, but rather in virtue of his identity as the Son, so that instead of his human nature sustaining his hypostasis, at God's right hand it is now the case that his hypostasis sustains his human nature.

The Incarnation as the ground for the orders of reconciliation and glory

The fourth evangelist says that in taking flesh the Word gives us all 'the power to become children of God' (John 1.12), and that this happens just insofar as we come to be 'born, not of blood or of the will of the flesh or of the will of man, but of God' (John 1.13; cf. Rom. 9.8) – that is, insofar as our life is sustained not by the secondary, created causal structures of flesh and blood or by human effort, but directly by God. In other words, John thus teaches that in the wake of Jesus' ascension to God's right hand, a new possibility for human existence is established. It is not a possibility that has its roots in any power of human nature, but solely in the fact that this nature has been elevated by being taken into God's own life and, on that basis, sustained in its creaturely character in a new way. Maximus the Confessor describes it as follows:

> The life that God will give does not consist in the breathing of air, or in the flow of blood from the liver, but in the fact that God in God's entirety will be participated in by human beings in their entirety [*theos holos holois metechomenos*], so that God will be in relation to the soul as the soul is to the body, and through the soul will likewise be present in the body . . . In this way the whole human being will be deified, being made God by the grace of the God who became human, so that the individual will remain entirely human in soul and body on account of his nature, and entirely God in soul and body owing to the grace and the splendour of the blessed glory of God.[21]

The upshot of Maximus' words, like those of John, is that insofar as they have been called to be children of God, in glory human beings will no longer relate to God indirectly through the causal structures of the created order ('the breathing of air . . . the flow of blood from the liver'), but rather will be sustained directly by God (who 'will be in relation to the soul as the soul is to the body').[22] And the claim that 'the individual will remain entirely human in soul and body on account of his nature, and entirely God in soul and body owing to . . . grace' means that the nature will remain human, but will be sustained divinely, through the Word that calls the hypostasis to life with God and thus sustains it before God.

That state is, of course, only reached eschatologically, yet it begins even now insofar as the order of glory is anticipated in the gospel and its message of reconciliation, according to which we 'are God's children now' (1 John

3.2), by virtue of having received the forgiveness of sins. For what does it mean to be forgiven? It means that one's identity is not determined by one's past actions (i.e. by the chain of secondary causes, including the actions of our own wills, that have brought us to whatever state in which we currently find ourselves), but rather by God's address to us as hypostases, declaring that our life is not determined by what we have done or failed to do, but solely on that word.[23] Insofar as we live in this way, 'not by bread alone, but by every word that comes from the mouth of God' (Matt. 4.4 and par.), we are not to be regarded 'from a human point of view', not because we have ceased to be human, but because our humanity is no longer to be understood *kata sarka*, according to the possibilities of created cause and effect within space and time. We remain as much creatures of the Word as we ever were, but in and through Christ, that Word is now spoken to us directly and sustains us by its power alone, rather than by way of secondary causes.[24]

And, of course, if we are no longer to be regarded from a human point of view, neither is Jesus, who as 'the pioneer and perfecter of our faith . . . has [already] taken his seat at the right hand of the throne of God' (Heb. 12.2). This certainly does not mean that we no longer regard Christ as a human being; on the contrary, in the ascension and session it is precisely the fullness of Jesus' humanity as defined by the life he led between Christmas and Good Friday that is vindicated as the life of God, the maker of heaven and earth. But it is a human life now lived by divine means and thus on divine terms. By virtue of the Incarnation, God is no longer hidden from the creature by virtue of the divine transcendence; on the contrary, by virtue of that transcendence, God has shown himself able to assume the life of the creature without ceasing for an instant to be God, and thereby to encounter the creature as creature – with the result that the creature can now know and love God.

In this way, we come back to Luther's claim that anyone who would deliberate and speculate about God soundly must disregard absolutely everything except Christ's humanity, but now with an explanation of how this coheres with Paul's insistence that 'even though we once knew Christ from a human point of view, we know him no longer in that way'. To recap, it is on the basis of the transformation of the conditions of human existence that both begins and has its ontological grounding in Christ that no one is henceforth to be regarded *kata sarka*, because no one any longer lives *kata sarka*, but by God's Word alone. Now, insofar as Jesus is the only human being who has to this point experienced the full fruits of the resurrection,[25] it might seem that the claim that he is no longer to be regarded *kata sarka* could be taken as read. And yet, arguably, it is just in the case of Jesus, whose earthly life was on the one hand ordinarily human, but on the other also distinguished by the capacity to do unheard of signs and wonders, that we are liable to confuse the humanity we can see with the divinity that we cannot. Here Luther's dictum comes into its own, for while it is indeed true that Christians rightly regard Jesus' humanity (including the inescapably human acts whereby he healed, forgave and fed his contemporaries) as the touchstone for all talk about God, they dare not confuse his humanity with his divinity, nor the life he lives now with the one he led in first-century Palestine. In this new life – the one that 'he lives to God' (Rom. 6.10) – he is no less human than he was in the stable or on the cross, but he is human differently, and in a way that exceeds our present experience. It can be tempting for us, precisely because what we know of the earthly Jesus is so rightly the focus of our theological attention, to limit our understanding of Jesus' humanity, and thus of the whole of humanity he came to save, to what we know of his earthly life. But while Jesus' humanity, as defined by the timespan between his birth at Christmas and his death on Good Friday, is rightly the criterion for all 'deliberation and speculation' about *divinity*, the ongoing effect of the divine work of reconciliation, by which ever new and unanticipated forms of the human are drawn into the body of Christ, means that our understanding of *humanity* continually exceeds what we see in the earthly Jesus. It is thus not out of a desire to avoid Jesus' humanity, but out of deference to our ignorance of its ascended form that we must not regard Christ *kata sarka*. For we do not know exactly what that humanity looks like, and we thus need to be careful what we say about it; but we do know that 'when he is revealed, we will be like him, for we will see him as he is' (1 John 3.2).

Notes

1 *quicunque velit salubriter de Deo cogitare aut speculari, prorsus omnia postponat praeter humanitatem Christi.* Martin Luther, 'Letter to Spalatin' (12 February 1519) in WA Br.1:226.

2 For a careful assessment of Luther's relation to Chalcedon, see Johannes Zachhuber, *Luther's Christological Legacy: Christocentrism and the Chalcedonian Tradition*, The Pere Marquette Lecture in Theology 2017 (Milwaukee, WI: Marquette University Press, 2017), especially p. 103: 'Luther situated his Christology within the Chalcedonian tradition, but his attitude toward the tradition was more flexible because he perceived doctrinal decisions as ultimately deriving from Scripture and therefore in need of justification in light of the biblical testimony.'

3 Heinrich Denzinger, Peter Hünermann, Robert Fastiggi and Anne Englund Nash, eds, *Compendium of Creeds, Definitions, and Declarations on Matters of Faith and Morals*, 43rd edn (San Francisco: Ignatius Press, 2012), p. 294.

4 In other words (and *pace* Victor Paul Furnish's claim in *II Corinthians* (Garden City, NY: Doubleday & Company, Inc., 1984), p. 332), Paul's argument here is not straightforwardly *a maiori ad minus*. Such an interpretation would be plausible if there were no conditional clause in the second half of the verse (i.e. if it read, 'From now on, therefore, we regard no one according to human standards, because we no longer know Christ in that way'); but the presence of the conditional serves precisely to raise the question of contrasting views of Christ (i.e. that some might

be tempted to continue to know him *kata sarka*), which otherwise would not be in view at all. Cf. the objections to Furnish's position raised by Margaret E. Thrall in *A Critical and Exegetical Commentary on the Second Epistle to the Corinthians*, 2 vols (Edinburgh: T & T Clark, 1994), vol. 1, pp. 418–19.

5 In this context, it is worth noting that in any earlier letter to this same congregation Paul had to deal with a faction who evidently denied that there would be a general resurrection of the dead, and he refutes them precisely by appealing to what he takes to be the unquestioned belief that Christ has risen (see 1 Cor. 15.12–18).

6 'God is causing this effect in things not just when they begin to exist, but all the time they are maintained in existence, just as the sun is lighting up the atmosphere all the time the atmosphere remains lit. During the whole period of a thing's existence, therefore, God must be present to it, and present in a way in keeping with the way in which the thing possesses its existence'. Thomas Aquinas, *Summa Theologiae*, 1.8.1, 60 vols (London: Eyre & Spottiswood, 1964–81).

7 Augustine, *Confessions*, 7.5.

8 Nicholas of Cusa, *Nicholas of Cusa on God as Not-Other: A Translation and Appraisal of* 'De li non aliud', trans. by Jasper Hopkins, 2nd edn (Minneapolis: Arthur J. Banning Press, 1983).

9 While this line of reasoning is generally associated with Kant, the idea is by no means absent in earlier Christian tradition: 'God is one, without beginning, incomprehensible, possessing in his totality the full power of being, completely excluding the notion of time and quality in that he is inaccessible to all *and not discernible by any being on the basis of any natural appearance [ek physikēs emphaseōs]*'. Maximus, *Chapters on Knowledge*, 1.1 (*PG* 90:1084A), in Maximus the Confessor, *Selected Writings*, trans. by G. C. Berthold (New York: Paulist Press, 1985), p. 129; translation altered.

10 It is on the grounds that the application of the designation 'cause' to God stretches the term past its breaking point that Katherine Sonderegger rejects the term as theologically appropriate in *The Doctrine of God*, vol. 1 of *Systematic Theology* (Minneapolis: Fortress, 2015), pp. 177–84. While I take the point, it seems to me that the distinction between primary and secondary causes provides the necessary framework for maintaining the analogical use of the term in a theological context.

11 Cf. Coleridge, who held the imagination to be 'a repetition in the finite mind of the eternal act of creation in the infinite I Am'. Samuel Taylor Coleridge, *Biographia Literaria*, ed. by Adam Roberts (Edinburgh: Edinburgh University Press, 2014 [1817]), p. 205.

12 It is necessary to address two seeming exceptions to this claim. The first is miracles (including the Incarnation), about which more will be said below, but the upshot of which is simply that such events are properly defined as precisely instances where God does not act by means of secondary causes. The second is the kind of inference to God's existence as first cause exemplified by Thomas in the second 'way' of the *Summa Theologiae*, 1.2. Here I would argue that Thomas's primary aim is to locate the word 'God' semantically (viz. as that which emerges at the horizons of human thought), as reflected in the fact that each of the five 'ways' concludes not, 'Therefore, God exists', but with some variant on 'and this is what everyone calls "God"'. He certainly wants to affirm that 'God' is an unavoidable concept, but (as he immediately goes on to argue in the preface to questions 3–11), the upshot is not that in running into the *concept* of God we come to know much of anything about God beyond this unavoidability: 'we cannot know what God is, but only what he is

not; we must therefore consider the ways in which God does not exist, rather than the ways in which he does'.

13 Again, this is not to gainsay the fact that human beings do make all sorts of claims about God apart from appeals to special revelation, but only to note that such claims, even if their content agrees with Christian accounts of the divine attributes, can refer only to God of the *philosophes et savants*, and not to the God of Abraham, Isaac and Jacob. That is, they can only testify to God's invisibility, which is quite different from the act, inseparable from Christian confession, of bearing witness to the God-who-is-invisible.

14 In this context, Jesus' virginal conception, while unique, does not in any fundamental sense qualify the ordinariness of the humanity thereby conceived; nor is it in any sense an ontologically necessary corollary of his being the Word incarnate, which (as discussed below) is a function of his hypostasis rather than his human nature.

15 When I speak of the Chalcedonian sense of 'hypostasis', I do not intend the meaning of the term as it was actually deployed by the bishops in the definition of 451, but rather as its meaning came to be clarified by Chalcedonian theologians over the subsequent 250 years (and, most especially, in the first half of the sixth century).

16 Importantly, this is not to say that the nature *causes* the hypostasis, for that would imply that the hypostasis was a part or attribute of the nature (and thus some *thing* – one property of the nature alongside others) rather than the identity of the one who instantiates the nature. One might say that my nature 'causes' me to have brown hair, two arms, the capacity to reason, even to exhibit particular personality traits; but it does not cause me to be Ian. In other words, I am the hypostasis I am as the one who has this particular body, with this personality, will, intellect and so forth; but because (as Christians will want to confess) as my identity as the particular hypostasis I am persists in spite of the most radical changes to any of these features, it cannot be derived from any of them. Though the hypostasis has no existence apart from the nature (since it is a hypostasis at all only as it is a hypostasis of that nature), it cannot be derived from any individual feature or set of features of the nature.

17 I put 'pre-exist' in inverted commas because although it is impossible to talk about the Incarnation except in terms that connote temporal sequence, the fact that the Word's taking flesh is not an evolution in the life of the Word (which, as eternal, does not subsist in temporal sequence), but simply the projection of an eternal reality into time, temporal relations are inexact and potentially misleading.

18 That is the force of the old Scholastic doctrine of 'enhypostasis', according to which this instance of humanity has no existence except as hypostatized by the Word.

19 This might seem to be a contestable ontological claim, insofar as a very traditional Christian understanding of death is the separation of the immortal soul from the corruptible body, according to which the hypostasis continues to subsist in the soul (insofar as it is precisely the soul of somebody or other). Even if one accepts this dualist anthropology, however, it remains the case that by virtue of its separation from the body the soul in question (and the hypostasis associated with it) is dead – and, absent some supernatural intervention, will naturally remain dead, and thus without a future characterized by life with God and other people that is the mark of human beings' earthly existence. That is, insofar as the complete human nature is a psychosomatic composite, the dissolution of that composite means death for the

soul and the hypostasis, even if they are understood to somehow continue to subsist as dead, as reflected in the Old Testament language of the dead having 'gone down to Sheol' (Gen. 37.35; 1 Kings 2.6; Job 21.13; Isa. 14.15; Ezek. 31.17; 32.27) from whence they do not come up (Job 7.9; cf. Ps. 6.5).

20 In this context, it is worth noting that Thomas in *Summa Theologiae*, 3.50 (following John of Damascus in *On the Orthodox Faith*, 3.27) insists that even in death the Word does not abandon Jesus' body. Notwithstanding that for Thomas (1) the soul was the means by which the Word was united to the body, and (2) death is defined as the separation of the soul from the body, the body is the Word's even after death, not simply in the sense that this body was the Word's, but that it remains so.

21 Maximus, *Ambiguum* 7, 1.113 (*PG*, 91:1088C); in *On the Difficulties in the Church Fathers: The Ambigua*, ed and trans. Nicholas Constas (Cambridge, MA: Harvard University Press, 2014); translation altered.

22 Although Maximus does not himself make the point, his vision of the way in which God will inhabit the soul of the blessed corresponds very neatly to Paul's language of the 'soul-driven' body being replaced by the 'spirit-driven' body in 1 Corinthians 15.

23 'Now to one who works, wages are not reckoned as a gift but as something due. But to one who without works trusts *him who justifies the ungodly*, such faith is reckoned as righteousness' (Rom. 4.4–5).

24 Cf. Maximus the Confessor, *Quaestiones ad Thalassium*, 61 (*PG*, 90: 640BC): 'the righteous man will not be in a "place" [*thesin*] describable in terms of "where" at all, having by grace received God himself as his "place" instead of any spatial "where" [*hyper to pou*] . . . For God does not admit of "where"; he is unqualifiedly beyond all "where". In him will be the sure foundation of all who are saved'. Maximus the Confessor, *On the Cosmic Mystery of Jesus Christ: Selected Writings from St. Maximus the Confessor*, trans. by Paul M. Blowers and Robert Wilken (Crestwood, NY: St. Vladimir's Seminary Press, 2003), p. 142; translation altered.

25 Those who confess the dormition or assumption of Mary will, of course, contest the accuracy of this statement.

5

Sound and Silence in Augustine's Christological Interpretation of Scripture

CAROL HARRISON

In *Confessions* Book 11 (11.6.8–7.9), Augustine contrasts the sound of spoken words and the silence of God's eternal Word: 'words, sounding in time, with your eternal Word in silence'. Spoken words are characterized by the fact that they are temporal and mutable; a voice begins and ends; the syllables sound in succession and then pass away; the words are fleeting and transient. In contrast, the Word of God, the Word that is with God in the beginning, is eternal and immutable; with him there is no time or change: 'no element of your word yields place or succeeds to something else, since it is truly immortal and eternal'. How then, Augustine wonders, can we hear the eternal, silent, Word? How does he speak and sound forth his silence so that he can be heard?

The fact that Augustine uses words and sound as a way of articulating something about the eternal and immutable silence of God is, of course, itself a 'manner of speaking'; in reality it is simply a very human, make-shift, rather inadequate analogy, in order to articulate something which cannot ultimately be captured by words, or indeed, by human thinking. The linguistic analogy is doubtless partly prompted by Augustine's prior training in the liberal arts and especially the language arts of grammar, dialectic and rhetoric; and partly by Scripture – especially the Prologue of John's Gospel. But as we will see, even though he is uttering words inspired by God, John the Evangelist, like Augustine, is still constrained by human speech. Neither can remain silent if the eternal Godhead is to be heard and communicated, but their words are really no more than a sound that gestures towards an inexpressible silence.

In fact, in making the distinction between silence and sound, Augustine is not so much describing two different types of word, but two very different orders of being: the eternal, immutable, silent Godhead and Creator, and temporal, mutable, successive creation. And that, I think, is the point. God sounds forth his silence in bringing the temporal order of mutable creation into being, in providentially ordering it, in inspiring his prophets and evangelists. Most especially, he is heard when, becoming incarnate, he speaks as both God and man; and, when resurrected, he continues to dwell within his body, the Church. So creation, providence, Scripture, the incarnate Christ, the body of the Church are all ways in which God's silence is, as it were, sounded for us to hear.

Before we go any further, however, we should also be aware that it is not only language that is a human analogy; so, also, is silence. We think of silence as the absence of sound, but what Augustine is trying to articulate in his distinction is that silence is in fact the fullness of God's eternal and immutable substance; that sound is simply a way of allowing us to be aware of it, of enabling us to apprehend something of what transcends our human capacity to know or express. We live and know in temporal, mutable, successive terms; God abides and knows in eternal, immutable, stillness and silence. Our question then must be, how *does* sound, how do words, how does Scripture convey what they cannot fully articulate; how do they communicate what is unknowable and ineffable to human beings because it belongs entirely to another order of being?

In examining Augustine's exegesis of Scripture, in the context of a sermon on the three natures of the Word of God (his eternal Godhead, his incarnate Godhead and manhood, and his union with the body of the Church) in this chapter, I hope we might begin to address these questions directly; Scripture and the words of the incarnate Word are arguably the closest that human words can come to expressing the divine. What I would like to suggest is that their sound or words are at once no more, and no less, than expressions of God's silence; in short, they are necessary, but necessarily limited. The most successful words or sounds, then, are ironically not those that capture, define or explain the divine, but those that are open-ended, allusive and indeterminate; those that indicate that there is more to know, that they are not ends but beginnings; those which make it clear that meaning is found *in* and *through* them, in the silence from which they originate. In short, words and sound give what might be said to be a bottom to the bottomless. The reader may well be wondering why I have mentioned sound as well as words; it is because at a number of points in this sermon Augustine appears to conclude that sound – wordless sound, songs without words, inarticulate groans and sighs – might actually fulfil this function better than words. But what does this mean for exegesis and Christology?

Augustine did not write a treatise directly devoted to exegesis;[1] nor did he compose a treatise specifically on the subject of the Incarnation,[2] although both subjects inform pretty much everything he writes. In a rather extraordinary sermon – sermon 22, discovered by François Dolbeau in 1990 – he addresses them both directly in order to give his congregation what he hopes will be a clear and unerring sense of just what is involved in understanding the nature of Christ and what this tells us about the nature of Scripture.[3]

His text is Psalm 22: 'They pierced my hands and feet. I may tell all my bones: they look and stare upon me. They part my garments among them, and cast lots upon my vesture' (Ps. 22.16–18). It is a text which clearly invites interpretation from the vantage point of the New Testament, in other words, a Christological interpretation. His congregation would be familiar with the traditional reading which related it to Christ's Passion, and he tells them that he wants to remind them of this, confirm it, and in so doing, clarify it for them. Having done so, he assures them that they will be better placed to tackle the less obvious, more obscure texts of Scripture, and to understand, as he puts it, 'how Christ is talked of there' (1).

His point therefore seems to be that, although this text might seem obvious, there are many which are not: that Christ's incarnate life and Passion is not the only way in which Scripture talks of him, but one of at least three ways: first, as Augustine puts it, according to his 'divine nature, which is coequal and coeternal with the Father before he assumed flesh'; second, 'after assuming flesh . . . as God who is at the same time man, and man who is at the same time God'; third, 'as in some manner or other the whole Christ in the fullness of the Church, that is, as head and body' (2). Just as a right understanding of the person of Christ requires that all three be considered, so also a right understanding of how to interpret Scripture requires an appreciation of the different ways in which he is presented in it.

As is well known, early Christian exegetes generally agreed that the whole of Scripture, Old Testament and New Testament, was to be understood and interpreted in relation to Christ: 'whether' as Augustine puts it here, 'he is being proclaimed in the law and the prophets, or in the letters of the apostles, or through . . . the gospel'. Christ was the ultimate meaning, or what we might call the 'horizon' of Scripture, which was therefore to be read in all its parts as a witness to and revelation of him.

To take this seriously is, of course, something of a stumbling block for modern historical critical exegesis, primarily concerned with establishing sources, textual redactions, forms and genres, authorial identity and intention, historically verifiable facts and so on. It is perhaps less of a challenge for some aspects of the sort of exegesis we find in the work of scholars such as Paul Ricoeur or David Tracy, for whom the text discloses its meaning, not through factual statements, but through analogy, metaphor and figures – through signs which signify in a manner which is more like the affective cognition characteristic of poetry than the intellectual cognition characteristic of scientific, historical criticism. This is not to say that what is thereby disclosed is not true, but that it is a truth which can only be cognized as an encounter which invites a response.[4]

This is to some extent demonstrated in what Augustine has to say in sermon 22 about the first way in which Scripture 'talks' of Christ: 'as God and according to that divine nature which is coequal and coeternal with the Father before he assumed flesh' (2). The best testimony to this, Augustine unhesitatingly affirms, is the 'noble and glorious one in the gospel according to St John', the Prologue of John's Gospel: John 1.1–5. He observes that 'These are wonderful and amazing words, even before they are understood; once understood (*intellecta*) they have to be wholeheartedly embraced (*ampletanda sunt*)'. These comments might well suggest that 'understanding', or some sort of intellectual cognition, precedes our wholehearted embracing, or affective cognition of them, but Augustine is quick to point out that what he means by 'understanding' is not something which can be taught by 'human aids', rather it is given by the same divine inspiration that inspired John to write: 'We are enabled, though, to understand them, not by human aids (*non opibus praebetur humanis*) but by being inspired to grasp them by the one who was good enough to inspire fishermen to utter them' (3).

If both Scripture and our reading of it are inspired, why, we might well ask, are the divinely inspired words, which describe Christ's eternal Godhead, not more readily comprehensible? More to the point, why is our divinely inspired hearing or reading of them not more conclusive? Is it because 'understanding', in the sense of intellectual comprehension and definitive statements, is not the purpose of divine inspiration (and so our modern historical critical questions are missing the point)? Well, it *is* partly this, and we are not the only ones who need to be reminded of it or to learn this lesson; so, evidently, do Augustine's hearers or readers, and so, too, do those who, in his day, thought precisely in these terms (he will later identify them with the Arians).[5]

Sermon 22 therefore identifies a number of factors which Augustine's congregation needs to bear in mind in order to appreciate just what 'understanding' Scripture entails. The first (as we might expect in an Augustinian context) is our fallen human nature: we need to learn the lesson of humility in order to counter our pride (4); to realize that, subject to original sin, we can neither will or do anything of ourselves, without the inspiration and work of God's grace. So, both the writing of Scripture and the hearing or reading of it are in fact a matter of grace – of inspiration. Augustine tells his congregation that God has made this abundantly clear by choosing to inspire, not educated, erudite, eloquent orators, but uneducated, ignorant, low-born fishermen, as authors of his word: 'The weak things of this world he chose, in order to disconcert the strong; and the foolish things he chose, in order to disconcert the wise' (1 Cor. 1.27–28) (4). Similarly, when the eternal Word of God became incarnate, he did not come to us as a wealthy, high-ranking inhabitant of an important city but as the illegitimate son of a craftsman, born in the back of beyond (4). The crudeness and rudeness of the Scriptures (which Augustine and his educated contemporaries were so acutely sensitive to), like the crude and rude circumstances of our Lord's incarnate life, were therefore, in the first instance, a lesson in humility.[6]

But of course, they were more than this, for what appears to be God's foolishness – his crudeness and rudeness – is in reality his wisdom: his eternal wisdom, which is beyond human comprehension and telling. This is the second factor that Augustine wants his congregation to bear in mind in understanding what interpretation of Scripture entails: when it talks of Christ, the eternal Word, begotten of the Father's substance, it is in fact doing the impossible: it is expressing what cannot be expressed or comprehended by created human beings or by human words.

So how *does* Scripture express the inexpressible? John's Prologue, which sets forth Christ, the eternal Word of God, before his taking on of flesh, is one that, Augustine comments, fills all who hear it with wonder and amazement. It is grasped by the few who understand, when they reflect upon it, to such effect 'that they are as it were struck by a kind of lightning flash of that everlasting and inexpressible light' (*ut quadam lucis illius sempiternae et ineffabilis quasi coruscatione perstringatur*) (5). In other words, Christ's Godhead is certainly not something that the few are able to grasp intellectually; it is not something they discover, but something that Scripture reveals or discloses to them. 'Knowledge' of Christ's Godhead, then, is a matter of wonder, amazement and a lightning flash of insight; it is a matter of divine inspiration: God's inspiration of the author, on the one hand, and the reader and hearer, on the other. The meaning (*sententia*), the intention (*voluntas*) and the truth (*veritas*) of Scripture, then, is God, who inspires it and who inspires our encounter with him in it. As Augustine tells his congregation: 'To save you from wasting your time seeking an understanding of these words from me, I told you that you can only understand them when you are inspired by the one whose inspiration was the cause of the uneducated fisherman proclaiming them' (5).

What is it, then, that we learn through an inspired reading of Scripture's inspired words? Augustine describes the way in which John was inspired to write his Gospel, and especially those 'wonderful and amazing words' of the Prologue, when, resting his head upon our Lord's breast at the Last Supper, the beloved disciple drank in what he would say about his divinity. 'Having drunk his fill', Augustine comments, he 'gave a good belch, and that very belch is the gospel. And so with the eyes of faith in the gospel you have seen the fisherman feasting, now listen to him belching "in the beginning was the Word, and the Word was with God, and the Word was God" (John 1.1–2)' (5). This does not quite answer our question, but it does rather effectively make the point that whatever it is we learn through an inspired reading of Scripture's inspired words, it is not a matter of intellectual cognition or even – always – of words! I suggested earlier on that sound – non-verbal sound – might be more effective in expressing what lies beyond the limits of words, and this is, I think, precisely what Augustine has in mind when he offers the analogy of a belch, or when, in his sermons on the Psalms, he describes the jubilation which wells up spontaneously from within the soul, issuing forth in wordless shouts of joy, thereby giving voice to what cannot be expressed in words but which cannot remain unuttered.[7] He has the same limitations and necessity in mind when he searches for names with which to refer to God (*Deus, Idipsum*), always acutely aware that God cannot be named, and yet, because we cannot and must not remain silent, we are constrained to refer to him with words, or better, sounds and voices, which are no more and no less than gestures to something that far transcends them.[8] It is for this reason, I think, that, preaching on Christ and John the Baptist as the Word and the Voice (*Uerbum* and *uox*), Augustine eventually chooses to limit his use of the term 'Word' only to the eternally begotten Word and the inner word which we conceive wordlessly within our minds, and contrasts this with all human language, teaching and prophecy, which is no more and no less than a voice which gestures and points towards the Word, but which can never fully articulate it.[9]

Thus, at every turn in the first part of this sermon, Augustine stresses the fact that Christ's Godhead is not something that can be known: even John, the author of the Gospel, 'was not of such genius or learning that his mind's eye could penetrate and soar above the whole of this atmosphere and all the ethereal powers . . . to reach "what no eye has seen or ear heard, nor has it come up into the heart of man" (1 Cor. 2.9)'. Rather, John knows Christ's Godhead because he is inspired, he drinks it in, as it were, and is 'filled' with it. As Augustine puts it, echoing the passage from *Confessions* 11 which we referred to at the beginning of this chapter:

> What sort of thing could the Father's Word be, how could it be a word? Was it thought, did it make a sound? Of course not. Because if it was thought, it took some time; if it made a sound, it was projected on air waves. Not so is the Word of God, but a Word that abides. (5)

As Augustine argues at much greater length in the *De trinitate*, the eternal begetting of the Word, then, is not to be thought of in terms of human words, and cannot be expressed in human words. Thus, struggling with words to express the ineffable begetting of the Word in sermon 22, he suggests that it is a begetting whereby the Word is expressed, or better, expresses/utters himself, even though *we* cannot express it. He observes: 'however it is to be said, nobody can express it with a human tongue. The Word is piously believed to be begotten; he can express himself, the Son of God alone can utter his own self (*ipse potest se effari et eloqui*). The person, though, to whom he expresses himself, can understand that Word, but cannot express it' (5). So what John 'understands' (or better, apprehends) and then belches forth, is, in effect, the unknowable, eternal, immutable begetting of the Word of God; his ineffable, wordless, expression.

Before he leaves the subject of the eternally begotten Word, Augustine confirms and illustrates what he has said by reminding his congregation of the Word's relation, not only to the Father, from whom he is begotten, but also to the Holy Spirit, by which the love and desire of God is 'inspired' or breathed forth within us, so that we might love and desire him through himself.

Like the eternally begotten Word, the Trinitarian Godhead to which the Spirit belongs transcends our knowing or saying: it is that, Augustine observes here (in a phrase which seems to have been taken over by Aquinas), 'than whom there is nothing better' (*quo nihil est melius*); it cannot be expressed, but God allows such words as we use 'because', he comments, 'if we wanted to say something worthy of him, we wouldn't be able to say anything at all' (7). Like the eternally begotten Word, then, the Trinity brings both the author and the reader of Scripture to 'knowledge' of Itself, by inspiring and filling them – in this case, the Holy Spirit fills us with love of and desire for God. Augustine observes: 'Now he breathes with the Holy Spirit; there, you see, you have the Trinity: the Father who begot, the Word which he begot, the Spirit by which charity is breathed forth or inspired. In order that this most delightful and surpassing and inexpressible Trinity may be loved . . . the Spirit desires the hearts of lovers' (7). Once again, then, what we know of the Trinity is not a matter of intellectual cognition or of words, but of affective cognition: the love which is shed abroad in our hearts by the Holy Spirit. Augustine therefore tells his congregation that when they are inspired and filled by the love and desire of God, they are thereby lifted up towards him, to 'reach that something else [ad aliud – again, words fail] which you have heard from the lips of the belching fisherman'.

This is hardly promising material for the modern exegete. What role, they might well ask, does Scripture have then, apart from being a suggestive belch – one that intimates a 'something else' that inspires a spiritual ascent?![10] Let us see whether things improve for the exegete as Augustine turns, in his sermon, from Christ's unknowable and ineffable Godhead to the second way in which Scripture talks of him: 'after assuming flesh . . . as God who is at the same time man, and man who is at the same time God' (2).

'And the word became flesh and dwelt among us.' Augustine has already demonstrated that there is an ontological divide between divine being and human beings, between the silence of the divine Word and the sound of human words, which only God can bridge. Now he teaches that God has done this pre-eminently in the Incarnation. As so often, he uses Philippians 2.7: although Christ was 'in the form of God, he emptied himself, taking the form of a servant', on which he comments: 'it was by appearing visibly in this way that he emptied himself, keeping back, that is to say, the majestic greatness of divinity, and presenting us with the fleshly garment of humility'. It is significant, I think, that in this section of the sermon Augustine repeatedly emphasizes the *mystery* of the Incarnation: Christ came 'in order to give shape to our little faith and nurture it by the mystery of his incarnation' (*ut parvam fidem nostram incarnationis suae sacramento informaret atque nutriret*) (10); as the 'mediator and head of the Church, through whom we are reconciled to God through the mystery (*per sacramentum*) of his humility and passion and resurrection and ascension and of the judgement to come' (11). Every aspect of Christ's incarnate life is a mystery (*sacramentum*), a sacrament of his Godhead, an earthly bearer of spiritual reality. The words in which his Incarnation are described in Scripture are no exception to this.

Augustine's emphasis on the mystery of the Incarnation and on its sacramentality is clearly aimed at those whom he describes as seeking to divide the natures of Christ. They ask how Christ can simultaneously be with God and at the same time be with Mary in the womb. The basic (philosophical) question is that of a whole and its parts: how can a whole be present in all its parts without being divided up? How can Christ be wholly God and wholly man? How can the two natures of Godhead and manhood be separate but undivided? Does Christ's taking of flesh not imply division, subordination, inferiority? Do passages such as John 14.28, 'The Father is greater than I', not indicate this?

Augustine likens the Arians to the serpent in paradise: they hiss with their promise of knowledge, trying to corrupt those in the Church by separating out Christ's manhood and Godhead (12). What they have failed to appreciate, or refuse to accept, he urges, is that there is no division; that as Philippians 2.7 makes clear, Christ remains in the form of God and, emptying himself, chooses to take the form of a servant for our salvation. The whole, then, is always fully present in the part, albeit obscured, hidden, veiled by the garment of flesh; the mystery of the Godhead is always fully present in the earthly, physical, temporal and mutable sacrament. Turning again to exegesis of Scripture, Augustine observes that the Arians have failed to understand the harmony of the gospel; that the same God is speaking in all its parts – in other words, that Scripture is inspired, harmonious and does not contradict itself – and so, in the form of God, in his eternal Godhead, equal to the Father, Christ is heard to say, 'I and the Father are one' (John 10.30); in the form of a servant, in his temporal manhood, less than the Father, he is heard to say 'The Father is greater than I' (John 14.28). And yet the same Christ, the one God, the one inspiration of Scripture, is speaking in both texts (13). The distinction between Christ's Godhead and manhood – in the form of God and in the form of a servant – is thus very much the same distinction we have seen Augustine make between silence and words or sound: silence and sound are inseparable; sound originates from silence and is a necessary constraint, whereby silence can be heard. We should not stop at sound but always seek – or better, be led to – silence, in and through it, for whereas sound can be heard, silence remains unknowable and ineffable. And, like Christ's manhood, what sound communicates can appear crude and rude – all too earthly, offensive and shocking – but we need to believe in its source and its unity with what cannot be heard or said, and not take sound as an end in itself.

In response to the Arians' heretical Christology, Augustine again invites his congregation to reflect on exegesis. We wondered if things would improve for the modern exegete as we followed Augustine in turning from an examination of the first way in which Scripture talks of Christ, that is in his Godhead, to the second, that is in his incarnate manhood and Godhead, but what Augustine has to say in this context very much confirms the exegetical principles which he has already applied to Christ's Godhead. Again, he emphasizes that nothing can be said worthily of God. As he observes in reference to the justice of God, 'And yet we say these things about God, brothers and sisters, because we cannot find anything better to say. I call

God just because in human terms I can't find anything better; in fact, he is beyond justice' (16).

This is the case whether Scripture is referring to God's power and wisdom, or whether it is using anthropomorphic metaphors to suggest that God repents or is ignorant (15–16). Indeed, the latter, like the crude and rude work of the fisherman evangelists, or John's belch, are no more than a particularly effective example (because they horrify the hearer or reader) of the inadequacy of all language to say anything about God. Augustine observes, 'That's why they also called him repentant and ignorant, which you now don't want to call him. So just as you realize that those things which now horrify you were said on account of your weakness, in the same way these things which you value highly were said on account of a tougher weakness of yours' (16).

So once again, we see that Scripture, when read rightly, does no more and no less than efface words, expose them, make them difficult (and even offensive), thereby setting out stumbling blocks in order to demonstrate that they are not ends in themselves, but beginnings; that meaning is found within and through its words, in the silence of divine unknowability and ineffability. As Augustine puts it, Scripture uses terms such as justice 'so that the human spirit might be led gradually by all sorts of words to that which cannot be said at all. Yes, you call God just, but you must understand something beyond the justice which you are in the habit of attributing to human beings' (16).

The end of words, then – even words such as courage, wisdom and justice – is to arrive where they began, in God's eternal, immutable silence. As Augustine strikingly comments, 'But any who have risen beyond even these words, and begun to think worthily of God as far as human beings are permitted to, will find a silence that is to be praised by the inexpressible voice of the heart' (*inueniet silentium ineffabili cordis uoce laudandum*) (16). So exegesis does not end in words but in wordless, heartfelt prayer and praise (which I suppose is slightly better than a belch!).

Returning to the subject of his sermon, Augustine therefore reminds his congregation of the rule of interpretation which should be applied to all references to Christ's incarnate humanity – the rule of the whole and the part: that, as he puts it, 'you cannot say he is equal in one part and unequal in another, because there are no parts in God . . . Wherever you find the Son called equal to the Father take it as being according to a certain essence of divinity. Wherever you find him less, take it as being according to the form of the servant he took on . . . In this way you will hold firmly both to what is in his nature and to what is in his mercy' (17). Just as Christ's Godhead and manhood, nature and mercy, are one, inseparable and indivisible, so, Augustine seems to suggest, is God's eternal silence and the temporal sound of his inspired words in Scripture.

His comments on Psalm 56 – 'Arise O my glory; arise psaltery and lyre' – are a good illustration of this. The psaltery and lyre, he comments, are both musical instruments which make a sound: the strings of the psaltery resonate from a sounding chamber in the upper part of the instrument; the strings of the lyre resonate from a sounding chamber which is in the lower part of the instrument. In the same manner, Augustine comments, Christ incarnate, acting in the fleshly body, resonated from above and from below: he worked miracles and he suffered; he sounded forth in his Godhead and he sounded forth in his manhood, but in both he did so through the physical organ or instrument of his flesh, through his body.[11]

Thus, whatever Christ incarnate does he does as God and man insepara- bly; his earthly works and words are always a sounding forth of his divine silence because in him, the two are inseparably united. When Christ rises, therefore, at the resurrection, he does so, as Augustine puts it, in 'one single flesh'.

Augustine makes a number of similar distinctions between the divine Word and the incarnate Word in the last three books of his *Confessions*, books 11–13, which I would like to suggest might well be read as a sustained reflection on sound and silence, and which I think might help us understand what he says in this sermon. As I noted at the beginning of this chapter, in book 11 of his *Confessions*, beginning a commentary on Genesis, Augustine distinguishes between the Word of God which is with God in the beginning and the Word which became man for our salvation. The Word in the begin- ning is a word that sounds eternally, simultaneously, in stillness, stability and silence, with none of the temporal succession that characterizes our words (11.7.9–11.13); the Word incarnate, however, 'sounded externally in human ears so that it should be believed and sought inwardly' (11.8.10). The question Augustine wishes to address in this book is the one we have so far been addressing in relation to sermon 22: how we move from words spoken in time to the eternal Word; from the mutable to the immutable; the fleeting to the still; from sound to silence. His answer in book 11 appears to be that this is achieved in and through the temporal, mutable sound of the divine Mediator, the Word incarnate. In contrast to the mind's tempo- ral distension in anticipating, attending to and remembering what it hears, when it listens to a poem or song being recited or sung (11.31.41 'a person singing or listening to a song he knows well suffers a distension or stretching in feeling and in sense perception from the expectation of future sounds and the memory of past sound'), in its anticipating, attending to and remember- ing the eternal Word of God incarnate, the fragmentation and distraction of temporal listening becomes one of concentration and stretching out, or intention, towards God himself (11.29.39 'not stretched out in distraction but extended in reach, not by being pulled apart but by concentration' *non distentus, sed extentus, non secundum distentionem, sed secundum inten- tionem*). In this way, listening to the incarnate Word, the human listener is formed and reformed towards the eternal Word (11.30.40 'I will stand still, then, and find firm footing in you, in your Truth who is shaping me to himself' *Et stabo atque solidabor in te, in forma mea, ueritate tua*).[12]

The second distinction which enables Augustine to illustrate the insep-
arability of sound and silence is found in book 12. Here, he distinguishes
between two different types of silence, which were both created by God 'in
the beginning' when he created 'the heavens and the earth'. First of all, there
is the silence of heaven, or the heaven of heavens – an intelligible, spiritual,
eternal silence of simultaneity and immutability, where there is no time, no
consecutiveness, no words that are fleeting or pass away, but everything is
always wholly present (12.11.1–13.16). Here, in unshakeable unity, peace
and concord, the host of heaven eternally delight in and enjoy God face to
face, ceaselessly and unfailingly cleaving to him.[13] In contrast to the heaven
of heavens is the earth's silence, a silence that is characterized by absence: the
'earth' is what Augustine understands by 'formless matter', the matter which
God drew from nothing in order to create; it is 'invisible and unorganised'
(12.4.4–5.5 referring to Genesis 1.2); a 'nothing something' (*nihil aliquid*),
an 'is-that-is-not' (*est non est*) (12.6.6), formless, not yet capable of change
because not yet possessing form or time (12.19.28). Again, Augustine is fighting for words to express the inconceivable. It is the silence of absence, of noth-
ingness, of formlessness, known by knowing what it is not (12.3.3–10.10).

Towards the end of book 12, Augustine returns to the contrast he has
drawn between the two different silences of earth and heaven. This time,
however, he explores the way in which the earth's silence is made present;
the way in which it sounds by receiving form in converting to God's call.
His contrast – or rather his illustration – is the *relation* between sound and
song: the relation between formless matter which simultaneously receives
form by becoming song. His point is that there is no sound without song; no
song without sound; sound is the matter of song; song is the form of sound –
'sound receives form to become song' (*idem quippe formatur, ut cantus est*)
(12.29.40). In other words, we only hear silence through sound, and sound
is only present as song – sound which is present because it has form.

The analogy of sound and song is thereby used to demonstrate what is,
in fact, one of the main points he wishes to argue in these last three books
of the *Confessions*, and which he makes explicitly in book 13: that the
creation, conversion and formation of human beings from nothing was not
a temporal process but a simultaneous, as it were instantaneous, sponta-
neous, timeless moment of what he calls 'concreation' (13.33.48–50).

So whereas God's silence is presence – the fullness of immutable, divine
eternity – the earth's silence is absence, the formlessness of matter drawn
from nothing, before it is called and formed by God. We only exist by being
brought forth, given form, sounded in time; we only come into being by
being called, and by responding to that call. So, when God speaks and says
'Let there be light', formless matter is drawn from nothing, it responds by
turning towards him, and in doing so it receives form: its silence becomes
sound (12.2.3; 13.1.1–3.4).[14]

This conviction that we are formed (or reformed) only by turning
towards God, and responding to the call of his Word (in the beginning and

incarnate), is, I think, confirmed by what Augustine has to say about the third way in which Scripture talks of Christ in sermon 22: 'how the whole Christ (*totus Christus*) is predicated with reference to the Church, that is as head and body' (19).

The idea of the Church as *totus Christus*, of Christ as the head of his body, the Church, is one of Augustine's favourite exegetical rules.[15] The whole of his vast commentary on the Psalms, the *Enarrationes in Psalmos*, is structured by it. This idea proves to be as much a pastoral strategy as an exegetical one, allowing his congregation to identify themselves not only with the psalmist but to join themselves to his prayers, which have effectively become the voice of the body of Christ, the Church, in dialogue with Christ, its head. The union is one that operates at a number of levels but it is first and foremost an ontological one: the Church, united with Christ, is animated by his Spirit, inspired by his love, breathes his desire, is joined to his Godhead by sharing his manhood, and partakes of his body and blood in the sacraments. The Church, his body, is also his voice: it composes, teaches, preaches and prays his words; it sounds forth his eternal and immutable silence. At a number of points in his sermon Augustine has hinted at these ideas: in his consideration of Christ's Godhead we saw that he described the Word's relation not only to the Father but to the Holy Spirit, by whom the love and desire of God is 'inspired' or breathed forth in us, so that we might love and desire him through himself (7). In the same passage, he refers to Christ the Word 'offering himself . . . asking somehow or other to be loved by the one he is not loved by'. This is a love that originates in the Trinity and draws the believer into contemplation of and union with the Trinitarian Godhead. In language which verges on the mystical, Augustine comments, 'In order that this most delightful and surpassing and inexpressible Trinity may be loved, soaring beyond the universal creation which it initiated, completed, arranged, soaring beyond it altogether, the Spirit desires the hearts of lovers' (7).

In a slightly less mystical vein, he also refers, in the section we have just examined on the incarnate Christ's manhood and Godhead, to the way in which Christ, the true light, enlightens others, so that they themselves become 'light-bearers or daystars' by receiving light (18). Both of these passages, on love and light respectively, are ways of expressing something of the mutual indwelling of Christ and the faithful; of the incorporation of believers into the life of the Godhead; and of the sacramental, mysterious unity of Christ and his body, the Church. Both are redolent of Augustine's comments in the Prologue to his *De doctrina christiana* where, commenting on the need for human teachers and preachers in order to communicate the word of God, he observes: 'For charity itself, which holds men together in a knot of unity, would not have a means of infusing souls and almost mixing them together, if men could teach nothing to men'.[16] This union, created by the sounding forth of the silent Godhead, by Christ, and by his evangelists, preachers and teachers, is made explicit in this third section of the sermon, where it is clearer than in the first two that it is not just that Scripture talks of Christ, but rather that the one who speaks in and through Scripture is Christ himself.

Augustine's first way of expressing this is a traditional one, often used in a mystical context, and especially in exegesis of the Song of Songs: the interpretation of the head and body, Christ and the Church, as a Bridegroom and Bride or a Husband and Wife (Eph. 5.31–32). The 'great sacrament' of marriage, of two becoming one flesh, described in Genesis 2.24 (20), allows Augustine and other Christian exegetes to express something of the inexpressible union of Godhead and manhood, of Christ and the Church, and of the heavenly city of God and the Church on pilgrimage in the world (19). He exhorts the Church to emulate the bride of the Song of Songs in being without stain or wrinkle, by enduring suffering, and stretching herself upon the cross, in order to iron out the wrinkles of sin, or by stretching out in love and desire for the future life (Phil. 3.13–14).

But in the context of this sermon it allows him to do even more than that: it allows him to say something about the nature of Scripture, and the way in which it sounds God's inexpressible silence. We should remember that this is a sermon preached extempore before a listening audience. Augustine's allegorical riffs on the Church as head and body have obviously invited the sort of response they probably also evoke in us, for he comments: 'All such passages, brothers and sisters, have a kind of sacramental meaning: anything in the scriptures that sounds absurd, sounds quite unnecessary, is under lock and key, not, however, locked up and empty; it's on something full of meaning that God turns the key, but he's looking for people to knock, so that he can open' (22).

Augustine is, in effect, summarizing what we earlier identified as the need for words or better, sounds, which are not definitive or conclusive, but which are, rather, open-ended and indeterminate; difficult and unsettling, and which invite search and discovery. He is also effectively summarizing the nature of Scripture: it is heavy with meaning, weighty with authority, filled with God's silent, unknowable and ineffable Godhead, guarding hidden, sacramental meanings. It may be obscure and closed, difficult to open, but its weight can be felt; its silence sensed. It is not to be sneered at or thrown away; it is not empty, but full (22). Augustine's illustration is on a par with John's belch: Scripture, he suggests, is like a bag of nuts which young boys hold in their hands, sense the weight of, rejoice over, but cannot open (22). Just as a young boy might hand over the nuts to a parent to crack open for him, so that he can eat them, so, he suggests, we should look to Scripture – in this case, to Paul – to reveal for us the presence of God in the sacraments, of Christ in the Church, of silence in sound, so that we, too, can be filled with them, and 'sit and eat'.

So give it to this father or mother . . . give him to break open what you are carrying around locked up, so heavy with such great authority. It's written in the book of Genesis; it's not a light matter, there's something hiding there, locked up. Doesn't he strike you as having said something when he said 'sacrament'? I can feel it; after all, it's heavy, but it's locked up. 'But I mean' he [Paul] says 'in Christ and in the Church' (Eph. 5.32). There you are, there's the food. Eat it. (22)

He might just as well have said, 'There you are, you can hear the silence, now listen to it.'

So what might we conclude? First, I think, that sound is not simply temporal, mutable and inarticulate; rather it is sacramental: it is the form that silence takes. Sound is like the flesh of the incarnate Christ, the words of evangelists, preachers and teachers, sounding forth the silent Godhead. Similarly, God's silence is not simply eternal, immutable and ineffable; rather it is the origin of sound. God's silence informs sound and is present in it, even though, in itself, it remains unknowable. In the context of this sermon, Augustine demonstrates that Christ is both the eternal and ineffable Word of the Father, and, in the unity of the Trinity, the Creator Word and the incarnate Word, the origin and inspiration of the words of Scripture and of all writing, teaching and preaching. It is through them that he is sounded, calling us, through participation in his mysteries, to his silent Godhead. In terms of exegesis, we might conclude, first, that Scripture is characterized as much by absence as presence, by the unknowability and ineffability of God. This means that it is often obscure, difficult, offensive, crude and full of stumbling blocks in order to inculcate humility and invite search; to give a bottom to the bottomless. But second, Scripture is also characterized as much by presence as absence: by the inspiration of the Spirit, the love of God, who is the whole present in its every part, as Christ's Godhead is united to his manhood, the head to the body, the Bridegroom to the Bride. We simply need to listen.

Notes

1 Though see *De doctrina christiana*. Pamela Bright, ed., *Augustine and the Bible* (Notre Dame IN: Notre Dame University Press, 1999); Anne-Marie La Bonnardière, ed., *Saint Augustin et la Bible*, Bible de Tous les Temps (Paris: Beauchesne, 1986); Bertrand de Margerie, *Introduction à l'histoire de l'éxègese III. saint Augustin* (Paris: Cerf, 1983); Frederick Van Fleteren and Joseph C. Schnaubelt, eds, *Augustine. Biblical Exegete* (New York, NY: Peter Lang, 2001).

2 Though see *De trinitate* books 4 and 13 and *Epistula*, 137. W. Geerlings, *Christus Exemplum. Studien zur Christologie und Christusverkündigung Augustinus*, Tübinger theologische Studien 13 (Mainz, 1978); Goulven Madec, *La Patrie et la Voie: Le Christ dans la vie et la pensée de saint Augustin* (Paris: Desclée, 2001); Gérard Remy, *Le Christ médiateur dans l'oeuvre de saint Augustin* (Paris, 1979); T. J. Van Bavel, *Recherches sur la Christologie de saint Augustin*, Paradosis 10 (Fribourg:

Editions Universitaires, 1954); Albert Verwilghen, *Christologie et Spiritualité selon saint Augustin: L'Hymne aux Philippiens* (Paris: Beauchesne, 1985).

3 Augustine, *Sermon* 341 (Dolbeau 22, Mainz 55) in *Vingt-Six Sermons au peuples d'Afrique, retrouvés à Mayence*, ed. François Dolbeau, Collections des Études Augustiniennes ' Série Antiquité 147 (Institut d'Études Augustiniennes: Paris, 1996).

4 See Cyril O'Regan, '*De doctrina christiana* and Modern Hermeneutics', in *De doctrina christiana: A Classic of Western Culture*, ed. by Duane W. H. Arnold and Pamela Bright (Notre Dame, IN: University of Notre Dame Press, 1995), pp. 217–43.

5 As Gregory Nazianzen (*Theological Oration*, 28.13) points out to Eunomius and Aetius, in thinking they can rationally comprehend the divine nature they are in fact taking a human image as an end in itself and idolizing it; God transcends what we can know.

6 Cf. *De doctrina christiana*, 2.6.7.

7 For example, *Enarrationes in Psalmos*, 26.ii.12; 32.ii.8; 46.7; 80.3; 94.3; 99.4.

8 *De doctrina christiana*, 1.6.6 'Hence the fact that he is called God: he himself is not truly known by the sound of these two syllables, yet when the word strikes our ears it leads all users of the Latin language to think of a supremely excellent and immortal being', in *Augustine De Doctrina*, ed and trans by R. P. H. Green (Oxford: Oxford University Press, 1995), pp. 18–19.

9 Tim Denecker and Gert Partoens, '*De uoce et uerbo*. Augustine's exegesis of John 1.1–3 and 23 in sermons 288 and 293A auct. (*Dolbeau* 3)', *Annali di Storia dell'Esegesi* 31.1 (2014), pp. 91–114.

10 The Word of God is not a word in our sense of the word. Words are, rather, a concession to human created-ness and fallen-ness; we are given them in all their crudeness and rudeness in order to inculcate humility and resist pride; because, however much they must inevitably fall short of expressing anything of the Divine, we otherwise would not be able to say anything at all (7).

11 Augustine, *Enarrationes in Psalmos*, 56.16, in *Expositions of the Psalms. The Works of St Augustine: A New Translation for the 21st Century, Vol.1, III/17*, ed. by John E. Rotelle, and trans. by Maria Boulding (Hyde Park, NY: New City Press, 2000), pp. 118–19.

12 Cf. 11.8.10: 'When some changeable creature advises us, we are but led to that stable Truth, where we truly learn as we stand still and listen to him, and are filled with joy on hearing the Bridegroom's voice, and surrender ourselves once more to him from whom we came.'

13 *Conf.* 12.11.12; 12.13.16; 12.15.19; 13.15.18.

14 Cf. *Conf.* 13 12.13–14.15 for similar insights, allegorically relating the days of creation to the Church, its Scripture, Sacraments and preachers as the sound/presence of God calling and converting, creating and recreating.

15 Michael Cameron, '*Totus Christus* and the Psychagogy of Augustine's Sermons', *Augustinian Studies*, 36.1 (2005), pp. 59–70; 'The Emergence of *Totus Christus* as Hermeneutical Center in Augustine's *Enarrationes in Psalmos*', in *The Harp of Prophecy: Early Christian Interpretation of the Psalms*, ed. by Brian E. Daley and Paul R. Kolbet (Notre Dame, IL: Notre Dame University Press, 2015), pp. 205–26.

16 *De doctrina christiana*, Prologue, 6 (Green, pp. 6–9).

6

How Could the Earthly Jesus
Have Taught Divine Truth?[1]

SIMON FRANCIS GAINE

How do we know the truth about God, we whose knowledge seems so limited by our finite and bodily constitution to the things of this world, the things we can know through our senses? It is true that, even though our minds are darkened by sin, nevertheless from our knowledge of this created universe, we can discover some knowledge of its Creator. But this is a knowledge that always leaves us dissatisfied because it falls so far short of the truth we can naturally desire concerning what and who God is. According to Catholic belief, divine revelation, which has its culmination in the life, death and resurrection of Jesus Christ, lifts us beyond the limitations of our natural knowledge of God, to faith in the Triune God, and in the mystery of his salvation which leads us by faith to a heavenly destination of beatifying knowledge of God just as he truly is. It is Jesus then, the head of the *totus Christus*, who is the Revealer in this saving plan of revelation, the one who teaches the members of his body the truth about realities that lie beyond our natural power to know. From this arises the question: how can he do it? What is it about Jesus that, even while he lived on earth, enabled him to teach human beings the truth about God and the kingdom of God? In what follows, I shall unfold various levels of answer to this question, seeing how some of this is answered with the help of defined dogma, some of it with the help of established Roman Catholic theological positions and the teaching of the ordinary Magisterium, and finally that some of it can be answered with the help of further theological speculation from within the Thomist tradition that derives from St Thomas Aquinas.[2]

We begin with the picture we find of Jesus in the Gospels, as one sent by God with a saving mission that includes teaching authoritatively about God, his creation and his people. All the Gospels present him as one who teaches with a distinctive authority. For example, there is Mark 1.21–22: 'They went to Capernaum; and when the Sabbath came, he entered the synagogue and taught. They were astounded at his teaching, for he taught them as one having authority, and not as the scribes.' Moreover, the formula Jesus uses in Matthew's Sermon on the Mount – 'But I say to you', rather than the typical prophetic, 'Thus says the Lord' – indicates in context a teaching authority transcending not simply the everyday scribes of Jesus' time but the whole historic line of divinely inspired prophets, a teaching authority on God's level. The readers of the Gospels are surely meant to realize that this authority is rooted in Jesus' unique and intimate relationship with God his Father, as witnessed by Jesus' words in Matthew 11.25–26:

> I thank you, Father, Lord of heaven and earth, because you have hidden these things from the wise and the intelligent and have revealed them to infants . . . All things have been handed over to me by my Father; and no one knows the Son except the Father, and no one knows the Father except the Son and anyone to whom the Son chooses to reveal him.

The Gospel of John provides a kind of extended commentary on this perfect mutual knowing of Father and Son as the basis of divine revelation to Christ's disciples: the Word is the one in the bosom of the Father who alone has seen God and makes him known (1.18). Moreover, Christ who is the Word made flesh (1.14) identifies himself as the Truth (14.6) and asserts that the word he speaks is true (8.39–47).

In answer to the question how Christ is equipped to teach divine truth, the Catholic faith replies that it is because he is God: the Word who was with God from the beginning *is* God (John 1.1). The precision of this reply is rooted in the debate about the precise character of the Saviour's divinity that raged especially through much of the fourth century. It was a presbyter of Alexandria in Egypt, Arius, who set the debate alight, and the deacon and later bishop of Alexandria, St Athanasius, who championed the solution of the *homoousios*, that the Son was consubstantial, of one being with the Father. Eventually the opponents of the Arians gathered support around the teaching of the Council of Nicaea that the Son is consubstantial with the Father, true God from true God.[3] Despite there being wider salvific concerns in the controversy, Christ's knowledge played some part in the arguments made. The Arians argued from limitations in Christ's knowledge allegedly found in the Gospels to the conclusion that he was not God in the sense that the Father was God but was rather a perfect creature to whom the title 'god' was due in some lesser sense.[4] The Nicenes argued from the knowledge of God, creation and human beings displayed by Christ in the Gospels to his full divine nature. This anti-Arian concern continued throughout the Patristic period. One can find it, for example, in the works on John penned by Cyril of Alexandria and Augustine of Hippo.[5] Any extraordinary knowledge manifested by Christ in the Gospels is used as evidence of his true divinity against the Arians. Orthodox Nicene theology thus provides us with part of the answer as to how Jesus could teach the truth about divine realities. As God, he knew all things.[6] As Son of the Father, he received all knowledge from the Father just as he received his being from the Father.[7] As the true Creator of all things, he knew all there was to know about creation.[8] Christ could teach divine truth because he was divine Truth. His teaching about God is true because it has its source in God, because he himself, the teacher, is divine.

To say that Christ is true God, however, can only be *part* of the explanation for how Christ teaches us about divine things *humanly*. In the Gospels, he teaches in a human way. There may be aspects of this teaching that can only be explained by his divinity, but I want to draw our attention here to the fact that he teaches through human words, images and concepts, when he teaches about the kingdom of God and about the Father and the relationship between Father and Son. Jesus is a man who tells stories, who tells parables, and who, within the context of Jewish tradition, presumably thought up these particular stories, formulated these particular parables, as vehicles of his teaching divine truth. It would surely not be true to the Gospel narratives to suppose that there was no place here for a human mind in the constitution of the human teacher of divine realities. Yet another of the great controversies of the fourth century was over whether or not Christ had a human mind, or whether in assuming a human body the Word itself took on the role of a human mind. That the Word did such a thing was held not only by the Arians, but also by some of the Nicenes, most famously Apollinarius. However, not only did the orthodox Fathers reject Arianism, but at the Council of Constantinople they also rejected Apollinarianism.[9] Again, the concerns were broader soteriological ones – it was because the human mind needed healing that the Word assumed a human mind.[10] The fact of the presence of a true human mind in the Incarnation certainly had implications for the nature of his teaching.

We should not be quick to assume, however, that just because people accepted that Christ had a true human mind, they accepted he had true human knowledge proper to his human mind. Reacting against the definition of the Council of Chalcedon that there were two natures in Christ, divine and human, there were those who sought what they held was a better way of maintaining the unity of Christ than the one person in two natures upheld by Chalcedon. Those who were convinced that Chalcedon had betrayed the legacy of Cyril on the unity of Christ thought that not only was there in Christ *one* nature of the Word incarnate, but that this meant that there was in him only one wisdom, one knowledge, one activity or operation, one will. The followers of Severus of Antioch refused to draw the conclusion from the reality of Christ's human mind that it had its own proper activity or operation of knowledge. Instead, the single divine knowledge did for Christ's human mind as well as for his divine mind. How the finite human mind could work with infinite divine knowledge did not seem to be a problem for them, and indeed the human mind did not really 'work' or operate on their view of things.

For those who were loyal to Chalcedon, however, such as Maximus the Confessor and John of Damascus, this could provide no solution. At the time of Chalcedon, Pope Leo the Great had taught that each nature, human and divine, had its own proper activity or operation,[11] and this was now confirmed as the orthodox position in opposition to any kind of Monothelitism or Monenergism. Not only did Christ have *two* minds, divine and human, but he also had two *wisdoms*, human and divine, and this passes down to medieval and modern Catholic theology. Aquinas, for example, who for his time was well informed about Patristic and conciliar developments, was aware that there had been those who had thought that Christ needed no knowledge besides his divine knowledge.[12] Aquinas was to argue, to the contrary, from the perfection of the Saviour's human nature to the fact that his human mind was perfected by its own knowledge, which he thus had in addition to the divine knowledge that came with his divinity. Without this specific perfection of the mind, Christ would have assumed an imperfect rather than perfect human nature, and according to Aquinas it was perfection that Jesus required here in order to bring us to perfection. From the perspective of our question, we can suppose that it is such knowledge proper to the human mind that is engaged in Christ's human act of teaching through images and ideas and parables and so on. Opposition to the Severan position on Christ's unity, however, did not mean that Maximus or John or the other Fathers had given much indication of what the human operation of Christ's human mind actually consisted in.[13] In general, when the Fathers found something extraordinary recorded in Scripture of Christ's human knowledge, such as that he had seen the Father, they tended to refer this to Christ's *divine* knowledge rather than the human knowledge in his human mind, since such passages were so important to oppose the lingering spectre of Arianism by proving his divinity from divine knowledge.[14] It was left to later theologians, such as Aquinas, to spell out the character of the knowledge in Christ's human mind more precisely.

At this point we should ask how an answer to the question of Christ's teaching us humanly about divine realities is shaping up. The Catholic doctrinal tradition indicates for us two crucial points, namely, that since he is truly divine, Christ has true divine knowledge, and that since he has a true and perfect human nature, he has a human mind perfected by *its* own proper knowledge. Hence Christ can teach us humanly about divine things because his divine knowledge is the source of this teaching and because through possession of a working human mind he has the capacity to communicate this knowledge in a human way. What remains to be explored, though, is precisely how Christ's divine knowledge is *able to be communicated* through his human mind. According to Chalcedon, though Christ's two natures are united in his one person, they retain their distinction, such that Christ's human and divine minds are in no way confused.[15] The Fathers certainly seem to suppose in their teaching that, nonetheless, the human mind of Christ somehow had the benefit of divine knowledge, but they do not really reflect on how this happened. What we need to explore is how Christ's two minds and two wisdoms are related, how we – or rather Jesus – gets from the divine knowledge in his divine mind to the human act of teaching his disciples in a human way through his human mind. Exactly how then does the human mind through which Christ teaches get the benefit of his divine knowledge?

Contemporary philosophical theology has tried to explore the relation between Christ's human and divine minds in various ways, largely by drawing on analogies from Freudian psychology, information technology, comparative religion or science fiction.[16] In some cases, however, the analogy of a divided mind can serve to keep the two minds isolated rather than united, contrary to the position of the Fathers, and sometimes this has even been the intention of contemporary philosophical theologians.[17] In my recent book, *Did the Saviour See the Father? Christ, Salvation and the Vision of God,* I have explored this question not from such analogies but from the analogy of faith, that is, by looking for illumination of the mystery of Christ's knowledge that underlies his teaching from among other mysteries of the Catholic faith, in this case the beatific vision of the saints. The eschatological character of Christ's earthly mission itself, and the intimate character of the saints' eschatological knowledge of God, encouraged me to look in this direction for a solution.[18]

As Aquinas explains the beatific vision of the saints, it is the highest participation of a created intellect in God's knowledge and has a very different means of knowledge from our normal, human knowledge. Our natural means of knowledge are abstract ideas or concepts based on what we sense from the world around us: we see sheep, hear sheep and smell sheep, and from all this sense data we form the idea or concept of sheep. Such ideas or concepts become the means by which we have knowledge of sheep and other finite realities, and all these ideas are limited and finite. None of our finite ideas can be an appropriate means for knowing the infinite God. But while our own natural means of knowledge, the finite ideas and concepts we form from sense data as the basis of our acts of knowledge, are inadequate for knowledge of the infinite God, God shares with the saints his own means of knowledge of himself. This means of knowledge is the divine essence. God has no body through which he comes to knowledge about himself or anything else, no distinct ideas or concepts to inform him about himself or the world. According to Aquinas, God knows himself only through himself, the only adequate means for knowing the infinite God, in which is included knowledge of God's power, of his creation, of salvation, of all he can do and does. In the beatific vision, God gifts himself to the minds of the saints so that his own being is now *their* means of knowledge as well as his. Thus they can know both the divine essence, and in the divine essence something of what God does, something of his creation and salvation.[19] Were God to grant this knowledge to Christ, he too would enjoy this intimate means of knowledge of God and of other things in God. Following on from the union of Christ's two natures on the level of being, that is, the hypostatic union, there would be a further union on the level of knowledge: Christ's human and divine minds, while remaining properly distinct, would be united by a common means of knowledge, because the divine essence itself, God's means of knowledge, would be shared with his humanity for a distinct operation of Christ's human mind, namely, his act of beatific vision.[20] While the Church has not solemnly defined Christ's beatific vision, not only is it supported by Aquinas, but it has also appeared in the Church's ordinary Magisterium, historically in two encyclicals of Pius XII in the 1950s, and again more recently, after a seeming absence of some decades, in the Congregation of the Doctrine of the Faith's notification concerning Jon Sobrino that was issued in 2006.[21] Where this leaves our question is with an account of how the human mind, while remaining distinct from the divine mind, can have the benefit of divine knowledge, since as a participation in divine knowledge the beatific vision is a kind of impact of divine knowledge on the human mind. This impact can thus help us see how Christ can take advantage of divine knowledge in his human mind, because this vision of God and of much in God is present in the human mind in this participated way, and the beatific vision can thus help explain the role of the human mind in teaching about God and the kingdom of God.

Aquinas himself explains the presence of the beatific vision in Christ's mind by saying that he had it in order to give it to us – Christ is perfect in this way in order to give us a share in his perfection.[22] In the twentieth century, Thomists unpacked and extended his argument by looking at how Christ brings us to the beatific vision in the next life *through faith in this life*, concluding that the beatific vision underlay the teaching that brought the disciples to believe in the truth he taught.[23] Various passages in Aquinas' *Commentary on the Gospel of John* support this approach.[24] However, I suggest that as early as the first question of the *Summa Theologiae* Aquinas is hinting at such a thing. When he asks in the second article whether *sacra doctrina* – a sacred teaching learned through revelation – is a science, he needs to ask where its basic principles, the articles of faith, come from, given that they are not in themselves self-evident. He answers that the articles of faith are derived from a higher science, which is 'the science of God and the blessed', *scientia Dei et beatorum*.[25] One might wonder why Aquinas bothers to add *et beatorum* here, since mention of *God's* knowledge is enough to establish where the principles on which sacred teaching proceeds are derived from: *God* reveals them to faith. I suggest that Aquinas adds 'and the blessed' because he is hinting at the revelatory role of Christ, who is of course pre-eminent among the blessed, in teaching us the basis of our faith. We may even suppose that *scientia Dei* et *beatorum* hints at knowledge in Christ's divine *and* human minds, both of which play a foundational role in the act of teaching by Jesus Christ that makes *sacra doctrina* a reality.

Thus it seems to me that, if we are to make sense of the role of Christ as human teacher of divine truth, we need to do more than identify the divine source of Christ's knowledge and its human term or end in the act of teaching. Rather, we need to gain some insight into the whole process from source to term, and Christ's possession of the beatific vision enables us to do this *up to a point*, because in it we can verify the impact of divine knowledge on the human mind. However, the act of beatific knowledge itself can hardly explain the *entire* process from source to term, and this is because of the *intrinsic inexpressibility* of this beatific act. Human teaching as such is something expressed, meaning that it must be expressible for the human mind in ideas and concepts and images, and thus somehow properly proportioned to the workings of the human mind. Beatific knowledge, however, is not like that at all, but is instead transcendently disproportionate to the workings of the finite human mind, because its means is no finite idea but the infinite essence of God. What this means is that the vision of the infinite God, which comes only through an infinite means of knowledge, that is, the divine essence, cannot *in itself* be expressed or articulated by the finite mind. In other words, the beatific vision in itself will not mean we are able to say or express what God is or who God is in any adequate way. Rather the beatific vision is in itself inexpressible, and even what is thus known in it is known inexpressibly *per se*, and we cannot suppose possession of the beatific vision to be equivalent to some articulated sets of knowledge. What this means for our question is that, in order to trace Christ's ability to teach divine truth in a human way from source *all the way* to term, we need not only to explore how divine knowledge is shared with the human mind by the beatific vision, but also to show how what is known in the beatific vision can be made somehow expressible and so communicable in Christ's teaching of the truth.[26]

Various theories have been proposed to manifest the path from Christ's beatific vision to his communicable knowledge. Each of these draws in some way on Aquinas' broader picture of the knowledge in Christ's human mind. In the knowledge of the blessed we have seen *one way* in which Aquinas sets out the perfection of Christ's human mind. But, as well as this participation in divine knowledge, Aquinas also names two other kinds of knowledge required by Christ for the perfection of his mind on Aquinas' account. One is infused knowledge, the kind natural to angels who do not draw ideas from any bodily senses, but as purely intellectual, spiritual though finite beings possess their ideas by nature as means of knowledge.[27] The other kind is acquired knowledge, the kind had naturally by human beings via the senses. Aquinas saw both as contributing perfection in different ways to the human mind of the Saviour.[28]

One theory of how Christ's beatific knowledge, which is in itself inexpressible, can be given some kind of finite expression, draws especially on Aquinas' account of acquired knowledge. We can find this approach in the work of the twentieth-century theologian Bernard Lonergan who, while unusually for his generation retaining Christ's beatific knowledge in his Christology, eventually seems to have eliminated Christ's infused knowledge from it. Lonergan thought of Christ's knowledge along the lines of the analogy of our own knowledge of the natural light of our intellects. By the light of our intellects we know so much, yet even philosophers have great difficulty in expressing exactly what our minds are. Lonergan compared

Christ to a scientist or philosopher seeking truth not yet possessed, where they already have a kind of knowledge of what they are looking for such that they can recognize it when they find it. In contrast, Christ *already* enjoyed the end of knowing God, and from this end used his human powers to render his ineffable knowledge 'effable' or speakable. The vehicle for this 'making effable' was the effable knowledge gained through the senses in the normal human way, but against the horizon of the light of the beatific vision which enabled Christ to judge well concerning the suitability of what was learned through the senses for speaking effably what was known ineffably in the vision.[29] Thus his experience of shepherds, fields, sowers, lost property, insistent neighbours, prodigal sons and their fathers equipped him with a natural knowledge that could become a vehicle for speaking the truth about God and his kingdom.

Whether, however, this can give us a *complete* picture of how Christ makes what is known in the vision communicable may be doubted. In the case of the biblical prophets, it is certainly true, according to Aquinas, that the prophetic light by which the prophet makes judgements is the chief element of prophecy. But the prophet may also have ideas infused into the mind, knowledge specially infused into the mind beyond the natural capacities of his intellect, by which he is able to prophesy God's action in the future or whatever it might be, and for Aquinas this *combination* of light and ideas is the most perfect kind of prophecy.[30] Surely we can see a more solid case for understanding Christ as a teacher of divine realities, the fulfilment of the prophets, if there is such a fuller picture of these extraordinary supernatural elements in his knowledge. Moreover, it is not clear that the light of the beatific vision, if in itself ineffable, can as such provide everything fitting for Christ to judge well of the fruits of acquired knowledge whether or not they are suitable vehicles of teaching divine truth in a human way. Perhaps it would be fitting for Christ to have some further knowledge of a prophetic kind in order to make comparisons with his acquired knowledge and so make these judgements. In contrast to Lonergan, Jacques Maritain provides just such a fuller picture in the second theory we are to consider.[31]

Although Maritain grants a role to Christ's acquired knowledge, the primary role in Christ's teaching knowledge is accorded to his infused knowledge. This theory Maritain develops from Aquinas. Like Lonergan, Maritain emphasizes the inexpressibility of the beatific vision. He compares one blessed with this vision to someone with only a thousand dollar note and no change to purchase an orange juice from a dispensing machine. Without a moneychanger, Maritain says, the man could die of thirst![32] According to Maritain, it is infused finite ideas and concepts that play the role of the moneychanger, so that what Christ knows inexpressibly in his vision he can 'translate' into finite knowledge suited to teaching by way of this infused knowledge. Rather than this vehicle of communication having an earthly source in the senses, it has a divine source in a divine infusion of ideas into Christ's mind.

A third theory, which I expound in my book, is based on the fact that Aquinas held that any of the blessed could draw from their vision similitudes or finite ideas of some things they saw there.[33] They can do this because what is known *in* the inexpressible vision of God is in itself finite and as such open to finite expression. So while the essence of God remains inexpressible, God's effects which are known in his essence *can* be expressed in ideas drawn by the blessed from their vision in a further series of willed supernatural acts distinct from the act of vision but dependent upon it. In the *De Veritate*, Aquinas makes it explicit that Christ's soul was capable of this too.[34] We can then suppose that, during his teaching ministry, Christ was able to make a series of such acts of translation for the sake of teaching the truth about God. However, it is true that when we examine Aquinas' biblical commentaries, we never find Aquinas appealing to this ability to explain the extraordinary, communicable knowledge had by Christ the teacher. I think this is because – and we almost certainly find this in some of Aquinas' interpreters – it is assumed that Christ did not *need* to draw ideas and concepts from his vision because he *already* had full sets of infused ideas covering all that could be known by finite means, already infused into his soul at conception.[35] As a result of such extensive infused knowledge, he never had any need to use his ability to form new ideas from his vision.

However, it seems to me that there is some advantage in supposing that Christ *did* form ideas and concepts in this way. For one thing, there is a clear line of continuity from Christ's divine knowledge through his beatific vision to the communicable ideas drawn from the vision, to his act of teaching humanly of divine realities through such ideas. Such a line of continuity is perhaps more important to us in a post-Enlightenment age that is more concerned carefully to articulate a fundamental theology of revelation than it was in the pre-Enlightenment age of medieval faith in which Aquinas lived. In particular, the engagement of the human will of Christ in individual acts of drawing ideas from the vision reinforces this continuity, in contrast to acquired knowledge which is drawn *from elsewhere*, from the senses, and infused knowledge which Aquinas holds is *divinely* infused into the soul quite apart from any act of Christ's *human* will. It seems to me, moreover, that where such communicable ideas are formed from the vision, they can be used by Christ in acts of *comparison* with ideas from elsewhere, whether infused or acquired, to confirm what is suitable to communicate the truth about God and his kingdom, and what is not. With such *connections* made, Christ can use finite knowledge from various sources as fitting vehicles for expressing in his teaching what he knows inexpressibly in the beatific vision.

In conclusion, we can make sense of the picture we find of Christ the teacher in the Gospels, of one who teaches us the truth about divine realities in a human way, by way of acts of theological discovery which take place under the guidance of Catholic dogma and the ordinary teaching of the Church, through speculation undertaken within the Thomist tradition.

Because he is true God, Christ's teaching has its source in divine knowledge. Because he is gifted with the beatific vision, his human mind has the benefit of divine knowledge. Because this vision, though inexpressible in itself, enables him to draw further communicable knowledge from it, he is able to teach in a human way, through his human mind, the truth about divine realities, about God and about the kingdom of God. While it is the picture of Christ in the Gospels that gives rise to this theological discovery and speculation, this very speculation should enable us to return to the Gospels once more and reread the story of Christ the teacher in a way that is more speculative and in some way fruitful in understanding the Saviour, the human teacher of divine truth, the head of the body, whom God has given us.

Notes

1 This is one of two chapters in this collection which supplement the papers given at the 2018 *Totus Christus* conference. An earlier version of the paper was given at a conference 'The Heart of Revelation: A Dominican Perspective' held at the Sapientia College of Theology, Budapest, on 19 November 2016, and published in Hungarian as Simon Francis Gaine, 'Hogyan taníthatott a földi Jézus isteni igazságokat?', in *Az Igazság ragyogása a Kinyilatkoztatás szívében: Domonkos megközelítések*, ed. by Ráhel Szabó (Budapest: L'Harmattan Kiadó, 2017), pp. 93–111.

2 Here I draw on and develop arguments contained in Simon Francis Gaine, *Did the Saviour See the Father? Christ, Salvation and the Vision of God* (London: Bloomsbury T & T Clark, 2016); and Simon Francis Gaine, 'Is There Still a Place For Christ's Infused Knowledge in Catholic Theology and Exegesis?', *Nova et Vetera*, English edn, 16 (2018), pp. 601–15.

3 Heinrich Denzinger, Peter Hünermann, Robert Fastiggi and Anne Englund Nash, eds, *Enchiridion symbolorum definitionum et declarationem de rebus fidei et morum, Compendium of Creeds, Definitions and Declarations on Matters of Faith and Morals*, 43rd edn (San Francisco: Ignatius, 2012), paras. 125–6. See also Lewis Ayres, *Nicaea and its Legacy: An Approach to Fourth-Century Trinitarian Theology* (Oxford: Oxford University Press, 2004).

4 For the Arian arguments, see Kevin J. Madigan, *The Passions of Christ in High-Medieval Thought: An Essay on Christological Development* (Oxford and New York: Oxford University Press, 2007), pp. 11–22.

5 Cyril of Alexandria, *Commentarii in Ioannem*, 1.10; Augustine of Hippo, *Tractatus in Ioannem*, 40.5.

6 Athanasius of Alexandria, *Contra Arianos*, 3.46.

7 Basil of Caesarea, *Epistulae*, 236.

8 Ambrose of Milan, *De Fide ad Gratianum*, 2.11.94; 5.16.199.

9 Denzinger–Hünermann, *Enchiridion*, para. 151.

10 Gregory of Nazianzus, *Epistulae*, 101.32.

11 Leo the Great, *Tomus ad Flavianum, Lectio dilectionis tuae*, 4. Denzinger-Hünermann, *Enchiridion*, para. 294.

12 Thomas Aquinas, *Summa Theologiae*, IIIa., q. 9, a. 1; *De Veritate*, q. 20, a. 1.

13 For example, John of Damascus, *Expositio Fidei*, 3.15–18.

14 Cyril of Alexandria, *Commentarii in Ioannem*, 1.10; Augustine of Hippo, *Tractatus in Ioannem*, 40.5.

15 Denzinger–Hünermann, *Enchiridion*, para. 302.

16 T. V. Morris, *The Logic of God Incarnate* (Ithaca, NY and London: Cornell University Press, 1986), pp. 102–7; Eleanore Stump, *Aquinas* (London and New York: Routledge, 2003), pp. 410–26; Richard Cross, 'Incarnation', in *The Oxford Handbook of Philosophical Theology*, ed. by Thomas P. Flint and Michael C. Rea (Oxford: Oxford University Press, 2009), pp. 452–75; Joseph Jedwab, 'The Incarnation and Unity of Consciousness', in *The Metaphysics of the Incarnation*, ed. by Anna Marmodoro and Jonathan Hill (Oxford: Oxford University Press, 2011), pp. 168–85; Andrew Loke, 'The Incarnation and Jesus' Apparent Limitation in Knowledge', *New Blackfriars*, 94 (2013), pp. 583–602.

17 For example, Richard Swinburne, *The Christian God* (Oxford: Clarendon, 1994), pp. 199–212.

18 Gaine, *Did the Saviour See the Father?*, pp. 73–4.

19 Aquinas, *Summa*, Ia., q. 12. For Aquinas on the beatific vision, see Jean-Pierre Torrell, *Recherches thomasiennes. Études revues et augmentées* (Paris: Vrin, 2000), pp. 177–97.

20 *Summa*, IIIa., q. 10. For the application of the Thomist theory of the beatific vision to Christ, see Gaine, *Did the Saviour See the Father?*, pp. 77–97.

21 Pius XII, *Mystici Corporis Christi*, 48; *Haurietis Aquas*, 56; Congregation for the Doctrine of the Faith, *Notificatio de Operibus P. Jon Sobrino, S. I.* Denzinger–Hünermann, *Enchiridion*, para. 5107; *Acta Apostolicae Sedis* 99 (2007), pp. 181–94.

22 Aquinas, *Summa*, IIIa., q. 9, a. 2. See also q. 10.

23 Reginald Garrigou-Lagrange, *Our Savior and His Love for Us* (St Louis, MO and London: Herder, 1951), pp. 143–71; Guy Mansini, 'Understanding St. Thomas on Christ's Immediate Knowledge of God', *Thomist* 59 (1995), pp. 91–124.

24 For example, *Commentary on the Gospel of John*, 7.3.

25 *Summa*, Ia., q. 1, a. 2.

26 Gaine, *Did the Saviour See the Father?*, pp. 97–9.

27 *Summa*, IIIa., q. 9, a. 3; q. 11. See Gaine, 'Is There Still a Place For Christ's Infused Knowledge in Catholic Theology and Exegesis?'.

28 *Summa*, IIIa., q. 9, a. 4; q. 12. See Simon Francis Gaine, 'Christ's Acquired Knowledge according to Thomas Aquinas: How Aquinas' Philosophy Helped and Hindered his Account', *New Blackfriars* 96 (2015), pp. 255–68.

29 Bernard Lonergan, *De Verbo Incarnato*, 3rd edn (Rome: Gregorian, 1964), pp. 406–7. On Lonergan's theory, see Jeremy Wilkins, 'Love and Knowledge of God in the Human Life of Christ', *Pro Ecclesia* 21 (2012), pp. 77–99.

30 Aquinas, *Summa*, IIa.IIae., q. 173, a. 2. For Aquinas on prophecy, see Serge-Thomas Bonino, 'Charisms, Forms, and States of Life (IIa IIae, qq. 171–189)', in *The Ethics of Aquinas*, ed. by Stephen J. Pope (Washington, DC: Georgetown, 2002), pp. 341–46.

31 Jacques Maritain, *On the Grace and Humanity of Jesus* (New York: Herder, 1969).

32 Maritain, *On the Grace and Humanity of Jesus*, pp. 72–3.

33 Aquinas, *Summa*, Ia., q. 12, a. 9 ad 2. See Gaine, *Did the Saviour See the Father?*, pp. 100–1; and Gaine, 'Is There Still a Place For Christ's Infused Knowledge

in Catholic Theology and Exegesis?'. Thomas Joseph White, 'The Infused Science of Christ', *Nova et Vetera*, English edn, 16 (2018), pp. 617–41, interprets me as holding that this supernatural ability to form similitudes is a natural one.

34 Aquinas, *De Veritate*, q. 20, a. 3 ad 4.

35 Aquinas, *Summa*, IIIa., q. 11, a. 1. See John of St Thomas [Jean Poinsot], *Cursus Theologicus in Summam Theologicam D. Thomae*, vol. 2 (Paris: Vivès, 1883), q. 12, a. 3, n. 1; P.-M. Margelidon, 'La science infuse du Christ selon saint Thomas', *Revue Thomiste* 114 (2014), pp. 379–416.

PART 3

Christ the Centre Indwelling and Perfecting All Things

Everything Holds Together[1]

Colossians 1.15–17 He is the image of the unseen God, the first-born of all creation, for in him were created all things in heaven and on earth: everything visible and everything invisible, thrones, ruling forces, sovereignties, powers – all things were created through him and for him. He exists before all things and in him all things hold together.

Everything holds together, everything,
From stars that pierce the dark like living sparks,
To secret seeds that open every spring,
From spanning galaxies to spinning quarks,
Everything holds together and coheres,
Unfolding from the center whence it came.
And now that hidden heart of things appears,
The first-born of creation takes a name.

And shall I see the one through whom I am?
Shall I behold the one for whom I'm made,
The light in light, the flame within the flame,
Eikon tou theou, image of my God?
He comes, a little child, to bless my sight,
That I might come to him for life and light.

---

1 Originally published in Malcolm Guite, *Parable and Paradox* (Norwich: Canterbury Press, 2016).

The Centre of Everywhere: Cosmic Christology in Early Franciscan Thought

LYDIA SCHUMACHER

In the second quarter of the thirteenth century, the first academic members of the Franciscan order made it their mission to articulate the spiritual and ministerial vision of their recently departed founder, Francis of Assisi, in theological and philosophical terms that would resonate with their colleagues at the recently founded universities. Those who worked at the University of Paris, which was the centre for theological study at the time, became particularly well known in their own day for collaboratively authoring what was undoubtedly one of the first great theological 'Summae' for which the period quickly became famous.

Named the 'Summa Halensis' for the man, Alexander of Hales, who oversaw the endeavour to produce it, this Summa was completed 20 years before Thomas Aquinas even set his hand to the task of authoring his own magisterial Summa, and in many respects it represents a structural and methodological prototype for this later work. As scholarship has succeeded in showing, the *Summa Halensis* formed the basis for the education of gifted Franciscan novices for much of the thirteenth century, through the time of Bonaventure and Duns Scotus, who further develop ideas that were first laid down by Alexander and his confrères.[1]

For many years, the significance of their collective work has been overlooked because of difficulties in determining which Franciscan authored which section of the text. As scholarship has well established, however, these difficulties do not undermine the fact that the Summa is precisely what its multiple authors intended it to be: an internally coherent and consistent as well as comprehensive indication of the distinctive features of the budding Franciscan intellectual tradition.[2] In this chapter, I would like to introduce readers to one aspect of that tradition which is particularly distinctive: this is what I describe as the Summa's 'cosmic Christology'.

The Summa takes the position, quite novel at the time, that it would have been fitting for Christ to become incarnate, and that he probably would have done so, even if humanity had not fallen into sin, such that his redemptive work on earth was not required. On this showing, the reason for his Incarnation was simply to bring to completion the work of creation that was initially enacted through him as the second person of the Trinity. To demonstrate this, I will start by explaining the understanding of creation that lies behind this 'supralapsarian' position, according to which Christ would have become incarnate regardless of the fall. I will then entertain the Summa's arguments as to why human nature was the most fitting one for Christ to assume, before enumerating the reasons why he actually did so.

These preliminary discussions lay the foundation for explaining what it means for early Franciscans to say that Christ completes his creative work by becoming a human being. They reveal what it means to say that he is at the centre of everything. At another level, they communicate the nature of our human calling to follow in the footsteps of Christ or bear his image in the world by engaging with our surroundings in light of his centrality. The closing section of this chapter will elucidate in part what this might entail.

Creation in the *Summa Halensis*

The Summa's doctrine of creation starts from the assumption that 'God is an infinite sphere, whose centre is everywhere and whose circumference is nowhere'.[3] This profound adage was drawn from the so-called 'book of twenty-four philosophers',[4] which was composed in the twelfth century by an unknown figure who wrote under the name of Hermes Trismegistus, the ancient Greek author of the so-called Hermetic corpus, who was regarded at the time as an enlightened pagan.[5] The goal of this book was quite simply to offer 24 statements defining the nature of God, on the model provided by Euclid's *Elements of Theology*.

Although the Summa adopts a later adaptation of the phrase from Alan of Lille, who spoke of God as an 'intelligible' rather than an infinite sphere, it furthered the then novel project of identifying infinity as the fundamental feature of the divine nature.[6] Previous authors had tended to describe God as first and foremost simple, and thus as a qualitatively different type of being to normal beings.[7] The construal of God as infinite certainly did not deny the otherness of God or proffer a theory in which God differs only quantitatively from the kinds of beings we know. Nevertheless, it allowed for the possibility of positing in God an infinite number of ideas for all possible and actual realities to which creatures correspond and through which they give direct if limited insight into some aspect of his nature.[8] Although creatures vary in the extent to which they are able to do this, the fact that they all instantiate some idea fully means that they are equal and equally valuable in God's sight.[9] It was apparently on this assumption that Francis of Assisi summoned his followers to treat all creatures, great and small, with care, generosity and compassion, especially the poor and lowly ones whose dignity is most often disregarded. Setting an example in this regard,

Francis famously interacted with animals 'as if they had reason',[10] speaking to them of God's love for them, which he saw reflected through them and which rendered them his brothers and sisters.

Though the fact that God knows and loves each one of these diverse creatures individually might seem to undermine his unity, the Summa claims that it does not, toeing the traditional line that the only proper object of God's knowledge is himself. By knowing himself, however, the authors of the Summa acknowledge that God knows the cause of all things and, by the same token, knows all the things he causes. Though in that sense, he has many ideas, the Summa insists that the multiplicity exists on the side of the things caused rather than on the side of God himself.[11]

The analogy that the Summa invokes to explain this phenomenon, drawn from Pseudo-Dionysius, and the Greek philosophical tradition before him, is that of a point or centre of a circle, from which many lines come and at which they terminate. In parsing this example, the Summa indicates that this is what it means to say that God's centre is everywhere, namely, that he is the source of all things that come from him and for that very reason limits and defines them. When considered in terms of his own circumference, however, he is outside all things and has no beginning or end. He cannot be encapsulated by any being, in much the same way that no one line can capture all the other lines that stem from the same central source.[12]

The one who determines which ideas to instantiate and who is responsible within the Godhead for instantiating them is the second person of the Trinity, that is, the Son. The Son is the obvious candidate to bring about creation because his role in the Trinity is to receive ideas or commands from the Father and carry them out in the Holy Spirit, who is the one in whom the goodness of God comes to be expressed in the goodness of creatures.[13] In the Middle Ages, some went so far as to describe the Spirit, or at least his work in the world, as the 'world soul', or 'a life-sustaining spirit directing the processes of the natural world'. The notion of the world soul stems from Greek philosophy and especially Plato's *Timaeus*.[14] It was passed on to medieval thinkers in the West through Calcidius' translation and commentary on the *Timaeus*, Macrobius' *Dream of Scipio* and other major works.[15]

As Bernard McGinn has noted, many twelfth-century thinkers adhered to the doctrine of the world soul in some form, not least Peter Abelard, whose identification of the world soul and the Holy Spirit was condemned at the Council of Sens in 1140.[16] After this time, enthusiasm for the doctrine waned but did not altogether disappear.[17] The *Summa Halensis* is no exception in continuing to reflect upon the doctrine of the world soul, which it summarizes in this way: 'some philosophers say that as the human being has its perfection in the rational soul, so the universe has its perfection in the world soul'.[18]

However, it casts doubt on the idea that God, not to mention any person in God, can be counted as the world soul. After all, God cannot be perfected as the world can and must be perfected; therefore, he cannot be the world soul.[19] Furthermore, God cannot be a world soul because he does not have a corporeal nature to which the soul can be united. Such responses to the doctrine seem designed at least in part to avoid pantheism, or the idea that God is one with the world, which had been condemned in 1225 in relation to the works of John Scotus Eriugena, who is known for furthering the Greek tradition in the West. This was evidently the risk of taking the idea that the Holy Spirit is the world soul too far, namely, that he could be reduced to a 'created principle of vitality in the universe'.[20]

Interestingly, the medieval conception of the world soul as the Spirit diverges widely from the one found in some early Christian writings, where 'soul is seen in parallel with intellect'.[21] Here, the Son is regarded as a kind of world soul, insofar as he is the locus of the divine ideas and the one through whom they are instantiated. In this capacity, the Summa proposes, the Son is not only the image of God himself but also, the Summa says, the 'Archetype' or Exemplar of all creation.[22] He is at the centre of everything because the basis for every being comes from him. As such he is also the obvious candidate to enter creation and indeed to become a creature. Although God in his absolute or unconditioned power could have determined that any member of the Trinity should become incarnate, consequently, in his ordained or determined power, he sent the Son.[23] To affirm that he did so, however, begs a number of preliminary questions whether it was even fitting for God to be united to a created being, and if so, which one.[24] The Summa's answers to these questions are ones I will explore below.

What kind of creature?

At the outset of this discussion, the Summa notes that a union between the Son and a creaturely nature would require some kind of similarity between them. This similarity cannot derive from sharing in a common nature, for there is no commensurability between the finite and the infinite, the one through whom all things exist and the ones that depend on him for their existence. However, there can be a likeness between them insofar as created things are caused by God and for this reason acquire qualities like goodness from him that are 'proportional', as the Summa says, to his goodness or reflect it in a particular way, without capturing it in full.

Another ground-clearing query the Summa strives to address at this point concerns the very question of positing potential in God for union with another entity. The problem with doing so, it observes, is that the notion of potential implies the possibility for change or improvement in God, which is unbefitting of a being that is already complete and perfect. To alleviate the problem, the Summa distinguishes between a passive potential and an active one.[25] God cannot be united to a creature through a passive potency, through which a quality or state is assumed that improves the assuming being. However, he can be united to a creature through an active power, where by his own initiative and volition he assumes a created nature not for his own benefit but for that of the created nature itself.

Here, the assumption of a creaturely nature by God only brings about change or improvement on the side of the creature that is assumed. For it activates a passive power in created nature to be joined to the Son of God.[26] The question therefore remains as to the kind of creature to which the Son would be most fittingly united. An initial option the Summa entertains in this regard is an angel, which is a purely spiritual being, albeit composed of what the Summa calls 'spiritual matter'.[27] This option is quickly eliminated, however, on the ground that the ideas for creatures or exemplars in God are not only for spiritual but also for corporeal beings, and even for beings, in specific, human beings, that are both corporeal or bodily and spiritual.[28]

Since human beings have a likeness to all creatures, both corporeal and spiritual, they enjoy a greater likeness to the full range of divine exemplars and are therefore more unitable to God than angels.[29] Further support for this conclusion is derived from the similarities the Summa mentions between human beings and the divine in terms of nature, personhood and power. With respect to nature, the Summa elaborates, the human soul governs its own body and the bodies that fall under its purview, much as God governs the world. Furthermore, human beings are similar to God in terms of their personhood. Here, the Summa notes a particular affinity between human persons and the second person of the Trinity, who originates from the Father and is with the Father the origin of the Spirit.

Like him, human beings originate from other human beings and have the potential to give rise to further human life. Although human beings are known as images of God in general, they are images of the Son more specifically who himself is the image of God that as such contains all the ideas God possesses for things he could make.[30] This brings us to the likeness that human beings, as spiritual beings, enjoy to God and specifically the Son in terms of their cognitive power. This power enables them to think of any item they like or may encounter in the world. Through reason, consequently, human beings can in principle encompass all created things and indeed can contemplate the whole of the created order.[31] In the words of the Summa, 'all natures are united in the human'.[32]

As a matter of fact, the Summa holds that 'the soul is a likeness to all things' not only in the sense that it is capable of knowing all things but also because it has something in common with all beings.[33] For instance, human beings are similar to the earth through the senses, to water through imagination, to air through reason, to the skies through the intellect, to the heaven of heavens through intelligence; to stones through essence, to trees through life, to animals through sense and imagination, to other humans through reason, to angels through intellect, to God through intelligence.[34]

This is why the Summa insists not only that all natures can be united in the human mind but also that all bodies are ordered to the human body, namely, because the human being has something in common with all bodies.[35] Lest we jump too quickly to the conclusion that the human being is the only viable candidate for union with God, however, the Summa considers another option, namely, that the whole universe is most fittingly united with God. To set up this discussion, it distinguishes between three kinds of world:[36] there is the archetypal or intelligible world that exists in the mind of God, that is the Son. And there is the actual sensible world we know and experience every day. But this itself is twofold.

First, there is the macrocosm (*maior mundus*), which is the whole of the universe, and then there is the microcosm (*minor mundus*), or the human being that has a likeness to all creatures in virtue of being bodily and spiritual. This distinction between macrocosm and microcosm was as old as some of the oldest Greek philosophy and continued to be popular in the Middle Ages, largely thanks to the transmission of Greek ideas to the west through Calcidius and Macrobius, among others like Martianus Capella and Boethius.[37] Despite the strong case that can be made that God is most unitable to the human being, this distinction is invoked by the Summa to show that there are some compelling reasons, listed below, why the universe is most appropriately united to God:

1　A universal effect is better assimilated to a universal cause than a particular effect. But God is a universal cause, and the universe is a universal effect, while the human being is a particular effect; therefore, the universe is more assimilated to God than a human being and thus more unitable to him.

2　Although human beings as microcosms can in principle contain the universe through reason, the macrocosm is more directly related to God's understanding of the world, as he created it, than a human being's understanding of it, as a mere microcosm. Thus, the universe is more unitable to God than the human being.

3　What is good is perfected by goodness; therefore a particular good is perfected by a particular goodness, and a universal good by a universal goodness. Since a human being is a particular good, it is perfected by a particular good, and the universe by a universal one. But the highest good or God is a universal good. Therefore the universe is more unitable with the highest goodness.

In typical scholastic fashion, the Summa then presents a number of further points on the other side of the argument:

1　Human beings are universal and one, given that all natures can be in principle united cognitively in the human mind. However, the universe consists of a vast multiplicity of beings. Since God is one as the universal cause of all things, human beings are closer and more unitable to him than the universe.

2 The universe is composed of multiple natures, while human beings have just one nature. Because God is one, he is more unitable to humans than to the universe.

3 Although the universe is more like God in a quantitative sense because it is universal as he is, the human being, though an individual, is more like God in a qualitative sense because all natures can be united in it.[38]

After considering these various arguments, the early Franciscans ultimately conclude that the human being rather than the universe is most fit for union with God. This is because a manifold effect like the universe is not properly united to a unified cause unless it is assimilated to a unified nature like the human being, which possesses the unifying power of rationality.[39] While the universe may be considered a greater likeness to the archetypal world if we think only in terms of where it is most widely diffused, the human being is a better likeness because it is a better expression of the way in which all beings are united in the mind of the Son.[40]

On account of the mind's power to unify things cognitively, the Summa goes even further to say that all creatures are ultimately ordered to the human being, who can contemplate a mental likeness of any one of them.[41] Among creatures, moreover, human beings are ultimate, because they alone are capable of knowing things as God knows them in himself as their source, that is, in relation to their divine models or exemplars.[42] Because human beings are oriented to God, in summary, and all beings are oriented to human beings, all beings are ordered through humans to God.[43] Without human assistance, in fact, non-human beings lacking the cognitive power would have no means of reconciling themselves to their Creator.

This means that it is not only possible but also fitting almost to the point of necessity that the Son of God become a human being. After all, no creature is complete until it is reconciled with its exemplar in him and thus with God. But this cannot happen until the exemplar himself becomes, in a sense, every creature: the universal every particular. That in turn entails assuming the only particular form of being that has something in common with all others and can virtually encompass them cognitively. This marriage of the universal and the particular is the feat Christ accomplished at his Incarnation, which the Summa regards as fitting, even if sin had never occurred, for the reasons outlined below.[44]

The fittingness of the Incarnation in the *Summa Halensis*

The first reason the Summa gives for the fittingness of the Incarnation is based on Pseudo-Dionysius' *Divine Names* 4, which states that 'the good is diffusive of its being'. On this basis, we say that in the divine, the Father diffuses his goodness in the Son through generation. From both, moreover, there is a diffusion of the Holy Spirit through procession. If we assume that creatures do not exist, then this diffusion that takes place in the Trinity is the highest diffusion. Where creatures do exist, however, the Summa notes that there would be a greater diffusion than that of God, if God did not diffuse himself in creatures. As the highest good, consequently, it is fitting that God should diffuse himself in creatures.[45] For the reasons outlined above, moreover, he should do this by taking on human nature.

The second reason for the fittingness of the Incarnation is as follows. There is no perfection unless in God, and the rational creature is able to be perfected. But the rational creature, or the human being, has two powers of cognition, namely, sensitive and intellectual. If therefore the whole person is to be perfected, this must happen according to sense and according to intellect. But God himself does not have a sensory or corporeal nature: he is pure intelligence or understanding. In order to make it possible for the embodied aspect of the human being to be perfected, consequently, God must become a corporeal and sensible being, and not just any such being. Rather he must unite himself with the human nature which possesses not only a body but also a rational soul.[46]

The third reason for the fittingness of the Incarnation is this. If there can be three persons in one substance – as in the Trinity – and three persons in three substances – as in the case of three persons or three angels – then there must be a possibility in the middle of one person that possesses three substances.[47] But such a person cannot exist except through the union of the divine and human natures, because this is the only case in which there are three substances in one being, namely, the divine substance as well as the spiritual and corporeal substances (or body and soul) that constitute the human being.[48]

In the aforementioned arguments, the Summa does not go so far as to affirm that the Son would have become incarnate regardless of sin *necessarily*. Presumably, the authors of the text avoid drawing this conclusion explicitly on the grounds that it is impossible to speculate as to God's will regarding a pristine world that is unknown to us. It is only possible to think in terms of necessities with regard to the world order that actually exists. Nevertheless, the Summa's arguments from fittingness in this section quite strongly support the conclusion that God's primary intention in becoming incarnate was to establish his place as the centre of everything by joining himself to the one being, the human being, to whom all beings are ordered and through whom he can be joined to all beings, thereby achieving their completion and perfection. Any effect of the Incarnation aside from or in addition to this was in a sense beside the point.

Our place in Christ's cosmos

From the discussion above, we can infer that Christ's Incarnation comes with a calling for those who consider themselves his followers. For if Christ is, in a sense, every creature, then the way we treat creatures is convertible to the way we would treat Christ. Although Christ has reconciled all creatures to himself once and for all, he has only done so in potency in the current order, thus anticipating but not yet accomplishing the final perfection and completion of creation at the end of time. The sign of our own anticipation of this event and indeed of our commitment to Christ, therefore, involves cognitively tracing all things back to the meaning and significance they have in him, ordering, governing and employing them on this basis.

That does not mean that human beings are qualitatively different to other beings in virtue of the rational power that makes these efforts possible. As modern scientific research has shown, and as the Summa already anticipated, there is tremendous continuity between humans and other beings, all of which share something in common with humans. The rational power does not therefore set human beings apart as 'superior' creatures to which all others should be subjected for exploitation. Rather, it simply signals that our unique role and place in creation is to contribute to and facilitate its flourishing. This is something that is possible to do even in cases where human rational powers are inhibited by physical or intellectual disability. In the Franciscan account, in fact, it is not the possession of rationality that makes us human but having a human soul united to a human body, however broken.

Any being that meets this description has a vital role to play in fostering a society that is attuned to its purpose to care well for the world. As this suggests, creation on this account does not exist for humanity in some anthropocentric fashion; rather, we exist on some level for the benefit of creation. That is not to say that creation somehow needs humanity to bring glory to God in its own way. This is something it achieves perfectly successfully independently of human involvement. Thus, the role we play in caring for creation is primarily for our benefit. For it is by harnessing the resources of creation in a way that 'makes more' of them than would otherwise be on offer that we bring glory to God in our own way. While we enhance our own flourishing at the same time, this cannot be regarded as our primary purpose. Indeed, we lose sight of our purpose when we become more preoccupied with making creation enhance life for us than with exercising good stewardship over creation for its own sake.

This perversion of our priorities inevitably has devastating effects both for creation and for human life overall, as is everywhere evident today. At the heart of the Summa's cosmic Christology is a call to remember our place and our role in the world. As has been suggested, this does not entail mastering and exploiting creation for our own ends but evaluating creatures in terms of the dignity and ends they have in Christ. This is something we are equipped to do as images of the Son, who stands midway between God and creatures, reconciling the two through the models he holds in his mind. To reflect his image, on this showing, is to consider how to order and employ creation in ways that are mutually beneficial and life-promoting and thus in accordance with God's design. It is to enjoy to a limited extent the perfection of creation that we anticipate by these very efforts.

As we have seen, the impetus to undertake these efforts comes from the Incarnation itself, where Christ, as God, actualized a potential latent in human nature to 'become' every creature. Because of this event, we confront him in every natural being we encounter, such that the way we treat beings other than Christ becomes the measure of how we would treat him. While it is relatively easy to show regard for those with an evidently high stature, who can clearly bring benefits to us, it is just as easy to neglect or undermine the wellbeing of those who for whatever reason cannot compel us to do so. In that sense, our dealing with 'the least of these', with those who cannot speak in their own defence, including the created order itself, becomes the real litmus test of our attitude and commitment to Christ. When we find the humility to attend to these – as Christ attended to us – we uncover the key to finding him, albeit where we least expected him, as the centre of everything.

Notes

1 Bert Roest, *A History of Franciscan Education* (Leiden: Brill, 2000), p. 126.

2 The coherence of the work has been emphasized by the editors of the Summa and by other authors: Victorin Doucet, 'Prolegomena in librum III necnon in libros I et II *Summa Fratris Alexandri*,' *Alexandri de Hales Summa Theologica* (Quaracchi: Collegii S Bonaventurae, 1948); Etienne Gilson, *History of Christian Philosophy in the Middle Ages* (London: Sheed and Ward, 1955), p. 327; Elisabeth Gössmann, *Metaphysik und Heilsgeschichte: Eine theologische Untersuchung der Summa Halensis (Alexander von Hales)* (München: Max Hueber, 1964); Lydia Schumacher, *Early Franciscan Theology: Between Authority and Innovation* (Cambridge: Cambridge University Press, 2019).

3 *Doctoris irrefragabilis Alexandri de Hales Ordinis minorum Summa theologica – Summa Halensis (SH)* (Quarrachi, 1924), vol. 3, Tr 1, Qu 2, Tit 1, Dist 2, Memb 1, Ch 1, Respondeo 1, p. 27: *Nam sicut dicit Trismegistus, divina essentia est sicut sphaera intelligibilis, cuius centrum est ubique, circumferentia vero nusquam. In quantum enim divina essentia consideratur ut res in se, perfecta est, cuius non est accipere finem bonitatis, et sic consideratur ut circumferentia, cuius non est accipere finem nec principium, sed est extra omnia: sic est de bonitate Dei. Vel potest considerari ut est in creatura, finiens ipsam et limitans et deducens, et sic dicitur centrum quia sicut centrum finit lineas et ab ipso lineae deducuntur, ita Creator finit creaturas et limitat et deducit eas.* There is an excellent doctoral thesis on the topic by Sarah McNeil Powrie, 'The Infinite Sphere: The History of a Metaphor in Theology, Science and Literature (1100–1613)' (unpublished doctoral thesis, University of Toronto, 2006). Powrie cites the following relevant works: Dietrich Mahnke's catalogue of references to an 'infinite sphere' from Parmenides to the German Romantics in *Unendliche Sphäre und Allmittelpunkt* (Stuttgart: F. Frommann, 1966); Jorge Luis Borges' brief essay on five centuries of discussion of the 'infinite sphere', from the *Liber XXIV* to Blaise Pascal, 'The Fearful Sphere of Pascal', in *Labyrinths:*

Selected Stories and Other Writings, ed. by Donald A. Yates and James E. Irby (New York: New Directions, 1964), pp. 189–92; Karsten Harries, 'The Infinite Sphere: Comments on the History of a Metaphor,' *Journal of the History of Philosophy*, 13 (1975), pp. 5–15.

4 See the *Liber Viginti Quattuor Philosophorum*, ed. by Francoise Hudry, Corpus Christianorum Continuatio Mediaevalis CXLIIA (Turnhout: Brepols, 1997).

5 Powrie, 'The Infinite Sphere', p. 20: half of the manuscripts of the *Liber XXIV* ascribe authorship to Hermes, possibly a combination of the Greek god Hermes and the Egyptian god Thoth.

6 Powrie, 'The Infinite Sphere', pp. 24, 57: on Alan of Lille's treatment of the metaphor in *Theologica regulae* ii, pp. 67, 177.

7 Lydia Schumacher, 'The Early Franciscan Doctrine of Divine Immensity: Towards a Middle Way Between Classical Theism and Panentheism', *Scottish Journal of Theology*, 70.3 (2017), pp. 278–94.

8 *SH*, 2.1, I1, Tr1, S1, Qu 2, Ti 1, C3, Ad objecta 1 (n. 11), p. 20: *unde omnium sive actualium sive possibilium est divina scientia.*

9 *SH*, vol. 1, P1, In1, Tr3, Q2, M2, C1, Respondeo (n. 91), p. 147. *SH*, vol. 1, P1, In1, Tr3, Q2, M2, C2, Respondeo (n. 92), p. 149. Vol. 1, P1, In1, Tr3, Q1, M2, C4, Solutio, Ad objecta 1, 3 (n. 80), pp. 130–1.

10 Jacques Dalarun, ed., *La Vie retrouvée de François d'Assise* (Paris: Editions Franciscaines, 2015).

11 Rega Wood, 'Distinct Ideas and Perfect Solicitude: Alexander of Hales, Richard Rufus, and Odo Rigaldus', *Franciscan Studies*, 53 (1993), pp. 7–31.

12 *SH*, vol. 2.1, In1, Tr, S1, Q2, T1, M3, C1, Ad objecta 1 (n. 14), p. 24; cf. *SH*, vol. 2.1, P1, In1, Tr1, S1, Q1, C6, Ad objecta 2 (n. 173), p. 256; cf. Pseudo-Dionysius, *The Divine Names* 2.5, 5.6: *sicut enim ad unum punctum, qui est centrum, omnes lineae rectae ductae ad circumferentiam ex omni parte terminantur, sic et per quamdam similitudinem omnia, quae sunt in universo, tendunt ad unum finem, et ille dicitur finis finium.*

13 *SH*, vol. 2.1, I1, Tr1, S1, Qu 2, Ti 1, C2, Ad contrarium a (n. 10), p. 19: *unus est mundus sensibilis et mundus sensibilis est exemplatum; multo ergo fortius est unum exemplar scilicet mundus archetypus: nam maior est unitas exemplaris quam exemplati.*

14 Margaret Gibson, 'The Study of the *Timaeus* in the Eleventh and Twelfth Centuries', *Pensamiento*, 25 (1969), pp. 183–94.

15 Bernard McGinn, 'The Role of the *anima mundi* as Mediator Between the Divine and Created Realms in the Twelfth Century', in *Death, Ecstasy, and Other Worldly Journeys*, ed. by John J. Collins and Michael Fishbane (Albany, NY: State University of New York Press, 1995), p. 302. The idea of the world soul came to the Middle Ages from Plato's *Timaeus* 30A via Macrobius, *In Somnium Scipionis* 1.14; and Boethius, *De Consolatione Philosophiae* III.9. It was employed in the twelfth century by William of Conches in his *Glosae Super Platonem*, ed. by Jeauneau (Paris: J.Vrin, 1965), pp. 144ff.; and Thierry of Chartres, in *Commentaries on Boethius by Thierry of Chartres and his School*, ed. by Haring (Toronto: PIMS, 1971), ii.21, p. 273. Regarding the late ancient sources, see Stephen Gersh, *Middle and Neoplatonism: the Latin Tradition*, Vol 2. (Notre Dame, IN: University of Notre Dame Press, 1986), pp. 474–9, 551–2. On the twelfth-century uses of the term, see Tullio Gregory, *Anima mundi: La Filosofia di Guglielmo di Conches e la Scuola di Chartres* (Florence: G. C. Sansoni 1955), as well as his article, 'The Platonic

Inheritance', in *A History of Twelfth-Century Philosophy*, ed. by Peter Dronke (Cambridge: Cambridge University Press, 1988), pp. 54–80. Irene Caiazzo, 'La discussione sull'Anima mundi nel secolo XII', *Studi filosofici*, 16 (1993), pp. 27–62; 'L'âme du monde: Un theme privilégié des auteurs chartrains au XIIe siècle', in *Le temps de Fulbert: Actes de l'Université d'ete du 8 au 10 juillet 1996* (Chartres: Société archéologique d'Eure-et-Loir, 1996), pp. 79–89.

16 Lesley Ann Dyer, 'Veiled Platonic Triads in Abelard's *Theologia Summi Boni*', in *Rethinking Abelard: A Collection of Critical Essays*, ed. by Babette S. Hellemans (Leiden: Brill, 2014). Lawrence Moonan, 'Abelard's Use of the Timaeus', *Archives d'histoire doctrinale et littéraire du moyen âge*, 56 (1989), pp. 7–90.

17 McGinn, 'The Role of the *anima mundi* as Mediator', p. 305.

18 Vol. 2.1, In1, Tr1, Q5, C4 (n. 96), p. 118: *Dixerunt enim quidam philosophi quod microcosmus suam habebat perfectionem et illud fuit anima rationalis, megacosmus suam habebat perfectionem et illud erat anima mundi.*

19 Vol. 2.1, In1, Tr1, Q5, C4, 3 (n. 96), p. 118.

20 McGinn, 'The Role of the *anima mundi* as Mediator', p. 295.

21 Johannes Zachhuber, 'The World Soul in Early Christian Thought', in *The Philosophical and Theological Sources of Byzantine Cosmologies*, forthcoming.

22 SH, vol. 2.1, In1, Tr1, S1, Q1, C3, Ar2, In contrarium a (n. 3), p. 8: *mundus sensibilis respondet archetypo, sicut exemplatum exemplari; sed idem est mundus archetypo quod ipse Deus.*

23 SH, vol. 3, Tr 1, Qu 2, Tit 1, Dist 2, Memb 1, Ch 4, Art 2, Respondeo, p. 32. Cf. SH, vol. 3, Tr 1, Qu 4, Tit 1, Dist 1, Ch 2, Responsio 1, pp. 49–50: *unde et indivisa est assumptio quantum ad actionem et non quantum ad personam cui convenit, quia uni et indivisae personae Filii.*

24 SH, vol. 3, Inq 1, Tract 1, Qu 1, Tit 1, Dist. 1, Respondeo 2, p. 26.

25 SH, vol 2.1, In1, Tr1, Q2, T1, D2, M1, C1, Respondeo 2 (n. 11), p. 27.

26 SH, vol. 3, In1, Tr1, Q2, T1, D2, M1, C1, Respondeo 2 (n. 11), p. 27.

27 David Keck, *Angels and Angelology in the Middle Ages* (Oxford: Oxford University Press, 1998), pp. 32, 94–5.

28 SH, vol. 2.1, In1, Tr1, Q2, T1, M2, C1 (n. 16), p. 33.

29 SH, vol. 2.1, In1, Tr1, Q2, T1, M2, C1, Respondeo 3 (n. 16), p. 35: *homo habet similitudinem cum omni creatura, scilicet corporali et spirituali, quarum rationes sunt in exemplari divino, quod non habet angelus; et ita homo est unibilior, cum secundum viam essendi magis exprimat similitudenim exemplaris divini.*

30 SH, vol. 2.1, In1, Tr1, Q2, T1, C4, Ar2, Ad objecta 1 (n. 15), p. 32: human beings are an express likeness (*simulitudo expressa*) of the image of God, the Son.

31 SH, vol. 3, Tr 1, Qu 2, Tit 1, Qu 2, Memb 2, Ch 1, Respondeo, p. 34.

32 SH, vol. 2.1, In1, Tr1, Q2, T1, C2, 3 (n. 17), p. 36: *omnes enim naturae uniuntur in homine.*

33 SH, vol. 2.1, In4, Tr1, S1, Q1, VI (n. 321), p. 387: *anima est omnium similitudo.* SH, vol. 2.1, In4, Tr1, S1, Q1, Solutio 1 (n. 321), p. 388: *[anima] convenit enim cum substantiis corporeis inanimatis in esse, licet non in corporeitate, cum animatis in vita, cum sensibilibus in sensu, et ex parte incorporearum cum angelis in intellect cum Deo, sive . . . in intelligentia* (The soul has something in common with inanimate corporeal substances in being, albeit not in being corporeal itself; with animated beings in life, with sensible beings in sense, with angels insofar as it is incorporeal and in the intellect or intelligence, with God).

34 *SH*, vol. 2.1, In4, Tr1, S1, Q1, Respondeo VI (n. 321), p. 385: *Similis est terrae per sensum, aquae per imaginationem, aeri per rationem, firmamento per intellectum, caelorum caelo per intelligentiam; similis est lapidibus per essentiam, arboribus per vitam, animalibus per sensum et imaginationem, hominibus per rationem, angelis per intellectum, Deo per intelligentiam.*

35 *SH*, vol. 3, Tr 1, Qu 4, Tit 1, Dist 2, Ch 2, Responsio 2, p. 52: *ad corpus humanum ordinatur omnia corpora, nec est aliquod corpus in universo cum quo non conveniat; propterea cum sit ultimum corporum in genere corporum, immediate se habet ad Deum et ideo unibile est* (All bodies are ordained to the human body, with which all things in the universe have something in common. Therefore as the human body is the ultimate in the genus of bodies, it is immediately related to God and unitable to him).

36 *SH*, vol. 2.1, In1, Tr1, Q2, T1, C2, 2 (n. 17), p. 36.

37 Rudolf Allers, 'Microcosmus: From Anaximandros to Paracelsus', *Traditio*, 2 (1944), pp. 319–408.

38 *SH*, vol. 3. Inq 1, Tract 1, Qu 2, Tit 1, Memb 2, Ch 2, Ad objecta 1, p. 37.

39 *SH*, vol. 3. Inq 1, Tract 1, Qu 2, Tit 1, Memb 2, Ch 2, Respondeo, p. 37: *concendum est quod universum non est unibile Deo, sed homo, quia effectui multiplicato non debet uniri unitas causae simplicissimae, nisi reducatur in unitatem naturae.*

40 *SH*, vol. 2.1, In1, Tr1, Q2, T1, C2, Ad objecta 2 (n. 17), p. 37: *dicendum quod similitudo mundi archetypi potest dupliciter repraesentari in mundo sensibili: vel magis diffuse, vel magis expresse. Si magis diffuse sic magis repraesentatur in universo: magis vero expresse repraesentatur in homine in quo repraesentatur unitas in natura, et secundum modum personae Filii Dei, qui dicitur mundus archetypus.*

41 *SH*, vol. 2.1, In1, Tr1, Q2, T1, M2, C1, 4 (n. 16), p. 35: *magis accedit anima ad Deum quam angelus quoad hoc: quoniam homo est ultima creatura et ultima in ordine universi et finis aliarum creaturarum, quod non angelus, et ita unibilior, quia magis accedens. SH*, vol. 3, Tr 1, Qu 4, Tit 1, Dist 2, Ch 2, Responsio 1, p. 52; cf. *SH*, vol. 3, Tr 1, Qu 4, Tit 1, Dist 2, Ch 2, Responsio 2, p. 52: *ad corpus humanum ordinatur omnia corpora, nec est aliquod corpus in universo cum quo non conveniat; propterea cum sit ultimum corporum in genere corporum, immediate se habet ad Deum et ideo unibile est. SH*, vol. 2.1, In1, Tr2, Q4, C3 (88), p. 111: *utrum omnia sint ordinata ad hominem. SH*, vol. 2.1, pp. 416-17: all things ordered to the human soul.

42 *SH*, vol. 3. Inq 1, Tract 1, Qu 1, Tit 1, Dist. 1, Respondeo 2, p. 26: *dicendum quod quaedam est distantia essentialis rei ad rem, et hoc modo infinita est distantia naturae divinae ad naturam creatam. Alia est distantia rerum secundum esse ordinis, et haec non est infinita creaturae ad Creatorem. Et secundum istam minus distat homo a Deo quam aliqua alia creatura, quia ultimum corpus in natura est corpus humanum, communicans cum omni corpore in natura; similiter ultima forma in natura est anima raionalis, et inde est quod omnia alia ordinantur ad hominem, et ideo est popinquior Deo, et ita est ei unibilis* (There is difference in essence between [any] two things, and in this way, the distance between the divine and created natures is infinite. Yet there is also a distance according to order, and here there is not an infinite distance between creature and Creator. Indeed, according to this type of distance, the distance between humanity and God is less than that of any other creature, because the ultimate body in nature is the human body, which has something in common with all bodies in nature. Likewise, the ultimate form in nature is the

rational soul, whereby all other things are ordained to humankind and therefore properly to God, such that it is unitable to him).

43 *SH*, vol. 2.1, In1, Tr1, Q2, T1, C2, c (n. 17), p. 37: *mundus factus est propter hominem, et homo propter Deum; si ergo rerum universitas ad hominem ordinatur et per hominem ad Deum, immediatius et propinquius se habet homo ad Deum quam universum.*

44 *SH*, vol. 3, Tr1, Q2, T2 (n. 23), pp. 41ff.; see also the excellent, unpublished dissertation of Justus Hunter on 'The Motive for the Incarnation from Anselm of Canterbury to John Duns Scotus' (unpublished doctoral thesis, Southern Methodist University, 2015).

45 *SH*, vol. 3, Tr1, Q2, T2, a (n. 23), p. 41.

46 *SH*, vol. 3, Tr1, Q2, T2, b (n. 23), p. 41.

47 Walter Principe, *Alexander of Hales*, p. 83: as God is the unity of nature in several persons, so Christ is the unity of person in diverse natures. Alexander discusses this topic in his Gloss I, 31, 32b, p. 315; and states that the union most fittingly occurs in the human being in his *Quaestiones* 15, 48, pp. 208–9.

48 *SH*, vol. 3, Tr1, Q2, T2, c (n. 23), p. 41.

8

Christ in the Eucharist

ANDREW LOUTH

It seems to me that if in this volume we are reflecting on the Divine Liturgy, the Eucharist, we need to do this by exploring the notion of *totus Christus* – a key theme in St Augustine's thought. So I am going to start by digging around in various works of Augustine, mostly his homilies, homilies preached to his congregation in Hippo, and on occasion in other places too, to discover the different aspects, the different dimensions of his notion of *totus Christus*. It is from this approach of unfolding Augustine's notion of *totus Christus* that I want to develop some understanding of Christ in the Eucharist. As often happens with Augustine, I found myself more and more fascinated by what I encountered.

Totus Christus. The whole Christ. In his twenty-eighth *Tractatus in Ioannis Evangelium*, Augustine puts it like this: 'For Christ is not in the head and not in the body, but Christ is whole, in the head and in the body – *Christus totus in capite et corpore*'.[1] And it is a theme that Augustine refers to again and again: the whole Christ, head and members, the whole Christ, head and body. I think it is very easy to think we know what that means – it is about the Church and the way he sees the Church and Christ as bound up together – but if we read it like that, that is, not really read it, but lazily think we know what Augustine is going to say, then I fear that we are going to miss most of what he has to say. Let us start, then, by exploring some of the ways in which Augustine himself expounds his notion of *totus Christus*. Elsewhere in the *Tractates on John*, Augustine seems to me to express with absolute clarity what it is that he means. Here, from the twenty-first homily: 'Therefore we call ourselves happy and give thanks that we have become not just Christians, but Christ. Wonder, rejoice, we have become Christ. Not just Christians, but Christ' – *non solum nos christianos factos esse, sed Christum*.[2] Then, a line later: *Christus facti sumus*, 'we have become Christ'. When we are baptized, I think this means, we do not just become believers in the Christian religion, a member of the Christian Church. We are not just Christians, a title which, as Augustine would have been perfectly aware, is a word first used by others to describe Christians in Antioch.[3] We do not just become Christians, *Christiani*. We become Christ, *Christus*, himself. This is something we must take absolutely seriously. We become Christ – not just Christians. That is the heart of Augustine's notion of *totus Christus*. This notion of *totus Christus* is explored by Augustine in a variety of ways. In several places, both explicitly and implicitly, it was 1 Corinthians 12.12 that he had in mind when thinking about *totus Christus*: 'For just as the body is one and has many members, and all the members of the body being many are one body, so also is Christ [οὕτως καὶ ὁ Χριστός/ *ita et Christus*]'. In his sermon on Psalm 142, Augustine comments, '. . . *ita et Christus*. He [the apostle] does not say: so is Christ and his body, but: one body, many members, so also is Christ. Christ is therefore the whole'.[4] For, in 1 Corinthians 12.12, which he is quoting here, it says the Church, one body, many members, is Christ himself. It is not for Augustine (or for Paul) a metaphor; it is a reality that has been created in baptism and is to be, as we shall see, celebrated and made manifest in the Eucharist. In an earlier sermon, one of the homilies on Psalm 30, speaking of the members of Christ, that is, of the faithful, Augustine notes that Paul 'does not say, so also the members of Christ, but this whole of which he speaks, he has called Christ'.[5] Many members – one body – Christ.

The notion of *totus Christus* comes up for Augustine in other contexts. One issue that comes up in any reflection on the Psalms is the question: Who is it who is speaking in the Psalms? Is it a Jew singing the psalm in the Temple (first or second), who perhaps composed it, a Christian for whom the Psalter has become his Christian book of prayers or songs, or is it Christ? This is a theme that had been discussed for many decades by Augustine's time. A famous example is Athanasius' *Epistula ad Marcellinum* where Athanasius considers precisely this question: Who is the person speaking in the Psalms? For him, it could be Christ speaking to us, it could be us speaking to Christ, or it could be Christ speaking (as the Church) to himself, as it were. We find this almost exactly the same in Augustine. For instance, on the homily on Psalm 30, from which we have already quoted, he says that it is right to say that Christ speaks even though it is the prophet David who is speaking in the Psalm. 'Christ, therefore', he says, 'speaks thus in the prophet. I dare to say Christ speaks [*Christus loquitur*], . . . for Christ speaks in the members of Christ'.[6] He develops this theme a little bit and then goes on: 'Let therefore Christ speak, because in Christ the Church speaks, and in the Church Christ speaks, both the body in the head and the head in the body'.[7]

There is another development of this that we find in Psalm 100.1, which reads, 'of mercy and judgment I shall sing to you, O Lord'. In this case, it is a matter, not of Christ's *speaking*, but of Christ's *singing*. Augustine comments:

> For let Christ sing this. If only the head sings, if this song is from the Lord, then it does not concern us. If the whole Christ [*totus Christus*], that is his head and body, let it be also in his members, to cleave to him in faith and hope and love. And if you sing in him, in him also you exult, because he is at work in you. In you, he is hungry. In you, he is thirsty. In you, he is troubled.[8]

Christ's voice and ours, his song and also ours; the song that we sing as we make our pilgrimage on earth is a song that, as we sing it, Christ is singing in us: 'In you, he is hungry. In you, he thirsts. In you, he is troubled.' That is what 1 Corinthians 12.12 affirms, in effect. We have already seen that this is one verse to which Augustine returns as he develops his notion of *totus Christus*. The end of the verse, *ita et Christus*, means Christ, one and many, the head and the members. In the apostle Paul's epistle, this verse comes in the middle of a section that moves from his account of the institution of the Eucharist, a tradition he says he has received from the Lord and has passed on (chapter 11), through to a discussion of the way in which many Christians are held together in unity in the one Christ, something which develops out from his understanding of the Eucharist, where we share in the oneness of Christ, where we realize the oneness of the body though we are many. He then goes on in the rest of chapter 12 to discuss the meaning of there being one body and many members, stressing the mutual coinherence and the mutual compassion that should be manifest in the Christian community. This leads into his hymn to *agape*, to love, in chapter 13, ending with looking beyond our experience of fragmentation to a union, to face-to-face knowledge of God in which we will know as we are known. It seems to me that Augustine is well aware of this sequence. He has not picked a verse out of the middle of nowhere; he has picked a verse very much from somewhere, where Paul's reflection moves from talking about the Eucharist, and what this means for Christians, to talking about love. What comes out of this is the notion of love as the lifeblood of the Church. This becomes even clearer as we reflect on the way Augustine's notion of *totus Christus* is rooted in his understanding of the Eucharist.

There is another passage from the *Enarrationes in Psalmos* where Augustine picks up the *caput–corpus* imagery in a rather different way. 'For not only is our head anointed', he says, 'but also His body which we are, for He is *King* because He reigns over us and leads us, He is *Priest* because He prays for us, and yet this Priest alone exists in such a way because He is also *Sacrifice*.'[9] This is not so much a matter of the *totus Christus* theme, but rather as exploring the way in which the different aspects of Christ are all one. He is King, he is Priest, he is Sacrifice. And in all these cases – as King, as Priest, as Sacrifice – he does not stand over and against us, but we are bound up in him. Thus Augustine writes of what is often opposed – ruler and ruled, priest and sacrifice. It recalls a wonderful passage in the *City of God*, where he speaks of

> the redeemed city, that is the assembly and congregation of the saints, offered to God as a universal sacrifice through the High Priest who in his passion offered himself for us in the form of a slave so we might be the body of so great a head. For it was this form that he offered, in this that he was offered, because in this way he is mediator, in this way he is priest, in this he is sacrifice.[10]

And Augustine concludes:

> This is the Christian sacrifice; though many, one body in Christ. And this
> sacrifice, the Church continually offers in the sacrament of the altar, well-
> known to the faithful, where it is demonstrated that in what she offers in
> that she is offered.[11]

As the theme of *totus Christus* is conceived of more explicitly in relation to
the Eucharist, this notion of our being Christ, not Christians, becomes more
and more central, more and more resonant. So back again to the Tractates
on John, 26: 'Let the faithful know the body of Christ, if they do not neglect
to become the body of Christ. Let them become the body of Christ, if they
want to live by the Spirit of Christ'.[12] That passage continues to conclude
with this:

> This is why, when the apostle Paul explains to us this bread – one bread,
> he says, one body, which we are though many: O, the sacrament of piety!
> O, the sign of unity! O, the bond of love! He who wants to live has where
> to live and whence to live. Let him approach, let him believe, let him be
> incorporated, that he may be given life.[13]

For Augustine, the *totus Christus* theme expresses his conviction that there
is some fundamental, as it were, ontological identity between Christ's head
and Christ's members. We become one, because we are not just Christians,
but Christ. This identity embraces other identities, for this identity is bound
up with Christ himself. In fact, I would suggest that Augustine's *totus
Christus* theme is founded on the way in which in the Eucharist bread and
body, head and members, are found together, and that in turn is rooted in
the conviction that in the Eucharist itself Christ is both priest and sacrifice, the One who offers and the One who is offered. And that identity too
embraces the unity of the Lord and his body. We have already encountered
this in the references to the Eucharist in the *City of God*, where Christ/the
Church are both Offerer and Offered.

This becomes vivid in a quite striking way if we look at the sermons
Augustine preached on the Eucharist. A good example is the homily that
seems to have been preached to a congregation which included people who
had recently been baptized, people who had just moved from being catechu-
mens to being Christians. And he says to them,

> This which you see, my dearest ones, on the table of the Lord is bread
> and wine. But this bread and wine, by the addition of a word, become the
> body and blood of the Word. For the Lord himself, who 'in the beginning
> was the Word, and the Word was with God, and the Word was God',
> on account of his mercy by which he did not despise that which he had
> created in his image: this Word became flesh and dwelt among us, as

you know; because this Word assumed humanity, that is a human soul and body, and became a man, while remaining God. On account of this, because he suffered for us, he has commended to us in this sacrament his body and blood, he who has also made us ourselves. For we have become his own body and by his mercy what we receive, that we are . . . Behold what you have received. How therefore you see what has been made one, that you also might be one, by loving yourselves [*diligendo vos*], by holding one faith, one hope, and an undivided love . . . And you, after that fasting, after toils, after humility and contrition, now in the name of Christ you have come to the chalice of the Lord. And here you are on the table, here you are in the chalice [*et ibi vos estis in mensa, et ibi vos estis in calice*]. You are this with us, for at the same time we are this, at the same time we drink, because at the same time we live [*Nobiscum hoc estis: simul enim hoc sumus, simul bibimus, quia simul vivimus*].[14]

Et ibi vos estis in mensa, et ibi vos estis in calice: 'Here you are on the table, here you are in the chalice'. There are two identities here: Christ is his body and blood, so we also are his body and blood, there on the altar, there in the chalice. So, Christ in the Eucharist. Our starting point, Augustine's doctrine of *totus Christus*, is based on the fact that Christ is the Eucharist, and that, participating in the Eucharist, we are Christ, we become who we are, who we have become, and therefore we, as his body, are one too.

All of this Augustine was preaching at the beginning of the fifth century, and also at that time we find similar ideas in a bishop who was an older contemporary of Augustine's, Theophilos, Pope of Alexandria until his death in 412 when he was succeeded by his nephew Cyril. In church history, Theophilos is presented very much as a 'Bad Thing', in the language of *1066 and All That*, but nevertheless, in the very last year of the fourth century, on Maundy Thursday, at the height of the Origenist controversy (one of the reasons for which he is regarded as a 'Bad Thing'), Theophilos preached a homily on the Mystical Supper, as the Last Supper is known in the East. I have argued elsewhere that this sermon marks a watershed in the way in which the Eucharist is understood in the Greek East.[15] And this remarkable shift at the end of the fourth/beginning of the fifth century is not something just noticed by scholars; it is something that became embedded in the Divine Liturgy itself. Towards the end of the sermon, as part of his summing up, Theophilos asserts: 'We should believe that he remains at once priest and victim, that he is both the one who offers and the one who is offered, that he receives and is distributed'.[16] These words have come to form the conclusion of the prayer said by the priest before the Great Entrance in the Byzantine Liturgy: 'for you are the one who offers and is offered, who receives and is distributed, Christ our body'. This expresses what we have seen lies at the core of Augustine's doctrine of *totus Christus*: not just the whole Christ, body and members, but Christ as the whole, expressing everything in the Eucharist – priest and sacrifice, the one who receives the sacrifice and what is distributed from the sacrifice. Every element of this involves us, as members of the body of which Christ is the head, the body that Christ *is*.

One of the books most influential for many of us in our understanding of the Divine Liturgy, the Holy Eucharist, is Dom Gregory Dix's astonishing work, *The Shape of the Liturgy* (1945).[17] One thing – *the* thing perhaps – that I have remembered and never forgotten from reading Dix is that the Liturgy, the Eucharist is an *action*, an action performed by Christ. It is not a collection of prayers and songs, or things said and done, it is not a gathering together of like-minded people who want to profess their common faith and hope. Remember what Augustine said: 'We are not just Christians, we have become Christ'. The Eucharist is not just a gathering together of Christians, it is Christ gathering us together as his own, even *as himself*. Christ's action is his offering himself to the Father and his gathering us together in that offering, so that Christ is both priest and sacrifice. As one with the Father, he is the one who receives the offering and he is what is distributed to us in the holy gifts, τὰ ἅγια δῶρα. We receive Christ himself so that we, gathered together in Christ, receive what we are, become what Christ has made of us.

This idea that Christ is the priest, the sacrifice, that Christ is the one who receives the Eucharist – the eucharistic offering, the eucharistic sacrifice – and the one who is distributed in the holy gifts, this is absolutely, totally and utterly radical, and it is hard for us to get anywhere near to grasping this. We easily fall back into thinking the Eucharist is some sort of holy communal activity – sometimes I get the impression that it is a kind of a religious prologue to the coffee hour that will follow afterwards – still less is it a gathering together of individuals making their own devotions: the Eucharist is Christ himself. Everything that happens in the Eucharist, the whole action, is Christ. This has some striking entailments. For instance, if we believe this, then we believe that if we stand in church and receive Communion, every person who comes back from the holy chalice is Christ, and that we, as we approach the chalice, are Christ too. In a kind of way, we are all gifts one to another because it is Christ given and Christ offered whom we receive in the Eucharist. If we are just slightly honest with ourselves, most (all?) of us find it very difficult to believe that every single person who comes up to the chalice is actually a gift to us. Yet that is something we should really genuinely believe. If we actually believe that Christ is the Eucharist, and everything that takes place – priest, sacrifice, the one who receives and the one who offers is Christ – then there is nothing left; everything is Christ. And that means that all of us who are partaking in it find ourselves not just in Christ but as Christ, we find ourselves to be Christ in the Eucharist, and not just we find ourselves but everybody else finds themselves in this way too. If we were to take that seriously, then it would have an enormous impact on how we gather together as Christians to celebrate the Eucharist.[18,19]

Notes

1 *Tract. in Ioannis Evangelium*, 28. 1. Text (the Maurist text) in *Homélies sur l'Évangile de saint Jean*, trans., introd., and notes by M.-F.-Berrouard, II (Paris: Études Augustiniennes, 1977); here p. 568.

2 *In Ioan*, 21. 8; pp. 286–8.

3 Cf. Acts 11.26.

4 Augustine, *Enarrationes in Psalmos*, 142. 3. Text from *Enarrationes in Psalmos*, ed. by D. Eligius Dekkers and Iohannes Fraipont, after the Maurist text, Corpus Christianorum Series Latina, pp. 38–40 (Turnhout: Brepols, 1956). Here vol. 40, p. 206.

5 Augustine, *In Psalmos*, 30, 2, 1.4 (38, p. 193).

6 Augustine, *In Psalmos*, ibid.

7 Augustine, *In Psalmos*, ibid.

8 Augustine, *In Psalmos*, 100. 3 (39, p. 1408).

9 Augustine, *In Psalmos*, 26. 2.2 (38, p. 155).

10 Augustine, *De Civitate Dei*, 10. 6 (text in Saint Augustine, *The City of God against the Pagans*, tr. David S. Wiessen, vol. 3, Loeb Classical Library [London: Heinemann/Cambridge, MA: Harvard University Press, 1968], tr. pp. 275–7, modified).

11 Augustine, *De Civitate Dei*, 10. 6 (tr. ibid., 277, modified).

12 Augustine, *In Ioannem*, 26. 13 (p. 516).

13 Augustine, *In Ioannem*, 26. 13 (p. 518).

14 Denis VI. 1–2, in *Sancti Augustini Sermones post Maurinos reperti*, ed. by Dom German Morin (Rome: Typis Polyglottis Vaticanis, 1930), pp. 29–30.

15 Cf. Andrew Louth, 'Late Patristic Developments in Sacramental Theology in the East: Fifth–Ninth Centuries', in *The Oxford Handbook of Sacramental Theology*, ed. by Hans Boersma and Matthew Levering (Oxford: Oxford University Press, 2015), pp. 170–83.

16 For the whole homily, see Norman Russell, *Theophilus of Alexandria* (London: Routledge, 2007), pp. 52–60.

17 Dom Gregory Dix, *The Shape of the Liturgy* (Westminster: Dacre Press, 1905, and often reprinted).

18 Some of the ideas in this paragraph have been inspired by, or encouraged by, my reading of Michon M. Matheisen, *Sacrifice as Gift: Eucharist, Grace and Contemplative Prayer in Maurice de la Taille* (Washington, DC: Catholic University of America Press, 2013), esp. pp. 92–116 (Chapter 3: The Ecclesial Sacrifice), though the pastoral application there is only implicit.

19 I am immensely grateful to Rebekah Vince for producing a transcript of the lecture I gave from notes, which formed the basis of the finished version.

9

An Augustinian Sensibility: The Whole Christ in Hooker's *Lawes of Ecclesiastical Polity*

PAUL DOMINIAK

Introduction: Christ at the centre

As the forbidding title *Of the Lawes of Ecclesiastical Polity* suggests, Richard Hooker's late sixteenth-century *magnum opus* concerns itself with the government of the Church. As the first apology for the Elizabethan Religious Settlement in the English vernacular, it had several intended audiences, from conformists through to Catholics.[1] Hooker's major interlocutors were drawn from the radical puritan wing of the English Church, 'them that seeke', as he puts it, 'the reformation of Laws, and orders Ecclesiastical, in the Church of England'.[2] Hooker takes as the voice of the radical puritans the writings of Walter Travers and Thomas Cartwright, whom the seventeenth-century historian Thomas Fuller famously described as the 'neck' and 'head' of the radical wing of Elizabethan puritanism.[3] Hooker's achievements in the *Lawes* draw many modern plaudits, ranging from his work eventually establishing him as the father of 'Anglicanism'[4] through to the more hyperbolic claim that he is the 'St Thomas Aquinas of Anglicanism . . . with his powers for systematic thinking'.[5] The historical obscurity of Hooker's apologetic context seems to relegate him, however, to the lecture hall of academia, rendering the *Lawes* as little more than a fascinating museum piece illustrating late sixteenth-century English conflicts over the life of the Church.[6]

Yet, Hooker's *Lawes* also has one other intended audience. Hooker claims to write so that 'posteritie may know we have not loosely through silence permitted things to passe away as in a dreame'.[7] Posterity remains perhaps Hooker's most significant intended and ongoing audience. Hooker writes that 'I have endeavoured throughout the bodie of this whole discourse, that every former part might give strength unto all that followe, and every later bring some light unto all before'.[8] Much of what Hooker writes exceeds his immediate apologetic purposes. Each part gestures back and forth, creating a doctrinal arc that spans from creation through to redemption and under which the reader can see and properly understand the ultimate meaning and purpose of the Church. In the *Lawes*, Hooker has an eye on capturing and defending for posterity's sake a greater vision of the Church as the ecclesial reception of the divine life through its participation in the whole of Christ.

Behind every claim in the *Lawes*, then, is one simple (but not simplistic) notion that frames the nature and purpose of the Church: namely, that all created things 'covet more or lesse the participation of God himselfe'.[9] Indeed, C. S. Lewis writes that Hooker's universe is 'drenched with Deity'.[10] For Hooker, Christ acts as the key unlocking creation and redemption as related modes of participation in God. We can go even further: Christ is at the centre of every claim in the *Lawes*, as the Word spoken or as the Wisdom informing.[11] Each gesture back and forth in the *Lawes* ultimately motions towards Christ and enlightens the entire shape of the Christian life *coram Deo et Christo*, in the presence of God and Christ. As will be shown, Hooker's vision of the ecclesial reception of divine life with Christ at the centre remains ultimately indebted to an Augustinian sensibility of the *totus Christus*, the whole Christ.

Christ the Word and Wisdom of God: the ecclesial reception of divine life

In the middle of a mini-treatise on Christology in Book Five of the *Lawes*, Hooker calls Christ the 'woord or Wisdom of God'.[12] This title manifests how participating in Christ through the Church as an extension of his body unlocks the entire economy of creation and redemption, a feature of Hooker's thought often overlooked in studies of his Christology, which often read this mini-treatise of Book Five in splendid isolation from the rest of the *Lawes*.[13]

On the one hand, all of creation participates in the eternal Word, the Wisdom of God, as the divine archetype for creation and as its end, since 'God hath his influence into the verie essence of all thinges'.[14] As such, Hooker can write that 'it must be confest that of Christ, working as a creator, and a governor of the world by providence, all are partakers'.[15] Hooker earlier grasps the essentially Trinitarian character of creation by the archetypal Word or Wisdom of God: echoing Acts 17.28, he writes, 'from the Father, by the Sonne, through the Spirit all things are'.[16] Indeed, all things desire union with God as the ultimate good, and (as Hooker puts it) 'by being unto God united we live as it were the life of God'.[17] In Book Five, Hooker grasps that this general desire for union with God also has a Trinitarian nature, resting in the Father as 'goodness', in the Son as 'wisdom' ordering all things, and in the Spirit as the divine 'power' of love.[18]

On the other hand, the incarnate Word or Wisdom of God restores and redeems this same creation broken by sin. Parsing the Johannine prologue that identifies the incarnate Jesus as the eternal Word, Hooker writes that 'wisdom to the ende that she might save manie made not *this or that man* hir habitation but *dwelt in us*'.[19] For Hooker, the Incarnation entails that by 'personal union', Christ's 'deitie' is 'inseparablie joined' to the body and soul of his humanity, deifying human nature.[20] While the incarnate 'Word' or 'Wisdom' has a particular deified human nature, this same nature is itself a corporate identity in Hebraic and Pauline thought, opening up the prospect of union with Christ.[21] Therefore, Hooker offers a Pauline Christology in which Christ recapitulates Adam as a corporate personality.[22] The germ of Adamic Christology can be seen in Paul's epistles (such as Rom. 5.12–21; 8.1; 13.14, or 1 Cor. 1.30; 15.20–23; 15.44–49). Patristic writers such as Irenaeus, Hippolytus, Origen, Methodius, Augustine of Hippo and Cyril of Alexandria developed and used Paul's Adam–Christ typology, rendering it as a key and enduring aspect of Christological thought then picked up and deployed by Hooker. Anything less than a realistic identity between Christ's humanity and ours would lead to 'too cold an interpretation', Hooker thinks, of our 'beinge in Christ',[23] another notably Pauline image that permeates the *Lawes*.[24] Through sharing in the whole Christ, fully divine and human, the second Adam, believers enjoy an analogous deification in which knowing God through the Word also entails the union of love with God, parsed as resting in Christ as Wisdom. The first Adam works as what Hooker calls 'an original cause of our nature and of that corruption of nature which causeth death'. Christ, as the second Adam, works as 'the cause original of restauration to life'. Thus, as 'wee are reallie partakers of the bodie of synne and death received from Adam', the hypostatic union instead makes us 'trulie partakers of Christ'.[25] Hooker sets this 'beinge in' (or the 'participation of') Christ within the context of 2 Peter 1.4, which he paraphrases as 'the *participation of divine nature*'. This biblical text is a *locus classicus* for Eastern theologies for deification, and Hooker's use sets the tone of what the drive in the *Lawes* really is. 'Being in Christ' welds believers in a chain linking us to Christ and so to the life of the Trinity. As such, Hooker writes that, through being in Christ, 'wee are therefore adopted sonnes of God to eternall life by participation of the onlie begotten Son of God, whose life is the wellspringe and cause of oures'.[26] Such participation in the whole of Christ unveils, as Owen Cummins puts it, 'the Athanasian *dictum* in Elizabethan language, "God became human that humans might be made divine"'.[27]

Under the canopy of this arc stretching from creation to redemption, Hooker places the Church as the corporate body of Christ. Bryan Spinks draws the arc in this way: for Hooker, 'the created universe itself, with its laws, allows participation in the divine . . . [and] election through Christ, justification, and the society of the church allows this participation to be achieved'.[28] The corporate body of Christ instrumentally fulfils the purpose of creation to return and rest in God inasmuch as it shares in the incarnate Word or Wisdom of God, Jesus Christ. Within and through the Church as the body of Christ, we come not only to know but also to love God and share in the unified life of the Trinity. As Robert Slocum phrases it, 'our participation [in God and Christ] involves us in a co-operative mutuality of unequals as we accept God's saving offer of a divine life'.[29] Hooker uses a number of reproductive, worldly images to describe how believers are re-created and drawn into the life of God through the Church: the Church is the 'verie mother of our new birth', providing the 'seede of regeneration' through the 'generative force' of the sacraments.[30] Most crucially, Hooker strongly identifies the Church with the crucified body of Christ: 'his Church he frameth out of the verie flesh, the verie wounded and bleeding side of the Sonne of man'; and we 'are in Christ because he knoweth and loveth us even as partes of him selfe'.[31] The sacraments establish participation in Christ as a Pauline notion of communion and Johannine pattern of mutual indwelling whereby 'Christ is in us' just as believers are in him.[32]

Hooker completely sets the sacramental economy of the Church, then, 'within an incarnational and soteriological framework'[33] in which Christ is the centre. For Hooker, participation in Christ is that 'mutual inward hold which Christ hath of us and wee of him, in such sort that ech possesseth other by waie of speciall interest propertie and inherent copulation'.[34] In baptism, believers are 'incorporated into Christ', which is to say they are brought into the body of Christ, a polyvalent image taken from Paul uniting both Christ and his followers as one.[35] In turn, the Eucharist conforms the recipient unto Christ as Wisdom. In his account of eucharistic reception in Book Five of the *Lawes*, Hooker emphasizes visceral union with and immediate tasting of the physical body of Christ on the cross. The eucharistic mysteries 'doe as nailes fasten us to his verie crosse' and 'in the woundes of our redeemer wee there dip our tongues' such that 'our hunger is satisfied . . . our thirst for ever quenched'.[36] The crucified and risen body of the whole Christ elicits and satiates our natural desire for God, incorporating believers into his being. Indeed, the Latin root of the verb 'to taste' (*sapere*) figuratively relates to wisdom (*sapientia*), identified by Hooker (following a long scriptural, Patristic and medieval tradition) as Christ. As we taste the incarnate Wisdom, so does the eternal Word lovingly unite us with himself, even as a prolepsis of heavenly union with God.

Hooker's Augustinian sensibility and the *totus Christus*

As Hooker unfolds this protean theological vision of participating in the whole of Christ, the 'woord or wisdom of God', he tacitly appeals to Augustine's idea of the whole Christ, the *totus Christus*. Hooker does so in order to work out the mystical nature of the Church as the corporate body of Christ, the site for the ecclesial reception of divine life. Augustine turns to the idea of the whole Christ across his works. Working from Paul's organic images of the Church as the body of Christ and Christ as the head of the Church (1 Cor. 12.12–27; Eph. 3.6; 4.1–16; 5.23; Rom. 12.4–5; and Col.

1.18–24), Augustine develops a realistic notion that Christ and his Church together form the *totus Christus* as a substantial unity.[37] Two examples of Augustine's use of the *totus Christus* image will suffice to illustrate that Christ's body takes on an ecclesial character. In his opening homily on the First Epistle of John, Augustine writes that 'The Word was made flesh, and dwelled among us; to that flesh is joined the church, and there is made the whole Christ, head and body'.[38] In another sermon, Augustine goes further: it is not that Christ would be incomplete without us; but Christ does not wish to be complete without us as the Church.[39]

When we compare what Hooker claims about how Christ relates to the Church, the close similarity with Augustine remains striking. In the middle of the *Lawes*, as he considers sacramental participation, Hooker writes that:

> It pleaseth [Christ] in mercy to accompt himself incomplete and maimed without us . . . Christ is whole with the whole Church, and whole with every part of the Church, as touching His Person, which can no way divide itself or be possest by degrees and portions . . . From hence it is that they which belong to the mysticall bodie of our Saviour Christ . . . are coupled everie one to Christ theire head.[40]

While Hooker does not explicitly refer to Augustine here, the derivation of the *totus Christus* image comes either from him or from one of his medieval interpreters. A likely alternative source would be Thomas Aquinas, who both recapitulates Augustine's idea of the whole Christ and represents another major influence on Hooker.[41] Given the sheer wealth and breadth of direct references to Augustine in the *Lawes*, however, he is the most likely source for Hooker's thought on the *totus Christus*. Of Hooker's 852 Patristic references, 95 of these are to 45 works of Augustine. In comparison, Hooker's 216 references to 86 medieval sources contain only 27 references to 7 works of Aquinas.[42] The real significance, however, of this derivation stretches beyond mere recapitulation of Augustine's idea of the *totus Christus*. While correlation does not always entail causality, there are compelling reasons to see Hooker's perpetual turn to Christ in the *Lawes* as exhibiting a deliberate Augustinian sensibility.

Pinning down what we might mean by an 'Augustinian sensibility' remains fraught with difficulty. There were, of course, manifold ways of reading and repurposing Augustine in the early modern period,[43] so much so that some scholars even question the usefulness of the label 'Augustinianism'.[44] Hooker's use of Augustine remains typical to the extent that the latter thinker was cited as a commonplace authority in theological discourse of the Reformation period.[45] Yet, like other contemporaneous readers of Augustine, Hooker reads 'for action', as Anthony Grafton and Lisa Jardine describe the purposeful nature of reading in the early modern period.[46] This 'reading for action' suggests the deliberate use of an 'Augustinian sensibility'. As already discussed, the *Lawes* exceeds its own apologetic, polemical and irenic aims. In addressing the audience of 'posterity', Hooker reads his sources in order to ensure that his participatory vision of the Church as an extension of Christ's body 'not passe away as in a dreame'. Hooker's unacknowledged use of Augustine's *totus Christus* image signals how a particular Augustinian sensibility implicitly infuses and shapes the *Lawes*. Indeed, the same turn to Christ, the same gesturing back and forth between doctrinal loci, and the same implications of the *totus Christus* image for Christian life can be seen in Hooker as they can in Augustine such that we can say they exhibit a theological genealogy.

What, then, more precisely is the 'Augustinian sensibility' evident in Hooker's *Lawes*, especially in its use of the *totus Christus*? If it is true that 'Christ simply pervades all of Augustine's theology as a ubiquitous and familiar subject',[47] and that there are multiple 'Christs' at work across Augustine's works,[48] then we need some kind of heuristic device in order to grasp the 'Augustinian sensibility' of the *Lawes*. Thankfully, the same sermons in which Augustine slowly developed the idea of the *totus Christus* offer such a heuristic device, namely the *Enarrationes in Psalmos* (the 'Expositions of the Psalms'). Michael Fiedrowicz insists that the *Enarrationes* represent an 'encyclopedia' or 'microcosm' of Augustine's broader thought.[49] Hooker both knows and references these sermons in the *Lawes*. Again, while the *Enarrationes* may not be the direct cause behind an 'Augustinian sensibility' in Hooker's thought, they offer a suitable cipher through which we can unfurl what that sensibility is and how it shapes what the *Lawes* bequeaths to posterity about the ecclesial character of Christ's body. Three related features of an 'Augustinian sensibility' shed light on the character of the Church as the whole Christ in the *Lawes*. These features are *method*, *gestures* and *purpose*.

Augustine's exegetical method as he preaches on the Psalms is to interpret them as being spoken by the head (Christ), by the body (the Church) or by both together as one voice, namely the *totus Christus*.[50] As Carol Harrison puts it, through his prosopological reading (that is, his person-centred exegesis) of the Psalms, for Augustine 'the Church, so to speak, is the visible, tangible continuation of Christ's Incarnation'.[51] The 'unity and indivisibility' of Christ and his Church are confirmed for Augustine by an array of other scriptural texts which only make sense in light of an actual union (such as Acts 9.4; 1 Cor. 12.12–27; John 15.5; or Matt. 25.42–45). Augustine casts the unity of voice between head and body in the mystical terms of marriage, using scriptural texts about marriage (such as Gen. 2.24; Matt. 19.6; and Eph. 5.31–32) to indicate a substantial union that does not obliterate difference, but which does make a new redemptive reality. One example from Augustine will suffice to illustrate all of this method. As he considers Psalm 30, Augustine writes the following of Christ and the Church:

But in fact he who deigned to assume the form of a slave, and within that form to clothe us with himself, he who did not disdain to take us up into himself, did not disdain either to transfigure us into himself, and to speak in our words, so that we in our turn might speak in his. This is the wonderful exchange, the divine business deal, the transaction effected in this world by the heavenly dealer . . . Without him, we are nothing, but in him we too are Christ. Why? Because the whole Christ consists of Head and body. The Head is he who is the saviour of this body . . . but the body is the Church, toiling on earth.[52]

Augustine goes on to make it clear that, in the Psalms, 'Christ is speaking', but Christ's speech also takes on the corporate voice of believers too. As such, Church and Christ become one grammatical and substantial subject because, as Augustine puts it in his sermon on Psalm 30, 'in the members of Christ there is Christ' and 'Head and body together are called one Christ'.[53] Augustine then immediately appeals to Ephesians 5.31–32 to describe the deep reality of this unity: 'so out of two people one single person comes to be, the single person that is Head and body, Bridegroom and bride'. Hooker's claim that 'it pleaseth [Christ] in mercy to accompt himself incomplete and maimed without us' echoes, then, Augustine's own sense that Christ 'suffered as our Head, and he suffers in his members, which means us'.[54] Christ's body, incorporating the Church, extends over time and space, encompassing and speaking into the entirety of human existence as it speaks itself back into Christ.

While Hooker does not share the exegetical method of the *Enarrationes* as such, he does show the same attentiveness to the voice of Christ and the Church's participation in that voice. Hooker gives a Christocentric shape to Scripture and scriptural exegesis in the *Lawes*.[55] While the Old and New Testaments both make believers 'wise unto salvation', they do so in a different regard: 'the difference betwene them consisting in this, that the old did make wise by teaching salvation through Christ that should come, the newe by teaching that Christ our Saviour is come'.[56] Hooker therefore distinguishes between central and peripheral ideas in Scripture, rather than giving all texts an equal weighting, but still sees them as united in their relation to Christ as the saving 'woord or Wisdom'.

While this Christological hermeneutic takes Christ to be the subject matter rather than the subject of Scripture, it is not the only way that Hooker turns to Christ as the voice to which our ears need to be attuned. The coda of Book One in the *Lawes* casts law in terms very close to the divine Wisdom of the sapiential books of Hebrew Scripture: 'her seate is the bosome of God, her voice the harmony of the world'.[57] That Christ is the divine Wisdom who orders creation remains the background to this coda and explains Hooker's high estimation of nature. For Hooker, then, the eternal Word speaks into the world. As he begins his polemical defence in Book Two of the *Lawes*, Hooker crucially returns to the scriptural figure of divine Wisdom in order to address the origin and manner of human knowing. Hooker uses Thomas Cartwright's 'pretended proofe' from Proverbs 2.9

for biblical omnicompetency to show, on the contrary, the 'sundry' divine influences on human understanding:

> Whatsoever either men on earth, or the Angels of heaven do know, it is as a drop of that unemptiable fountaine of wisdom, which wisdom hath diversly imparted her treasures unto the world. As her waies are of sundry kinds, so her maner of teaching is not meerely one and the same. Some things she openeth by the sacred books of Scripture; some things by the glorious works of nature: with some things she inspireth them from above by spirituall influence, in some thinges she leadeth and trayneth them onely by worldly experience and practise.[58]

For Hooker, then, Christ (as 'woord or Wisdom') acts as the *principium* or beginning principle who speaks in nature, Scripture and the worldly practice of the Church. When he turns to the *totus Christus* image in his Christ-centred ecclesiology, then, it is clear that our participation in Christ is his speaking into us and our being heard in him. Like Augustine, Hooker images the *totus Christus* as a mystical marriage: the Church is Christ's 'spouse'; and the Church enjoys 'mystical conjunction' and 'copulation' with Christ, thereby sharing in his deified life as one.[59] That the whole arc from creation to salvation represents Christ speaking, and that the Church ought to listen for the voice of Christ, remains fundamental to Hooker's theological vision in the *Lawes*, and the first aspect of his Augustinian sensibility.

We can also see in Augustine's *Enarrationes* the same set of mutually reinforcing gestures arching from creation to redemption that we have already seen in Hooker's work, indexed against Christ and within which the Church is nestled.[60] As David Meconi puts it, creation is a 'prologue to Augustine's theology of divine union'.[61] For Augustine, as it will be for Hooker, the phrase 'in the beginning' found in Genesis really means 'in the Word'.[62] Creation is the speech of the Word, as it were. The incarnate Word then speaks human nature afresh. Augustine writes in the *Enarrationes* that 'He who originally formed [the soul] came himself to reform it, for all things were created through the Word and through the Word the image was stamped on us'.[63] So it is that, as Meconi sums up Augustine's vision, 'the ultimate purpose of God's establishing the world is ecclesial communion, the church of praise appearing as the *telos* [goal] of all creation'.[64] Real and substantial union with Christ in the Church represents, for Augustine, the sharing in the life of the Trinity through participation in Christ, nourished by the dominical sacraments.[65] In the *Lawes*, Hooker silently follows Augustine, who sees that the ecclesial reception of the divine life in the *totus Christus* represents a kind of deification through becoming like Christ.[66] In another sermon, Augustine makes explicit the deification implied in the 'wonderful exchange' of the *totus Christus*: 'we carry mortality about with us', writes Augustine, 'we endure infirmity, we look forward to divinity. For

God wishes not only to vivify, but also to deify us'.[67] In the whole Christ for Augustine, as Ployd comments, 'we come to know both earth and heaven, both the incarnate and eternal Christ, both *scientia* [knowledge] and *sapientia* [wisdom], through Christ himself, who brings humanity and divinity together'.[68] Christ as Word and Wisdom brings creation to know and love the Trinity, for Augustine as it will for Hooker.

Most crucially, then, we can see how Hooker's Augustinian sensibility lends to the *Lawes* the same kind of purpose as is found in Augustine's *Enarrationes*. Augustine's expositions of the Psalms and his notion of the *totus Christus* in particular, take aim against the Donatist schismatics who divide the unity of the body of Christ. Yet, just as Hooker's *Lawes* exceed their own polemical context, so too does the disputatious character of Augustine's thought act as a necessary but not an ultimately sufficient way to grasp what the purpose of his work is in what it bequeaths to posterity. The genre of the *Enarrationes* is the sermon. As Ployd puts it, Augustine 'preaches with a purpose: to cultivate love and faith in his audience'.[69] Teubner likewise points out that Augustine's sermons take place within actual Christian worshipping communities, and that accordingly 'the *totus Christus* as lived reality is thus the form of the non-ideal community becoming sanctified'.[70] Since Augustine's *totus Christus* is the 'hermeneutical centre'[71] of Augustine's expositions of the Psalms, reciting the Psalms 'ushers the congregation into sharing in Christ's voice, as both expressive of human life before God and transformative of human life into divine life'.[72] Rowan Williams puts it this way: 'singing the psalms . . . becomes a means of learning what it is to inhabit the body of Christ and to be caught up in Christ's prayer'.[73] Augustine's *totus Christus* is thereby a performative and transformative notion. 'Everything written here is a mirror for us', Augustine would write of the Psalms, using an image picked up by Jean Calvin in the sixteenth century in the preface to his own commentary on the Psalms; and in the Psalms Augustine thinks 'we discover our voice' as one with the voice of Christ.[74] As such, Augustine's sermons (as Michael Cameron points out) 'were instruments for deepening Christian conversion, contributions to a vast re-orientation of thought, feeling, and practice'[75] in order that believers may not only know God but be joined with Christ in love for God and neighbour. We should not neglect or underestimate this ethical aspect to being Christlike through the *totus Christus* dynamic, even though Augustine's concept of the whole Christ historically led in a different, hierocratic direction towards papal supremacy.[76] Indeed, modern scholars have begun to retrieve the critical, ethical and liberating dimensions of Augustine's thought in order to recover its radical potential for the Church, both in its ecumenism and in its relation to the powers and principalities of the world.[77]

It is in the ethical aspect of being Christlike that we see the ultimate purpose of Hooker's *Lawes* for the sake of posterity. Some pejoratively describe the *Lawes* as merely 'window-dressing for the command structure of Elizabethan society' against its opponents.[78] The Augustinian sensibility of the *Lawes* surely aims, however, to lead people by the hand to a greater vision and goal, namely the 'participation of God himselfe'. For Hooker, divine influence leads creation by the hand (*manuductio*) towards its beatitude through natural and supernatural means. As a text addressed to his opponents out of love, Hooker's *Lawes* attempts to persuade them not only to obey the ecclesiastical polity of the Church of England, but also freely to embrace it as a way in which they can experience God's call to heal and restore creation in Christ.[79] Hooker's very method in the *Lawes* is, as Andrea Russell puts it, 'intensely participative'[80] since it imitates (as a text seeking to 'resolve the conscience') the manuduction by God of a broken world such that it enjoys the peace and order that is the 'participation of God himselfe'. As for interpretations of the *totus Christus* that conflate and flatten God's kingdom and the Church, or eschatology and history, Hooker carefully avoids them. His stress in the final 'books on power' in the *Lawes* remains on the provisional quality of the secular order, and even of the visible Church, in comparison with the eschatological fullness of union with Christ.[81] Hooker's real emphasis remains on the role of the visible Church in transforming society through a Christlike ethic of love flowing from the liturgical training of 'godliness' as the 'welspringe of all true virtues'.[82] Indeed, his account of worship constructs the Church as a school of virtue preparing for the fullness of beatific union given gratuitously through God's grace and participation in the ascended and glorified Christ.[83]

It is perhaps no accident, then, that Hooker sets the *totus Christus* image amidst the liturgical concerns of Book Five of the *Lawes*. Public worship 'deals with the whole of that humanity assumed by Christ', as Rowan Williams phrases it.[84] As Hooker well knows in the tribulations of his age, and as we may appreciate in our own, the life of the visible Church is halting and hesitant; but the Church is the site in which we can receive, and grow in, the life of God. Common prayer is a locus of unity with one another before the Triune God. Hooker argues that the established liturgy affords 'mutuall conference and as it were commerce to be had betwene God and us'.[85] Worship crafts appropriate 'holie desires' which lead believers both to know and also to love God in sacramental union with Christ, and so to experience ethical as well as ontological transformation in that union.[86] Indeed, he provocatively writes that in the Eucharist 'there ensueth a kind of transubstantiation of us'.[87] The plural 'us' suggests the corporate, mystical union of body and head, the *totus Christus*, which dramatically transubstantiates or changes believers into Christ. As we have seen, Augustine similarly uses the word 'transfiguration' to describe the great exchange of the whole Christ that asymmetrically perfects our human nature as it meets with the eternal Word. Indeed, in the *Confessions*, Augustine hears the voice of the Lord saying, 'I am the food of the fully grown; grow and you will feed on me. And you will not change me into you like the food your flesh eats, but you will be changed into me'.[88] We might use the more ordinary verb 'transform' to grasp the elevation of humankind in Christ as he speaks into the hollow of our being, as well as the eucharistic raising up of the broken and complex historical reality of the Church into union with the ascended and glorified Christ. For Hooker, as for Augustine, the praise of the Church, mystically united with Christ, makes our voice in worship the voice of the body of Christ, the whole Christ, Word and Wisdom. Hooker's final word and wisdom to posterity is, above all else, simply the 'woord or Wisdom of God'. In Christ we are spoken, and into Christ we speak our entire selves. The whole Christ speaking and being spoken is that which Hooker does not wish to pass away loosely through silence, as in a dream.

Notes

1 See William H. Harrison, 'The Church', in *A Companion to Richard Hooker*, ed. by W. J. T. Kirby (Leiden and Boston: Brill, 2008), pp. 305–66. Harrison recognizes the 'practical and polemical' (p. 305) concerns of the *Lawes* but balances this context with the theological gestures between ecclesiology, soteriology and Christology in Hooker's thought in a vein which this essay attempts to continue.

2 Richard Hooker, *Of the Lawes of Ecclesiastical Polity*, 1:1.2–4; Pref.1.1. All quotations are taken from W. Speed Hill, ed., *The Folger Library Edition of the Works of Richard Hooker* (vols 1–5, Cambridge, MA: Belknap Press, 1977–90; vol. 6, Binghamton, NY: Belknap Press, 1993; vol. 7, Tempe, AZ: Medieval & Renaissance Texts & Studies, 1998). For ease of locating references, I employ a dual reference system: the first refers to the volume, page and line numbers of the *Folger* edition; the second refers to the comparable location in Keble's edition, which gives book, chapter and section (*The Works of Richard Hooker*, ed John Keble, Oxford 1841).

3 Thomas Fuller, *The Church History of Britain from the Birth of Jesus Christ until the Year MDCXLVII* (1655; new edn, ed. by John Sherren Brewer, 6 vols, Oxford, 1845), vol. 4, p. 26.

4 See Peter Lake, '"Anglicanism": Business as Usual? The Immediate Reception of Hooker's Ecclesiastical Polity', *Journal of Ecclesiastical History*, 52.3 (2001), pp. 456–86 (p. 456).

5 Dionisio De Lara, 'Richard Hooker's Concept of Law', *Anglican Theological Review*, 44 (1962), pp. 380–9 (p. 388).

6 See Charles Miller, *Richard Hooker and the Vision of God: Exploring the Origins of 'Anglicanism'* (Cambridge: James Clarke & Co., 2013), pp. 11–15; and Rowan Williams, 'Foreword', in *A Companion to Richard Hooker*, ed. by W. J. T. Kirby (Leiden and Boston: Brill, 2008), pp. xv–xxvi.

7 Hooker, *Lawes*, 1:1.9–10; Pref.1.1.

8 Hooker, *Lawes*, 1:57.24–33; I.1.2.

9 Hooker, *Lawes*, 1:73.8–10; I.5.2. See Charles Irish, '"Participation of God himselfe": Law, the mediation of Christ, and sacramental participation in the thought of Richard Hooker', in *Richard Hooker and the English Reformation*, ed. by W. J. T. Kirby (Norwell: Kluwer Academic Publishers, 2003), pp. 165–84; and Paul Anthony Dominiak, *Richard Hooker: The Architecture of Participation* (London: T & T Clark, 2019).

10 C. S. Lewis, *English Literature in the Sixteenth Century, Excluding Drama* (Oxford: Clarendon Press, 1954), p. 462.

11 See Egil Grislis, 'Jesus Christ – The Centre of Theology in Richard Hooker's *Of the Lawes of Ecclesiastical Polity*, Book V', *Journal of Anglican Studies*, 5.2 (2007), pp. 227–51; and Egil Grislis, 'The Hermeneutical Problem in Hooker', in *Studies in Richard Hooker*, ed. by W. Speed Hill (Cleveland, OH and London: Case Western Reserve University Press, 1972), pp. 159–206.

12 Hooker, *Lawes*, 2:213.13–23; V.52.3.

13 For example, see W. David Neelands, 'Christology and the Sacraments', in *A Companion to Richard Hooker*, ed. by W. J. T. Kirby (Leiden and Boston: Brill, 2008), pp. 369–401.

14 Hooker, *Lawes*, 2:236.22–23; V.56.5.

15 Hooker, *Lawes*, 2:242.11–13; V.56.10.

16 Hooker, *Lawes*, 1:59.28–29; I.2.2.

17 Hooker, *Lawes*, 1:112.17–20; I.11.2.

18 Hooker, *Lawes*, 2:237.10–13; V.56.5.

19 Hooker, *Lawes*, 2:213.22; V.52.3.

20 Hooker, *Lawes*, 2:216.4–18; V.52.4.

21 See Grant Macaskill, *Union with Christ in the New Testament* (Oxford: Oxford University Press, 2013), pp. 128–71.

22 Hooker, *Lawes*, 2:237–240; V.56.6–8.

23 Hooker, *Lawes*, 2:239.13–16; V.56.7.

24 See Macaskill, *Union with Christ*, pp. 219–50.

25 Hooker, *Lawes*, 2:240.3–11; V.56.7.

26 Hooker, *Lawes*, 2:240.3–11; V.56.7.

27 Owen Cummins, *Eucharist and Ecumenism: The Eucharist across the Ages and Traditions* (Eugene, OR: Pickwick Publications, 2013), p. 74.

28 Bryan D. Spinks, *Two Faces of Elizabethan Anglican Theology: Sacraments and Salvation in the Thought of William Perkins and Richard Hooker* (Lanham, MD and London: The Scarecrow Press, 1999), p. 133.

29 Robert B. Slocum, 'An Answering Heart: Reflections on Saving Participation', *Anglican Theological Review*, 84.3 (2002), pp. 1009–15 (p. 1015).

30 Hooker, *Lawes*, 2:207.13–19; V.50.1.

31 Hooker, *Lawes*, 2:239.5–6, 22–24; V.56.7.

32 See John Booty, 'Book V', in *The Folger Library Edition of the Works of Richard Hooker*, ed. by W. Speed Hill (vol. 6, Binghamton, NY: Belknap Press, 1993), pp. 197–9.

33 Christopher Cocksworth, *Evangelical Eucharistic Thought in the Church of England* (Cambridge: Cambridge University Press, 1993), p. 38.

34 Hooker, *Lawes*, 2:234.29–31; V.56.1.

35 Hooker, *Lawes*, 2:255.6–13; V.60.2.

36 Hooker, *Lawes*, 2:343.7–31; V.67.12.

37 See Tarcisius van Bavel, 'The "Christus Totus" Idea: A Forgotten Aspect of Augustine's Spirituality', in *Studies in Patristic Christology*, ed. by Thomas Finan and Vincent Twomey (Portland, OR: Four Courts Press, 1998), pp. 84–94.

38 Augustine, 'First Homily', I.2, in *Homilies on the First Epistle of John. The Works of St Augustine: A New Translation for the 21st Century*, III/14, ed. by Daniel E. Doyle and Thomas Martin, and trans. by Boniface Ramsay (Hyde Park, NY: New City Press, 2008), p. 22.

39 Augustine, 'Sermon 341', 341.1 and 11, in *Sermons 341–400. The Works of St Augustine: A New Translation for the 21st Century, III/10*, ed. by John E. Rotelle, and trans. by Edmund Hill (Hyde Park, NY: New City Press, 1995), pp. 19, 26.

40 Hooker, *Lawes*, 2:242.6–243.23; V.56.10–11.

41 See, for example, Aquinas' recapitulation of Augustine's *totus Christus* in Thomas Aquinas, 'Commentary on Psalm 3', no.5, found in *Expositio in Psalmos, Opera Omnia*, vol. 14 (Parmae: Typis Petra Fiaccadori, 1813), pp. 148–353 (p. 157); or *Summa Theologiae*, III.19.4 and III.48.2 ad. 1 in the Blackfriars edition, 61 vols, Latin and English with notes and introductions (London: Eyre & Spottiswoode, and New York: McGraw-Hill Book Company, 1964–80). On the broader impact of Augustine on Aquinas, and the latter's interpretation of the former, see Thomas F. Ryan, *Thomas Aquinas as Reader of the Psalms* (Notre Dame, IN: Notre Dame University Press, 2001), esp. p. 41; and Michael Dauphinais, Barry David and Matthew Levering, eds, *Aquinas the Augustinian* (Washington, DC: The Catholic University of America Press, 2007). On Hooker's relationship to Thomism, see Paul Dominiak, 'Hooker, Scholasticism, Thomism, and Reformed Orthodoxy', in *Richard Hooker and Reformed Orthodoxy*, ed. by Scott Kindred–Barnes and W. Bradford Littlejohn (Göttingen and Bristol: Vandenhoeck & Ruprecht, 2017), pp. 101–26.

42 See A. S. McGrade, 'Classical, Patristic, and Medieval Sources', in *A Companion to Richard Hooker*, ed. by W. J. T. Kirby (Leiden and Boston: Brill, 2008), pp. 51–88 (esp. p. 52).

43 See Jay T. Collier, *Debating Perseverance: The Augustinian Heritage in Post-Reformation England* (Oxford: Oxford University Press, 2013), pp. 1–19, esp. n.25 and n.26, pp. 12–13, for an extensive list of studies. See Thomas F. Martin, *Our Restless Heart: The Augustinian Tradition* (Maryknoll, NY: Orbis Books, 2003), esp. pp. 113–37 for the reception of Augustine across the Protestant and Catholic reformers of the sixteenth century. See also Henri Marrou, *St Augustin et l'augustinisme* (Paris: Seuil, 1955), esp. p. 180 where he describes multiple 'Augustinianisms' always at play in the reception of Augustine; and Arnoud S. Q. Visser, *Reading Augustine in the Reformation: The Flexibility of Intellectual Authority in Europe, 1500–1620* (Oxford: Oxford University Press, 2011) on the ways Augustine was read and the purposes for which he was used.

44 See R. James Long, 'On the Usefulness of "Augustinianism" as a Historical Construct: Two Test Cases from Oxford', *Medieval Perspectives* 16 (2001), pp. 74–83; and Eric Leland Saak, *Creating Augustine: Interpreting Augustine and Augustinianism in the Later Middle Ages* (Oxford: Oxford University Press, 2012), esp. pp. 1–22.

45 For a full list of references, see *The Folger Library Edition of the Works of Richard Hooker* (vol. 7, Tempe, AZ: Medieval & Renaissance Texts & Studies, 1998), pp. 20–4.

46 Anthony Grafton and Lisa Jardine, 'Studied for Action: How Gabriel Harvey Read His Livy', *Past and Present*, 129 (1990), pp. 3–51; discussed in Visser, *Reading Augustine*, pp. 96, 114.

47 Hubertus R. Drobner, 'Studying Augustine: An Overview of Recent Research', in *Augustine and His Critics: Essays in Honour of Gerald Bonner*, ed. by Robert Dodaro and George Lawless (London: Routledge, 2000), pp. 18–35 (p. 28). See also Martin, *Our Restless Heart*, pp. 27–36.

48 Joanne McWilliam, 'The Study of Augustine's Christology in the Twentieth Century', in *Augustine from Rhetor to Theologian*, ed. by Joanne McWilliam (Waterloo, ON: Wilfrid Laurier Press, 1992), pp. 183–206 (p. 183).

49 Michael Fiedrowicz, 'Introduction', in *Expositions of the Psalms. The Works of St Augustine: A New Translation for the 21st Century, Vol.1, III/15*, ed. by John E. Rotelle, and trans. by Maria Boulding (Hyde Park, NY: New City Press, 2000), p. 64.

50 On Augustine's prosopological exegesis, see Michael Cameron, *Christ Meets me Everywhere: Augustine's Early Figurative Exegesis* (Oxford: Oxford University Press, 2012), esp. pp. 166–212; and Adam Ployd, *Augustine, the Trinity, and the Church: A Reading of the Anti-Donatist Sermons* (Oxford: Oxford University Press, 2015), esp. pp. 57–84. The most complete study of the *Enarrationes* is Michael Fiedrowicz, *Psalmus Vox Totius Christi: Studien zu Augustins 'Enarrationes in Psalmos'* (Freiberg: Herder, 1997). For a short but comprehensive account of Augustine's Christ-centred ecclesiology, see Stanislaus J. Grabowski, 'St Augustine and the Doctrine of the Mystical Body of Christ', *Theological Studies*, 7.1 (1946), pp. 72–125.

51 Carol Harrison, *Beauty and Revelation in the Thought of Saint Augustine* (Oxford: Oxford University Press, 1992), p. 226.

52 Augustine, *Enarrationes*, 30(2).3, in *Expositions of the Psalms. The Works of St Augustine: A New Translation for the 21st Century, Vol.1, III/15*, pp. 322–24. See Michael Cameron, 'Transfiguration: Christology and the Roots of Figurative Exegesis in St Augustine', *Studia Patristica*, 33 (1997), pp. 40–47.

53 Augustine, *Enarrationes*, 30(2).4, in *Expositions of the Psalms*, Vol. 1, p. 324; compare *Enarrationes*, 130.1, in *Expositions of the Psalms. The Works of St Augustine: A New Translation for the 21st Century, Vol.6, III/20*, pp. 138–40.

54 Augustine, *Enarrationes*, 61.4, in *Expositions of the Psalms, The Works of St Augustine: A New Translation for the 21st Century, Vol.3, III/17*, p. 204. The background to both texts is Colossians 1.24 where Paul writes that he suffers so that his experience 'may fill up what is lacking to the sufferings of Christ'.

55 See Grislis, 'The Hermeneutical Problem in Hooker', pp. 191–92.

56 Hooker, *Lawes*, 1:128.3–21; I.14.4.

57 Hooker, *Lawes*, 1:142.8–9; I.16.8.

58 Hooker, *Lawes*, 1:147.23–148.6; II.1.4.

59 Hooker, *Lawes*, 2:234.31; 2:239.3; V.56.1; V.56.7. On Hooker's comparison between participation in Christ and marriage, see Robert C. Schwarz, 'Dignified and Commodious: Richard Hooker's "Mystical Copulation" Metaphor', *Sewanee Theological Review*, 43.1 (1999), pp. 16–30.

60 See Jonathan D. Teubner, *Prayer after Augustine: A Study in the Development of the Latin Tradition* (Oxford: Oxford University Press, 2018), p. 69: 'In this doctrine [i.e. the *totus Christus*], prayer becomes the intersection of Christology and soteriology, doctrine and practice'. Similarly, see Rowan Williams, 'Augustine and the Psalms', *Interpretation*, 58.1 (2004), pp. 17–27 (p. 20): 'The interconnection between hermeneutics, Christology, and the doctrines of grace, salvation, and the church is extraordinarily tight'.

61 David Vincent Meconi, *The One Christ: St Augustine's Theology of Deification* (Washington, DC: The Catholic University of America Press, 2013), p. 31.

62 Augustine, *De Genesi contra Manichaeos*, I.3, in *On Genesis. The Works of St Augustine: A New Translation for the 21st Century, I/13*, ed. by John E. Rotelle, and trans. by Edmund Hill (Hyde Park, NY: New City Press, 2002), p. 40. Compare Augustine, *Enarrationes*, 32(1).9; 32(3).12, in *Expositions of the Psalms*, Vol. 2, pp. 389; 413; and Augustine, *Confessions*, 11.3.5–9.11, trans. by Henry Chadwick (Oxford: Oxford University Press, 2008), pp. 223–8.

63 Augustine, *Enarrationes*, 32(3).16, in *Expositions of the Psalms*, Vol. 1, p. 416.

64 Meconi, *The One Christ*, p. 33.

65 See Augustine, *Enarrationes*, 17.36, in *Expositions of the Psalms*, Vol. 1, p. 195; and *Enarrationes*, 47.8, in *Expositions of the Psalms*, Vol. 2, pp. 343–44.

66 See Gerald Bonner, 'Augustine's Concept of Deification', *Journal of Theological Studies*, 37 (1986), pp. 369–86; and Norman Russell, *The Doctrine of Deification in the Greek Patristic Tradition* (Oxford: Oxford University Press, 2006), pp. 329–32.

67 Augustine, 'Sermon 23B', 1.1–6, in *Newly Discovered Sermons. The Works of St Augustine: A New Translation for the 21st Century*, III/11, ed. by John E. Rotelle, and trans. by Edmund Hill (Hyde Park, NY: New City Press, 1997), p. 37.

68 Ployd, *Augustine*, p. 80. On Christ as knowledge and wisdom, see Augustine, *De Trinitate*, 13.19.24, in *Nicene and Post-Nicene Fathers*, Vol. 3, ed. by Philip Schaff (Peabody, MA: Hendrickson, 2004), pp. 180–81.

69 Ployd, *Augustine*, p. 56.

70 Teubner, *Prayer after Augustine*, p. 83.

71 Allan D. Fitzgerald, ed., *Augustine through the Ages: An Encyclopedia* (Grand Rapids, MI: William B. Eerdmans, 1999), pp. 292–93.

72 Teubner, *Prayer after Augustine*, p. 75.

73 Williams, 'Augustine and the Psalms', pp. 19–20. See also Jason Byasee, *Praise Seeking Understanding: Reading the Psalms with Augustine* (Grand Rapids, MI: William B. Eerdmans, 2007), pp. 56–100.

74 Augustine, *Enarrationes*, 30(2).3, in *Expositions of the Psalms*, Vol. 1, pp. 322–4; and *Enarrationes*, 40.6; 45.1, in *Expositions of the Psalms*, Vol. 2, pp. 231–2; 310–1.

75 Michael Cameron, 'Totus Christus and the Psychagogy of Augustine's Sermons', *Augustinian Studies*, 36.1 (2005), pp. 59–70 (p. 60).

76 See Michael Horton, *People and Place: A Covenant Ecclesiology* (Louisville, KY: Westminster John Knox Press, 2008), pp. 155–89. Compare Jürgen Moltmann, *The Coming of God: Christian Eschatology* (London: SCM Press, 2000), p. 184.

77 For example, see Anthony J. Chvala-Smith, 'Augustine of Hippo', in *Empire and the Christian Tradition: New Readings of Classical Theologians*, ed. by Kwok Pui-Lan, Don H. Compier and Joerg Rieger (Minneapolis: Fortress Press, 2007), pp. 79–93; Kimberley Baker, 'Augustine's Doctrine of the *Totus Christus*: Reflecting on the Church as Sacrament of Unity', *Horizons*, 37.1 (2010), pp. 7–24; Michael J. Iafrate, 'The *Totus Christus* and the Crucified People: Re-Reading Augustine's Christology from Below with the Salvadoran Jesuits', *Journal of Postcolonial Theory and Theology*, 2.4 (2011), pp. 1–49; and Simon Chan, 'Mother Church: Toward a Pentecostal Ecclesiology', in *Pentecostal Ecclesiology: A Reader*, ed. by Chris E. W. Green (Leiden: Brill, 2016), pp. 23–46.

78 Robert Eccleshall, 'Richard Hooker and the Peculiarities of the English', *History of Political Thought*, 2 (1981), pp. 63–117 (pp. 63, 83).

79 On this irenic aspect, see Daniel Eppley, *Reading the Bible with Richard Hooker* (Minneapolis: Fortress Press, 2016), pp. 167–218.

80 Andrea Russell, *Richard Hooker, Beyond Certainty* (Oxford: Routledge, 2016), pp. 101–2.

81 For example, see Hooker, *Lawes*, 3: 356–363; VIII.4.1–6.

82 Hooker, *Lawes*, 2:17.9–10; V.1.2.

83 See Egil Grislis, 'Richard Hooker and Mysticism', *Anglican Theological Review*, 87.2 (2005), pp. 253–71; and Paul Dominiak, '"From the Footstool to the Throne of God": *Methexis, Metaxu,* and *Eros* in Richard Hooker's *Of the Lawes of Ecclesiastical Polity*', *Perichoresis*, 12.1 (2014), pp. 57–76.

84 Rowan Williams, *Anglican Identities* (London: Darton, Longman & Todd, 2009), p. 31.

85 Hooker, *Lawes*, 2:65.7–8; V.18.1.

86 See Paul Dominiak, 'The Logic of Desire', *Reformation and Renaissance Review*, 16.1 (2014), pp. 37–51.

87 Hooker, *Lawes*, 2:339.7–8; V.67.11.

88 Augustine, *Confessions*, 7.10.16; p. 124.

10

Reasoning upon the Essentials: Chalcedonian Sacramentalism in Andrewes and Bramhall[1]

DAVID CURRY

The first two essays in T. S. Eliot's *For Lancelot Andrewes* are on Lancelot Andrewes (1555–1626) and John Bramhall (1594–1653).[2] A collection of essays intended to 'indicate certain lines of development'[3] belonging to Eliot's conversion to orthodox Christianity in the form of Anglo-Catholicism, the essays on Andrewes and Bramhall suggest something of their importance for the understanding of classical Anglicanism, to use a later term. They illumine an approach to Christology. For Andrewes and Bramhall, and the tradition which they embody, the interplay and conjunction of human and divine, temporal and eternal, earthly and heavenly in the person of Christ belong to the determination of what is essential to the faith and to our participation in it.

Subtitled, '*essays on style and order*', Eliot understood the necessary relation between form and content, arguing that in Andrewes 'intellect and sensibility were in harmony',[4] something which he argues was lost after Andrewes and John Donne and 'from which we have never recovered'.[5] This was not just in literature but also in theology in terms of the harmonious interplay of word and sacrament, itself a critical feature of classical Anglicanism which Andrewes's sermons illustrate.

In these first two essays, Eliot connects both Andrewes and Bramhall directly to the seminal figure of Richard Hooker. 'The achievement of Hooker and Andrewes was to make the English Church more worthy of intellectual assent'.[6] With respect to Bramhall, he suggests that 'for ordonnance, logical arrangement, for mastery of every fact relevant to a thesis', Bramhall may 'surpass even Richard Hooker'.[7] In Eliot's view, 'the writings of Hooker and Andrewes illustrate that determination to stick to the essentials, that awareness of the needs of the time, the desire for clarity and precision on matters of importance, and the indifference to matters indifferent'.[8] Such remarks equally apply to Bramhall's writings.

Andrewes and Bramhall argue for the essential catholicism of the English Church as reformed and catholic. Their works reveal a form of thinking the essentials of the Christian faith centred on Chalcedonian and Trinitarian orthodoxy expressed in the Catholic Creeds. They offer a way of reasoning upon the essentials of the faith that is at once principled and clear about the essentials to which 'nothing can be added and nothing taken away' and yet allows for a certain generosity of spirit about things indifferent. But things indifferent or secondary are not things indifferent or unimportant in exactly the same way. There is an order of importance and an order of relation with respect to things essential and things indifferent and there is always the more primary question about the relation of things indifferent to the essential doctrines of the faith. Sometimes the distinction between what is essential and what is not essential has been mistaken requiring *correction*; sometimes it has been confused requiring *clarification*; sometimes it is assumed and implicit requiring *explication*; and sometimes it is forgotten or ignored requiring *recollection*.[9]

Such reasoning upon the essentials shows the formative character of what Bramhall calls the 'fundamentals or essentials of Faith'.[10] Reasoning upon the essentials, upon the proper order and conjunction of the natural and the supernatural, the outward sign and the inward grace, also characterizes the way in which Bramhall and Andrewes, along with Richard Hooker especially, understand and describe our participation in the divine life through the sacraments.

The Chalcedonian definition will largely determine the understanding and nature of Anglican sacramental theology, what Robert Crouse describes as 'Chalcedonian sacramentalism'.[11] Nicholas Lossky in his magisterial treatment of Lancelot Andrewes describes Andrewes's eucharistic theology as 'Chalcedonian realism'.[12] This suggests the formative role that essential doctrine plays in the shape of devotion and practice for the theology of the English Church.

'Stick[ing] to the essentials': nothing added, nothing taken away

The treatment of the sacraments by Andrewes and Bramhall is about a reasoning upon the essentials. 'That which was once an essential part of the Christian Faith is always an essential part of the Christian Faith', Bramhall argues, 'that which was once no essential, is never an essential'.[13] The things which are essential are 'plain' and 'necessary', Andrewes says.[14]

The essentials of the faith are grounded in the dogmas of the Trinity, the Incarnation and redemption. Andrewes's *apologia* for the English Church, stated in a sermon in 1613, became famous and was often repeated: 'One Canon of Scripture put in writing by God, two Testaments, three Creeds, the first four Councils, five centuries and the succession of the Fathers therein, three centuries before Constantine, two centuries after Constantine, draw for us the rule of religion'.[15] Bramhall refers to the rule of faith as that to which 'nothing can be added, nothing taken away': 'We have a certain rule of Faith, the Apostles' Creed, dilated in the Scriptures, or the Scriptures contracted into the Apostles' Creed'.[16]

The conjunction of Scripture and Creed provides the ground for a reasoning upon the essential doctrines of the Christian faith and acts as a measure and guide for subsequent doctrinal development without allowing for any additions to what is necessary to salvation. 'The Scripture and Creed are not two different rules of Faith but one and the same rule, dilated in the Scripture, contracted in the Creed; the end of the Creed being to contain all fundamental points of Faith, or a summary of all things necessary to salvation'.[17] The Creeds come out of the Scriptures and return us to the Scriptures – an interpretative principle evident in Andrewes's sermons. Such a form of reasoning also applies to the understanding of the sacraments through which we participate in what is believed. 'Into this Faith were we baptized, unto this Faith do we adhere', Bramhall argues.[18] This belongs to the harmony of intellect and sensibility, to the relation between form and content, between sign and thing signified, between Word and sacrament. This is a constant point of emphasis for both Andrewes and Bramhall.

'The Desire for Clarity and Precision': Chalcedonian exegesis in Andrewes

Hooker's explication of the Chalcedonian Definition became paradigmatic for classical Anglican sacramental theology. His preamble to the treatment of the sacraments in the *Lawes* is a reasoning upon the principles of Chalcedon.

> There are but four things which concur to make complete the whole state of our Lord Jesus Christ: his Deity, his manhood, the conjunction of both, and the distinction of the one from the other being joined in one.[19]

He presents a summary of essential doctrine in terms of the heresies and controversies of the early Church through which these principles are achieved and established.

> Four principal heresies there are which have in those things withstood the truth: Arians by bending themselves against the Deity of Christ; Apollinarians by maiming and misrepresenting that which belongeth to his human nature; Nestorians by rending Christ asunder, and dividing him into two persons; the followers of Eutyches by confounding in his person those natures which they should distinguish. Against these there have been four most famous ancient general councils: the council of Nice [*sic*] to define against Arians, against Apollinarians the council of Constantinople, the council of Ephesus against Nestorians, against Eutychians the Chalcedon council.[20]

'In four words', Hooker sums up concisely the principles that belong to our reasoning upon the nature and person of Christ:

ἀληθως, τελέως, ἀδιαιρέτως, ἀσυγχύτως, truly, perfectly, indivisibly, distinctly, the first applied to his being God, and second to his being Man, the third to his being of both One, and the fourth to his still continuing in that one Both, we may fully by way of abridgement comprise whatsoever antiquity hath at large handled either in declaration of Christian belief, or in refutation of the foresaid heresies.[21]

Indeed, for Hooker, all heresies concerning the person of Jesus 'in any age' are comprehended in these terms.

Following Hooker, Andrewes employs the measure of Chalcedon frequently and consistently in his sermons. He does so explicitly in his Nativity Sermon of 1611, unpacking the Christmas mystery in terms of the interplay of divinity and humanity united in the person of Christ. His text is John 1.14, the Word made flesh, *Verbum caro factum est*. 'He that "in the beginning" was *apud Deum* and *Deus*', with God and is God – He '"in the fullness of time" was *apud homines* and *homo*', with men and is man.

'Made' it was; against Manicheus holding that He had no true body; as if factum had been fictum, or making were mocking. Made it was, but how made? Not *convertendo*, 'the Word converted into flesh,' as Cerinthus; of 'flesh converted into the Word,' *Verbum caro facta est*, as Valentinus; for the Deity cannot be changed into any thing, nor any thing into it. Nor made *conciliando*, as friends are made, so as they continue two several persons still; and while the flesh suffered the Word stood by and looked on, as Nestorius. That is *cum carne*, not *caro*; 'made with flesh,' not 'flesh;' and never was one person said to be made another. Nor made by compounding; and so a third thing produced of both, as Eutyches. For so, He should be neither of both, Word nor flesh, neither God nor man.[22]

Echoing the Athanasian Creed, he argues that 'into the Godhead was the manhood taken; the natures preserved without confusion, the person entire without division', and then proceeds to quote Chalcedon.

Take the definition of the fourth General Council: *Sic factum est caro ut maneret Verbum, non immutando quod erat, sed suscipiendo quod non erat; nostra auxit, sua non minuit; nec Sacramentum pietatis detrimentum Deitatis*; 'He was so made flesh that He ceased not to be the Word, never changing that He was, but taking that He was not; we were the better, He was never the worse; the mystery of godliness was no detriment to his Godhead, nor the honour of the creature wrong to the Creator'.[23]

This way of interpreting Chalcedon emphasizes the preservation of the distinctions of natures within the unity of person. Andrewes extends that thinking to the *agenda* that follows from the *credenda*. In short, like Hooker, he extends the measure of Chalcedon to the sacraments.

> The mystery of godliness, or exercise of godliness – call it whether ye will – which we call the Sacraments; the Greek hath no other word for it but Musterion, whereby the Church offereth to initiate us into the fellowship of this day's mystery. Nothing sorteth better than these two mysteries one with the other; the dispensation of a mystery with the mystery of dispensation. It doth manifestly represent, it doth mystically impart what it representeth.[24]

Such is the necessity of our participation in the scriptural and creedal mysteries sacramentally.

> Because He hath so done, taken ours of us, we also ensuing His steps will participate with Him and with His flesh which He hath taken of us. It is most kindly to take part with Him in that which He took part in with us, and that, to no other end, but that He might make the receiving of it by us means whereby He might 'dwell in us, and we in Him.'

This is an explicit reference to the Prayer Book Liturgy.

> He taking our flesh, and we receiving His Spirit; by His flesh which He took of us receiving His Spirit which He imparteth to us; that, as He by ours became *consors humanae naturae*, so we by His become *consortes Divinae naturae*, 'partakers of the Divine nature.' Verily, it is the most straight and perfect taking hold that is. No other union matches it.[25]

Hooker argues that 'wherefore taking to Himself our flesh, and by His incarnation making it his own flesh, he had now of his own although from us what to offer unto God for us'.[26] Andrewes, in turn, applies this to the sacraments:

> For look how we do give back that He gave us, even so doth He give back to us that which we gave Him, that which He had of us. This He gave for us in Sacrifice, and this He giveth us in the Sacrament, that the Sacrifice may by the Sacrament be truly applied to us.[27]

The constant point is about our being 'partakers of the Divine Nature' through the grace of the sacraments imparted to us. As he puts it in one of his Whitsunday sermons,

> If 'partakers of the Divine nature' we hope to be, as great and precious promises we have that we shall be, that can be no otherwise than by

receiving One in whom the Divine nature is. He being received imparts it to us, and so makes us *Consortes Divinae naturae*; and that is the Holy Ghost.[28]

At issue are the sacramental forms of our participation in the mysteries of God.

Sacramentum memoriae: the essential catholicism of classical Anglicanism

A subject on which the English reformers were greatly preoccupied was the doctrine of transubstantiation. While the argument changes over more than a hundred years, there is a remarkable consistency about the nature of a sacrament based upon a Chalcedonian understanding of the distinction of natures in the unity of the person of Christ.

Cranmer's Article XXVIII of the Thirty-Nine Articles states that

> Transubstantiation (or the change of the substance of Bread and Wine) in the Supper of the Lord, cannot be proved by holy Writ; but is repugnant to the plain words of Scripture, overthroweth the nature of a Sacrament, and hath given occasion to many superstitions.

The article emphasizes that 'the Body of Christ is given, taken, and eaten . . . only after an heavenly and spiritual manner'. This identifies a number of key features that remain constant: the integrity of natural substances, the lack of basis for transubstantiation in the Scriptures, and above all else a concern for the nature of the sacrament. The receiving of the sacrament 'after an heavenly and spiritual manner' becomes a common emphasis and relates to a consistent way of thinking about the real presence of Christ. The arguments are about the nature of the sacrament and the real presence.

Cranmer, writing mostly before the Council of Trent (1546–1564), is largely responding to the sacramental practices of the late medieval Church. On the one hand, his concern is about 'many superstitions'; on the other hand, it is about a fundamental reform in practice as well. At the risk of an oversimplification, there is a profound shift from Mass as spectator event to Mass as Communion. Cranmer and Calvin wanted (and largely failed) to achieve the practice of frequent Communion.

In the rubric of the Communion rite of 1549, Cranmer says,

> although it bee redde in aunciente writers, that the people many yeares past receiued at the priestes handes the Sacrament of the body of Christ in theyr own handes, and no commandment of Christ to the contrary: Yet forasmuche as they many tymes conueyghed the same secretelye awaye, kept it with them, and diuersly abused it to supersticion and wickednes:

139

lest any suche thynge hereafter should be attempted, and that an uniformitie might be used, throughout the whole Realme: it is thought conuenient the people commonly receiue the Sacrament of Christes body, in their mouthes, at the Priestes hande. (Book of Common Prayer, 1549)

It is a direction about receiving the sacrament to prevent an abuse of the sacrament. It becomes the basis for the infamous Black Rubric in the 1552 rite, which forbade the adoration of any 'real and essential presence of Christ's natural Flesh and Blood'. This rubric was removed in Elizabeth's 1559 rite but restored with one significant alteration in the 1662 Book of Common Prayer, when what was proscribed was the adoration of any 'corporeal' presence, a change suggesting that what the formularies had always opposed was a 'corporeal' presence, not what was understood by a 'real' presence.

Robert Crouse recognizes that Cranmer and subsequent English reformers were countering 'a superstitiously materialistic notion of the Presence, popularly associated in his time with a debased idea of transubstantiation'.[29] The questions were about sacrifice and about the presence of Christ in the sacrament.

Cranmer defends himself against the accusation that he denies the sacrifice of the Mass and that he denies 'that we receive in the sacrament that flesh which is adjoined to God's own Son'.[30] He says, 'the controversy is not, whether in the holy communion be made a sacrifice or not, . . . but whether it be a propitiatory sacrifice or not, and whether only the priest make the said sacrifice'.[31] About the eucharistic presence, Cranmer rightly protests that he has made the point a hundred times,

that we receive the self-same body of Christ that was born of the Virgin Mary, that was crucified and buried, that rose again, ascended into heaven, and sitteth at the right hand of God the Father Almighty: and the contention is only in the manner and form how we receive it.[32]

Cranmer states,

For I say (as all the old holy fathers and martyrs used to say), that we receive Christ spiritually by faith with our minds, eating his flesh and drinking his blood; so that we receive Christ's own very natural body, but not naturally nor corporally.[33]

Spiritually not corporally, not carnally. The sentence is characteristic of Cranmer's thinking and contributes to the sacramental theology of the English Church as expressed in the classical Prayer Book liturgies. We thank God after receiving Communion, 'that thou dost graciously feed us, in these holy mysteries, with the spiritual food of the most precious Body and Blood of thy Son our Saviour Jesus Christ', words present in both 1549 and 1552 along with other rich phrases such as 'our Sacrifice of prayse and thanks geuing' and of 'our selfes, our soules, and bodies, to be a reasonable, holy, and lively [living] sacrifice unto thee'.

For Cranmer, the only propitiatory sacrifice is Christ's sacrifice on the cross to which nothing can be added and nothing taken away. The question is about the form of our participation in his saving work sacramentally. As he puts it,

> We should understand the sacrament, not carnally, but spiritually, being like eagles in this life, we should fly up into heaven in our hearts, where that Lamb is resident at the right hand of his Father which taketh away the sins of the world . . . by whose passion we are filled at His table . . . being made the guests of Christ, having Him dwell in us through the grace of his true nature . . . assured and certified that we are fed spiritually unto eternal life by Christ's flesh crucified and by his blood shed.[34]

The passage conveys much of what belongs to Cranmer's eucharistic theology and contributes to the character of Anglican sacramental theology. Crouse argues that Cranmer inaugurated

> a distinctive tradition of sacramental theology, firmly grounded in the Scripture and the ancient Fathers, which remained remarkably consistent through the theology of the Elizabethan Settlement and the Caroline Divines, so as to constitute a defining characteristic of Classical Anglicanism.[35]

Cranmer's doctrinal approach, largely drawing on Chalcedon, becomes definitive for Anglican sacramental theology. As Crouse observes, it is by 'following the Christological paradigm', meaning the Western and Latin understanding of the Chalcedonian definition, that 'the Anglican conception of the nature of a sacrament is developed'.[36] He explains:

> Characteristic of that conception is the insistence that the natural element, the outward and visible sign, retains always its natural integrity, while it becomes the instrument of a supernatural presence; thus exemplifying the basic Augustinian and Thomistic theological principle, that grace does not destroy nature, but perfects it.[37]

Associated with the questions about real presence is the concept of locality, about the place of Christ's body. Here Cranmer largely follows Calvin rather than Luther in opposing the Lutheran concept of 'consubstantiation' and rejecting the idea of the ubiquity of Christ's body as inconsistent with the nature and properties of bodies. Thomas Aquinas also argues that 'Christ's body in the sacrament is in no way localized'[38] and that 'Christ is not in the sacrament as if he were in a place'.[39] Christ's real body is in heaven, 'at the right hand of God the Father Almighty', a creedal and scriptural teaching emphasized by many of the Fathers as well and reflected in Cranmer's image about being 'like eagles in this life' and 'flying up into heaven, where that Lamb is resident at the right hand of his Father'.[40]

This counters the carnal, corporeal and physical forms of late medieval piety and what Crouse rightly calls 'a debased idea of transubstantiation'.[41] By the sixteenth century, the various opinions of the schoolmen about the meaning and nature of transubstantiation had proliferated into a profusion and a confusion of contradictory positions. In terms of the Tridentine dogma about transubstantiation, there were many competing points of view and conflicting opinions. Bramhall would observe almost a century after Cranmer that it was 'as if Pandora's box had been newly set wide open, whole swarms of noisome questions and debates did fill the schools'.[42]

The question for Cranmer is about the nature of Christ's presence in the sacrament and the purpose of the sacrament. Thus, he argues for 'a sacramental mutation'[43] and 'a spiritual mutation in us',[44] which will be taken up by Hooker who argues for 'a transubstantiation in us'.[45] The point really is about the nature and the purpose of the sacraments. What are they and what are they for?

Sacraments, Hooker notes, have a mixed nature. They are, as Crouse puts it,

> a mixture or conjunction of the natural and the supernatural, the divine word and the natural element, of the finite and the infinite, of the outward sign and the inward grace. They are means or instruments of human participation in the divine life.[46]

Maintaining those distinctions becomes the primary concern for Cranmer and for Hooker, for Andrewes and for Bramhall, albeit in different registers of discourse.

Hooker provides the basic paradigm in terms of his reading of Chalcedon particularly by unpacking that mystery in terms of 'the gift of eternal generation, the gift of union and the gift of unction'.[47] The *tendency* in Hooker's teaching is *towards* the so-called extra-Calvinisticum (or extra-Catholicum), albeit cautiously and with reservations about what can and cannot be said on the controversial questions about the sacraments. He is arguing for one way of preserving the integrity of the natures of divine and human in the unity of person of Christ, a way that follows from a sense of the primacy of the divine transcendence and a refusal to collapse God into the categories of the finite, on the one hand, and to negate the fundamental qualities of finite humanity, such as locality, on the other hand. One might note the parallels in argument with the disputes about predestination. There is the same concern: not to overstate what can and cannot be known with respect to the interplay of human and divine, about what can and cannot be predicated of each, about not collapsing one into the other, and, in the case of the predestination debates, about reading temporal moments into the eternity of God in terms of the 'when' of the divine decrees about election.

Hooker and Andrewes uphold, first, the deity of Christ, second, the humanity of Christ, third, characteristics of Christ that belong to both divinity and humanity but not simply to one or another alone, and, fourth, the association of certain attributes of divinity with his humanity and certain attributes of humanity with his divinity; in short, a kind of interchange. This is about the different ways of understanding the *communicatio idiomatum*, the exchange of properties.[48] It is a kind of dialectical reasoning upon the creedal essentials of the faith.

Andrewes follows Hooker in this understanding with respect to the gift or grace of eternal generation. Such is the *Verbum Deus* which is 'too high for us', he says; instead, the *Verbum caro* is 'what concerns us', and, as often in Andrewes's sermons, the question is what benefit is derived from the mystery under consideration and what duties and obligations follow.[49] Thus Andrewes moves from the grace of the union of divine and human in Christ to the grace of unction. What flows from the union of the divine and human nature in Christ cannot, however, extinguish the fundamental characteristics of either nature. This is the necessary tension.

Hooker is emphatic about the grace of unction in Christ that 'supernatural endowments are an advancement, they are no extinguishment of that nature whereto they are given'.[50] With respect to the sacraments, the concern is how to understand our participation in Christ. The answer is through the nature of the sacraments themselves as 'visible and outward signs of an inward and spiritual grace'. They are, as Andrewes says, the 'conduit-pipes of His grace, and seals of His truth'[51] by which Christ may be with us and we with him. Grace does not destroy nature but perfects it. This could almost be the mantra for the essential catholicism of Anglicanism.

Negotiating the relation of the human nature to the divine person of Christ is critical. The later-named extra-Calvinisticum was already present in such late medieval figures as Gabriel Biel and anticipated by a number of Patristic writers concerned to uphold the essential attributes of an impassible deity. Hooker argues against the physical ubiquity of Christ's body because that would deny a fundamental characteristic of bodies, yet the conjunction of the divine and human 'after a sort' and what follows from that conjunction in terms of the grace of unction means that 'presence by way of conjunction is in some sort presence'.[52]

On that score, Andrewes sees the essential connection between resurrection and ascension and applies it to the sacrament as 'a badge of the one, a pledge of the other'.

For which cause, as it is called 'the living Bread,' so that it shall restore us to life and raise us up at the last day, so it is also, 'the Bread that came down from Heaven;' came down from thence, to make us go up thither, and in the strength of it to ascend into God's holy hill, and there rest with Him in his Tabernacle for ever.[53]

Such things belong to the determination of what is essential to the faith and to our participation in it. It reveals the constant conjunction of Word and sacrament.

That so the truth of the feast, and of the text both, may be fulfilled in us everlastingly with God (*Patrem vestrum*) our Father; and with Christ (*fratres Meos*) our Brother, and with the blessed Spirit, the love of them both one to the other, and of them both to us.[54]

Andrewes's reasoning follows the Chalcedonian paradigm.

And the gathering or vintage of these two in the blessed Eucharist, is as I may say a kind of hypostatical union of the sign and the thing signified, so united together as are the two natures in Christ. And even from this Sacramental union do the Fathers borrow their resemblance, to illustrate by it the personal union in Christ; I name, Theodoret for the Greeks, and Gelasius for the Latin Church, that insist upon it both, and press it against Eutyches. That even as in the Eucharist neither part is evacuate or turned into the other, but abide each still in his former nature and substance, no more is either of Christ's natures annulled, or one of them converted into the other, as Eutyches held, but each nature remaineth still full and whole in His own kind. And backwards; as the two natures in Christ, so the signum and signatum in the Sacrament, *e converso*.[55]

This is the basis of Andrewes's argument against transubstantiation: as if

the substance of the bread and wine to be flown away and gone, and in the room of it a remainder of nothing else but accidents to stay behind, was to them unknown, and had it been true, had made for Eutyches and against them.[56]

Bramhall in his *Answer to Milletiere* in 1653 states clearly the position of the English Church:

Not one of your arguments comes home to Transubstantiation, but only to a true Real Presence; which no genuine son of the Church of England did ever deny . . . Christ said, 'This is my Body;' what He said, we do steadfastly believe. He said not, after this or that manner, *neque con, neque sub, neque trans*. And therefore we place it among the opinions of the schools, not among the articles of our Faith. The Holy Eucharist, which is the Sacrament of peace and unity, ought not to be made the matter of strife and contention.[57]

He enquires into the history of transubstantiation to show that it is a later development, that it is not found in the Fathers, and that in the Schools there are a host of positions that are inconsistent with one another and, most importantly, with the Chalcedonian emphasis which is so critical to the English reformers. Bramhall largely draws upon Gabriel Vazquez (1549/51–1604), a Spanish Jesuit deeply steeped in the teachings of Aquinas but known for his concise descriptions of the different and differing schools of thought about transubstantiation. By way of Vazquez, Bramhall provides a kind of survey on the state of the question in its historical development to show that transubstantiation can only be a matter of opinion and not an article of faith, *necessitate medii*, necessary to be believed. His concern throughout is to uphold the fundamental nature of the sacrament as 'a visible and outward sign of an invisible and spiritual grace', and to counter any arguments that seem to compromise the integrity of the natural elements as the instruments of grace.

For the English reformers, the sacraments are not empty signs but effective signs which effect what they signify. Andrewes sums up the understanding of the English Church. Following Augustine's *haec sunt Ecclesiae gemina Sacramenta*, he notes that in baptism and Communion we have not two sacraments simply but the two twin-sacraments of the Church and, that 'with us', 'there are two rules' which capture the essential understanding of the sacraments. The first rule is '*Quicquid Sacrificio offertur, Sacramento confertur*' – what the sacrifice offers, the sacrament confers. The second rule is '*Quicquid Testamento legatur, Sacramento dispensatur*' – what the Testament bequeaths or legislates, the sacrament dispenses or provides.[58]

Word and sacrament are both instruments which have, as Hooker says, a 'generative force and virtue'[59]: the Scriptures are 'in the nature of a doctrinal instrument' of salvation[60]; 'The Sacraments are the powerful instruments of God to eternal life'[61]; 'Grace is the very end for which these heavenly mysteries were instituted'.[62] Word and sacrament go together as the essential forms of mystical participation in the life of God in Christ, the whole Christ. And this, Hooker and Andrewes argue, is to follow the Fathers in their reasoning upon the essentials.

> Christ is personally there present, yea present whole, albeit a part of Christ be corporeally absent from thence; that Christ assisting this heavenly banquet with his personal and true presence doth by his own divine power add to the natural substance thereof supernatural efficacy, which addition to the nature of those consecrated elements changeth them and maketh them that unto us which otherwise they could not be; that to us they are thereby made such instruments as mystically yet truly, invisibly yet really work our communion or fellowship with the person of Jesus Christ as well in that he is man as God.[63]

Communion is about our mystical participation in Christ including 'in the fruit, grace and efficacy of his body and blood, whereupon there ensueth a kind of transubstantiation in us, a true change both of soul and body, an alteration from death to life'.[64]

In the Holy Eucharist, Andrewes says, 'we do not gather to Christ or of Christ but Christ himself'.[65] Synaxis, he notes, is one of the ancient terms for the Holy Eucharist. Critical to that gathering is the integrity of the natures of God and man and the integrity of the sacrament which has both a heavenly and an earthly part.

> For as there is a recapitulation of all in Heaven and earth in Christ, so there is a recapitulation of all in Christ in the holy Sacrament. You may see it clearly: there is in Christ the Word eternal for things in Heaven; there is also flesh for things on earth. Semblably, the Sacrament consisteth of a Heavenly and of a terrene part.[66]

Such is the harmony of intellect and sensibility in Andrewes, the constant balance and interplay of Word and sacrament. The constant recalling of Christ in his sacrifice and the perpetual remembering of our participation in his sacrifice is the *sacramentum memoriae* which belongs to the essential catholicism of the English Church. 'Holy Communion', Andrewes says, 'is the blessed union, the highest perfection we can in this life aspire unto'. *Sacramentum memoriae* is about our being 'gathered to Christ, and by Christ to God'.[67]

> Find the gathering, you shall find fulness; find Christ, and you shall find the gathering, for the gathering is full and whole in Christ.[68]

Notes

1 This is one of two chapters in this collection which supplement the papers given at the 2018 *Totus Christus* conference.

2 T. S. Eliot, *For Lancelot Andrewes: Essays on Style and Order* (London: Faber & Faber, 1971). Though published in 1928, a version of the essay 'Lancelot Andrewes' first appeared in the *Times Literary Supplement* on 23 September 1926.

3 Eliot, *For Lancelot Andrewes*, p. 7.

4 Eliot, *For Lancelot Andrewes*, p. 16.

5 T. S. Eliot, review of *Metaphysical Lyrics and Poems of the Seventeenth Century: Donne to Butler*. Selected and edited, with an Essay, by Herbert J. C. Grierson (Oxford: Clarendon Press. London; Milford) in the *Times Literary Supplement*, October 1921.

6 Eliot, *For Lancelot Andrewes*, p. 14.

7 Eliot, *For Lancelot Andrewes*, p. 38.

8 Eliot, *For Lancelot Andrewes*, p. 14.

9 David Curry, *The Recovery of Reformed Catholicism*, Machray Review, Number 3 (Toronto, Prayer Book Society of Canada, 1993). An address given at Nashotah House, Wisconsin, upon the occasion of its 150th anniversary.

10 John Bramhall, *A Replication*, II in *Works*, ed. by A. W. H., 5 vols, Library of Anglo-Catholic Theology (Oxford: J. Parker and Co., 1842–45), p. 279.

11 Robert D. Crouse, *The Biblical and Patristic Foundations of Anglican Sacramentalism as Understood by the English Reformers*, Mere Anglicanism Conference, Charleston, SC, 1 February 2008.

12 Nicholas Lossky, *Lancelot Andrewes. The Preacher (1555–1626), The Origins of the Mystical Theology of The Church of England*, trans. by Andrew Louth (Oxford: Clarendon Press, 1991).

13 Bramhall, *A Replication*, II, p. 279.

14 Lancelot Andrewes, *Sermon III*, Vol. I in *Works*, ed. by J. P. Wilson, James Bliss, 11 vols, Library of Anglo-Catholic Theology (Oxford: J. Parker and Co., 1841–54), p. 35.

15 Lancelot Andrewes, 'Concio Latine Habita, In Discessu Palatini' (*Opuscula Posthuma*) in *Works*, IX, p. 91. As Jean-Louis Quantin reminds us, this was in a sermon preached before King James and the Elector Palatine, Frederick V, 'the chief champion of Calvinism in Germany'. Jean-Louis Quantin, *The Church of England and Christian Antiquity: The Construction of a Confessional Identity in the Seventeenth Century* (Oxford: Oxford University Press, 2009), p. 155.

16 Bramhall, *Schism Guarded*, in *Works* II, p. 630.

17 Bramhall, *Schism Guarded*, in *Works* II, p. 597.

18 Bramhall, *A Reply to S.W.'s Refutation*, in *Works* II, p. 288.

19 Richard Hooker, *Lawes of Ecclesiastical Polity*, Bk. V, ch. Liv in *The Works of Richard Hooker*, ed. by John Keble (Oxford, 1841), p. 237.

20 Hooker, *Works* V, ch. Liv, p. 237–8.

21 Hooker, *Works* V, ch. Liv, p. 238.

22 Andrewes, *Sermon VI*, in *Works* I, p. 90.

23 Andrewes, *Sermon VI*, in *Works* I, p. 91.

24 Andrewes, *Sermon III*, in *Works* I, p. 43.

25 Andrewes, *Sermon I*, in *Works* I, p. 16.

26 Hooker, *Works* V, ch. Li, p. 222.

27 Andrewes, *Sermon II*, in *Works* I, pp. 30–1.

28 Andrewes, *Sermon V*, in *Works* III, p. 190.

29 Crouse, *The Biblical and Patristic Foundations*, p. 2.

30 Thomas Cranmer, *Writings and Disputations of Thomas Cranmer . . . Relative to the Sacrament of the Lord's Supper* (Cambridge: Parker Society, 1844), p. 365.

31 Cranmer, *Writings*, p. 369.

32 Cranmer, *Writings*, p. 370.

33 Cranmer, *Writings*, p. 284.

34 Cranmer, *Writings*, p. 398.

35 Crouse, *The Biblical and Patristic Foundations*, p. 3.

36 Crouse, *The Biblical and Patristic Foundations*, p. 6.

37 Crouse, *The Biblical and Patristic Foundations*, p. 6.

38 Thomas Aquinas, *Summa Theologiae*, 3a, 76, 5.

39 Aquinas, *Summa Theologiae*, 3a, 76, 6.

40 Cranmer, *Writings*, p. 398.

41 Crouse, *The Biblical and Patristic Foundations*, p. 2.

42 Bramhall, *Answer to Milletiere*, in *Works* I, p. 14.

43 Cranmer, *Writings*, p. 269.

44 Cranmer, *Writings*, p. 276.

45 Hooker, *Works* V, ch. Lvii.11, p. 358.

46 Crouse, *The Biblical and Patristic Foundations*, p. 1.

47 Hooker, *Works* V, ch. Liv.2, p. 232.

48 Joseph N. Tylenda, 'Calvin's Understanding of the Communication of Properties', in *An Elaboration of the Theology of Calvin*, vol. 8 of Articles on Calvin & Calvinism: A Fourteen Volume Anthology of Scholarly Articles, ed. by Nicholas C. Gamble (New York and London, Garland Publishing, 1992), p. 151. See also Joseph N. Tylenda's analysis of Calvin's *communicatio idiomatum* in Theodore Zachariades, *The Omnipresence of Jesus Christ: A Neglected Aspect of Evangelical Christology* (Milton Keynes: Paternoster, 2015), ch. 6.

49 Andrewes, *Sermon VI*, in *Works* I, p. 86.

50 Hooker, *Works* V, ch. Lv.6, p. 241.

51 Andrewes, *Sermon VI*, in *Works* I, p. 100.

52 Hooker, *Works* V, ch. Lv, p. 8.

53 Andrewes, *Sermon XVI*, in *Works* III, p. 58.

54 Andrewes, *Sermon XVI*, in *Works* III, p. 58.

55 Andrewes, *Sermon XVI*, in *Works* 1, p. 281.

56 Andrewes, *Sermon XVI*, in *Works* 1, p. 282.

57 Bramhall, *Answer*, in *Works* I, p. 8.

58 Andrewes, *Sermon XVIII*, in *Works* III, p. 102.

59 Hooker, *Works* V, ch. L.1, p. 219.

60 Hooker, *Works* V, Vol.II, p. 85.

61 Hooker, *Works* V, ch. L.1, p. 220.

62 Hooker, *Works* V, L.1, p. 220.

63 Hooker, *Works* V, ch. Lxvii.11, p. 357–8.

64 Hooker, *Works* V, ch. Lxvii, 11, p. 358.

65 Andrewes, *Sermon XVI*, in *Works* I, p. 280.

66 Andrewes, *Sermon XVI*, in *Works* I, p. 281.

67 Andrewes, *Sermon XVI*, in *Works* I, p. 283.

68 Andrewes, *Sermon XVI*, in *Works* I, p. 267.

The Christology of the French School

ROBIN WARD

O Jesus living in Mary:
Come and live in Thy servants,
In the spirit of Thy holiness,
In the fullness of Thy power,
In the perfection of Thy ways,
In the truth of Thy virtues,
In the fellowship of Thy mysteries,
Rule Thou over every adverse power,
In Thy Spirit, for the glory of the Father.

This prayer, the authorship of which is uncertain but which is usually associated with Jean-Jacques Olier, founder of the Sulpicians and one of the three principal inspirers of what is known as the French School of spirituality, exemplifies the particular and distinctive Christology that this chapter intends to consider. The prayer is evidently the product of a fulsome baroque piety, but one that crops up subsequently in some unexpected places: Gerard Manley Hopkins renders it in a version beginning 'Jesu that dost in Mary dwell . . .'; and rather more surprisingly it turns up in the decent obscurity of a dead language in that exemplary text of moderate Tractarian devotion, *The Cuddesdon Office Book*.[1] But the first line raises hackles still. I once put the prayer into a confirmation booklet when I was a parish priest: the bishop's chaplain asked me to change it, so I sent it back suggesting *O Jesus not living in Mary*, and heard no more. I think it works its way back into the Anglican patrimony through H. P. Liddon, E. B. Pusey's disciple and a student of the spirit of the revival of seminary life in France when he was Vice Principal of Cuddesdon in the 1850s.

What was the French School? Well, to begin with, it is perhaps easiest to say it had little to do with St Francis de Sales, who for the purposes of the history of spirituality is essentially an Italian who happens to speak French, and who is much closer to the mind and method of Lorenzo Scupoli than any of the theologians I intend to consider. And although the principal exponents of the School are closely associated with St Vincent de Paul and his disciples, this is more a matter of ecclesiastical zeal than intellectual co-working. Three figures dominate the foreground: Pierre de Bérulle (1575–1629), founder of the French Oratory and cardinal, the most prolific author of the School; Charles de Condren (1588–1641), Bérulle's successor as superior of the Oratory congregation, the mystic of the School whose spiritual legacy is preserved in Amelot's biography; and Jean-Jacques Olier (1608–1657), whose extraordinary ministry as parish priest of St Sulpice in Paris and his founding of the Sulpician congregation exemplified the teaching of the School about the importance of the mission and dignity of the priesthood. All three are somewhat complex characters: none has been canonized, and with the exception of the relatively mute Condren, they were diffuse, unsystematic authors who wrote in the interstices of demanding apostolic and political endeavours, very often at the cost of lucidity and clarity.

Why bother with them then? Well, their teaching has the sort of 'chronic vigour' that has proved itself able to refresh the Church in times other than their own: among Anglicans, Liddon's interest in England is followed by H. Sidney Lear's study *Priestly Life in France* written in 1903, and by M. V. Woodgate (the biographer of Father Benson) who wrote on Charles de Condren in 1949. There is also an immense biography of Jean-Jacques Olier by Edward Healy Thompson, published in 1861. More recently, the English translation of Henri Huvelin's wonderful series of catechetical lectures on the period, *Some Spiritual Guides of the 17th Century*, published in 1927, coupled with the reception of Brémond's vast *A Literary History of Religious Thought in France* of 1928 and Pourrat's *Christian Spirituality*, translated and published by the SPCK, made the thought of Bérulle, Condren and Olier accessible to a wide readership. Huvelin's lectures are remarkably acute, not least because he and Olier suffered from similar psychosomatic disorders: his description of M. Bourdoise's seminary at St Nicholas-du-Chardonnet – 'I should not have liked to attend his seminary, but I would have liked to live opposite it, for the beauty of the services in the church'[2] – is an appealing insight. And, in more recent years, French scholars have given a huge amount of attention to the work of the French School, in synthetic studies such as Krumenacker's *L'école française de spiritualité* and the identically named work by Raymond Deville, and in the immense labours of Michel Dupuy and others to bring almost to completion a critical edition of the complete works of Bérulle in 14 volumes.

Out of what setting did the French School work, and why did that work find as a consequence an enduring value? The French Church after the Wars of Religion in the latter part of the sixteenth century was in a bad way. The clerical state was entered largely as a means of acquiring an income, the episcopate was almost exclusively manipulated as a means of exercising royal patronage, and the ravages of war and the remaining powerful Huguenot presence had brought Catholic life at a parochial level to a squalid state. When Jean-Jacques Olier, having turned down the reversion of one of the peerage sees of France to become parish priest of St Sulpice in Paris (much to the fury of his mother), arrived in his new charge, he found a scene of massive urban poverty, virtually no religious practice, the church used partly as a nightclub, a sinister undercurrent of active Satanism, clerical colleagues who wore the seventeenth-century equivalent of combat fatigues all day, and churchwardens who argued with him about having Benediction. But it is Bérulle in particular who laid down the lines of reform and renewal: first, the renewal of the spiritual life, to be achieved working with Madame Acarie to introduce the Carmelite Reform into France, work begun in 1602 and resulting in some 40 houses by the time of his death; second, the revival of priestly life, through the foundation of the congregation of the Oratory in 1613, in which priests lived a common life without religious vows; third, the revival of political Catholicism in opposition to the policy of Richelieu, the failure of which precipitated Bérulle's fall from influence with Louis XIII in 1629, and his death saying Mass some two weeks later, as he pronounced the words of the Roman Canon, *Hanc igitur oblationem servitutis nostrae*.

Bérulle had the classic late scholastic theological training proper to a Doctor of the Sorbonne who had been taught by Jesuits and who was in his early years very close to the Order. But his writings, although they clearly demonstrate a fluent command of this sort of learning, are emphatically closer to the sort of vernacular discursive, even ecstatic, meditations which are characteristic of the most effective of Counter-Reformation ascetic and mystical theology. His most acute critic, Jean Dagens, in the first portion of what proved to be an abortive attempt at a comprehensive study of Bérulle's theology,[3] identifies a rich hinterland of influences and themes: a reverence for Augustine as both theological and literary master; a mysticism that carries forward the apophaticism of the Rhineland mystics; a sympathy with the Christian Platonism of Pico della Mirandola; a sympathy with the work of the English Capuchin Benet of Canfield – rediscovered by Aldous Huxley[4] – in reintegrating to the mystical life a devotion to the humanity of Christ in his Passion. But Dagens is clear too that Bérulle's work is distinctive not for its synthetic quality but for its originality: the Copernican Revolution in the spiritual life as Brémond calls it, which apparently led to Pope Urban VIII declaring him to be 'the Apostle of the Incarnate Word', hardly an epithet that suggests only an incremental contribution to theological science.

What did Bérulle write to justify this? There are just two long works: the seminal *Discours de l'état et des grandeurs de Jésus*, and the shorter *Vie de Jésus*, both works of his maturity published in the 1620s. To these may be added a rich collection of *Opuscules de Pieté*, assembled in 1644 by his disciples after his death, a series of *Élevations*, including a celebrated one on St Mary Magdalen dedicated to Queen Henrietta Maria of England, whose marriage to Charles I he had negotiated and whom he had accompanied to England in 1625. Those expecting an anticipation in Bérulle of the sort of French 'Life of Jesus' that culminated in Renan will be disappointed: the work, consisting of 140 pages in the critical *Oeuvres Complètes*, stops at the Nativity. This rather startling fact gives us the clue to Bérulle's force and importance: he is the affective theologian of the doctrine of the mysteries of

Christ's incarnate life, a doctrine which finds its classical enunciation in the Latin theological tradition in the *Tertia Pars* of the *Summa Theologica* of St Thomas Aquinas, and which is carried over into the Anglican theological patrimony by Richard Hooker, who in the Fifth Book of the *Ecclesiastical Polity* writes concerning the Incarnation that,

> For his body being a part of that nature which whole nature is presently joined unto Deity wheresoever Deity is, it followeth that his bodily substance hath everywhere a presence of true conjunction with Deity. And forasmuch as it is by virtue of that conjunction made the body of the Son of God, by whom also it was made a sacrifice for the sins of the whole world, this giveth it a presence of force and efficacy throughout all generations of men.[5]

Bérulle puts it thus: the mysteries of the life of the incarnate Christ

> are past with regard to execution, but present with regard to their virtue, and their virtue will never pass away, nor will the love ever pass away by which they were accomplished. The spirit, then, the state, the virtue, the merit of the mystery is ever present . . . This obliges us to treat the things and mystery of Jesus not as past and extinguished, but as living and present, and even eternal, the source from which we can reap a fruit that is present and eternal.[6]

Miklos Vetö, in his outstanding study of Bérulle's theology *La Christo-Logique de Bérulle*, printed as an introduction to the selection from the *Opuscules* published apart from the projected complete critical edition in 1997, identifies as the key theological characteristic of his Christology the role of the incarnate Christ as the perfect adorer of the Father. From this everything else follows: the *religious* character of Christ's work; the perennial efficacy of the various states of his incarnate life; the theological significance of the divine infancy as an exemplary state of abasement, what the French School theologians call *anéantissement*; the importance of the Blessed Virgin as the 'first altar' on which divine praise is paid; the continuation of this immolation in the Eucharist and by the priesthood; the moral consequences of Christ made flesh and sin for our own moral life, and in particular the controversial and distinctively Bérullian emphasis on the vow of servitude as giving effect to the teaching of St Paul in Galatians 2.20, 'I have been crucified with Christ; it is no longer I who live, but Christ who lives in me; and the life I now live in the flesh I live by faith in the Son of God, who loved me and gave himself for me'. The vow of servitude, the most controversial aspect of Bérulle's teaching during his own time and subsequently, has recently benefitted from an astute study by Erik Varden, published as *Redeeming Freedom*, in which the fundamental importance in the Christian moral life of exchanging the yoke of the old Adam for the yoke of Christ is set out both in terms of Bérulle's spiritual teaching and his work for church reform.

Bérulle is clear that in our fallen state the Incarnation is for our redemption, and that the particular self-emptying of the Son of God in order to be made sin is the definitive way in which his life becomes our own. But in various places he also makes clear that the Incarnation is the exemplary way in which the created order gives honour to its Creator by imitating the mysterious relations that constitute the inner life of the divine Trinity, and that the Incarnation follows from the logic of the creation, although in an unfallen world Christ would have come not as redeemer but as *glorificateur*, the one who gives glory.

As Bérulle writes in the seventh *Discours*, 'By the Incarnation, the Son of God wished to make a reflection of himself, that is on his unique and intimate operation in Eternity.' This accomplished, God who is adorable from all eternity in due time receives the homage of a perfect adorer, one who in himself as incarnate Word of God gives to the Church a perfect offering at the altar and in the Christian cult. We see here a theme that connects intriguingly with subsequent Anglican Christology, especially the work of those associated with the *Lux Mundi* school. Bérulle by no means anticipates the psychological anxieties about the personal self-awareness of Christ that preoccupied the Anglican kenoticists, but he does come close to them in his emphasis on the self-offering of Christ in expiatory adoration from the first moment of the Incarnation, and the way in which the oblation of the Son of God is a characteristic mystery of his entire incarnate life. This emphasis has unsatisfactory consequences in the eucharistic theologies of Charles Gore and Maurice de la Taille, in which offering occludes immolation. It is also distorted in the work of some of Bérulle's followers, most notably Condren, who goes so far as to describe Christ as being in heaven in a state of death. But the fundamental point remains sound, in relating the Incarnation to the homage of creation to its maker through the oblation of the Son.

When we turn to key Bérullian texts, we are immediately confronted with shortcomings that Varden expresses very frankly in the introduction to his survey:

> Bérulle's often indigestible prose, his ponderousness and impermeability to humour . . . can make for heavy going. There are occasional passages of great beauty, especially in his last works, when a new spontaneity is in evidence. But an expanse of desert sand lies between watering holes.[7]

Of course, this is not a fundamental handicap for a theologian, and given the unreadability of the vast bulk of early modern university theology, we should perhaps recall that Bérulle's works have at least been thought worthy of a modern critical edition, something more mellifluous writers of his age such as Jeremy Taylor have been denied. The first printing of the

Discours contained only six texts, to which a further six and then the *Life of Jesus* were added in the course of the 1620s as the controversy about the vow of servitude intensified. Briefly put, Bérulle as superior of the Carmelite houses in France had introduced formal vows of servitude to Jesus and to Mary as fundamental parts of the formation of the nuns, and opponents both within and without the Order criticized this as a novelty and as alien to the Carmelite spirit, which through translations from the Spanish of Teresa of Avila and John of the Cross was becoming better known at first hand in France. The 12 *Discours* are therefore written out of a political setting of some bitterness, in which Bérulle is constrained to defend the key theme of his spiritual system for the French Oratory and the French Carmelites.

The polemical context of the publication of the *Discours* shapes in particular the earlier texts, and is exemplified in the remarkable second *Discours*, in which Bérulle – writing of course at the time that the Galileo controversy was coming to its bitter climax in Rome – embraces a theological Copernicanism, with Christ as the Sun whose worship is anticipated by the cult of the Egyptians. This second *Discours* contains the heart of Bérullism: Christ who is sun of justice and centre of the universe, around which the worlds revolve, submits to an *anéantissement* of his glory, which is a more fundamental mastering than that of the initial act of creation out of nothing itself. Consequently, the response of the redeemed sinner to this act of self-obliteration on the part of the Word made flesh is a corresponding deliberate and chosen vow of servitude, in which the old Adam is renounced by a formal *désappropriation*, and in its place the divinized humanity of the Word is adopted by an act of *appartenance*. By making this act, the one who makes it is incorporated into the work of the 'perfect adorer', the Word made flesh whose human nature is now glorified in heaven. Here it is worth recalling also the hierarchical preferences that are so apparent in Bérulle's theology, and which Paul Cochois identified with a strong pseudo-Dionysian influence: the hierarchical ascent of adoration that the Incarnation makes possible, and which is continued visibly in the cult of the Church and in particular in the Eucharist offered by the ministerial hierarchy, is prominent as an inspiration in all the principal proponents of the French School, in their writings and in their reform agenda. This is clearly evident in the way that Bérulle concludes the second *Discours*: 'You are, sacred humanity, the sacred Temple of Divinity . . . a Temple in which the Divinity abides with more holiness, more dignity and more admirably even than in the order and state of glory.'[8]

Bérulle connects this adoration explicitly to the Eucharist in the sixth *Discours*, in which the Christian religion is explained under the heading of three distinct mysteries: that of the Trinity, which properly honours the Father as being according to Dionysius the *fontal deity*; the Incarnation, in which the Son is honoured as subsistent in human nature as redeemer; and the Eucharist, in which the Holy Spirit is invoked in the spirit of religion to transform the eucharistic elements. As to the Eucharist itself, it is to us 'the return of a sacred deposit, which having been taken from us and given a new dignity in itself, is returned to us with interest'[9] as a communication making for eternal life. The latter portion of the *Discours* reveals Bérulle's anxiety to address particular criticisms of the vows of servitude, and there is a certain degree of repetition and a much more diffuse sense of argumentation. But the final three *Discours* return to a much more systematic treatment of his Christology, a treatment which is based around the three-fold begetting of the Word: in the bosom of the Father; in the womb of the Virgin; and in the glory of the resurrection.

The eternal begetting of the Son in the bosom of the Father gives rise to some curious Patristic speculation from Bérulle: following Clement of Alexandria, he uses the term 'matri-pater'[10] to illustrate how although the eternal begetting of the Son is without a mother, nevertheless it is not without a womb, which is the Father's bosom. This divine paternity that gives birth is itself honoured by the Church, which begets and gives birth herself to her children in baptism. The begetting of the Word in the womb of the Virgin – the first altar from which the Father receives acceptable praise – is the foundation of Bérulle's intense and distinctive Marianism, which finds its particular expression in the *Vie de Jesus*, confined as it is to the nine months spent by the 'Redeemer in the womb', the title of John Saward's short book on the subject.[11] It is indeed 'Jesus living in Mary' that informs both the doctrinal and the devotional expression of Bérullian Christology, both in his own most finished works and in the practice of his disciples, most notably Condren and Olier.

The incarnational character of this Christology is perhaps most emphatically expressed in the conclusion of the *Discours*, where the Passion and Cross of the Saviour himself are presented in terms of a third Nativity – a Nativity into glory. Bérulle's account of the redemption sees the death of the Son as a sort of Sabbath rest, in which the human nature taken by the Word becomes for us an 'Ark of the Covenant', into which is poured the plenitude of divinity. The key scriptural text here is Colossians 2.9: for Bérulle, it is the fullness of the Godhead that dwells in the glorified humanity of the Word, a fullness which is the third and culminating Nativity of the Son, and which we follow, in the remarkable comparison he makes between the redeemed and those who follow on as captives in the triumphant procession of the victor. But the key theme here is that of successive births: begotten of the Father, a divine birth in which the Word has sovereignty as God; a human birth, human among humans but sovereign even in the womb; a birth into glory, by which the plenitude of divinity and the fullness of sovereignty are given in the session of the risen Christ at the right hand of the Father. Bérulle, a child of his time and place, anticipates the cult of the Sun King in calling Christ 'sun of the empyrean heaven'.[12]

The cult of the Sun King, the vow of servitude, the exaltation of the priesthood and the eucharistic cult, pious devotion to the childhood of Christ, and indeed the Redeemer in the womb, all this might well seem impossibly remote, hierarchical and hieratic for the Church and for a work-able Christology in our own age. And as we read the ponderous baroque circumlocutions of Bérulle, we can see something of the spirit at work that subsequently produced the whole lush subculture of French Catholic *bon-dieuserie*: the seminary priest – the third sex – formed in the sort of hothouse piety that Zola captures scathingly in *La Faute de l'abbé Mouret*; the cultus of the hearts of Jesus and Mary, begun by Bérulle's younger con-temporary St John Eudes; Jesus, the prisoner in the tabernacle, in which the eucharistic presence is conceived as an ongoing annihilation of the glory of the Son of God. In fact, we can find in Bérulle much of the dis-tinctive ethos of pre-Vatican II European Roman Catholic devotional life that, at the University of Oxford, was consigned to the dust heap in that magisterial work of respectable Anglo-Catholic one-upmanship, Leighton Pullan's Bampton Lectures *Religion since the Reformation*. Even where the Christology of the French School appears to escape the sacristy for a moment, in the 'heavenly offering' school of eucharistic thought sponsored principally by Maurice de la Taille, the Thomists fight back with panache: Anscar Vonier devotes much of *A Key to the Doctrine of the Eucharist* to demolishing what Dom John Chapman in his Letters calls at one point 'bad French' eucharistic theology.

What can we reclaim from all this? First, I think the theme of Jesus Christ as perfect adorer of the Father, which is perhaps the most funda-mental insight of the French School as Bérulle and his followers expound it, remains important, both for Christology in its strict sense and in the moral theology that follows from it. The Redemptorist moral theologian Bernard Häring developed, in response to the evident collapse of superficial Christian piety in Germany in the 1930s, a new understanding of the lived moral life that places a particular emphasis on the virtue of religion as the coordinating principle of our growth in virtue, a theme that receives simi-lar attention in the liturgical morality of the Orthodox theologian Christos Yannaras. Religion, the cult owed to and given to God by Christ as perfect adorer, preserves the preference of contemporary moral theology to begin from the person rather than from acts in themselves, but does justice to both parts of the Pauline injunction, 'For Christ is the end of the Law' (Rom. 10.4). Similarly, in an environment in which liturgical worship is reduced to an ever more unattractive pedagogic and didactic grind, restoration of adoration as the end of cult is a fundamental driver of reform and renewal. Second, although with the exception of John Saward few contemporary theologians have been drawn to the Bérullian cult of Christ in the womb, his sense of the servitude of Christ to the most abject deprivations of our nature, and in turn our own need to follow that servitude if we are to find freedom in the new Adam from the old, offers both a rich solidarity for the dispossessed and powerless with the work of the Redeemer, and a powerful coming to terms with the existential crisis of our being thrown into living – and so into dying – without power to help ourselves: 'Take my yoke upon you, and learn of me; for I am meek and lowly in heart: and ye shall find rest unto your souls. For my yoke is easy, and my burden is light' (Matt. 11.29).

Notes

1 Cuddesdon College, *The Cuddesdon College Office Book*, new edn (London: Oxford University Press, 1961), p. 170.

2 Henri Huvelin, *Cours sur L'Histoire de L'Église Tome 10: Le Renouveau de la Vie Spirituelle au XVIIe Siècle* (Paris: Editions Saint-Paul, 1969), p. 237.

3 Jean Dagens, *Bérulle Et Les Origines De La Restauration Catholique (1575–1611)* (Paris: Desclée De Brouwer, 1952).

4 Aldous Huxley, *Grey Eminence: A Study in Religion and Politics* (London: Triad/Granada, 1982).

5 Richard Hooker, *Ecclesiastical Polity*, Book V (London: J. M. Dent & Sons Ltd, 1907), pp. 224–5.

6 Pierre de Bérulle and Miklós Vetö, *Opuscules De Piété* (Grenoble: J. Millon, 1997), p. 241.

7 Erik Varden, *Redeeming Freedom: The Principle of Servitude in Bérulle* (Rome: Studia Anselmiana, 2011), p. 9.

8 Pierre de Bérulle et al., *Œuvres Complètes. Oratoire De Jésus* (Lyon: Editions Du Cerf, 1995) vol. 7, p. 129.

9 De Bérulle et al., *Œuvres Complètes. Oratoire De Jésus*, p. 226.

10 De Bérulle et al., *Œuvres Complètes. Oratoire De Jésus*, p. 376.

11 John Saward, *Redeemer in the Womb: Jesus Living in Mary* (San Francisco: Ignatius Press, 1993).

12 Saward, *Redeemer in the Womb*, p. 476.

PART 4

Christ the Universal Paradigm and the Local Habitation

Ascension Day[1]

We saw his light break through the cloud of glory
Whilst we were rooted still in time and place,
As earth became a part of heaven's story
And heaven opened to his human face.
We saw him go and yet we were not parted,
He took us with him to the heart of things,
The heart that broke for all the broken-hearted
Is whole and heaven-centered now, and sings;
Sings in the strength that rises out of weakness,
Sings through the clouds that veil him from our sight,
Whilst we ourselves become his clouds of witness
And sing the waning darkness into light;
His light in us, and ours in him concealed,
Which all creation waits to see revealed.

1 Originally published in Malcolm Guite, *Sounding the Seasons* (Norwich: Canterbury Press, 2012).

12

What is Christ's Humanity?
Some Nineteenth-century Answers
and their Patristic Roots

JOHANNES ZACHHUBER

Introduction

A contribution on nineteenth-century German theology to a volume dedicated to the *totus Christus* may seem problematic from the outset. Often,
this theological epoch is thought to have accomplished very nearly the
opposite – not representing the 'whole' Christ, but a partial Christ, a Christ
stripped of his divinity and reduced to a merely human figure, the so-called
historical Jesus. No less a person than E. B. Pusey himself led the charge
as suggested by the following recollection of his 1825 visit to Göttingen,
which was recounted by his biographer as follows:

> Here also Pusey used to attend the Lutheran church, and he often would
> describe one of his experiences at its services. The preacher of the day
> was a Rationalist, and was engaged in showing – but in language which
> the educated only would understand – the general untenableness of some
> portion of the Gospel history. In doing this he had occasion, of course,
> constantly to mention the Holy Name of Jesus. The church was full of
> country-people or simple townsfolk, and each time our Lord's Name
> was mentioned they bowed their heads reverently; 'evidently making
> each mention of our Saviour the occasion of an act of devotion to Him.'
> Of the drift of the sermon to which they were listening they had no
> idea; to them it was edifying on account of the frequent mention of our
> Saviour's Name. Pusey would frequently refer to this when insisting that
> God overrules human error so completely as, at times, to make the teach-
> ers of error the unintentional servants and friends of truths.[1]

If in my chapter I shall sound a somewhat dissenting note to this established
assessment of theological historiography,[2] my intention is not to deny that
the historicizing tendencies of nineteenth-century German Christology *could*
lead to an inadequately reductionist picture of Jesus Christ. Rather than
reiterate this well-worn criticism, however, I will focus on the considerable

theological potential in this approach which, I will argue, is by no means as detached from the kind of Christological reflection that has emerged since the Patristic period as is sometimes alleged. Perhaps no Christology will ever represent the 'whole Christ'; what I hope to show is how an approach to Christology through history, as it was practised by some of the most distinguished nineteenth-century theologians, can contribute an important dimension to our own understanding of the Saviour today.

The first thing to note is the absolute centrality of Christology within a whole strand of nineteenth-century German theology.[3] This centrality is as evident in Schleiermacher's *Christian Faith*[4] as it is in Isaak August Dorner, whose history of the Christological dogma is arguably one of the most remarkable scholarly products of the entire century and, in a way, unrivalled even in our own time.[5] Yet Christology was equally important for Dorner's great rival, F. C. Baur and his Tübingen school, including not least the notorious D. F. Strauß.[6] It may not be possible to identify one, single factor that could exclusively explain this theological preference for the doctrine of the Incarnation.[7]

A major influence, certainly, was the philosophical interest in the Incarnation that came to the fore in the various facets of the philosophy of German idealism.[8] What is fascinating to observe here is the intimate link between the acceptance of history as an intellectual paradigm, a historical interpretation of Christianity and a speculative, philosophical interest in Christology as a bridge between the two. This connection is fully in evidence in F. W. J. Schelling's influential lectures *On Academic Study*.[9] These lectures were part of a popular genre in German intellectual life of the time, initiated by Kant's *Conflict of the Faculties*, but perpetuated in the early nineteenth century with a particular interest in university reform, which was an urgent task at the time.[10] Like his peers, then, Schelling addressed the traditional faculties seeking to inscribe them into an overall, philosophical framework. One of his arguments for the retention of theology, which other reformers were keen to expunge,[11] was its intimate relationship with history:

> This is the great historical tendency of Christianity; this is the reason that the science of religion, in Christianity, is inseparable from history – is, indeed, one and the same with it. This synthesis with history, without which theology itself cannot even be conceived, presupposes, on the other hand, the higher Christian view of history.[12]

This statement deserves careful attention. At first sight, one could detect here the kind of reductionist view of Christianity Pusey was so concerned about. Schelling, after all, calls for a purely historical interpretation of the religion. And yet, he only does so because, and insofar as, he believes that the way we understand history is itself fundamentally affected by Christianity. The two, he seems to say, mutually interpret each other – the purely historical interpretation of Christianity depends on a 'higher' view of history, which itself is only enabled by the Christian tradition.

It becomes clear in what follows that the conceptual foundation holding these two ideas together is Christology.[13] For Schelling, this doctrine expresses and embodies the idea of an ultimate coming together of God and world, the infinite and the finite in a way that preserves both and does justice to both. This, obviously, is a 'philosophical Christology', not a theological one; Schelling appropriates Christian ideas without committing to their doctrinal truth claims. All the more remarkable is that his interpretation of the person of Jesus Christ fastens on the concept of Incarnation – unlike most eighteenth-century and twentieth-century liberal attempts, which usually appropriated Christology on the basis of Christ as a moral exemplar.[14]

Let us now look at the other aspect of Schelling's claim: What is the 'higher Christian view of history'? What is this novel understanding of history and why does it matter? We need to take a step back here and consider briefly the significance of the emergence of early historicism at the turn of the nineteenth century.[15] This movement encompassed much more than the amassing of an unprecedented amount of historical knowledge and historical scholarship (although this played its part). Equally important for it was the idea that having a history and being part of a historical process was a fundamental dimension of human nature, perhaps the most fundamental dimension. This basic assumption did not only underwrite an extensive agenda of historical research but motivated as well profound reflections on the character and the meaning of history. How can history be understood in such a way as to facilitate a better grasp of what human beings are? If it was characteristic for this early phase of historicism, which extended throughout much of the former half of the nineteenth century, that this latter question, which was philosophical, and the actual exploration of historical knowledge went hand in hand, it was equally characteristic of that time, as we have already seen in the case of Schelling's lectures *On Academic Study*, that this historico-philosophical reflection was inscribed into a theological framework.[16] And the key to achieving this end was Christology, more specifically the concept of the Incarnation. Historical, philosophical and theological concerns were thus constantly blended together and conceived in their interdependence.

At the risk of simplifying things a little, one can distinguish two different approaches that were taken by early historicist thinkers to understand history and, through it, unlock the mystery of the human being. One of them conceived of history essentially as a process: here the art of the historian was to piece together the disjointed facts scattered across a variety of documents or sources into a single narrative. 'History' ultimately was this narrative, and if history had meaning, this meaning resided in this story. History was therefore by necessity supra-individual even though it could not exist without the active participation of individual agents. The danger for the historian was not to see the forest for the trees, to get distracted by the plurality and heterogeneity of individual events and occurrences and overlook the bigger trends, patterns and developments.

The alternative approach started from starkly reversed assumptions. Here, the essence of history was the perception and understanding of individuals. The art of the historian, from this perspective, was to study and describe people, events and cultural formations on their own terms. The implication of this imperative was a critique of the tendency to apply cultural universals without proper regard for the individual case, to deduce from general assumptions what must be the case in a particular situation, or to judge any part of history by a standard that was taken from a different context.

Both approaches would claim that they used history to elucidate what it meant to be a human self. The former – let us call it history as process – emphasized the need to place the self in continuity with the bigger picture, as part of traditions and long-term developments and indeed, in important ways, as their results. The latter – let us call this history as individuality – would make us aware that in all this flow and flux we are nonetheless not merely a drop of water in an ocean but discrete, individual people with our own moral choices and personal identity distinguishing us from other individuals who have existed in the past and exist with us in the present.

Christology and history: Schelling

These two ways of thinking about history and about human historicity obviously have wide-ranging consequences for the way historical research is conducted, but I cannot pursue this question here. More pertinent for my chapter is another question. Given the way Christology was connected with the problems of early historicism, how did these different approaches affect Christological reflection?

Let us begin with the view of history as process. Here we have to return one more time to Schelling's lectures *On Academic Study*. In this text, the Incarnation underwrites the idea of the unity of all history. The philosophically valuable idea to be gained from the Christian doctrinal tradition was that God became incarnate in history; but this did emphatically not mean, for Schelling, that God became human for about 30 years at the beginning of the common era. Rather, it signified the more universal process by which God and world become one. The 'eternal Son of God', according to Schelling, is 'the finite itself'.[17]

History was, on the one hand, crucial for understanding this process because it participates both in the natural order of causality and in the spiritual order of freedom.[18] History is where the two meet; for this reason, historical study has in and of itself a theological dimension. On the other hand, however, theological, Christological reflection is oriented towards history in order to come to its fulfilment:

The highest religious feeling, expressed in Christian mysticism, holds the secret of Nature and the Incarnation of God for one and the same.[19]

Historical study, philosophical reflection on history and Christology are thus closely tied together. The foundation of their unity is the notion of history as process. Therefore, the human nature of the incarnate Christ is universal and ultimately cosmic. Schelling is clearly harking back to some of the earliest Patristic Christologies with roots in the biblical testimony itself.[20] Yet the consequence for him is that the historical individuality of the Saviour becomes impossible to conceptualize. Christ is no longer an individual, historical person but the principle of the union of the infinite and the finite.

F. C. Baur: historicist theology

Schelling's line of argument was taken over by F. C. Baur (1792–1860) who from the mid-1820s became the most prominent – albeit controversial – historical theologian in Germany.[21] He put his cards on the table in this regard in the preface to his first, major monograph published in 1824. All historical investigation, he argued there, must ultimately choose between one of two approaches:

> . . . either that of separation and isolation, which, consistently pursued, necessarily leads to atomism, fatalism and atheism, or that on which dawns a purer and higher consciousness of the divine to the degree to which the spiritual life of the peoples is recognised in its great interconnectedness as a great whole, thus leading to an ever more sublime idea of the divine. . . . I am not scared of the well-worn charge of mixing philosophy and history. Without philosophy, history for me remains forever dead and dumb.[22]

This principle, and in particular the role of Christology for it, was then worked out subsequently throughout the 1830s and early 1840s in three major monographs: *Christian Gnosis or the Christian Philosophy of Religion in its Historical Development* (1835); *The Christian Doctrine of Reconciliation* (1838); and *The Christian Doctrine of the Trinity and the Incarnation of God* (3 vols, 1841/42).[23]

Baur's fundamental insight is that the unique characteristic of Christian theology is its relation both to philosophy and to history. Christianity both enables and necessitates a philosophical interpretation of history and a historical interpretation of religion, the latter culminating in Christianity. Key is the Incarnation: the arc formed by these three major monographs written in the space of just seven years corresponds to this complex argument as Baur moved from an account of 'the Christian philosophy of religion' to the concept of reconciliation as the heart of soteriology to the twin doctrines of Trinity and Christology as the fully conceptualized outworking of the Christian impulse.

All these monographs are histories; this is not merely due to Baur's own specialization as a historical theologian but reflects his conviction that history is the ultimate medium revealing the full truth of Christian teaching. The truth of Christianity is only fully and truly captured in and through an account of its historical development.[24]

In the course of discussing these histories, Baur was mindful to emphasize precedents for the position he himself sought to defend. Unsurprisingly perhaps, he explored in some depth Patristic reflection about the humanity of Christ. Textbook descriptions of the emergence of classical Christology may give the impression that the one and only question that had to be resolved during those centuries concerned the precise relationship between humanity and divinity in the person of the Saviour. But while this impression can, perhaps, be gained from an isolated reading of the Chalcedonian formula of faith, any broader survey of Patristic Christologies immediately reveals the centrality of reflections about Christ's humanity as somehow both particular and universal.[25]

While the Jesus of the Gospels was evidently a historical individual, with his own family, place and time of birth, national and cultural background and so forth, even the earliest Christological reflections interpret this person in the light of collective or corporate personalities:[26] he is the suffering servant (Matt. 8.17); he is the true Israel (Matt. 2.15); he is (the second) Adam (1 Cor. 15.45). At least from Irenaeus onwards, this assumption takes centre stage wherever Christological and soteriological reflections overlap. The identity of Christ's and our humanity – expressed through the notion that Christ somehow *is* Adam – explains how the injection of divinity into one individual can have a salvific effect on many (or possibly all[27]) others.[28]

Baur reported these Patristic views, which he called 'mystical theory',[29] with considerable sympathy – remarkable certainly for those who are familiar with the much more critical evaluation the same Patristic accounts will receive 50 years later in Harnack's *History of Dogma*.[30] In his account, Baur referred specifically to Hilary of Poitiers and Cyril of Alexandria,[31] but it is Gregory of Nyssa whom he followed in his sketch of this type of atonement theory. According to Baur, the mystical theory focused essentially on one insight: through the Incarnation of the Logos a higher, spiritual principle has been imparted to humanity allowing its reintegration into unity with the divine. This idea was encapsulated in Athanasius' celebrated statement that 'Christ had to become man, so we would become gods'.[32] Christ, then, is the individual representing humanity. He is a member of the human race, part of the whole, but he also contains within himself the principle dominating the totality of human beings. Baur saw a twofold symmetry at work here:[33] on the one hand, whatever happened to Christ must also happen to everyone else – this is the mechanism by means of which salvation spread from him to all humankind. Yet at the same time and by the same token, it was equally necessary that everything that was characteristic for humankind had to be found in Christ too. This is why, he suggested, Gregory argued that Christ had to die; in fact, Gregory of Nazianzus even intimated the need for Christ to have assumed sin.[34]

It is because of this perceived balance between Christ's humanity and ours that Baur found this approach at work in those Fathers for whom, he wrote, the two natures in Christ formed a particularly close and organic relationship; their distinction was not emphasized to the detriment of their actual union.[35]

Interestingly, Baur denied that this Patristic approach neglected the subjective side of the atonement. It was true that Christ is redeemer, initially, by representing within himself the process of an ever-increasing domination of the lower, material principle through the higher, spiritual one. This did not, however, preclude the subjective aspect, according to Baur, because the individual appropriation of the renewed unity of divine and human had to happen within each individual's consciousness. This was the case, he maintained, even though the Church Fathers tended to emphasize the 'objective' aspect of the union of divine and human, which they, rightly, saw as the basis without which the subjective appropriation would be impossible.[36]

Baur did certainly not identify his own solution to the Christological problem with the views of these Fathers. Yet he was clearly keen to stress the link between their position and his own one. His reason for emphasizing this connection appears rather obvious: what he found prefigured there was an understanding that, due to a clear sense of the unity of the divine and human in Christ, his humanity became associated with ours in a particular way. Christology is thus key to an understanding of our humanity, while the latter task required the integration of what was particular and individual into the overarching solidarity and cohesion of the race.

The main step Baur felt he was taking beyond those Fathers was to inscribe this view of Christ's humanity into a historical paradigm as a particularly suitable intellectual frame for understanding how human individuality was connected with humanity as a whole.[37] Ultimately, however, this link was somewhat one-sided and Baur, as Schelling before him, understood the subject of God's Incarnation as collective, not individual. The Incarnation, according to Baur, was fully understood when leaving behind the identification of the human being assumed by the Logos with the particular individual, Jesus of Nazareth, in favour of its dissolution into the historical succession of individual persons.

This Christological position is more commonly associated with Baur's student David Friedrich Strauß, who saw in the identification of Christ's humanity with humanity as a whole the only viable solution of the Christological dilemma, as he called it.[38] But in some ways, it is more instructive to study it in Baur because we can there perceive much more clearly how this Christological view is aligned with a particular understanding of history. Throughout his entire career, Baur was committed as a historical theologian to the ideal of history as a total process. In his view, failure to perceive universal coherence would result in 'fatalism, atomism, and atheism'.[39] This understanding of history as process shaped his approach to Christology. In the doctrine of the Incarnation, he hoped to find a solution to this very problem: unity over division; coherence over isolation; continuity of tradition over rupture from it.

Isaak August Dorner: history as individuality

If such an emphasis on history as process could jettison Christ's human individuality and historical particularity, does this indicate a fundamental flaw in the underlying understanding of history as process?

This was certainly the view of Baur's great younger colleague, rival and opponent, Isaak August Dorner (1809–1884). Dorner's masterpiece, a full account of the doctrine of Christology (*History of the Development of the Doctrine of the Person of Christ*), was in many ways prompted by concerns arising from the kind of Christology emerging from the thought of Baur and Strauß. Against them, Dorner sought to establish the significance of Christ's Incarnation as a unique historical event and this as the basis for the Church's Christological reflection. Thus far, one can see in Dorner a defender of Christological 'orthodoxy'. Yet it would be utterly mistaken to ignore his own involvement in the historicist movement of the time. In many ways, he represents what I called earlier the second main strand of early historicism for which history was only worth its salt if it focused on the individual. As we shall see, Dorner was, in his own way, as much interested in Patristic speculations about Christ and Adam as Baur had been.

If Baur's understanding of history as process could be traced back to Schelling's lectures *On Academic Study*, Dorner's view of the relationship between history and Christology ultimately derived from Friedrich Schleiermacher's *Christian Faith*.[40] This influential theological text contained its own reflection about history and individuality as the foundation of Christian theology. In a way reminiscent perhaps of Robert Jenson's argument in the late twentieth century,[41] Schleiermacher prescribed to the Christian theologian a form of reflection willing to embrace historical particularity: the origin of Christianity in the first century, the particular person of Jesus, the received forms in which Christian thought has been expressed and so forth. None of that, he suggested, could be philosophically deduced from some sort of universal truth but had *prima facie* to be accepted as historically contingent facts.[42] This endorsement of individuality and particularity is, however, justified in a thoroughly and fascinatingly philosophical reflection on history.

Schleiermacher did not deny that history was, in some sense, a continuous, evolutionary process. Yet while for Baur this insight was the result of a philosophical reflection on history, for Schleiermacher it was an almost trivial starting point: it was, we might say, history considered merely as a fact of nature. By contrast, it was the identification of discrete individuals in this continuous stream which, according to Schleiermacher, required historical and philosophical ingenuity. In order to explain that, he presented an intriguing model of the historicity of human nature:

> The origin of every human life may be regarded in a twofold manner, as issuing from the narrow circle of descent and society to which it immediately belongs, and as an act (*Tatsache*) of human nature in general.[43]

Human individuals, Schleiermacher suggests here, can and must be understood in two ways: in terms of their 'physical' continuity and in terms of discrete individuality. Only this dual perspective maintains their continuity with humankind as well as their individuality and originality; their shared identity with their fellow humans as much as their difference from them.

Individuals are, therefore, part of nature, but they are more than just elements of this reality. They represent, we might say, quanta of energy, flashes of activity inserted into otherwise inert nature. Their very individuality is thus the heartbeat of nature's life. In and through individuals – albeit certainly not through all of them equally[44] – new things happen; without them the world could not progress and would thus be unable to approach its future perfection.

While Schleiermacher's view of history does not neglect its unity and coherence, for him the more remarkable fact is the emergence of genuine novelty which is only possible in and through individuality. This individuality, incidentally, is not just limited to human and other particulars but encompasses collective entities too; Schleiermacher's theory thus seeks to account for the emergence of new nations, cultures and not least religions.[45] A theory of history that is worth its salt, he believed, must be able to explain precisely such new beginnings.

As in Schelling and Baur, Christ's humanity in Schleiermacher is aligned with humanity in its historical extension.[46] Due to his different conception of history, however, Schleiermacher's Christ did not have to give up on his human individuality in order to be related to all humanity. On the contrary, it was only as an individual that Christ could have had his unique importance for humankind.[47] He was, so to speak, the strongest bundle of energy, the brightest flash issuing forth from humanity's universal nature. In this way, he is the ideal, paradigmatic human being (*Urbild*) from whom and towards whom all human history is directed.[48] But he can only exist as such a paradigm insofar as he is also a proper historical individual.

Dorner's approach to Christology was, in many ways, based on Schleiermacher's theory. In his humanity, Dorner suggested, Christ was the 'central individual' of the human race, the culmination of human perfection which, however, as such had to exist as and in one individual:

As a deeper reflection on nature considers the lower stages of existence as disjoint and separate parts of a whole or an Idea, which then recapitulates itself (*sich zusammenfasst*) in the noble, godlike form of humanity, which as such is the head and crown of natural creation: in the same way, humanity must be understood as the disparate plurality of a higher whole, a higher Idea that is, Christ. And as nature could not collect itself into unity merely in the Idea of a man (*in der Idee eines Menschen*) but in real man (*im wirklichen Menschen*), in the same way humanity does not recapitulate itself in a mere Idea, in an ideal Christ, but in the real God-man who as a person represents its totality and recapitulates in himself all the paradigms (*Urbilder*) or ideal personalities of all particular individualities.[49]

This passage is taken from a two-part article containing Dorner's initial intuition about his historical and systematic project. This article, although proposing a sweeping overview of the entire history of Christology was, in reality, strongly tilted towards most recent developments. Moreover, it is evident that Dorner's own solution to the Christological problem – the conception of Christ as the 'central individual' of humanity as expressed in the present text – was developed from a critical study of Kant, Schelling, Hegel and Schleiermacher. By comparison, Dorner's historical understanding was as yet underdeveloped and his sweeping account of the Christological controversies of the early Church, in particular, appears to reflect the study of generic textbooks more than that of original sources.

In 1839, Dorner went on to publish the study in book form, and the considerably enlarged text, printed on over 550 pages, indicates the growth of the historical material he was able to include.[50] It is at this stage of his work that he evidently became fascinated by the Patristic period as a precursor of his own position. Drawing partly on Baur's *Versöhnungslehre*, published the previous year, Dorner inserts a 30-page account of early Patristic testimonies for an intuited sense of the unity of the divine and human in Christ. In other words, he believes to have detected in early Fathers, from Irenaeus to Gregory of Nyssa, a remarkably 'complete' Christology even though none of them is even familiar with the later, Chalcedonian conception of the hypostatic union of two natures. Dorner explains this fact with the *Totalanschauung* (total intuition)[51] which these early Fathers had of Christ himself and which, incidentally, provides further evidence for his own, theological view of the historical factuality of Christ's existence.[52]

In the first instance, Dorner cites Irenaeus and his doctrine of recapitulation. Christ, according to Irenaeus, is the second Adam and as such not only the redeemer of humankind but also their true representative. The Incarnation was necessary, Irenaeus argued against the Gnostics, because only in this historical act could the drama of salvation history come to its conclusion. Dorner writes, 'the Logos is to him [sc. Irenaeus] the paradigm (*Urbild*) of all human beings as well as their creator . . . The Incarnation is ultimately the full realization of this paradigm (*Urbild*). Thus, the real human being, Jesus Christ, who is himself the realized Logos, participates in that general relationship with universal humankind as well.'[53]

Dorner subsequently discussed Tertullian, Origen, Hippolytus, Athanasius,[54] Gregory of Nazianzus and Gregory of Nyssa. He summarizes by noting that this 'interesting but insufficiently noted' aspect of Patristic Christology demonstrated how 'not merely one or another, but the most respected teachers of the Church' are of the same mind in this regard: Christ did not only have the limited significance of any other human being, but 'his Person stands in an essential relationship with the race as a whole'.[55] While this view took different forms in its detail, Dorner argued, there can be no doubt the Church on this point simply stayed close to the faith of the apostles.[56]

Towards the end of his book, Dorner engaged with F. C. Baur's conception in a lengthy footnote. In his *Versöhnungslehre*, Baur, then Dorner's senior colleague at Tübingen, had included a rebuttal of the theory of Christ as the 'central individual' as contained in Dorner's original article.[57] In response, Dorner points out, in words that are strikingly similar to those he chose in summarizing the views of the early Fathers, that his concept 'cannot merely be considered the idea of one or another person but, as we have seen, persists in different forms throughout all centuries seeking to attach itself, with more or less success, to almost every form of Christology'.[58]

By comparison with Baur, let alone Schelling, Dorner easily appears as the more traditional proponent of an orthodox Christology. Yet while such an impression certainly corresponds to his own intention, it would be a mistake to ignore that his own views took shape under precisely the same intellectual influences that formed the thought of his contemporaries and rivals and that have been laid out at the outset of my chapter. In other words, Dorner's Christology is, once again, developed against the backdrop of the early historicism with its close ties to the philosophies of German idealism. Consequently, he too sought to inscribe the doctrine into a paradigm in which history had become the medium in and through which the deepest truths about humanity were expected to emerge.

Yet this very modern turn to history necessarily involved close engagement with older theological texts, and in this process the resources of Patristic thought had the opportunity to prove their enduring topicality. And thus, as much as Baur discovered in the Fathers his own views of Christ's humanity as ultimately transcending that of an individual, Dorner was able to find there the thought of Christ's humanity as representing all human beings in and through his personality.

Conclusion

To conclude, I propose to take a step back from the details of these historical figures and their Christological research in order to get a clearer sense of how these various Christological reflections that have been discussed in the foregoing contribute to the 'whole Christ'.

First, Christology and human identity: Christology, I have argued, is more than the problem of how a unity of human and divine natures can be conceptualized. In many ways, the person of Jesus Christ is the key to an understanding of ourselves, and Christology rightly conceived is therefore closely related to the problem of human identity. Christology has often been perceived as a particularly abstract and scholastic doctrine. Inscribing it into human historicity, as has been done by nineteenth-century German theologians, has the potential to connect it directly with some of the deepest intellectual and spiritual questions human beings are asking about themselves.

Second, an important dimension of this problem is the relationship between our individuality and our integration into larger communities and groups. As we have seen, this problem loomed large among nineteenth-century thinkers. Whether we observe this tension in a historicist key, as they mostly did, or whether we apply sociological, political or cultural analyses, there is no doubt about its enduring significance. Baur and Dorner rightly (re-)discovered that these questions were central for Patristic Christologies. This insight remains important today.

Third, as we have seen, the concept of history is ambiguous insofar as it can be focused on a process or development but also on the individuals making up this process. The comparison between Schelling and Baur on the one hand, and Schleiermacher and Dorner on the other has shown that the difficulty to fine-tune the relationship between these two is ultimately similar to the equally difficult balance between Christ's universal and his particular human nature about which there was much debate in the first millennium.[59] This points to the approximate character of Christology, the need to treat the quest for the 'whole Christ' as an open-ended reflection on the one person that stands at the very centre of the Christian faith rather than a doctrine that has, at some point, once and for all been settled.

Notes

1 Henry Parry Liddon, *Life of Edward Bouverie Pusey*, ed. by J. O. Johnston and Robert J. Wilson, 4 vols, 4th edn (London: Longmans, 1894), vol. 1, pp. 77–8.

2 The charge was originally led by Martin Kähler, *The So-called Historical Jesus and the Historic Biblical Christ*, trans. by Carl Braaten (Philadelphia: Fortress, 1964). It was subsequently central to the position of Karl Barth and his school. Cf. for a British view: Leighton Pullan, *Religion Since the Reformation* (Oxford: Oxford University Press, 1923), pp. 188–91. The most comprehensive account in English remains Alister McGrath, *The Making of Modern German Christology: 1750–1990*, 2nd edn (Eugene, OR: Wipf & Stock, 2005).

3 Robert Morgan, 'Christ', in *The Oxford Handbook of Nineteenth-Century Christian Thought*, ed. by Joel Rasmussen, Judith Wolfe and Johannes Zachhuber (Oxford: Oxford University Press, 2017), pp. 591–609.

4 Friedrich D. E. Schleiermacher, *The Christian Faith*, trans. by H. R. Mackintosh and J. S. Stewart (London: T & T Clark, 1999). Even Karl Barth conceded that Schleiermacher 'wished' to be 'a Christocentric theologian'. See Karl Barth, *Protestant Theology in the Nineteenth Century: Its Background and History*, trans. by Brian Cozens/John Bowden, new edition (Grand Rapids, MI: Eerdmans, 2002), p. 418.

5 Isaak August Dorner, *Entwicklungsgeschichte der Lehre von der Person Christi von den ältesten Zeiten bis auf die neuesten* (Stuttgart: Liesching, 1839); 2nd edn, 2 vols (1845–53). ET: *History of the Development of the Doctrine of the Person of Christ*, 5 vols (Edinburgh: T & T Clark, 1880–97). Unless otherwise indicated, references will be to the first edition.

6 David Friedrich Strauss, *Das Leben Jesu, kritisch bearbeitet*, 2 vols (Tübingen: Osiander, 1835–36), ET: *The Life of Jesus, Critically Examined*, 3 vols, trans. from the 4th edition by Marian Evans (London: Chapman, 1846); Ferdinand Christian Baur, *Die christliche Lehre von der Dreieinigkeit und Menschwerdung Gottes in ihrer geschichtlichen Entwicklung*, 3 vols (Tübingen: Fues, 1841–43).

7 In my view, one should not, for example, underestimate the continuing influence of the classical authors of Lutheran orthodoxy for whose emergence from the mid-sixteenth century Christology had been absolutely central. Cf. Richard Schröder, *Johann Gerhards lutherische Christologie und die aristotelische Metaphysik* (Tübingen: Mohr Siebeck, 1983).

8 Hans Küng, *The Incarnation of God: An Introduction to Hegel's Theological Thought as Prolegomena to a Future Christology*, trans. by John R. Stephenson (Edinburgh: T & T Clark, 1987).

9 Friedrich Wilhelm Joseph Schelling, *Vorlesungen über die Methode des akademischen Studiums* (1803), in Friedrich Wilhelm Joseph Schelling, *Sämmtliche Werke*, ed. by Karl Friedrich August Schelling, vol. I/5 (Stuttgart/Augsburg: Cottag, 1859), pp. 207–35. ET: *Lectures on Academic Study*, trans. by Ella S. Morgan, in *The Journal of Speculative Philosophy*, 11 (1877), pp. 92–100, 160–77, 225–44, 363–70; 12 (1878), pp. 205–13; 13 (1879), pp. 190–8, 310–19; 14 (1880), 145–53; 15 (1881), 1–8, 152–8.

10 Cf. Zack Purvis, *Theology and the University in Nineteenth-Century Germany* (Oxford: Oxford University Press, 2016), pp. 86–102.

11 Johann Gottlieb Fichte, 'Deduzierter Plan einer zu Berlin zu errichtenden höhern Lehranstalt', in *Die Idee der deutschen Universität: Die fünf Grundschriften aus der Zeit ihrer Neubegründung durch klassischen Idealismus und romantischen Realismus*, ed. by Ernst Anrich (Darmstadt: WBG, 1956), esp. pp. 154–5, 161–2; cf. Johannes Zachhuber, 'Wissenschaft', in *The Oxford Handbook of Theology and Modern European Thought*, ed. by Nicholas Adams, George Pattison and Graham Ward (Oxford: Oxford University Press, 2013), pp. 479–98 (pp. 484–5).

12 Schelling, *Vorlesungen*, p. 291; ET: p. 209.

13 Cf. Christian Danz, *Die philosophische Christologie F. W. J. Schellings* (Stuttgart/Bad Canstatt: Frommann-Holzboog, 1996).

14 This was, for example, Kant's view: cf. Manfred Kuehn, 'Kant's Jesus', in *Kant's Religion within the Boundaries of Mere Reason: A Critical Guide*, ed. by Gordon E. Michalson (Cambridge: Cambridge University Press, 2014), pp. 156–

74. Cf. also, for example, Don Cupitt, *Jesus and Philosophy* (London: SCM Press, 2009).

15 Cf. Johannes Zachhuber, 'The Historical Turn', in *The Oxford Handbook of Nineteenth-Century Christian Thought*, ed. by Joel Rasmussen, Judith Wolfe and Johannes Zachhuber (Oxford: Oxford University Press, 2017), pp. 53–71.

16 Cf. Johannes Zachhuber, *Theology as Science in Nineteenth-Century Germany: From F.C. Baur to Ernst Troeltsch* (Oxford: Oxford University Press, 2013), pp. 4–12.

17 Schelling, *Vorlesungen*, p. 294; ET: p. 213.

18 *System des transcendentalen Idealismus* (1800), in *Sämmtliche Werke*, ed. by Karl Friedrich August Schelling, Vol. 1/3 (Stuttgart: Cotta, 1858), pp. 327–634 (p. 593). ET: *System of Transcendental Idealism*, trans. by Peter Heath (Charlottesville, VA: University of Virginia Press, 1978), p. 203.

19 Schelling, *Vorlesungen*, p. 290; ET: p. 209.

20 Cf. Matthew Craig Steenberg, *Irenaeus on Creation: The Cosmic Christ and the Drama of Redemption* (Leiden: Brill, 2008).

21 On Baur cf. Peter C. Hodgson, *The Formation of Historical Theology: A Study of Ferdinand Christian Baur* (New York: Harper, 1968); Horton Harris, *The Tübingen School* (Oxford: Oxford University Press, 1975).

22 Ferdinand Christian Baur, *Symbolik und Mythologie oder die Naturreligion des Alterthums*, 2 vols (vol. 2 in 2 parts) (Stuttgart: Metzler, 1824–25), p. xi.

23 Ferdinand Christian Baur, *Die christliche Gnosis oder die christliche Religions-Philosophie in ihrer geschichtlichen Entwiklung* (Tübingen: Fues, 1835); *Die christliche Lehre von der Versöhnung in ihrer geschichtlichen Entwicklung von der ältesten Zeit bis auf die neueste* (Tübingen: Fues, 1838); *Die christliche Lehre von der Dreieinigkeit und der Menschwerdung Gottes in ihrer geschichtlichen Entwicklung*, 3 vols (Tübingen: Fues, 1841–3).

24 Zachhuber, *Theology as Science*, pp. 47–48.

25 Cf. for what follows: Johannes Zachhuber, 'L'individualité de l'humanité de Jésus Christ selon quelques Pères de l'Église', *Revue des sciences religieuses*, 90 (2016), pp. 35–50.

26 C. F. D. Moule, *The Origin of Christology* (Cambridge: Cambridge University Press, 1977).

27 Gregory of Nyssa used this logic to argue for universalism: Morwenna Ludlow, *Universal Salvation: Eschatology in the Thought of Gregory of Nyssa and Karl Rahner* (Oxford: Oxford University Press, 2000), pp. 89–95.

28 Cf., for example, Eric Osborn, *Irenaeus of Lyons* (Cambridge: Cambridge University Press, 2004), pp. 101–8.

29 Baur, *Versöhnungslehre*, p. 118. This is a reference to Schleiermacher who used this term to designate his own, preferred understanding of salvation: *Christian Faith* §100, pp. 428–9; Baur, *Versöhnungslehre*, p. 618.

30 Adolf Harnack, *History of Dogma*, trans. from the 3rd German edition by Neil Buchanan et al. (New York: Dover, 1958), vol. 3, p. 297 and n. 580.

31 Baur, *Versöhnungslehre*, pp. 116–17, n. 1.

32 Baur, *Versöhnungslehre*, pp. 112–16.

33 Baur, *Versöhnungslehre*, pp. 111. Cf. Athanasius, *de incarnatione* 54,3.

34 Baur, *Versöhnungslehre*, p. 114. Cf. Gregory of Nazianzus, *or* 30, 5,6–9.

35 Baur, *Versöhnungslehre*, p. 111.

36 Baur, *Versöhnungslehre*, p. 118.

37 Baur, *Versöhnungslehre*, pp. 729–37.

38 Strauss, *Life of Jesus*, p. 895.

39 Baur, *Symbolik*, p. xi.

40 Dorner's attachment to Schleiermacher can be seen from the order in which he discussed the most recent thinkers in his historical account of Christology: Schelling, Hegel, Schleiermacher (*Entwicklungsgeschichte*, pp. 340–529). For Baur, by contrast, the order was inevitably Schelling, Schleiermacher, Hegel (for example, *Gnosis*, pp. 611–735). While Dorner would critique Schleiermacher (pp. 509–27), there is no doubt that he felt his own position followed naturally from that of the author of the *Glaubenslehre*.

41 Robert Jenson, *Systematic Theology*, vol. 1: *The Triune God* (Oxford: Oxford University Press, 2001), p. 47.

42 Schleiermacher, *Christian Faith* § 19.4, pp. 91–2.

43 Schleiermacher, *Christian Faith* § 94.3, p. 388.

44 For Schleiermacher's view of great people or 'heroes' as those 'who in any respect give character to an age or a district', cf. Schleiermacher, *Christian Faith* § 94.1, p. 386.

45 Schleiermacher, *Christian Faith* § 94.1, p. 386.

46 On Schleiermacher's Christology cf. Jacqueline Mariña, 'Schleiermacher's Christology Revisited. A Reply to his Critics', *Scottish Journal of Theology*, 49 (1996), pp. 177–200; Jacqueline Mariña, 'Christology and Anthropology in Schleiermacher', in *The Cambridge Companion to Friedrich Schleiermacher*, ed. by Jacqueline Mariña (Cambridge: Cambridge University Press, 2005), pp. 151–70; Ralph Del Colle, 'Schleiermacher and Spirit Christology. Unexplored Horizons of *The Christian Faith*', *International Journal of Systematic Theology*, 1 (1999), pp. 286–307; Lori Pearson, 'Schleiermacher and the Christologies behind Chalcedon', *Harvard Theological Review*, 96 (2003), pp. 349–67.

47 Schleiermacher, *Christian Faith* § 93, p. 377.

48 Schleiermacher, *Christian Faith* § 93, p. 377.

49 Isaak August Dorner, 'Über die Entwicklungsgeschichte der Christologie, besonders in den neueren Zeiten', *Tübinger Theologische Zeitschrift* (1835), pp. 4, 81–204; (1836), pp. 1, 96–240 (p. 239).

50 From 1845, he published a much enlarged second edition which was to become the classical version: see n. 5 above.

51 Dorner, *Entwicklungsgeschichte*, p. 52.

52 Dorner, *Entwicklungsgeschichte*, p. 28.

53 Dorner, *Entwicklungsgeschichte*, p. 61.

54 Relying for Athanasius, interestingly, on Johann Adam Möhler, *Athanasius der Grosse und die Kirche seiner Zeit, besonders im Kampfe mit dem Arianismus*, 2 vols (Mainz: Kupferberg, 1827): Dorner, *Entwicklungsgeschichte*, p. 70.

55 Dorner, *Entwicklungsgeschichte*, pp. 77–8.

56 Dorner, *Entwicklungsgeschichte*, p. 79.

57 Baur, *Versöhnungslehre*, pp. 729–33.

58 Dorner, *Entwicklungsgeschichte*, p. 370.

59 Zachhuber, 'L'individualité'.

13

The Oxford Movement and the Incarnation

GEORGE WESTHAVER

Introduction: contending for the Incarnation[1]

Each day at Evensong at Pusey House, we remember E. B. Pusey as one who contended 'by his life and learning earnestly for the truth of the Incarnation'. In some ways this is a surprising description, because, unlike questions associated with apostolic succession, the real presence, baptismal regeneration or private confession, the doctrine of the Incarnation was generally not an explicit focus in the disputes in which the leaders of the Oxford Movement were caught up or involved. However, not only Pusey, but also John Henry Newman and John Keble argued that a proper apprehension of the truth of the Incarnation was fundamental to understanding the sacraments or Christian ministry, how to read the Bible or to understand the created order. What was contentious, what is behind the 'contending' in the Pusey prayer, is the all-embracing or comprehensive character of the doctrine of the Incarnation that leaders of the Oxford Movement put forward. Pusey and his colleagues argued that the kind of apologetic theology common in their day was often tainted with an empiricism which suggested that the ways of God and the great truths of Christianity are available to be comprehensively analysed by the powers of human reason – not just probed or contemplated, but mastered and judged, anatomized and dissected. An emphasis on what was practical or useful led, in their view, to a lack of appreciation of doctrines that did not meet acceptable standards of utility or whose results could not be measured. They argued that it was possible to keep all the words and doctrinal formulations of orthodox Christianity while promoting a sensibility which made it impossible to apprehend the realities which the formulations were meant to communicate.

To explore the all-embracing or comprehensive character of the doctrine of the Incarnation put forward by the leaders of the Oxford Movement, we can begin by considering, first, what they say about our participation in the Incarnation, how Christ dwells in us and we dwell in him. Second, for the Tractarians, the Incarnation serves as a lens to see how God is manifest in the flesh, how divine truth is grasped and seen through sensible signs and things. Finally, we will consider why it is important for the Tractarians that what we know about the Incarnation is held in tension with what we do not know; it is a mystery, 'a truth sacramental'.

Christ in us and we in him

How then does Christ dwell in us? While the Incarnation is, first of all, a doctrine about the union of the divine and human natures in Christ, Keble, Newman and Pusey saw it also as the key to understanding the union of Christ and his body, the Church: 'It is this realisation that God gives us not just His gifts, but Himself, that is the deepest conviction of the Fathers of the Oxford Movement.'[2] Pusey emphasizes that the gift of the Christian life is nothing less than 'union with that mystery, whereby we are made partakers of the Incarnation'.[3] God has 'so taken our poor nature into Himself, that in Him it is In-Godded, Deitate'.[4] One finds the same emphasis on partaking of the divine nature in Newman's sermons. 'He', the one who is 'the brightness of God's glory', writes Newman, 'came in that very nature of Adam, in order to communicate to us that nature as it is in His Person, that "our sinful bodies might be made clean by His Body, and our souls washed through His most precious Blood;" to make us partakers of the Divine nature'.[5] This manner of expressing the gift of the Incarnation in sacramental language emphasizes the way in which participation in Christ through the sacraments was intrinsic to a proper understanding of the Incarnation for Pusey, Newman and Keble. Newman, for example, describes the Incarnation in terms borrowed from the eucharistic rite: 'Christ then took our nature . . . and then He imparted it to us. He took it, consecrated it, broke it, and said, "Take, and divide it among yourselves".'[6]

At the same time, for the Tractarians, the sacramental presence of Christ, our dwelling in him, is not isolated to the sacraments. For Newman, the real presence of Christ in the Church means that the historical existence of Christ, his coming in and going out among his disciples, is not simply past and gone. Rather, by the indwelling Spirit, the histories to which the gospel bear witness constitute the present life of the Church. To be a member of the body of Christ is to be a *sacramental sign*, of the One Invisible Ever-Present Son of God', it is to live the life of 'the Ever-Present son of God' who *mystically reiterates* in each of us all the acts of His earthly life'.[7] Pusey extends this notion of the presence of Christ being repeated or lived again in his body through the ages to include not only the acts of Christ's earthly life but also the histories and prophecies which reveal or manifest different aspects of the life or character of the incarnate Son before his coming in the flesh.[8] For Pusey, 'Every history in the Bible is a prophecy, which is fulfilled throughout all centuries and in the soul of each individual.'[9] According to this approach, the history of King Asa, the godly and reforming king of Judah and Jerusalem who reigned 900 years before the birth of Christ, is not simply over and gone (see 2 Chron. 14). Rather, King Asa's 'taking away the altars of the strange gods' describes the purifying reform which constitutes the life of the Church and the path of sanctification in every generation. Asa's prayer is a prophecy which is fulfilled, mystically reiterated, in the soul of each member of the body of Christ who 'cries to the

Lord his God' in the face of what seems to be impossible circumstances or overwhelming odds: 'help us, O Lord our God, for we rest on thee, and in thy name we go against this multitude'. As part and parcel of rejecting a meagre or merely external relationship to Christ, a sacramental reading suggests that the struggles of Asa do not offer the Church mere metaphors or principles of godly action, examples from which to learn. More profoundly, these histories are taken into the historical life of the eternal Son of God who takes on human history as well as human nature, who both represents and fulfils the history of Israel of which Asa's struggles are a part. By constituting his history, they become histories which the members of his body inhabit, means of both communion and communication, and in them we live and move and have our being (Acts 17.28).

God manifest in the flesh: the Incarnation as a stereoscopic lens

It would be possible, of course, to reject Newman and Pusey's view of history that is mystically reiterated or lived again as a kind of outmoded and fanciful Platonism. Newman expressed the idea of mystical reiteration in terms that could be open to this charge, arguing that 'All that is seen, – the world, the Bible, the Church, the civil polity, and man himself, – are types, and, in their degree and place, representatives and organs of an unseen world, truer and higher than themselves.'[10] On the other hand, one might discover something more creative or insightful in the Tractarian approach by putting their all-embracing view of the Incarnation alongside an account of how we know or see anything at all, like that which we find in Iain McGilchrist's *The Master and his Emissary: The Divided Brain and the Making of the Western World*. As part of his analysis of how the right and left hemispheres of the brain perceive or attend to the world in different ways, McGilchrist offers an apologetic for the kind of perception that both attends to the world in analytic detail and sees through the surface of things. 'In order truly to see the thing as it is', he argues, attention 'needs both to rest on the object and to pass *through* the plane of focus'. According to the sacramental approach which Newman's characterization of 'all that is seen' suggests, 'the object' in McGilchrist's account could refer to biblical histories, Old Testament ceremonies, a person, a verse in a psalm, a contemporary political event or some natural phenomenon. McGilchrist continues: 'Seeing the thing as it is depends also on seeing through it, to something beyond, the context, the "roundness" or depth, in which it exists.'[11] In Newman's terms, this 'context' or 'roundness' is that truer and higher 'unseen world'. The idea that the fullest kind of vision 'needs both to rest on the object and pass through the plane of focus' also evokes George Herbert's description of a kind of sacramental or stereoscopic sight in his poem 'Elixir', a poem known more widely through the hymn version, 'Teach me my God and King'. This form of seeing both 'stays' the eye on the history or the person, the object or the image, and on the other hand sees or passes through it, 'And then the heav'n espy'.[12] For the Tractarians, the Incarnation serves as a lens for seeing how divine life and truth – the inexhaustible depth or context which gives reality to all created things – is communicated not only in the Bible or the sacramental life of the Church, but in sensible signs and realities more generally.

Apprehending sacramental truth

McGilchrist also casts light on another key feature of the Tractarian approach to the Incarnation. For them, 'mystery' refers not only to the sacramental character of all knowledge, but also to the way in which that which is apprehended is at the same time beyond all strictly human comprehension. McGilchrist argues that the most integrated, holistic form of human knowing, a vision that sees not only the details on the surface but also the depth, is a kind of knowing that goes beyond 'what can be grasped or explicitly stated'.[13] In more theological terms, Pusey argued that 'our highest knowledge must be our indistinctest; for that which is most elevated must most surpass our comprehension'. Or, in Newman's words, the Incarnation is a 'truth sacramental', a truth which is both revealed and also hidden, 'neither light nor darkness, but both together'.[14] In the perceptive description by the Newman scholar Denis Robinson, 'The mystery of the Incarnation, its real sense, lies somewhere between what we know and what we do not know . . . Christ, like the mystery in which he is inculcated, lies somewhere between . . . He is both between and within the human and the divine'.[15] For the Tractarians, the truth of the Incarnation includes not only what the truth is, but how it is apprehended. On the one hand, in the Incarnation, God takes on not only flesh, but also language and the categories of human thought. On the other hand, the divine Word remains incommunicable and inexhaustible, so we can never leave the apophatic moment behind without fundamentally marring or misunderstanding what is revealed and known.

Reading Psalm 49 with the help of St Augustine serves as a useful illustration of what it means to grasp or apprehend a 'truth sacramental', a mystery: 'O hear ye this, all ye people: ponder it with your ears, all ye that dwell in the world' (Ps. 49.1). For Augustine, the appeal to all people that dwell in the world makes it clear that it is Christ who is speaking in this psalm – no merely human voice has this kind of reach in space or time: 'Our Lord Christ has shouted through his apostles; he has shouted in as many tongues as he has sent', the voice 'addresses us now', and 'not just you who are present', but 'all over the world and in all the churches'.[16] Giving voice to this idea, the Matin Responsory for Advent, which is often heard at Advent carol services, describes those who will 'go out and meet' the Lord in the season of Advent with words from the second verse of the psalm, the 'high and low, rich and poor, one with another' (Ps. 49.2).[17] The psalm offers a classic expression of the Tractarian principle of reserve – 'wisdom' does indeed come to us, but in 'parables'; the 'understanding' is shaped, but indirectly, in a reserved manner, in a mystery, by 'musing' on 'dark speech' or enigmas should be (Ps. 49.3–4).[18] While Christ speaks more clearly in other places, we cannot resolve the unclear into the clear without marring, lowering or perverting the very truth which we seek.

The truth of the Incarnation is offered, but it comes as a kind of a trial, like that faced by those who, on the one hand, seek to become followers of Christ, but who, on the other hand, hold themselves back for various reasons, or for different forms of family obligations (see Luke 9.57–62). For the Tractarians, apprehending the truth of the Incarnation was not merely a problem of knowledge, but one of sanctification. Augustine begins his commentary by stating the problem bluntly: 'All the words that God speaks to us are salutary for those who understand them right, but perilous for those who attempt to twist them to suit the perversity of their own hearts, instead of reshaping their hearts to the rectitude of God's word.'[19] However much we agree or disagree with the particularities of the Tractarian approach, this kind of 'contending', with the confusions or not-seeing of our own hearts, in whatever form we know they take, is surely one that we can take up for ourselves. 'The mystery of Christ is not something remote, but a movement that is being played out within us', even now.[20]

Notes

1 This chapter fills out a sermon given at the conference (readings: Ps. 49; 2 Chron. 14; Luke 9.51–62).

2 Andrew Louth, 'Manhood into God: The Oxford Movement, the Fathers and the Deification of Man', in *Essays Catholic and Radical: A Jubilee Group Symposium for the 150th Anniversary of the beginning of the Oxford Movement 1833–1983*, ed. by Kenneth Leech and Rowan Williams (London: The Bowerdean Press, 1983), pp. 70–80 (p. 74).

3 Edward Bouverie Pusey, *Scriptural Views of Holy Baptism*, Tracts for the Times 67, vol. II, Part II, 4th edn (London: J. G. F. and J. Rivington, 1842), p. 49.

4 Edward Bouverie Pusey, Sermon 4: 'God with Us', in *Parochial Sermons, vol. I: For the Seasons from Advent to Whitsuntide*, 3rd edn (Oxford: John Henry Parker, 1852), p. 53.

5 John Henry Newman, Sermon 12: 'The Gospel Feast', in *Parochial Plain Sermons*, 8 vols, new edn (London: Rivington, 1868), vol. 7, pp. 92–93.

6 Newman, Sermon 9: 'Christian Sympathy', in *Parochial Plain Sermons*, vol. 5, pp. 117–18.

7 Newman, Sermon 1: 'Fasting a Source of Trial', in *Parochial Plain Sermons*, vol. 6, p. 3.

8 Cf. Newman, Sermon 19: 'Regenerating Baptism', in *Parochial Plain Sermons*, vol. 3, pp. 277–78.

9 Edward Bouverie Pusey, 'Lectures on Types and Prophecies of the Old Testament' (1836–37), manuscript in the Pusey House Library, p. 27, drawing on Johann Georg Hamann (1730–88).

10 John Henry Newman, 'Milman's View of Christianity', in *Essays Critical and Historical*, vol. 2, 5th edn (London: Pickering & Co., 1881 [1841]), p. 193.

11 Iain McGilchrist, *The Master and his Emissary: The Divided Brain and the Making of the Western World* (New Haven, CT: Yale University Press, 2010), p. 182.

12 George Herbert, 'Elixir': 'A man that looks on glass,/ On it may stay his eye;/ Or if he pleaseth, through it pass,/ And then the heav'n espy'.

13 McGilchrist, *The Master and his Emissary*, p. 179.

14 Newman, Sermon 18: 'Mysteries in Religion', in *Parochial Plain Sermons*, vol. 2, p. 211; and John Henry Newman, 'On the Introduction of Rationalistic Principles into Religion', No. 73, *Tracts for the Times*, iii (London: J. G. and F. Rivington, 1839), p. 9.

15 Denis Robinson, 'Preaching', in *The Cambridge Companion to John Henry Newman*, ed. by Ian Ker and Terrence Merrigan (Cambridge: Cambridge University Press, 2009), pp. 241–54 (p. 249).

16 'Exposition 1' of Psalm 48. Saint Augustine, *Expositions of the Psalms*, Vol 2: Psalms 33–50, trans. by Maria Boulding (Hyde Park, NY: New City Press, 2000), pp. 350–1. Psalm 48 in the LXX numbering is the Psalm 49 referred to in the text.

17 The Greater Responsory for Matins on Advent Sunday: 'I look from afar: and lo, I see the power of God coming, and a cloud covering the whole earth. Go ye out to meet him and say: Tell us, art thou he that should come to reign over thy people Israel? High and low, rich and poor, one with another: Go ye out to meet him and say: Hear, O thou shepherd of Israel: thou that leadest Joseph like a sheep. Stir up thy strength, O Lord, and come: to reign over thy people Israel'.

18 For the Tractarian principle of reserve, see Isaac Williams, 'On Reserve in Communicating Religious Knowledge', Parts I–III, No. 80, *Tracts for the Times*, iv, 2nd edn (London: Rivington, 1840).

19 Augustine, *Expositions of the Psalms*, p. 350.

20 Robinson, 'Preaching', p. 249.

14

Christ and the Poetic Imagination

MALCOLM GUITE

It may be, that after some already weighty chapters, what I have to contribute will come as a little light relief, though perhaps the poetic imagination can also offer a new perspective on ancient mysteries. In any case we can certainly enjoy a little bit of poetry together, as we move from Shakespeare, through to Coleridge, and finally circle back to Oxford and a reflection on C. S. Lewis.

I'm going to start with Shakespeare, and in particular with a passage in which Shakespeare lets us into the mystery of his craft, into the secrets of his workshop, as it were, answering the central question: How is poetry made? How does the poet work? It is, of course, the famous passage from *A Midsummer Night's Dream*. I shall be focusing particularly on those words:

> The poet's eye, in fine frenzy rolling,
> Doth glance from heaven to Earth, from Earth to heaven.[1]

I am going to let that passage tell us about poetry but then I want to ask, 'How might that kind of language be available to us as theologians?' We need as many tongues, as many languages and vocabularies as we can get, in order to voice the praise and make the great doxology that we need to make. How might this account of poetry be available to theology? And might Shakespeare even have been conscious of the particular way in which his words might have theological resonance?

But just to set a little bit of context, this famous and beautiful passage, about the poet's eye and the making and shaping of poetry, comes towards the end of *A Midsummer Night's Dream*. It functions as both an epilogue to the main action of the play and a prologue to the play within the play. The four lovers, it will be remembered, leave the day-lit rationalism of the Athenian court to encounter the moonlight transformations of Puck and find themselves caught up in the elemental quarrel of Oberon and Titania. They leave the court mismatched and miserable, caught in a chain of frustration and betrayal; they return rightly matched and joyful, ready to enter into the fruitfulness of love, of which the play's closing nuptials are a sign. Puck has so cast a spell on the lovers who are now at last, through the play of magic, rightly linked again to one another, and on waking they imagine that their transformations have only been a dream. They tell their story to Theseus and Hippolyta, not knowing whether they will be believed or whether to believe themselves. Theseus claims not to believe them and inveighs against their 'shaping fantasies' (though the audience of course know that, within the world of the play they are speaking truth). So it is, that in a kind of playful irony, Shakespeare puts his best account of the poetic imagination as a truth-bearing faculty into the mouth of a hostile witness. So Theseus says:

> More strange than true. I never may believe
> These antique fables nor these fairy toys.
> Lovers and madmen have such seething brains,
> Such shaping fantasies, that apprehend
> More than cool reason ever comprehends.
> The lunatic, the lover, and the poet
> Are of imagination all compact.
> One sees more devils than vast hell can hold—
> That is the madman. The lover, all as frantic,
> Sees Helen's beauty in a brow of Egypt.
> The poet's eye, in fine frenzy rolling,
> Doth glance from heaven to Earth, from Earth to heaven.
> And as imagination bodies forth
> The forms of things unknown, the poet's pen
> Turns them to shapes and gives to airy nothing
> A local habitation and a name.
> Such tricks hath strong imagination,
> That if it would but apprehend some joy,
> It comprehends some bringer of that joy.[2]

On the surface and most straightforward level he is simply saying, 'I don't believe it! I deny that these events, which the lovers have narrated, actually took place. I think they have been deceived by their overwrought imaginations, and their imaginations were overwrought because they were in love.'

But Theseus goes on to describe the way imagination itself works, and in so doing concedes to imagination almost everything his reason hopes to deny. What is more, he generalizes from this particular denial to a denial of all 'antique fables' and fairy toys and in so doing, cuts off, in a fine piece of dramatic irony, both the branch on which he is sitting and the stage on which he is standing. For here is Theseus, whose entire existence to us and to our minds and imaginations rests on the fact that he has come down to us from antiquity through the medium of 'antique fables', saying 'well of course you can't believe these antique fables, I don't believe them myself'. Here is Theseus remade in the imagination of Shakespeare, and engendered or embodied in us by the power of Shakespeare's poetry, telling us, in the very medium of that poetry, 'well of course you all know there's nothing in poetry'. So, acknowledging that he is meant to be denying the very thing, Shakespeare gently affirms it through him. And I want to focus on what he says about the poet but I want to observe, just before I do, the pair of verbs: two different verbs about ways of knowing are paired like bookends or like poles of a magnet or words that are going to cast a sort of field of force over the whole passage, on either side of the account of poetry. That pair of words of course is *apprehend* and *comprehend*. So we are told that there is a shaping fantasy that *apprehends* more than cool reason ever *comprehends*. We are told later that in order to *apprehend* some joy we must *comprehend* some bringer of that joy.

Now let us turn to the work of poet. 'The poet's eye, in fine frenzy rolling,/ Doth glance from heaven to Earth, from Earth to heaven'. So the first thing we need to notice is the comprehensiveness of the poet's glance. We can say, in one way, that the phrase 'Heaven and Earth' is a way of saying 'everything'. Shakespeare certainly knew the Creed that said 'I believe in God, the father almighty . . . Creator of Heaven and Earth, And of all things visible and invisible'. And in fact his play is very much about the relationship between things visible and things invisible. So you could say 'Heaven and Earth, Earth and Heaven' is one way poetically of expressing that nothing is to be outside the poet's glance. There is an inclusiveness, there is a comprehensiveness there. But maybe there is more going on: Heaven to Earth; Earth to Heaven. Perhaps the words 'apprehend' and 'comprehend', exerting their field of semantic flow on either side of this passage, are already working on us: we move through *comprehending* the earthly towards *apprehending* the heavenly. Perhaps if Shakespeare is echoing the Creed, 'Creator of heaven and Earth', the pairing of 'visible and invisible' is implicit. Perhaps we can begin to think that on the one hand we have the heavenly: the not yet visible, that which is apprehended but which we have not yet seen fully embodied, we have not got the full vision for. And on the other hand we have also got the earthly: the thing we can see and comprehend. Maybe 'heaven' and 'earth' are picking up 'apprehend' and 'comprehend' in that way. But of course what we have is this sense also of the gap between them and we ask: How do I bridge this gap? How might heaven and earth in any sense find that commonality or a place of connection or cohesion? How might 'apprehension' be wooed and brought into the realm of 'comprehension'? How might the simply comprehended suddenly open up a door or a window in towards that mystery which is beyond them, from which it comes? Well, Shakespeare goes on to say:

The poet's eye, in fine frenzy rolling,
Doth glance from heaven to Earth, from Earth to heaven.
And as imagination bodies forth
The forms of things unknown, the poet's pen
Turns them to shapes.

There is an astonishing juxtaposition here between the word 'imagination' and the word 'bodies'. And 'bodies' is not even a noun, it is a verb in the present continuous. 'Bodies', 'imagination.' Shakespeare holds these two very different words together and shows us that the art of imagination, which is going up and down, back and forth between heaven and earth, is to *body*, to *embody*. There is no poetry without a bodying forth. And what does that bodying forth actually do? It makes a shape, which is habitable. It is not simply making something opaque and inaccessible. It is making something that invites you into it, that has doors and windows:

> imagination bodies forth
> The forms of things unknown, the poet's pen
> Turns them to shapes and gives to airy nothing
> A *local habitation* and a name. [emphasis mine]

You notice by the way that Theseus, for all his championing of 'cool reason', has made a logical error here, a false argument. He says, 'imagination bodies forth/ The forms of *things unknown*, the poet's pen/ Turns them to shapes and gives to *airy nothing*/ A local habitation and a name' [emphasis mine]. He has simply presumed that because a thing is unknown it does not exist. But just because a thing is unknown it is not necessarily 'airy nothing'. It is precisely when a thing is unknown or, unknowable, or only a fleeting apprehension, that we need a poet to come in on the scene and make for this 'airy nothing', that is not nothing at all, but this 'unknownness', a local habitation and a shape that it can inhabit. Theseus has already engaged in a cheap sleight of hand, the same reductive assumption that has been perpetrated on us ever since by the Dawkinses of this world.

So there it is. The poet makes this place where the imagination can body forth the form of things unknown. 'The poet's eye . . . Doth glance from heaven to Earth, from Earth to heaven', you can see some poets that start with the earthly glance and they look at something and they really just give you what it is in such wonderfully, lovingly realized detail, that in the very act of telling you what it is they open it up to another kind of becoming. The classic example of that would be Seamus Heaney and perhaps the classic poem would be 'Digging', a poem which appears at first to be entirely about the things of the earth:

> The cold smell of potato mould, the squelch and slap
> Of soggy peat, the curt cuts of an edge
> Through living roots.[3]

But by the end you have got back to the pen:

> Between my finger and my thumb
> The squat pen rests.
> I'll dig with it.

You could not get a better last line than that. Suddenly we go back through the entire poem. This poem that has been so earthly, so rooted, so palpable, so full of what Heaney would in a later poem call the 'the rough porous language of touch',[4] so particular, so obviously about digging and generations and families and the culture of the peat bog and Irish potatoes and all of those things. You would not think it was about anything else on the first reading. And then you get this superb surprise: 'I'll dig with it'. And you realize that all through the poem he has been telling a truth about telling the truth, a truth about what poetry is and how poetry works, and 'telling it slant' as it were. Telling it right along the slant of the spade as it goes into the earth until the spade becomes again the slant of the pen in the poet's hands.

So Heaney is a poet who starts there at the earthly end of the axis. You can see other poets who may start in a kind of moment of completely extraordinary, wordless realization and start off with the glance at heaven, with an unembodied apprehension and then seek for that apprehension a series of different, if partial embodiments. T. S. Eliot in the *Four Quartets* is like that. He has no sooner given you some beautiful image than he says,

That was a way of putting it – not very satisfactory:
A periphrastic study in a worn-out poetical fashion,
Leaving one still with the intolerable wrestle
With words and meanings.[5]

And so he tries again offering one image after another as possible habitations for his apprehensions. Both of those poets are successful because, whether their 'glance' starts at heaven or whether it starts with earth, they are concerned to bridge the two, to make the connection and to make the shapes that make a habitation for insight. That is how poetry works.

But we asked earlier, might this account of how poetry works also be available to us for our thinking as theologians? When I came to write *Faith, Hope and Poetry*, I was trying to bring together two deep, kindling loves and energies in my mind: my love of poetry, which preceded my conversion to Christ, and my later understanding of the richness of Christ as the living and incarnate Word.[6] I was trying to get those two together. And I returned to this Shakespeare passage and I looked at it again and I thought, 'How can I not have seen this? Look at what he's doing! This whole passage is a riff, not only on the Creed, but it's a riff on the Prologue to John's Gospel!' Does Shakespeare's poetry help us to apprehend something about the Incarnation, the great mystery at the heart of Christian theology? Theologians hoping to reflect on what we might mean by saying 'The Word was made flesh and dwelt among us, full of grace and truth' may find this very passage, for all its imaginary pre-Christian setting, full of 'antique Fables and fairy toys', has a direct bearing on the heart of Christian faith. In the Incarnation, the Word which dwells in the beginning richly with God, the divine Logos which would otherwise be an apprehension or an abstraction in the human mind, is literally 'bodied forth', literally given 'a local habitation and a name', so that in John's Gospel the first question of the disciples to Jesus is 'Master, where are you staying?'. In Jesus Christ, who 'bodies forth' from the Father truths that would otherwise have remained 'the form of things unknown', we see a continuous movement between 'earth and heaven, heaven and earth'; we see Jesus 'bodying forth' again and again the love which is the essence of heaven, and we see the disciples glimpsing in him not only the physical body but also a kind of window or doorway into heaven itself, as at the Transfiguration. Indeed, in John's Gospel Christ declares himself to be the Door and the Way.

Shakespeare's account of the poetic imagination as the bodying forth in earthly terms of heavenly apprehension provides us with a model for understanding the Incarnation as the supreme act of divine poiesis. If this is so then it has rich implications for our understanding of humanity as made in God's image; for it means that we are made as makers ourselves, as imaginative 'embodiers'. If that is the case then we might regard the successful embodiment of truth in Christ, the word made flesh, as the prime imaginative or communicative act which underwrites and makes possible all others. We might see this divine poiesis in Christ as answering exactly to that need of which George Steiner spoke in *Real Presences*:

> any coherent understanding of what language is and how language performs . . . is in the final analysis under-written by the assumption of God's presence . . . the experience of aesthetic meaning in particular that of literature and the arts . . . infers the necessary possibility of this "real presence" . . . this study will contend that the wager on the meaning of meaning . . . when we come face to face with the text and work of art or music . . . is a wager on transcendence'.[7]

Though one might add that this wager on the meaning of meaning is in fact a wager on God's immanence as well as his transcendence. We wager that God has enabled our imagination to create symbols which are energized between the poles of immanence and transcendence; the 'Earth' and 'heaven' of Shakespeare's lines. Tom Wright puts it beautifully in his chapter. He speaks of Jesus as 'the place where, and the means by which, heaven and earth were coming together'. And all of that makes me feel that Shakespeare was, in that celebrated passage, quietly providing us with some new way of thinking about the mystery of the Incarnation.

I want very briefly now to turn to a couple of passages about the poetic imagination from Coleridge, before finally landing as it were in the arc of this chapter, back both in Athens but also in Oxford with C. S. Lewis. So here is a passage from the *Biographia Literaria*, which I think is about apprehension and comprehension, and about how the imagination makes and holds shapes which the reason can subsequently comprehend:

They and only they can acquire the philosophic imagination, the sacred power of self-intuition, who within themselves can interpret and understand the symbol, that the wings of the air-sylph are forming within the skin of the caterpillar; those only, who feel in their own spirits the same instinct, which impels the chrysalis of the horned fly to leave room in its involucrum for antennae yet to come. They know and feel, that the potential works in them, even as the actual works on them.[8]

Here Coleridge advances the beautiful suggestive idea that the poetic imagination can hold open for us a shape or a space we have yet to grow into. The great works of art and literature are, as it were, making room for our future insights, giving us the shapes, the stories, the images into which the undeveloped antennae of our inner life can grow.

That is why we need artists and poets and painters and musicians. It is not that we are abandoning the knowledge we have already acquired by reason; it is just that artists and poets are making and creating a shape into which knowledge itself will eventually grow. By doing that 'the poet's pen turns them to shapes' that will move us gradually from that tentative apprehension into comprehension. But the apprehender must make the shape into which the comprehension can grow, which the comprehension can inhabit. Now Coleridge himself, at first and early on in his life, before various tragedies struck him, had by God's gift an almost extraordinary capacity to know the heavenly through the earthly. He could write with such confidence to his son, before his son grew up, imagining how he might grow up:

But thou, my babe! shalt wander like a breeze
By lakes and sandy shores . . .
so shalt thou see and hear
The lovely shapes and sounds intelligible
Of that eternal language, which thy God
Utters, who from eternity doth teach
Himself in all, and all things in himself.
Great universal Teacher! he shall mould
Thy spirit, and by giving make it ask.[9]

This presents clear evidence, by the way, that Coleridge was never a pantheist. There is a God who utters. He is not the utterance; he is the utterer. And yet because he is the utterer you may find him in his utterance. But he will call through the utterance and lead you to ask for something more. Later in life, Coleridge began a serious reading and re-reading of John's Gospel. He is the most Johannine of all the English poets, and he began to think more and more about what it meant to speak of God himself as Logos and as Word. And he soon moved away from his flirtation with Unitarianism and back into a really thoroughgoing and life-restoring Trinitarian faith. Here is a little glimpse of that happening in a notebook of 1805 when curiously, just like the mariner whose life was transformed by a moonrise, Coleridge looks and he says:

> In looking at objects of nature while I am thinking, as at yonder moon, dim glimmering through the window-pane, I seem rather to be seeking, as it were asking, a symbolical language for something within me, that already and forever exists, than observing anything new. Even when the latter is the case, yet still I have always an obscure feeling, as if that new phenomenon were the dim awaking for a forgotten or hidden truth of my inner nature.[10]

Now at that stage in 1805 he is still a long way from working all this through, but Coleridge eventually comes to see that the Logos, the Word in whom and through whom and for whom all things were made, who is involved in 'an eternal act of creation', of breathing all these things into being, is the 'filial Word', the only-begotten son, Jesus Christ. I love this idea that the project of making man is ongoing and that though in one sense it is finished on the cross, it needs to be finished in us. That God is still creating and that he is breathing everything into being, like a poet uttering a poem. Coleridge realized that there is something 'in here', an image of the Logos, corresponding with the Logos himself 'out there'. Eventually, he came to realize that one aspect of that *imago Dei* is itself the power of imagination, as an active and shaping agent of both divine creation and human perception. And so in the famous thirteenth chapter of the *Biographia Literaria* he says: 'The imagination, then, I consider either as primary or secondary. The primary Imagination I hold to be the living Power and prime Agent of all human Perception.' Then he adds, and this is the key theological point, it is 'a repetition in the finite mind of the eternal act of creation in the infinite I AM'. So the eternal act of creation, as it is outside time and is therefore equally close to every moment in time, is just as close, just as immediate for us now as it was 'in the beginning'. So Coleridge is saying that when you perceive anything, when you begin to read the extraordinary text that God has given you in his creation, there is something in you, the image of the Logos within you, helping you to perceive, indeed, in some sense to co-create what the Logos himself is saying through creation as he makes the cosmos new in every moment, in an eternal act of creation. Some of the implications of this way of understanding, especially as Coleridge grounded it in a renewed understanding of the Trinity, become apparent at the end of the *Biographia*, when he looks up at the starry heavens and perceives the cosmos itself as the echo of the exchange of love between the Father and the Son:

> The upraised Eye views only the starry Heaven which manifests itself alone: and the outward Beholding is fixed on the sparks twinkling in the aweful depth, though Suns of other Worlds, only to preserve the Soul steady and collected in its pure *Act* of inward Adoration to the great I

AM, and to the filial WORD that re-affirmeth it from Eternity to Eternity, whose choral Echo is the Universe.[11]

However, I promised something on C. S. Lewis, so in conclusion I want to just show you a little passage of his prose and a great passage of his poetry where some of these themes – the themes of how reason and imagination might be reconciled, how comprehension and apprehension might refresh rather than contradict one another, how Christ as Word incarnate might be the centre of that reconciliation – are all gathered together. The first passage is Lewis giving us a bit of McGilchrist *avant la lettre*. Lewis famously wrote – and he wrote this much later, this is in *Surprised by Joy*, so he is looking back over 20 years – about what it was like to be an atheist in Oxford in the 1920s:

> The two hemispheres of my mind were in the sharpest contrast. On the one side a many-sided sea of poetry and myth; on the other a glib and shallow 'rationalism.' Nearly all that I loved I believed to be imaginary; nearly all that I believed to be real I thought grim and meaningless.[12]

I wonder if that rings any bells? I think Lewis has expressed a dilemma that is more than personal, it goes right to the heart of our experience of modernity. This bifurcation of vision between reason and imagination is also the subject of one of his best poems (titled 'Reason' by Hooper, but the title, I think, closes down rather than opens up the possibilities of the poem):

> Set on the soul's acropolis the reason stands
> A virgin arm'd, commercing with celestial light,
> And he who sins against her has defiled his own
> Virginity: no cleansing makes his garment white;
> So clear is reason. But how dark, imagining,
> Warm, dark, obscure and infinite, daughter of Night:
> Dark is her brow, the beauty of her eyes with sleep
> Is loaded, and her pains are long, and her delight.
> Tempt not Athene. Wound not in her fertile pains
> Demeter, nor rebel against her mother-right.
> Oh who will reconcile in me both maid and mother,
> Who make in me a concord of the depth and height?
> Who make imagination's dim exploring touch
> Ever report the same as intellectual sight?
> Then could I truly say and not deceive,
> Then wholly say that I BELIEVE.[13]

There are a number of remarkable things going on in this poem. First is the sense of inner space, of height and depth in the psyche itself. The soul, the inner Athens, has its heights, its Acropolis, but also depths and caves. Second, there is the bodying forth of the soul's distinct powers of reason and imagination in the form of the two goddesses, Athene and Demeter. This is no glib classical allusion in the eighteenth-century manner, but a symbolic reimagination of the inner self in which more than personal, perhaps more than human, powers are at work, and it is highly significant that at this point both these powers are figured as feminine. Lewis is sometimes caricatured at this stage of his life (the late 1920s) as a bluff, masculine, conservative, probably misogynistic, dogmatically bigoted bachelor don, yet here he is expressing his inner life by saying essentially, 'My problem is I can't get my inner goddesses together'!

After exploring many paired contrasts – touch and sight, light and dark, maid and mother, depth and height – the poem ends with a plea that subtly summons the echoes of its own answer:

Oh who will reconcile in me both maid and mother
Who make a concord of the depth and height?

These lines point and give new significance to the paradox of Incarnation which is at the heart of the integrative faith which Lewis was on the cusp of embracing. The pagan goddesses must be *either* maid *or* mother, but the Virgin Mary, in whom their numina is subsumed for Christian devotion, is *both* maid *and* mother. In and through her 'Yes' to God, the archetypal assent of all faith, Christ the reconciler comes into the world, the one who not only reconciles man to God, and time to eternity, but is also in himself the concord of all depth and height, inner and outer. Lewis's language here summons echoes of Saint Paul:

that ye, being rooted and grounded in love, May be able to comprehend with all saints what *is* the breadth, and length, and depth, and height; And to know the love of Christ, which passeth knowledge, that ye might be filled with all the fulness of God. (Eph. 3.17–19)

These are of course anticipatory echoes; the poem as it stands witnesses to an impasse and points to a hoped-for 'concord' which has not yet arrived.

The way Lewis found out of this personal impasse was at once spiritual, theological and literary, and it brings us to the heart of both his Christian belief and his poetic practice. In Christ he sees the linking of the broken parts and the severed dimensions of our divided being: the height and depth, the east and west, outer and inner, reason and imagination. Lewis's great task at a personal, spiritual level is obedient and humble reintegration under the guidance of the shaping and creative Word of God incarnate in Christ, but this is also his task as a writer. There is no place in his theory for 'originality', for a fragmented privatized vision, because the task is not simply to comment privately on our present disintegration of sensibility but to learn afresh the profound and given, unfallen 'stock responses'. Because Christ is the Logos who is himself a *mimesis* of the Father, so poetic mimesis can become a kind of *Imitatio Christi*. So, for both Coleridge and Lewis, Christ came as the liberator and reconciler of both reason and imagination. Perhaps this is another aspect of the *totus Christus* we are exploring in this volume.

Notes

1 *A Midsummer Night's Dream*, Act V, Scene 1.

2 *A Midsummer Night's Dream*, Act V, Scene 1, lines 2–21.

3 'Digging', in Seamus Heaney, *Opened Ground* (London: Faber & Faber, 1998), pp. 3–4.

4 'Bone Dreams', in Heaney, *Opened Ground*, p. 107.

5 T. S. Eliot, 'East Coker', II, lines 18–21.

6 Malcolm Guite, *Faith, Hope and Poetry: Theology and the Poetic Imagination* (Farnham: Ashgate, 2012 [2010]).

7 George Steiner, *Real Presences* (London: Faber, 1989), pp. 3–4.

8 Samuel Taylor Coleridge, *Biographia Literaria*, ed. by James Engell and W. Jackson Bate, 2 vols (Princeton: Princeton University Press, 1983), vol. 1, pp. 241–2.

9 'Frost at Midnight', lines 54–64. Available from <https://www.poetryfoundation.org/poems/43986/frost-at-midnight>.

10 Kathleen Coburn, ed., *The Notebooks of Samuel Taylor Coleridge* (Princeton: Princeton University Press, 1957–73), vol. 2, p. 2546.

11 Coleridge, *Biographia Literaria*, vol. 2, pp. 247–8.

12 C. S. Lewis, *Surprised by Joy* (London: Fount Paperbacks, 1977 [1955]), p. 138. For McGilchrist *avant la lettre*, see Iain McGilchrist, *The Master and his Emissary: The Divided Brain and the Making of the Western World* (New Haven, CT: Yale University Press, 2010). McGilchrist is discussed also in the chapter in this volume by George Westhaver, 'The Oxford Movement and the Incarnation'.

13 *The Collected Poems of C. S. Lewis* ed. by Walter Hooper (London: Fount Paperbacks, 1994), p. 95.

PART 5

Christ the Saviour Irreducible and Complete

Before Abraham Was I AM[1]

John 8.58: Jesus said unto them, Verily, verily, I say unto you, Before Abraham was, I am.

Oh pure I AM, the source of everything,
The wellspring of my inner consciousness,
The song within the songs I find to sing,
The bliss of being and the crown of bliss,
You iterate and indwell all the instants
Wherein I wake and wonder that I am,
As every moment of my own existence
Runs over from the fountain of your name.

I turn with Jacob, Isaac, Abraham,
With everyone whom you have called to be,
I turn with all the fallen race of Adam
To hear you calling, calling 'Come to me'.
With them I come, all weary and oppressed,
And lay my labours at your feet, and rest.

---

1 Originally published in Malcolm Guite, *Parable and Paradox* (Norwich: Canterbury Press, 2016).

15

The Work of a Theologian
in the Body of Christ

LEWIS AYRES

Introduction

We are saved through the unity of the Word with the human nature that he took as his own. In all manner of ways might we have been saved; in reality the Father chose to save us in Christ, through the unity of the incarnate Word. Consequently, there is no way to the Father except through the one mediator, the man Jesus Christ. This is not a statement about the centrality of verbal confession, but a theological statement about the mysterious structure of the divine economy. Whether we know it or not, *if* we are drawn to the Father, *if* we are drawn into the communion of the divine life, it is so because we have been drawn into the body of Christ through the animating gift of his Spirit. Only so have we come to share in Christ's atoning work, and in his eternal love for and praise of the Father. The Father draws us into this atoning and restoring work through engrafting us into a complex set of relationships with the humanity of the incarnate Word, that which is, as Thomas Aquinas tells us, both the *caro Dei* (the flesh of God) and the *caro humanae naturae* (the flesh of human nature).[1] We address prayers through him, and to him, he is our *exemplum*, he is our head gone before to set out the way, it is into him that we are assumed as we travel along that way, and beneath an impenetrable veil it is he who is priest and victim at the holy mysteries, and it is him whom we consume at that feast.

Through the course of this chapter, I want to think about some key aspects of the theologian's work by setting that work within the broader context sketched in the previous paragraph. Reflecting on how Christians find themselves in a multiplicity of relationships to the one mediator will provide us with a number of principles and analogies that will fuel what I hope will be a reasonably entertaining series of complaints about the tendencies of academic theology in our day. Put more positively, I hope to show, first, that one of the oldest dynamics of Christian intellectual life should remain ever with us. Since the second century of the Church's life, theological minds have devoted much attention to the tensions between the faith of the unlearned Christian, the faith into which we are all baptized and the speculations of those with appropriate intellectual gifts who feel the draw to explore the riches of our faith. My argument will be that attention to the dynamics of our relationship to the humanity of Christ can help us penetrate to the heart of how the tension between unlearned and learned faith should be held.

De occulto mysterio[2]

We must first, then, establish a doctrinal point. How do Christians relate to the human flesh of the incarnate Word? In a multiplicity of ways irreducible to a simple pattern or concept that may be grasped beyond the stark imagery of flesh on flesh, flesh in flesh, and flesh consumed by flesh. This is not at all to say that theological exploration of this multiplicity of ways is inevitably fruitless, but it is to say that theological thinking here can only perform its task well by ever circling a mysterious vortex of imagery that stimulates but also binds imagination and intellect.[3]

Allow me to begin with one of the best known of Christological tensions. The incarnate and risen Word is both our head and the body of which we are members. As head of his body, the incarnate Word has gone before us and, to use a spatial metaphor that is, of course, problematic, he turns back to draw us to him. As Augustine writes,

> Our Head intercedes for us: some members He is receiving, others He is chastising, others cleansing, others consoling, others creating, others calling, others recalling, others correcting, others renewing.[4]

It is also as the one who has gone before that Christ is our example, and is viewed as it were at a distance – sometimes at a distance summed up in the great icons of Christ *pantokrator*, Christ as ruler of all, sustaining us and preparing for judgement – and sometimes as the Christ whose virtuous and loving life is now laid out before us, lived toward God's work in all the events that the Scriptures narrate. 'Example' here has many resonances, and summary of them is near impossible.

But as the one who draws Christians together into his body, Christ is not distant from us; we are incorporated into him. Christ has chosen, we might say, again following Augustine, that he will be complete with us as his body. Our lives, our suffering and our virtue make up what is missing (Col. 1.24). And all of these, of course, are given us by him even as they are ours.[5] From this perspective, our relationship to the life-giving humanity of Christ almost defies imagination and representation. His humanity touches ours – the language is warranted by the Thomist insistence that Christ's humanity is an instrumental *efficient* cause[6] – but touches in a way that is ever mysterious. As Christians we are *in* the events of Christ's incarnate life; we are baptized into his death and we have begun to rise with him.[7] But, of course, the Church is not in Christ such that all that is true of the incarnate Word's humanity is true of us. Through the outpouring of his Spirit – Christ's Spirit – we are also adopted sons and daughters of the Father (2 Cor. 6.18). The first chapter of Ephesians, for example, while it speaks ultimately of the Church as Christ's body, and thus as the 'fullness' of Christ, the one in whom we are redeemed by sharing in his blood, also insists that we are individually 'sons' (of the Father). The two languages sit together, but with little explanation of how that may be so (cf. Gal. 4.5). Our relationship to the incarnate Word is thus multilayered, both inviting and defeating intellect and imagination, and it is so because this is a relationship to a body – transformed for sure, but still a body.

We must take one step more. The complexities of our relationship to the Word's own body are focused by the Eucharist like the sun's rays through a lens. But, rather than continuing with Augustine, allow me to turn briefly to Thomas. Perhaps surprisingly, his more developed account of the eucharistic presence in the elements will better help us see the paradoxes of Christ's fleshy presence focused to intensity. At one level, Thomas's account is deeply and starkly realist. Famously he states that 'the whole body', is present, 'the bones and nerves and all the rest'.[8] Indeed, his defence of the term 'transubstantiation' (which was defined for him at the fourth Lateran Council),[9] juxtaposes a stark realism, and a relentless insistence that we confess the incomprehensibility of how this realism is effected. The term 'transubstantiation' names the complete change of the substance of the bread into Christ's true body and flesh, and yet the term is used precisely because this unique form of change must have a name of its own.[10]

There is work for theology to do here, but that work seems only to heighten complexities. We might note two (of the many) qualifications Thomas introduces. First, this body is not marked by space and, second, this body is present as substance without any accidental presence, and hence may be known, not by sense or imagination, but *only* by the intellect.[11] In the light of the first qualification, the assertion of Christ's true giving of his body in the consecrated elements shimmers before us as a true mirage. This is his true body, animated by his soul and rendered life-giving by the power of the Word who assumed both body and soul. Yet, our power to imagine that body is torn from us once we accept that our spatial conceptions of body will not do. This is the crucified, risen and ascended body, truly there and truly beyond the imagination. And thus, the second qualification. The eucharistic presence can be confessed by the grace-aided and grasped by the intellect. But the more the mind attends well to this reality, the more it is thrown back onto the virtue of faith. Indeed, within Western liturgies, there are few greater reminders of what faith entails than the elevation of the host after consecration. What some will have expected, when I mentioned St Thomas, to be an overly technical and speculative account of the eucharistic elements, turns out to be a precise, incisive exploration of narratives, images and terminologies that offer an invitation to the Christian mind, but which ever show us how faith must remain faith.

Although I distinguished Thomas and Augustine here, they could be reunited were we to take time to explore how Thomas includes and adapts Augustine's account of Christians being taken up mystically into Christ as the priest who offers to the Father, and into Christ as the lamb that is slain and offered.[12] Both theologians put before us a complex and interrelated matrix of biblical symbolism. An interrelated and sometimes tensional set of themes generates a catalogue of relationships to the enfleshed Word. Body gazes at body, flesh touches flesh and body finds itself in the body of another. But, this catalogue of relationships is no theological confusion that we might unravel. The divine body whose reality founds this matrix of symbolism exceeds our capacity to grasp. Indeed, the transcendence we have here is not one that relativizes all representation, but one in which the divine excess reveals itself to us and takes up for our use a range of terminologies and images that may guide and shape our meditation until the end.

In saying all this, it should be noted, I am *not* offering any implied critique of the complex eucharistic theologies with which my tradition is filled; my aim is only at renewing our focus on the complexity that founds all such theology if it is worth the name. And so, one of the fundamental conclusions I want to draw from this brief examination may follow on from a point made with characteristic passion by the Russian polymath and martyr Pavel Florensky:

> . . . the more massively and metaphysically crudely and archaically we conceive religious concepts, the more profound will the symbolism of their expression be and therefore the closer we will come to a genuine understanding of strictly religious experience. This compressed, densified character of religious concepts characterizes our entire liturgy.[13]

If we want to 'understand' the reality of what happens to us when we are drawn into the body of Christ we cannot do better than speak attentively the basic language that Scripture and the liturgy give us. But 'speaking *attentively*' has many modes. The Christian uninterested in intellectual exploration, but who speaks this language in direct faith, the one who believes simply that 'this is my body', sets an example to all. Their attentiveness to the one who is present and who effects this change, their willingness to speak this language as their own, should surely humble those gifted with the desire and ability to explore further. And yet 'speaking attentively' may also refer to that speaking which occurs as part of a lifelong struggle to advance in understanding through thought and prayer.[14]

But, in both cases, 'this is my body' and '[h]e who eats my flesh and drinks my blood abides in me, and I in him' (John 6.54) are most deeply understood when they are heard in their full strangeness. Of course, to hear the latter in 'full strangeness' is already to have heard Christ say that he is the 'living bread which came down from heaven' (John 6.51) and to know that we have in this chapter of John's Gospel complex metaphorical fields (seen for example in the chapter's insinuation of much that attends on the significance of manna in Jewish tradition), and the brute realism of Christ's command that we eat his flesh. The languages with which we have to deal here invoke images deeply rooted in Israel's history and yet turn them to new ends in the light of Christ. There is much for the theological mind to do here, but the images remain images until the end, to entice and defeat the fallen mind. Attenuation of the linguistic resources present in these images runs the risk of failing us, leading us to attempt a theological move 'beyond' – but in fact simply away from – the reality of the enfleshed Word's presence in the eucharistic sacrifice. Simple faith may grasp what the gifted intellect may miss, and there are lessons here for all who attempt to think theologically.[15]

Ad divinae revelationis fontes[16]

There is nothing in what I have written here so far, I hope, that does anything other than present – from my own particular angle – some fundamental canons of Catholic orthodoxy. The question I want to ask in the remainder of my chapter is this: if what I have presented is a description of the water in which the theologian swims, how should she swim such that the nature of the water is not forgotten or mistaken? In case the allusion is not obvious to you, I allude here to the famous commencement address delivered at Kenyon College in 2005 by the late David Foster Wallace. That address is built around a simple story which runs as follows:

> There are these two young fish swimming along, and they happen to meet an older fish swimming the other way, who nods at them and says, 'Morning, boys. How's the water?' And the two young fish swim on for a bit, and then eventually one of them looks over at the other and goes, 'What the hell is water?'[17]

The 'water' – and the wine – in which theologians swim is the body and blood of Christ, both in the sense that this is the ontological context of our existence, and in the sense that theologians should (if they honour the name) swim in a sea constituted by a set of terminologies and images which constantly push us beyond the limit of human understanding. There is no escape from this sea, because it is into this sea that the Father pushed us when the Son assumed our human nature and spoke to us in the language of Israel's Scriptures.

In this section of my chapter, then, I want to look at ways in which awareness of our complex relationship to the flesh of God may shape how we understand the theologian's task at this point in the history of Christian thought. But, first, I think we need to take a few moments for a little ground clearing, and answer the basic question: What do I mean by theology? How one answers this question makes a great difference to how one conceives its relationship to the engagement of Christians with the humanity of Christ.

Theology, I suggest, is one of the ways in which Christians proclaim, speculate, wonder and praise.[18] It is, in other words, an activity inseparable from the modes of thinking, speech and imagining that are simply intrinsic to being one of the baptized. For the sake of argument, allow me to suggest that theology may be considered under two basic headings, those of 'handing on' and 'speculating' – *traditio* and *speculatio*. The task of handing on that which we have been given, handing on so that its promise is embraced by a new generation, is surely one of the most basic dynamics of the theological act. That which we hand on involves not only propositions, statements of faith and a symbolic universe, but also a sense of the promise and tensions that flow from the complexities of our relationship to the incarnate Word. In this last sense, I allude to that strain of thought from Maurice Blondel to Yves Congar that founds tradition in the possession of a sense of the faith.[19]

Handing on is also a *prophetic* act, but I understand this term in a fairly traditional Christian sense, not as the prophesying of what will happen, but as a testifying to the work of God. Testimony of course involves calling out that which is not of God and speaking about what will be; but at its root all Christians are prophets insofar as they testify to the work of God in the world. To see the dynamics of the prophetic here one can do much worse than look to the discussion that occupies the first half of Congar's early *True and False Reform in the Church*.[20]

Theology is also speculative. I used the Latin term *speculatio* for a reason; it carries both the sense of scrutiny, of examining and judging a reality that is before one, *and* the sense of a looking out over a broad horizon – speculation in the sense of an intellectual attempt to stretch established principles to new cases, or to bring into theological orbit new questions and new theoretical resources. The articulation and rearticulation necessary when one hands on – even using well-established terms and concepts – shows that *traditio* and *speculatio* are interwoven. But there is also a speculation that is part of the invitation God extends to his people. To restore and exercise human reason we are invited to think with, in and through the Word that has been spoken among us. Through meditation on this Word we may with grace and in time come to see more of the created order both in glory and (for now) in tragedy. In this sense though, it will be reasonably obvious that speculation can never be anything other than deeply rooted in the act of tradition.

The act of *traditio* and *speculatio* has different aspects shaped by the manner in which different resources for thought and different contexts intervene. Most obviously in our day, and in the context of theological thinking when it is practised in universities, the act may be focused on biblical texts, or on resources from the tradition, or with particular philosophical questions in mind (to give just three examples). But a great deal is lost when these different aspects are not perceived as necessarily part of a conversation, and as aimed at the same goal, and as at handing on the same faith – from another perspective one might say, when they are not understood as actions within the symbolic world and the reality of body of Christ as it heads toward union with the Father. An extra level of difficulty exists here because, of necessity, the conversation that constitutes the theological act occurs amid and is nurtured by a wide variety of other secular conversations that have little interest in (and often only animosity towards) the Christian tradition. These secular conversations are thus both generative and seductive. It is the negotiation of the boundaries thus created (boundaries which might also be construed as debates over ends and over assumptions about the nature of the created order and the activities of knowing and reasoning) that have caused so much of the controversy over the very nature of theology in the past few hundred years.

If one construes the nature of theology in something like this fashion – and I recognize that what I have said is inescapably abstract in tone – then it becomes clear that the core of theological thinking consists in handing on and thinking through Christ crucified and risen, and the God and the created order revealed through the Word's mission. Theology in this sense is rarely far from the need to think about Christ's person, in human and in Trinitarian perspective. It is important, I think, for this to be stated frequently; around this task in the modern theological world many other tasks and concerns have come to circle – some of necessity, some falsely, most partaking of some truth, but some only naked emperors.

What attitude will enable us to sustain attention to the complexities of these conversations and to return our focus (as it so easily is drawn away) on that which should draw our attention? Last year, I was asked to speak on theology and spirituality at a Benedictine monastery in Kent. The topic was 'what do the saints know?' While there are many ways in which I might have answered this question, I suggested that the saints were those attentive to the *disruption* that the gospel effects to our reasoning and to our imagining of the world. By 'disruption' I refer to the manner in which, first, the language of the Christian faith – its fount of images and narratives – *generates* particular avenues of thought that cut across those that may have been common currency in a particular culture or in a particular life. But, second, I also refer to the way that this generative force is also a *binding* one, restricting, rejecting and often interrupting paths of thought and imagination that otherwise might have seemed attractive, rational or just simply obvious.

I hope that my use of the word 'imagination' here gives a sense of the sheer range of ways in which the gospel generatively and bindingly disrupts. Through the Spirit's work, this disruption happens in and is modelled for us by those of many intellectual gifts and by those with few. The direct and persevering faith of the parishioner who attends daily Mass and believes in the words of the liturgy played out before him or her exemplifies the disruption of the gospel every bit as much as the philosopher who confesses

Christ and abandons the patterns of reason that seem hallowed by tradition to follow a new rationality (say an Origen, a Victorinus or an Edith Stein), or every bit as much as the dramatic decision of one who sells all and heads for the desert (say an Antony). Each of these, under the power of the Spirit, exemplifies the generative and binding disruption that the gospel causes in the fallen world, and each offers lessons for the theologian about the brute reality of the terms, commands and images through which the Word has been spoken to us. And at the very heart of that generative and binding disruption is the continually nurturing symbolic field through which we speak of, worship and touch the humanity of Christ. The development of attention to ways in which this field generates and disrupts is essential if we are to avoid the seductions of entering without theological critique into the secular conversations that are also essential nurturing features of the Christian tradition. This disruption occurs in aid of the mind's reformation, and this leads to one of the perennial ironies of Christian attempts to develop in knowledge of God.

Early Christian theologians devoted considerable energy to meditating on what should be a constant question: how should we articulate the relationship between, on the one hand, the faith delivered in catechesis and, on the other hand, the speculative work of intellectual gifted and active Christians? Because of the legacy of the Gnostic dispute, it was fundamental that the one who engaged in speculative work could not reject that which is given us in catechesis and in the bare language of the Scriptures. But *how* this non-rejection should be understood was open to many interpretations.

I want to consider just one meditation on the question, but one of the richest, that which is to be found in a striking and complex passage of Augustine's 98th Tractate on John, probably written in the second decade of the fifth century. But we must note where he begins. Through this text, Augustine asks whether there is any extra knowledge that 'spiritual' persons possess that is not also possessed by those who are still 'carnal'. Augustine asks whether those who, through the gift of the Spirit and through the exercise of their intelligence, see something of the treasures of wisdom and knowledge (Col. 2.3), see more or different things than those who can take only the milk of Christ's teaching. Augustine gets to the heart of his answer thus:

> Mother Wisdom herself, who, although on high she is the solid food of the angels, deigned in a manner of speaking to turn into milk for the little ones, 'when the Word was made flesh and dwelt among us.' But this very man Christ who, in his true flesh, true cross, true death, true Resurrection, is called the pure milk of little ones, when he is correctly apprehended by spiritual men, is found to be the Lord of the angels.[21]

For the 'little ones', Wisdom became the 'milk' that could nurture us, incarnate in a manner that could be seen and heard by us. Those who are 'spiritual' come to see that this very same one is the Lord of the angels. The increase that is vouchsafed the 'spiritual' is an increase in understanding of the very realities given to us all that we might understand something of God's purposes. Indeed, Augustine takes the question further:

> little ones neither must be suckled in such a way that they always fail to understand [that] Christ [is] God, nor must they be weaned in such a way that they forsake Christ the man . . . the crucified Christ is both milk for those suckling, and food for those advancing.

The crucified Christ comes in here because of Augustine's insistence that progress across the sea of this world involves increasing adherence to the wood of the cross, increasing humility before the event that is a constant stumbling block to the philosophers of this world. Christ is, in a famous image, both the homeland to which we travel and the road we must travel if we are to arrive.

At one level, Augustine is concerned with describing the faith of those who deserve the title 'spiritual'. Being one of the 'spiritual' has nothing to do with one's degree of learning, or one's place in the Church, but everything to do with the gift of grace and the consequent character of one's faith, hope and love. And yet, at another level, Augustine is using his account of the relationship between the simple in faith and the spiritual to condition and critique all that he also says about the intellectual task of thinking the divine. Thus, Augustine tends to present the very transcending of the material in our imaginations, the increasing recognition of the consequences of divine transcendence for how we understand biblical language, as one of the central tasks for the speculative imagination. But even this attempt to think towards a better conception of God serves us ill without also a constant recognition of our failure to understand, and a prayer for grace that we may love God more intensely. The 'spiritual' are thus the model for all intellectual Christians *both* in providing an example of some features at which we should aim – submission to Scripture, love for Christ, recognition of divine transcendence, recognition of the need for grace – *and* in offering a constant critique of the sense of intellectual mastery that may accompany intellectual prowess. When Augustine, in *Confessions* Book 13 offers a parallel portrayal of the 'spiritual', he presents this class as those who are taught by God 'to see the Trinity of the Unity and the Unity of the Trinity', but also as those who do not judge the Scripture that is set above them as a firmament; it is only a short step to read this attention to the firmament as parallel in many ways to the generating and interrupting force of Scripture of which I spoke above.[22]

With Augustine we might compare how Newman celebrates and yet undercuts both the university and the 'liberal' mind at whose production it should be aimed. Towards the end of the nine discourses that make up *The Idea of the University*, Newman, after lauding the potential of the liberal arts, undercuts much of what he might seem to have offered, by emphasizing the impossibility of the university teaching true humility, the virtue essential for true Christian growth:

> humility or condescension . . . may be said to consist . . . in placing ourselves in our thoughts on a level with our inferiors; it is not only a voluntary relinquishment of the privileges of our own station, but an actual participation or assumption of the condition of those to whom we stoop . . . it is an abdication, as far as their own thoughts are concerned, of those prerogatives or privileges to which others deem them entitled.[23]

Newman names humility here 'a virtue of conduct', slicing through what intellectuals call 'modesty'. Such modesty is an 'embellishment of the exterior' only, and so can be part of a 'philosophical morality' which may be 'proud at the very time that it is unassuming'. This kind of modesty is the very opposite of that which Christianity holds up before us.[24] But he names also an intellectual virtue, a virtue that follows when we are attentive to what it is that the saints know; humility is that which St Philip Neri and others know, and that which the university will always hold of no regard. And the school in which we learn the force, the generative power and the strictures of a humble submission to the disruptions of the gospel is the body of Christ. The lesson that Augustine and Newman join in recommending to us is one that we learn as we journey with all of the baptized, it is learned by attending to, submitting to and believing upon the symbolic universe through which we are drawn into contact with the saving humanity of Christ.

How, then, can we imagine a conception of theological practice that will best bring to our attention the struggles of theologians to inhabit the symbolic universe of the Word's own body? Here I am happy to declare my hand as a student of those theologians who encouraged the Church toward a project of *ressourcement* in the first half of the last century. Most certainly, any articulation of their programme – or, better, programmes – in our day involves a radical rethinking of some emphases, but one remains as important now as it was then: the importance of turning to the work of pre-modern Christian theologians in the round. *Ressourcement* in this sense involves turning back to consider the great and foundational theologians of our tradition as living minds struggling, growing, changing, tacking one way and then another as they seek to hand on and articulate the faith in particular contexts. This is not a preliminary educational task (what was named from the fifteenth century as 'positive' theology), but at the very heart of grasping the speculative core of Christian teaching.[25]

Now, to argue such a case is to make a statement about the theological nature of tradition, about how we view the theological history that God has gifted to us. As I have suggested in a number of papers over the last few years, arguing that the Church's tradition is gift rather than simply a historical succession of opinions is one of the most basic tasks for anyone attempting to set out a *theology* of the theological task today. The theologian who came closest to expressing the theology of tradition required here is Yves Congar. He writes,

> Sacred history, the history of the Church as the Church of God, is made out of the succession of God's 'visitations' thanks to which men elicit those responses of faith and love by which the city of God is built up. In a theological analysis, this moment of the divine activity, which logically precedes our free decisions or reactions, is attributed simultaneously to God and to the sacred humanity of Christ, our head . . .[26]

'Sacred history' is the consequence of the work of divine grace in history, operating through the sacred humanity of Christ (and Congar's very choice of words shows his own deeply rooted Thomism – *ressourcement* and Thomas are no enemies!). The sheer diversity of realities which must be included in that history is beautifully conveyed by Congar a few paragraphs later:

> . . . the history of the Church is . . . that of the achievement or consolidation of [the covenant] relationship, already perfectly established, but not yet fully consummated. This history could be formulated as in Hebrews 11: 'it was by faith, fulfilling the gospel and by a mission of the holy spirit that the Council of Nicaea . . . it was by faith . . . that Augustine . . . by faith . . . that Francis Xavier . . . that Thérèse Martin, and so on.' This history recalls Christians' responses to the calls of God and of time; it is made up of councils, acts of the magisterium, missionary endeavours, and religious foundations, of conversions and of decisions taken for God; but also the more secret history, to be disclosed only at the last judgement, of all the movements of faith and love drawn from our human freedom by God's grace.[27]

Congar speaks here not only of the history of magisterial teaching, but also of the broader tradition of theological reflection and spiritual vision that is that teaching's context. A theology of tradition along these lines – and Congar offers us only the barest hints – can help us develop patterns of attention to the struggles of Christian thinkers to articulate the Christian faith and stay faithful to the symbolic world of Christ's body.

There is much that follows from this suggestion that theological thinking should root itself far more deeply in a particular vision of the tradition and its lessons. There is much, for example, that I might suggest about how we should envisage the various subdivisions of the theological act. Space prevents me from sketching much here. But, for the sake of stimulating conversation, allow me to suggest that, perhaps, we should imagine good discussions of Christian doctrine as the efflorescence of long historical and scriptural exploration (not as the product of a distinct discipline called 'systematic' theology). Perhaps we should imagine historical work by theologians as a negotiation of boundaries, a constant struggle to understand the contexts and questions that formed the horizons of those we find in the Christian tradition (thus engaging positively the canons of a good deal of post-renaissance historiography), and yet learning to see those figures and periods as also the outworkings of a divine providence (and thus simultaneously attentive to where the canons of our faith demand rather different accounts of human agency). Perhaps we should imagine Christian exegesis as not only a similar negotiation of canons, but also as a pluralistic exercise in which the history of reception takes increasing prominence as we recognize ways in which the Spirit draws out of the text its full resources.[28] Perhaps we should imagine the theologian's engagements as always caught between an attempt to grasp the world as it is and an attempt to understand the failures of human knowing that can only be completed by submission to the disruptions of the gospel. There is no space to consider any of these suggestions in detail, but each suggestion is aimed at pushing us to think how we might imagine theology's task and its subdivisions in the light of a truly theological conception of the tradition as a school for thinking and imagining within the body of Christ.

I want to bring these reflections to a close by reflecting again on the dangers of the university. I write all this, of course, as someone who teaches in one and is happy to receive a cheque at the end of every month! Now, the university is not the home for all theological thinking, *Deo gratias*, and it may well be that, if things continue as they are in this country, less and less theological thinking will occur directly in that context. But the university has, over the last couple of centuries, deeply shaped how we conceive the task. And this shaping has been both a gift and also a curse.

Why has it been a curse? Precisely because it has made harder an appreciation of the generative and binding disruption that is intrinsic to our relationship with the flesh of God. In the last discourse of *The Idea of a University*, Newman turns again to the manner in which the university works against the very structures of 'revealed religion'. He writes:

> This then is the tendency of that Liberal Education, of which a University is the school, viz., to view Revealed Religion from an aspect of its own – to fuse and recast it, – to tune it, as it were, to a different key, and reset its harmonies, – to circumscribe it by a circle which unwarrantably amputates here, and unduly develops there; and all under the notion, conscious or unconscious, that the human intellect, self-educated and self-supported, is more true and perfect in its ideas and judgements than that of Prophets and Apostles, to whom the sights and sounds of Heaven were immediately conveyed. A sense of propriety, order, consistency, and completeness gives birth to a rebellious stirring against mystery and miracle, against the severe and the terrible.[29]

What I find particularly interesting is that Newman writes these words at the end of a series of discourses in which he has insisted that theology has a vital place *within* the university, and that the liberal arts are the *core* of any decent education. It is not that theologians should leave the university to its own self-delusions. It is, however, that any attempt to practise the theological act within this context must constantly be aware of how it will subtly be circumscribed and reshaped by the very culture it seeks to enhance. Now one of the ways in which life within the university has sought to tune us to a different key in the century and a half since Newman wrote is through the gradual professionalization of theological subdisciplines.

The term professionalization, of course, refers in a rather general sense to the process by which a group of people engaged in an activity take on common work practices, common standards for their activity and develop institutions that will sustain a common vision of their role. Professional is, of course, often used in opposition to amateur, and it has so been used since at least the nineteenth century, very often (and rightly) with the sense that the transition from the latter to the former involves a certain loss. Here, I use the term to refer to the manner in which the various constitutive aspects of the theological act have gradually been seduced into developing professional cultures and institutions to the detriment of their common task and conversation. I am hardly the first to point out that the gradual professionalization of theological subdisciplines occurred alongside the development of other secular disciplines and alongside complex developments in conceptions of research and argument. Often in a hidden and gradual manner, but sometimes with open if (I think) deeply misguided celebration, the various aspects of the theological act have been rendered apart and imbued with assumptions about the nature of investigation and discovery that work against the unity of the theological act.

It is in this context that calls for a greater attention to the rich symbolic universe of Christ's body, calls to the disruption of the gospel and calls for us to shape a theology of tradition that can reground our attention in the providential history of our responses to divine action, all easily fall into stony ground. They do so because of our indebtedness to visions of the discipline that war against our best instincts. In some ways, the past 30 years have seen the emergence of a new willingness to think outside the boxes of our subdisciplines; in other ways, this is a battle whose outcome is still very much in the balance.

Now, those who laud or even only defend the process of professionalization will, of course, point to the necessity of training students in increasingly specialized subfields of study; without this process surely successful training is in jeopardy? It is against this charge that I want to end by opposing the importance of what I will term 'theological expertise' to 'professionalization'. True theological expertise should focus around two skills or habits.

The first is skill in negotiating the link between Augustine's milk and solid food, knowing what an increase in theological knowledge actually involves and knowing the constant relevance of the symbolic world of the faith into which we are baptized. Now, obviously enough, one is hardly going to be proficient at this task without knowing a good deal of that symbolic universe, and one will need good models of submission to it, good models of humble and attentive speakers. Once again, we come back to the importance of Christians' relationship to the incarnate Word's flesh as a school for theological thinking.

The second skill is negotiating well the boundaries of Christianity's relationship to the humanities. Whatever subdivisions of the theological act we make our own, we will find ourselves in a symbiosis with the study of the liberal arts; this has been ours since antiquity. Yes, of course, the modern historicisms that I see as offering such a promise for theological thinking, and yet such a seductive danger, are the product of developments that began only a few hundred years ago. Yet, insofar as they represent one stage in the development of humanity's tools for analysing human culture and human texts, their emergence is only part of a story with which Christianity has been engaged since at least the second century. If we are to engage well now with such secular traditions, it is vital that we become attuned to where and how theological thinking is pressed into a retuning as Newman has it, and where it is not. There are many who can undertake this discernment well, but in their very professionalization our subdisciplinary boundaries fight against this more deeply than I think many are prepared to admit. And if we have become inept at noticing when we have left a fruitful path, I suggest it is precisely because we have forgotten the lessons taught to us by attending to the complexities of how we relate to the flesh of God.

Now, this has been all very grand and all very abstract. I am under no illusion that one can usefully achieve much by sketching a general plan for reorganizing how theology is taught in our universities or how theologians are trained. The forces at play are too complex and powerful. But there may be value in thinking about strategies for resistance, and what should commend itself to us better than a strategy that focuses on attending more deeply to the lessons we should learn as those who inhabit and consume Christ's body?

Notes

1 Thomas Aquinas, *Summa Theologica*, IIIa, q. 48, a. 2, ad 3; q. 48, a. 4, ad 1.

2 Pius XII, *Mystici Corporis Christi*, 79.

3 Concise theological works which attempt to give a sense of the fundamental structure of the divine economy through attention to the complex patterns of imagery Scripture delivers us, and the adaptations of such terminologies through the course of Scripture, are rare in recent decades. For two examples, see Yves Congar, *The Mystery of the Temple, or the Manner of God's Presence to His Creatures from Genesis to the Apocalypse*, trans. by Reginald F. Trevett (Westminster, MD: Newman Press, 1962); and Jean Daniélou, *The Bible and the Liturgy* (Notre Dame, IN: University of Notre Dame Press, 1960).

4 Augustine, En. in Ps. 85.5 (quoted in *Mystici Corporis* 59). On the theme of the *totus Christus* in Augustine see esp. *Serm.* 341, and the chapter by Fr Andrew Louth in this volume.

5 On the priority of Christ's action, see for example *Mystici Corporis* 51: 'He gives increase of grace and prepares future glory for souls and bodies. All these treasures of His divine goodness He is said to bestow on the members of His Mystical Body, not merely because He, as the Eucharistic Victim on earth and the glorified Victim in heaven, through His wounds and His prayers pleads our cause before the Eternal Father, but because He selects, He determines, He distributes every single grace to every single person "according to the measure of the giving of Christ".'

6 References here might abound, and the secondary debates are extensive. As a point of departure, consider Thomas's discussion of whether Christ's passion brought about salvation as an efficient cause, *ST*, IIIa, q. 48, a. 6.

7 See Michael Cameron, *Christ Meets Me Everywhere: Augustine's Early Figurative Exegesis* (Oxford: Oxford University Press, 2012).

8 *ST*, IIIa, q. 76, a. 1, ad 2.

9 For the relevant text, see H. Denzinger and P. Huenermann (eds), *Enchiridion Symbolorum*, 43rd edition (San Francisco, CA: Ignatius Press, 2012), no. 802.

10 *ST*, IIIa, q. 75, a.5, r.

11 *ST*, IIIa, q. 75, a.2, ad. 3: *sed quodam speciali modo, qui est proprius huic sacramento*; *ST* IIIa, q. 76, a.7, r.

12 For the original discussion in Augustine, one should begin with the famous discussion at *City of God* 10.20 and *serm.* 229a. For a good introduction to the dynamics of the Eucharist as sacrifice in Thomas, see Bruce D. Marshall, 'The Whole Mystery of Our Salvation: St. Thomas Aquinas on the Eucharist as Sacrifice', in *Rediscovering Aquinas and the Sacraments: Studies in Sacramental Theology*, ed. by Matthew Levering and Michael Dauphinais (Chicago, IL: Hillenbrand Books, 2009), pp. 39–64.

13 Pavel Florensky, *The Pillar and Ground of the Truth: An Essay in Theodicy in Twelve Letters*, trans. by Boris Jakim (Princeton, NJ: Princeton University Press, 2004), p. 63.

14 Bruce D. Marshall, '*Quod Scit Una Vetula*: Aquinas on the Nature of Theology', in *The Theology of Thomas Aquinas*, ed. by Rik Van Nieuwenhove and Joseph Wawrykow (Notre Dame, IN: University of Notre Dame Press, 2005), pp. 1–35.

15 Christ's humanity is that through which God addresses us, and transforms us, but we should not make the mistake of assuming that this humanity is thereby and *a priori* comprehensible to us. On this principle and its consequences see, for example, Henri De Lubac, *A Brief Catechesis on Nature and Grace,* trans. by Richard Arnandez (San Francisco: Ignatius Press, 1984), pp. 81–8.

16 Pius XII, *Humani Generis*, 21.

17 See David Wallace, 'This is Water', <http://www.metastatic.org/text/This%20is%20Water.pdf> [accessed 31 January 2019].

18 This brief account draws on my 'What is Catholic Theology?', in *The Oxford Handbook of Catholic Theology*, ed. by Lewis Ayres and Medi Ann Volpe (Oxford: Oxford University Press, 2019), pp. 5–41; and my '*Totius Traditionis Mirabile Sacramentum*: A Theology of Tradition in the Light of *Dei Verbum*', in *Ad Limina Apostolorum*, ed. by Thomas Joseph White, Bruce McCormack and Matthew Levering (Washington, DC: Catholic University of America Press, forthcoming).

19 Maurice Blondel, *The Letter on Apologetics & History and Dogma*, trans. by Alexander Dru and Iltyd Trethowan (Grand Rapids MI: Eerdmans, 1995), p. 267: '[Tradition] preserves not so much the intellectual aspect of the past, as its living reality . . . It relies, no doubt, on texts, but at the same time it relies primarily on something else, on an experience always in act which enables it to remain in some respects master of the texts, instead of being strictly subservient to them.' Cf. Yves Congar, *Tradition and Traditions*, one volume edition, trans. by Michael Naseby and T. Rainsborough (London: Burns and Oates, 1966), p. 279.

20 Yves Congar, *True and False Reform in the Church*, trans. by Paul Philibert (Collegeville, MN: Liturgical Press, 2011).

21 Augustine, *Io. ev. tr.* 98.6; John W. Rettig, *Tractates on The Gospel of John 55–111* (Washington, DC: Catholic University of America Press, 1994), p. 214.

22 See *Conf.* 13. 23.33. Here I use the translation of Henry Chadwick, *Saint Augustine. Confessions* (Oxford: Oxford University Press, 1991).

23 John Henry Newman, *The Idea of a University*, introduced by Martin J. Svaglic (Notre Dame, IN: University of Notre Dame Press, 1982), p. 156 (discourse 8).

24 Newman, *The Idea of a University*, p. 157 (discourse 8).

25 I discuss this principle further in 'Theology and the *Historia Salutis*: Post-Conciliar Renewal and One Recent Thomism', *The Thomist*, 79 (2015), pp. 511–50, and make use of the same quotations from Yves Congar in '*Totius Traditionis Mirabile Sacramentum*'. I would also like to acknowledge here a debt to the third chapter of Marie-Dominique Chenu's powerful *Une école de théologie: le Saulchoir*, ed. by G. Alberigo et al. (Paris: Éditions du Cerf, 1985), esp. pp. 134–4.

26 Yves Congar, *Tradition and Traditions: An Historical and a Theological Essay* (London: Macmillan, 1967), pp. 262–63. Cf. 406ff.

27 Congar, *Tradition and Traditions*, p. 263.

28 I explore this further in 'The Word Answering the Word: Opening the Space of Catholic Biblical Interpretation', in *Theological Theology: Essays in Honor of John B. Webster*, ed. by R. David Nelson, Darren Sarisky and Justin Stratis (London: Bloomsbury, 2015), pp. 37–53.

29 Newman, *The Idea of a University*, p. 165 (discourse 9).

16

Salvation in Christ: Six Models

KALLISTOS WARE

Safety in numbers

Some years ago, I was travelling by railway train when a stranger came and sat opposite me. After staring at me for some time he said, in a low but clear voice, 'Are you saved?' How did I reply? How would *you* reply to that question? I will not say at this point what my reply was, but I will tell you at the end of this chapter.

If we consult the New Testament, what we find is not a single way of understanding the saving work of Christ, not one exclusive and systematic theory, but a series of different images and symbols set side by side. They are images and symbols of profound power, yet for the most part they are not explained or interpreted but left to speak for themselves. If, then, we seek to enter more deeply into the living mystery of Christ's saving work, it is best to follow the example of the New Testament and to have a number of different images in our mind. We should not isolate any single image, treating this as the sole and exclusive key to the doctrine of salvation, but we should combine the various images together. Our guiding motto should be 'safety in numbers'.

Let us look at six possible models of salvation. This list is not meant to be exhaustive; it would certainly be possible to add other models as well. We should not regard these models as mutually exclusive alternatives, but we should work with all of them, for each one reveals part of the truth to us.

This leads me to recall the first time that I travelled to America, some 60 years ago, as a graduate student in 1959. In those days, only the wealthy could afford to travel by air, and so I went by boat, on one of the vast Cunard Liners, the Queen Elizabeth. The voyage lasted five days, and the ticket included not just the sleeping accommodation but also the meals. To my considerable satisfaction, I found that at mealtimes the menu was not divided up into a limited selection of courses. I was given a huge card indicating all the various things that I might choose to eat, and I was left free to devise as many courses as I wished. At breakfast, for example, I could have porridge and cereal and fruit juice, and after that both fried eggs and smoked haddock, if I felt like that in the heaving waters of the mid-Atlantic. In the evening, the other people at my table were somewhat unimaginative, choosing just three courses: soup, meat or fish, and then pudding. I worked out a programme of at least seven courses: melon, then hors d'oeuvres, then soup, fish, meat, cheese and the sweet, with perhaps one or two other items such as a lemon sorbet inserted between the main courses. I remember walking up and down on deck each afternoon for over an hour, so as to provoke a good appetite for the gastronomic challenge of the evening meal. This Cunard system of feeding was highly satisfactory for me as a hungry student, eager to get the full money's worth for my ticket (although it was Princeton University who had actually paid for my journey).

Let us apply the system of the Cunard menu to our present topic, and include in our spiritual meal all the various items on our menu of salvation. Of our six models, let us not say 'either/or' but 'both/and'.

Underlying all six models, there is one fundamental truth: Jesus Christ, as our Saviour, through his cross and resurrection has done something for us that we could not do alone and by ourselves. We cannot save ourselves; we need help. As our Lord affirms, 'Apart from me you can do nothing' (John 15.5). In one of my favourite books, *Ghost Stories of an Antiquary* by M. R. James, the author recounts in 'A School Story' how the boys in class were being taught to write conditional sentences in Latin, that is, sentences beginning with the word 'if'. The master told them each to write down a conditional sentence of their own invention. The boys handed in their pieces of paper, and the master looked at the one on top of the pile. At once he made an odd noise in his throat and rushed out of the room. The boys wondered who had made a grammatical error so horrendous as to upset the master in this alarming way. The piece of paper on top read, *Si tu non veneris ad me, ego veniam ad te*: 'If you don't come to me, I'll come to you'. And strangely, the handwriting was not that of any of the boys in the room.

How the story continues – what it was that the schoolmaster so greatly dreaded and how it eventually came to him – I shall not tell you; you must read the story for yourselves, and I do not want to spoil it for you. Let us simply apply the words on the bit of paper to the work of Christ. We could not come to God, so he has come to us. We could not by our own efforts traverse the chasm that sin has interposed between us and heaven; so God in Christ has crossed over the abyss and himself drawn near to us. Salvation is not the result of our own exertion but a divine act. Our cooperation is indeed essential, but it is never sufficient.

In regard to each model of salvation, let us ask four questions:

1 *Does the model in question envisage a change in God or in us?* Some theories of Christ's saving work seem to suggest that God is angry with us, and what Christ has done is to satisfy God's anger. But that cannot be right. It is we who need to change, not God. As St Paul said, 'God was in Christ, reconciling the world to himself' (2 Cor. 5.19). It is the world that needs to be reconciled to God, not God who needs to be reconciled to the world.

2 *Does the model separate Christ from the Father?* Some theories of atonement appear to imply that God the Father is punishing his Son when

Christ dies on the cross. I remember as a student in Oxford hearing that great evangelist Billy Graham assert, 'At the moment when Christ died on the cross, the lightning of God's wrath hit him instead of you.' I did not find that a happy way of interpreting the doctrine of our salvation. Surely we should not separate Christ from the Father in such a way, for the two are one God, members together of the undivided Trinity. As St Paul states, in the words quoted above (2 Cor. 5.19), 'God was in Christ'. When Christ saves us, it is God who is at work in him; there is no separation between Father and Son.

3 *Does the model isolate the cross from the Incarnation and the Resurrection?* We are to regard Christ's earthly life as a single unity. We should not interpret salvation solely in terms of the cross, but we should also take into account what went before the crucifixion, and what came after.

4 *Does the model presuppose an objective or a subjective understanding of Christ's saving work?* Does Christ's saving work merely appeal to our subjective feelings, or did he do something to alter our objective situation in an actual and effective manner?

Model one: teacher

First of all, we may think of Christ as teacher, as the one who reveals to us the saving truth, who illuminates us and disperses the darkness of ignorance from our minds, 'the true light that enlightens everyone who comes into the world' (John 1.9). He saves us by teaching us about God. This was exactly the way in which his disciples thought of him initially, when they called him 'Rabbi', which means 'Teacher'. Later, of course, they came to realize that he was not just a human teacher but something far greater. This first model was adopted in particular by the second-century Apologists, most notably by Justin Martyr.

Recalling our four questions, we may say of this first model:

1 Yes: the change is in us, not God.

2 No: there is no separation between Jesus and the Father; Christ's teaching is the teaching of God.

3 No: the cross is not isolated; Christ's teaching role embraces his whole life, all that he said and all that he did and was.

4 So far, so good. But difficulties arise over the fourth question. Through his teaching, Christ opens our minds to the truth, but does he then leave us to carry out that teaching simply by our own efforts? Has he actually altered our objective situation? More specifically, as fallen human beings, we do not merely require to be instructed, but we need to be set free from sin. So this first model expresses part of the truth but not the whole, for it leaves out the tragedy and the anguish of sin.

Model two: ransom

In this second image of Christ's work, we think of him as paying a ransom on our behalf: 'The Son of Man came not to be served but to serve, and to give his life as a ransom for many' (Mark 10.45). The point of this ransom metaphor is that previously we were enslaved to sin, but now we are liberated: 'Christ has set us free' (Gal. 5.1). But this act of saving liberation on Christ's part was enormously costly. The ransom that Christ paid on our behalf was nothing less than his own life, laid down for us on the cross. It was no easy task to set us free; an arduous act of reparation was required.

Let us keep in mind that this is only an image or metaphor, and let us not press this metaphor too far, turning it into a systematic theory. It is wise to refrain from asking, '*To whom* is the ransom paid?' In fact, the New Testament does not actually ask that question. If we say, 'The ransom is paid to God the Father', then we are in danger of separating Christ from his Father, and of regarding the Father as cruel and vindictive, relentlessly demanding payment and recompense. Surely God is not like that; he does not require payment but forgives us freely. Should we then say that the payment is paid to the devil? That is an answer that the Fathers, Greek and Latin, have sometimes given; but it creates serious problems. It suggests that the devil has rights or claims upon us, and that cannot be true. The devil has no rights; he is a cheat and a liar. The essential point of the ransom metaphor is not transaction or bargain but liberation. It is better, then, not to ask to whom the payment is being made. Let us stick to the basic point: Christ has set us free.

Applying our four questions to the ransom model, we respond:

1 No problem: the change is in us, not in God.
2 Again, no problem, so long as we do not envisage Christ as paying the ransom to the Father. But if we do assume that Christ is making a payment to his Father, then there will indeed be a danger of separating the first and the second members of the Trinity from one another.
3 Certainly, the ransom model concentrates more especially upon the cross, but it need not do so exclusively. It is the whole earthly life of Christ, from his conception in the womb of his mother to his ascension into heaven – and including notably his transfiguration and his resurrection – that has set us free.
4 Here lies the major strength of the second model, compared with the first. In setting us free, Christ has indeed altered our objective situation.

Model three: sacrifice

Here we enter deep water. For us today, the idea of sacrifice has lost much of its meaning, but in the worship of peoples in the ancient world, whether

Hebrew, Greek or Roman, sacrifice was everywhere taken for granted. In the Old Testament, there are a number of different kinds of sacrifice, yet nowhere do we find a clear definition of what sacrifice is and how it works. In the New Testament, Christ is seen as fulfilling the sacrifices of the Old Covenant more particularly in two ways:

1 'Christ our Paschal Lamb has been sacrificed' (1 Cor. 5.7); 'Behold, the Lamb of God who takes away the sin of the world' (John 1.29). Here Christ is envisaged as the Paschal Lamb, eaten at the Passover in memory and re-enactment of the Exodus from Egypt (see Ex. 12.1–14, 21–27). Christ's death on the cross and his resurrection constitute the New Passover.

2 'He is the atoning sacrifice (*hilasmos*) for our sins' (1 John 2.2). This recalls the sacrificial ritual on the Jewish Day of Atonement (Yom Kippur), when the worshippers are sprinkled with blood to cleanse them from their sins (Lev. 16.23, 27–32). In a similar way, the blood of Jesus, sacrificed for us, cleanses us from all sin (1 John 1.7). The sacrifice of the Day of Atonement is recalled in particular at the institution of the Eucharist, when our Lord says, 'This is my blood of the New Covenant, which is poured out for many for the forgiveness of sins' (Matt. 26.28).

To appreciate the meaning of sacrifice, let us hold fast to four ideas:

1 A sacrifice is fundamentally an *offering* or *gift* made to God.
2 The true sacrifice is to offer to God, not wheat or an animal, but *ourselves*. Sacrifice signifies above all self-offering: 'In burnt offerings and sin offerings thou hast taken no pleasure. Then I said, "Lo, I have come to do thy will, O God"' (Heb. 10.6–7, quoting Ps. 40.6–7).
3 It is often assumed that the essence of sacrifice lies in the death of the sacrificial victim – lamb, goat, calf or whatever. This is misleading. The true purpose of sacrifice is *not death but life*. If the victim is slain, that is not because its death has value as an end in itself, but so that its life may be released and offered to God. According to the viewpoint of the Old Testament, the life of an animal or human being resides in the blood; and thus, by the pouring out of the victim's blood, its life is set free and made available, so that it can be offered up to God.
4 A sacrifice, in order to be truly a gift or offering, has to be *voluntary*. That which is taken from us by force, through coercion and against our will, is not genuinely a sacrifice.

Now we can apply all this to the sacrifice of Christ:

1 Christ, as sacrifice, is offered up to God (but here care must be taken to not separate Christ from the Father).
2 It is Christ who offers himself in sacrifice.

3 When Christ dies on the cross, it is that we may have life. This is made transparently clear when we reflect that his death on the cross is followed on the third day by his life-creating resurrection. Death and resurrection are not to be regarded as two separate moments but they constitute a single event or drama.

4 Christ was not under any compulsion to die, but he laid down his life freely on our behalf: 'I lay down my life for the sheep . . . No one takes it from me, but I lay it down of my own accord' (John 10.15, 18). If Jesus had not gone voluntarily to his death, the crucifixion would have been no more than a miscarriage of justice, an act of violence, a murder. But because he laid down his life willingly, his death became a life-creating sacrifice for the sins of the world.

Underlying the whole notion of sacrifice as voluntary self-offering, there is one all-important factor: *love*. Why does Christ lay down his life? Out of love: '. . . having loved his own who were in the world, he loved them to the end' (John 13.1); 'For God so loved the world that he gave his only Son' (John 3.16). Love, then, is the key to the entire idea of sacrifice. What is sacrifice? It is voluntary self-offering, inspired by love – love to the uttermost, love without limits.

Recalling our four questions, we may say: there is indeed a danger of stating the 'sacrifice' model in such a way as to imply that the change is in God, not in us (see question 1), that Christ is separated from the Father (see question 2), and that the cross is to be isolated from the rest of our Lord's life (see question 3). But this danger is largely avoided if the element of love is emphasized. In that case, Christ's sacrifice is seen as an expression of God's unchanging love; the sacrifice of love alters us, not God, and there is no separation between Father and Son. Moreover, the entirety of Christ's life, from the incarnation onwards, is a sacrifice or offering to God; so the cross is not isolated. Finally, as a sacrifice inspired by love, Christ's self-offering is made in full freedom, with willing and kenotic generosity.

Closely linked to the notion of sacrifice, there are two other ways of thinking about Christ's saving work:

Model three, variant (1): satisfaction

Anselm (*c*.1033–1109), Archbishop of Canterbury, interpreted Christ's sacrifice in terms of satisfaction. His theory of the atonement has been widely popular, not only in the West but in the East, primarily because it possesses a firmly 'objective' character (see question 4). His interpretation of the doctrine of salvation is based on the principles of the medieval feudal society in which he lived. Human sin, he argued, has offended God's honour; satisfaction has to be given to the Father in recompense for his offended honour, and this satisfaction has been rendered by Christ on our behalf. For all its popularity, this theory has two grave disadvantages: (i) it interprets salvation in legalistic categories, rather than as an act of divine love; (ii) the notions of honour and satisfaction, while reflecting medieval feudalism, are not to be found in the New Testament.

Model three, variant (2): substitution

Unlike variant (1), the concept of substitution – that Christ bears our sins in his own person, suffering instead of us – does indeed possess clear biblical roots. Christ is here seen as fulfilling two Old Testament prototypes:

(i) He resembles the sacrificial *scapegoat* on whose head were placed the sins of the people, before it was driven out into the wilderness (Lev. 16.20–22).
(ii) Christ is the *Suffering Servant* described in Isaiah 53.4–7 (compare Acts 8.30–35):

Surely he has borne our infirmities and carried our sorrows . . . He was pierced for our transgressions, crushed for our iniquities; upon him was inflicted the punishment that made us whole, and by his wounds we are healed . . . The Lord has laid on him the punishment of us all . . . He was led like a lamb to the slaughter.

Jesus, then, when he suffers and dies on the cross, is taking our sins upon himself and is enduring the punishment that we deserve to undergo: 'For our sake [God] made him to be sin who knew no sin, so that in him we might become the righteousness of God' (2 Cor. 5.21).

Now in this substitution model it is evident that the change is in us, not in God (see question 1); yet we must be careful not to interpret the model in such a way as to separate Christ from God, as Billy Graham unfortunately did (see question 2). Also, there is a danger that the notion of substitution may turn Christ's ministry into a transaction that is somehow external to us, in which we are not directly and personally involved. Jesus does indeed suffer for our sins, but we need to be associated with his act of sacrificial suffering in such a way as to make that act our own. It is certainly legitimate to say, 'Christ *instead of* me', but we should balance that by also saying, 'Christ *on behalf of* me'. Substitution language has to be combined with the language of indwelling: 'Christ in me, and I in him'. The element of mutual love needs to qualify the notion of substitution.

Model four: victory

Here Christ's work of salvation is seen as a cosmic battle between good and evil, between light and darkness. Dying on the cross and rising from the dead, Christ is victor over sin, death and the devil. This victory is summed up in the last word that he spoke on the cross, *Tetelestai* (John 19.30), usually translated, 'It is finished'. This, however, is not to be seen as a cry of resignation or despair. Christ is not just saying, 'It's all over. This is the end', but he is affirming, 'It is accomplished, it is fulfilled, it is completed.' For other examples of the victory motif, see Colossians 2.15: '[God] disarmed the principalities and powers and made a public example of them, triumphing over them [through the cross]'; and also Ephesians 4.8: 'When he ascended up on high, he led captivity captive' (compare Ps. 68.18).

The writer who makes particular use of this theme of victory is St Irenaeus of Lyons (late second century). And if we want to see the idea of victory lived out liturgically, then let us call to mind the paschal midnight service, with its ever-repeated refrain *Christos anesti ek nekron*, 'Christ is risen from the dead, trampling down death, by death'. Let us recall also the marvellous sermon attributed to St John Chrysostom, read during the course of the midnight celebration, with its overwhelming sense of triumphant joy. The same note of victory occurs in the Latin paschal hymns: 'Death and life have contended in that combat tremendous. The Prince of Life who died reigns immortal.'

There is a story told from the early days of the Communist persecution in Russia that strikingly illustrates this experience of paschal victory. An atheist lecturer came to a village, and all the inhabitants were assembled to listen to him. At some length he explained to them that there is no God. At the end, he invited questions. At the back of the audience, the local parish priest stood up and said, 'I'd like to say something.' Sensing trouble, the atheist lecturer told him, 'You must be brief. I can only allow you half a minute.' 'That's all right', the priest replied. 'I don't need nearly as much time as that. What I want to say is this: Christ is risen!' At once the audience shouted back, 'He is risen indeed!' Turning to the atheist lecturer, the priest rejoined, 'That's all I wanted to say.' Such indeed is our answer to the world's alienation and misery. The risen Christ is victor over sorrow and darkness.

The outstanding advantage of this victory model is that it holds together the cross and the resurrection. They are regarded as a single event, an undivided drama. Christ's death on the cross is already a victory, but his victory is at that moment hidden. When the myrrh-bearing women come early in the morning to the tomb and find it empty, and when Christ appears before them, alive once more (Matt. 28.9), then the victory is made manifest. This victory model has, however, a problematic aspect. It can sound militaristic. The saving work of Christ seems to be understood in terms of superior force, of coercive power. So we need to make clear that Christ's death and resurrection, while they are indeed a victory, are a victory of an unusual kind. What the cross of Christ sets before us is the victory not of superior force, not of military might, but of suffering love. On the cross, Christ is victorious through his voluntary self-emptying, through his weakness and vulnerability. A victory, yes, but a *kenotic* victory.

The full meaning of this becomes evident when we note the connection between Christ's cry on the cross – *Tetelestai*, 'It is finished' (John 19.30) – and what is said by the Evangelist before the account of the Passion: 'Having loved his own who were in the world, he loved them to the end' (John 13.1). In Greek, the word for 'end' in this sentence is *telos*, which comes from the same root as the verb *tetelestai*. Now everything in St John's Gospel is closely interconnected, forming a single structure. When I was at school, our history master had a characteristic phrase. In a curiously high-pitched voice, he used to say, 'It all ties up, you see, it all ties up.' That is a good way to study history, and it is also a good way to interpret the Bible. So when Jesus says, 'It is finished', *Tetelestai*, the Evangelist intends us to think back to what was said six chapters earlier, 'He loved them to the end (*eis telos*).' This interconnection discloses precisely what has been 'finished' and fulfilled by Christ's death on the cross: it is the victory of love. Despite all the suffering, both physical and mental, that has been inflicted upon him, Jesus goes on loving humankind. His love is not swallowed up. It is not changed into hatred. We are to see his victory, then, not as a military or coercive victory, but precisely as the victory of suffering love, of inexhaustible and unchanging love, love without limits. God incarnate is never so strong as when he is most weak. In the words of Karl Barth, 'The Christian God is great enough to be humble.' That is what we see above all in his victory on the cross.

Model five: example

Just as the 'satisfaction' model of the atonement is associated with a particular Latin writer, Anselm of Canterbury, so this fifth model is likewise associated with another Latin writer, Peter Abelard (1079–1142/3), Anselm's younger contemporary. Abelard regards Christ's life and sacrificial death as the supreme example of love in action. Love, so he maintains, is deeply attractive, and in this way the love of God made manifest in Christ's life and death evokes a corresponding response of love in us. As is said in the Anglican hymn that I used to sing as a child: 'Oh dearly, dearly has he loved/ And we must love him too'. Christ's love, revealed most intensely on the cross, acts as a spiritual magnet, drawing us all to him: 'I, when I am lifted up from the earth, will draw all people to myself' (John 12.32).

Many Christians in modern times have been particularly attracted by this fifth model, because it moves completely away from the notion of God the Father as angry and vindictive, demanding as satisfaction the blood of his Son. It does not employ legalistic categories or the militaristic imagery of an armed conflict. Instead, it interprets God's saving work in terms of love. It does not separate Christ from the Father, because the love that Christ displays is specifically God's love (see question 2). It does not isolate the cross from the other moments in Christ's life, because the whole of Christ's life is an expression of love (see question 3). But difficulties arise regarding question 4. If Christ has done no more than set us an example, does that mean we have to follow that example by our own efforts? Has Christ objectively changed our predicament?

There is a story told of Robert the Bruce, the great Scottish commander in the thirteenth century, that illustrates this difficulty. Fighting against the invading English, he was repeatedly defeated. One day, sitting alone after a severe reverse, he reflected, 'It's no good. I must give up. No point in continuing to fight.' Then he noticed a spider that had fallen out of its web and was trying to get back again. It kept pulling itself up by the thread on which it was hanging, but continually it fell back. Yet it went on trying until at long last it succeeded in getting back into its web. Robert applied the lesson to himself: he decided to go and fight the English just one more time, and on this final occasion, he defeated them.

Now the spider may have encouraged Robert subjectively by setting him an example, but it did not actually change his outward, objective situation. It did not *directly* determine the outcome of the subsequent battle. So we are to ask ourselves: has Jesus on the cross done no more for us than the spider did for Robert the Bruce? Has he merely set us an example, leaving us to follow the example by our own efforts? Surely that is not enough. We need the help of his active and effectual grace.

This objection, however, based on the story of Robert of Bruce, misconceives the true scope and dynamism of love. Love is creative. It is not merely a subjective feeling. If we love someone with all our heart, then we change the world for that person. Love is an objective energy in the universe. If a child has been loved by parents when growing up, that will influence the way in which the child experiences the world in later life. Because of the love of parents, the child will have a courage, trust and hope not otherwise available to him or her. By the same token, hatred also is an objective force. If a child has not been loved but has been rejected in early years, that will prove an influence later on. The child on growing up will find it more difficult – but not of course impossible – to trust and love others.

From this it is evident that love is a potent, enabling force. Our love alters the lives of others. And if this is true of our human love for each other, how much more is it true of the suffering, divine-human love of Christ our Saviour! By loving us, he does not just set us an example, but he changes the world for us, giving our life a direction and power that it could not otherwise possess. The love of another for us – and above all the love of Christ our God – infuses into our life a transfiguring force. Love enables, just as hatred depotentiates. Where love is concerned, the subjective/objective contrast breaks down.

If we now join together models three, four and five, we can discern a common theme that unites them together, and that is the theme of *suffering love*. What makes Christ's death a redeeming sacrifice is precisely that he offers himself willingly in love (Model three). The victory of Christ is nothing else than the victory of kenotic, suffering love (Model four). And the example of this suffering love alters our lives, filling us with grace and spiritual energy (Model five). Models four and five, interpreted as we have sought to do, are simply two sides of the same coin: his victory is nothing else than the example of his unchanging love, and the example of his unchanging love is itself the victory. Combining these three models, understanding each in the light of the others, we reach a firm and convincing doctrine of atonement.

Model six: exchange

To appreciate this our final model, we may think of Christmas. What do we do each December? We send one another greetings; we exchange presents. And that is exactly the meaning of Christ's incarnation that we are celebrating at Christmas. When Jesus was born in Bethlehem, there took place the greatest and most wonderful of all possible exchanges. He took our humanity – our gift to him, offered through the Blessed Virgin Mary – and in exchange he bestowed upon us the gift of participating in his divine glory.

In this sixth model, then, salvation is understood in terms of mutual sharing, of reciprocal participation. As St Paul affirms, using the metaphor of riches and poverty: 'Though he was rich, yet for your sakes he became poor, so that through his poverty you might become rich' (2 Cor. 8.9). The riches of Christ are his divine life, while our human poverty signifies our fallen condition, our alienation and brokenness. Christ takes upon himself our brokenness – our mental and physical pain, our loneliness and sorrow – and so by way of exchange we are enabled to share in his eternal life, becoming 'partakers of the divine nature' (2 Peter 1.4).

St Irenaeus of Lyons makes the same point when he states, 'In his unbounded love, he became what we are, so as to make us what he is.'[1] St Athanasius of Alexandria is yet more succinct: 'He became man that we might be made god.'[2] We can also translate the words of Athanasius, 'He became incarnate that we might be in-godded', or 'He was humanized that we might be deified.'

This sixth model encourages us to think of salvation in terms of *theosis* or 'deificiation'. Salvation is not merely a change in our legal status before God, it is not merely an imitation of Christ through moral effort, but it signifies an organic, all-embracing transformation of our created personhood through a genuine participation in divine life. This sixth model can also be spelt out in terms of *healing*. St Gregory of Nazianzus – 'Gregory the theologian', as he is termed in the Orthodox tradition – adopts this approach when he insists, 'The unassumed is unhealed.'[3] Christ, that is to say, has assumed our human nature in its entirety, and thereby he has imparted to us the possibility of salvific healing. Another way of expressing this sixth model is to think in terms of *anakephalaiosis* or recapitulation (see Eph. 1.10). Assuming our humanness, Christ has summed up or recapitulated all humankind in himself; and so his incarnation, death and resurrection become by grace an event in the personal life of each one of us.

Let us recall the four questions that we emphasized earlier. The sixth model presupposes a change in us (see question 1). At the same time, it posits a change in God, in the sense that, without ceasing to be true God, the second person of the Trinity has also become truly human. As the Church proclaims at Vespers on Christmas Eve: 'What he was, he has remained, true God; and what he was not, he has taken upon himself, becoming man through love for mankind.'[4] The sixth model, stressing as it does the Godhead of Christ, holds closely together Christ and the Father (see question 2). Also, and most importantly, it treats Christ's 'economy' as a single unity: incarnation, transfiguration, Gethsemane, Golgotha, the empty tomb, the ascension are all seen as essentially connected (see question 3). And the 'exchange' model is also fully objective (see question 4).

As was indicated at the outset, these six models are not mutually exclusive; we can and should make use of all of them. Equally, our list of six makes no claim to be exhaustive: we can find other models in the New Testament and in tradition. Two aspects of salvation in particular, of which I have not so far spoken, need to be kept in view. First, salvation is not solitary but social. We are saved *in the Church*, as members of it and in union with all the other members. Second, salvation is conferred *through the sacraments*: we are saved by participating in the 'mysteries' of Baptism and Holy Communion.

'Are you saved?'

It remains for me to say how I replied to the man in the train when he asked me, 'Are you saved?' Suppose that I answered, 'Yes: I am saved', might that not have been over-confident? Long after his conversion on the road to Damascus, St Paul voiced the fear that 'after preaching to others, I myself should be disqualified' (1 Cor. 9.27). God is faithful, and he will never let us down. But we humans retain free will, and so, up to the end of this earthly life, we are in danger of falling away. As St Antony of Egypt warned us, 'Expect temptation until your last breath.'[5] We are each of us on a journey and that journey is not yet completed.

So perhaps I should have answered the man, 'No, I'm not saved.' But that would have been to deny the fellowship in Christ that even now I enjoy. Possibly, then, I might have replied, 'I don't know whether I am saved or not.' The man would surely have found that a feeble response. He could have rejoined, 'If you don't know, you'd better go and find out. And if you don't know, why do you go about in black and keep writing books about religion?' Thus I thought the best way to answer was to say, 'I trust by God's mercy that I am *being saved*.' In other words, it is wisest to use the continuous present: not 'I *am* saved' but 'I am *being* saved.' Salvation, that is to say, is a process. It is not just a single event but an ongoing journey that is only completed at the moment of our death. That, then, was my answer to the man in the train. But if any of my readers can think of a better answer, please let me know.

Notes

1 See St Irenaeus of Lyons, 'Preface', *Against the Heresies*, Book V.

2 St Athanasius of Alexandria, *On the Incarnation*, 54:3.

3 St Gregory of Nazianzus, *Letter 101, to Cledonius*.

4 *The Festal Menaion*, trans. by Mother Mary and Archimandrite Kallistos Ware (London: Faber & Faber, 1969), p. 253.

5 See 'Antony 4', in *Sayings of the Desert Fathers: The Alphabetical Collection*, trans. by Benedicta Ward (London/Oxford: Mowbray, 1981), p. 2.

17

Christ and the Oriental Orthodox 'Miaphysite' Tradition

POLYCARPUS AUGIN AYDIN

Introduction

The ancient Latin axiom, *Lex orandi lex credendi* – the law of prayer is the law of belief – suggests that worship and belief are closely related. In fact, the liturgy serves as a source of theology in the Syriac tradition. One of the major features of the West Syrian liturgical family is the number of anaphoras (i.e. the book of the divine or eucharistic liturgy); there are more than 80 known anaphoras in the Syriac tradition.[1] Today, a dozen of these anaphoras are in current use.[2] In this contribution, I will look at three of these – the Anaphora of St James (the brother of our Lord), the Anaphora of St Dionysius Bar Salibi and the Anaphora of Sixtus of Rome – to examine how Christ is portrayed in them. Such a comparison is interesting in part because these eucharistic anaphoras were composed by Church Fathers living in different times and coming from different geographical regions of the Syriac Orient. Studying the wealth of the eucharistic anaphoras and rich prayers that have come down to us helps us to see the beauty, variety, abundance and richness of this unique liturgical treasure and recognize its significance, in addition to shedding light on how Christ is portrayed – whether as heavenly physician, judge or any one of the many images used by the Oriental Orthodox 'miaphysite' liturgical tradition.

In his *West Syrian Liturgical Theology*, the Syriac liturgical scholar, Fr Baby Varghese remarks:

> the early Church has always insisted on the intrinsic relationship between doctrine and the Eucharistic liturgy. Thus, Irenaeus of Lyons wrote: 'Our doctrine agrees with the Eucharist and the Eucharist confirms our doctrine.' The Eucharistic prayers were first composed in the interests of doctrinal, not liturgical, uniformity. The Eucharistic prayer itself with its account of salvation history, is the proclamation of the community's common faith. In later centuries, the introduction of the Nicene Creed further emphasized the doctrinal dimension of the liturgy. The prayers of all the sacramental and liturgical celebrations were written within the limits of orthodoxy, so that they should express the mind of the Church.

Prayers were always carefully formulated, selected and introduced in the liturgy to imprint the faith of the Church in the mind of believers. Thus, doctrines are 'lived', that is expressed, celebrated and transmitted in and through the liturgy.[3]

It is well known that one of the most visible common characteristics of the Eastern Christian liturgies is their Trinitarian emphasis. It is also significant that all the prayers of the West-Syriac eucharistic anaphora, except the concluding prayer, are addressed to God the Father. The Church, as the body of Christ, gathers together in the Spirit of sonship and offers the Eucharist. In the Spirit, the faithful of the Church address God 'Abba, Father',[4] because he has authorized them to do so in Christ, and we have been given the 'Spirit of sonship'. True Christian prayer is always Trinitarian. Trinitarian invocation is required because, outside the Trinitarian faith, it is impossible to know Christ, to recognize in Jesus the incarnate Lord, 'One of the Holy Trinity'.

Also, as we shall see, the Christian liturgy has its foundation in the Incarnation of the Second Person of the Holy Trinity. Incarnation is an act of God's philanthropy, to restore us to communion with himself. God became man in order to restore God's image in man that was impaired by the fall. The liturgical texts regularly evoke the meaning and goal of the Incarnation in vivid phrases. A hymn to be found in the *Shimo*, the Book of Common Prayer in the Syriac Tradition, summarizes the goal of Incarnation. It says:

Glory to the holy Father, who sent His holy Son and He descended and dwelt in a pure and holy womb in a holy manner; He came in our image and likeness, that we might become like Him; He became a son of man that He might make us sons of His Father and partakers of His holy Spirit.[5]

The Syriac Orthodox anaphoras have attracted the attention of both Western and Eastern scholars because of their reputation for rich theological content and diversity. Most of the extant anaphoras were composed in the first millennium of the Common Era. A few of them were originally composed in Greek and then translated into Syriac in the Golden Age of Syriac Christianity, the period between the fourth and eighth centuries. The majority of the shorter anaphoras were composed during the second millennium and can be easily identified because of their style and content, reflecting the decline in the literary and theological activities of Syriac Christianity.

Regarding the main structure of the Syriac Orthodox anaphoras, or the eucharistic liturgies, we see that it consists of two basic parts: the Order of Offering and the Anaphora proper. The Order of Offering is composed of the Liturgy of Preparation and the Liturgy of the Word and concludes with the Creed. The Anaphora opens with the Prayer of the Kiss of Peace, directed to God the Father, and includes the Blessing of the Bread and Wine, the Anamnesis, Invocation of the Holy Spirit, the six Prayers of Intercession, the Prayer of Fraction and Commixture, the Lord's Prayer, the

Great Elevation, the Communion, Prayer of Thanksgiving, Dismissal of the Faithful, and the Post-Communion Prayers.

Having established this, now I would like to look at the three Syriac anaphoras, namely, the Anaphora of St James, the Anaphora of St Dionysius Bar Salibi and the Anaphora of Sixtus of Rome, to examine how Christ is portrayed in them. Before doing so, it may be helpful to say something about each one of them.

The Syriac eucharistic anaphoras

The Anaphora of St James bears the following title in Syriac: ܐܢܐܦܘܪܐ ܕܡܪܝ ܝܥܩܘܒ ܐܚܘܗܝ ܕܡܪܢ ܗܘ ܪܫܐ ܕܐܦܝܣܩܘܦܐ ܩܕܡܝܐ ܕܐܘܪܫܠܡ ܫܠܝܚܐ ܘܣܗܕܐ. ܕܫܡܥ ܘܝܠܦ ܡܢ ܦܘܡܗ ܕܡܪܝܐ܆ (The Anaphora of St James, the Brother of our Lord, the First Archbishop of Jerusalem, Apostle and Martyr who has heard and learned from the mouth of the Lord). The Anaphora of St James of Jerusalem is considered the oldest and pre-eminent among the Syriac anaphoras and served as a model for all the subsequent anaphoras in the Syriac tradition. There is a Greek recension of this anaphora, wrongly attributed to Jacob of Edessa (+708), and a shorter version in Syriac which was done by the Syriac Orthodox prelate and polymath Catholicos Mor Gregorius Bar 'Ebroyo in the thirteenth century. The Anaphora of St James is the one most frequently used in the Syriac Orthodox Church today. Its use is obligatory at all the major festivals of the Church, at the ordination of deacons and priests, and the consecration of a bishop or a patriarch, and at the celebration of the Holy Eucharist for the first time by a newly ordained priest.

The Anaphora of St Dionysius bar Salibi bears the Syriac title: ܐܢܐܦܘܪܐ ܕܡܪܝ ܕܝܘܢܘܣܝܘܣ ܝܥܩܘܒ ܒܪ ܨܠܝܒܝ ܡܝܛܪܦܘܠܝܛܐ ܕܐܡܝܕ܂ (The Anaphora of St Dionysius Jacob bar Salibi, the Metropolitan of Amid). St Dionysius bar Salibi was native of Melitene and the Metropolitan of Amid in the twelfth century. He was a prolific writer and the first Syriac Orthodox theologian to provide a commentary on the entire Bible. He has also written or commented upon works in philosophy, canon law, doctrine and poetry, including a commentary on the liturgy. Three anaphoras attributed to St Dionysius are known, but only the first (which is also sometimes attributed to Dionysius the Areopagite) has been published so far.

The Anaphora of Sixtus bears the following title in Syriac: ܐܢܐܦܘܪܐ ܕܡܪܝ ܟܣܘܣܛܘܣ ܕܪܗܘܡܝ (The Anaphora of St Sixtus of Rome). Sixtus was the Bishop of Rome and died in 258 CE.

Upon examining the above-mentioned anaphoras, one encounters passages and prayers in which they offer a number of specific themes or images of Christ that are of particular importance and significance. Furthermore, they shed light on how Christ is portrayed – whether as heavenly physician, the medicine of life, the heavenly bridegroom, judge or any one of the many images used by the Oriental Orthodox 'miaphysite' liturgical tradition.

Portrayal of Christ in Syriac liturgical and spiritual tradition

1 Christ the 'Good Doctor' or the 'Heavenly Physician'

In the early Syriac tradition, sin is frequently viewed as a wound which is in need of healing. Accordingly, Christ is portrayed as 'the Good Doctor' or 'the Heavenly Physician' who comes to heal the wounds of fallen Adam, of humanity. Thus St Ephrem, the greatest poet and theologian of the Syriac Church, in his *Commentary on the Diatessaron* writes: 'when Adam sinned and was deprived of that glory with which he was clothed, he hid his nakedness with the fig tree. Our Lord came and endured suffering for him, to heal the wounds of Adam, and to provide a garment of glory for his nakedness.'[6]

Likewise, a prayer in the Anaphora of St James, a prayer recited by the priest following the Kiss of Peace, says:

O God the Father, Who by Your great love toward mankind, did send Your Son into the world to bring back the sheep that had gone astray. Reject not, O my Lord, the service of this bloodless sacrifice for we rely not on our righteousness, but on Your mercy. Let not this Mystery, which was instituted for our salvation, be for our condemnation, but for the remission of our sins and for the rendering of thanks to You and to Your Only-begotten Son and to Your all holy, good, adorable, life-giving and consubstantial Spirit, now, always and forever.[7]

Another passage, following the Sanctus, has the following relevant prayer:

In truth You are Holy, and You make Holy, O King of the worlds, and Holy is Your Son, our Lord Jesus Christ, and Holy too is Your Holy Spirit Who searches out hidden things. You created man out of earth and placed him in paradise, and when he transgressed Your commandment, You did not leave him straying, but did guide him by the prophets, and in the fullness of time You sent Your Only-begotten Son into the world, Who when He had taken flesh of the Holy Spirit and of the Virgin Mary, renewed Your image which was worn out.[8]

Similar prayers are also to be found in the Anaphora of St Dionysius bar Salibi as well as that of Sixtus of Rome.

2 Medicine of life

In the Syriac Patristic and liturgical tradition, Christ is portrayed not only as the 'Good Doctor' or the 'Heavenly Physician', but also as the 'medicine of life'. Thus Ephrem, in his *Hymns on the Nativity*, says:

Let Eve today rejoice in Sheol,
For her daughter's Son
Has come down as the Medicine of Life
To revive His Mother's mother.[9]

Also, in his *Hymns on Unleavened Bread,* Ephrem comments on the Last Supper saying: 'the Life-giver of all blessed the food and it became the Medicine of Life for those who ate it'.[10] From that time onwards, this healing medicine of life is offered to every faithful Christian communicant at each celebration of the Holy Eucharist.

This theme is also clearly expressed in the institution narrative of all the anaphoras, as we have in the following passage taken from the Anaphora of St James:

> When He, the sinless One, was prepared to accept the voluntary death for us sinners, He took bread into His holy hands and when He had given thanks, He blessed and sanctified and broke and gave to His holy disciples, and said: Take, eat of it. This is My Body which for you and for many is broken and given for the remission of sins and for eternal life.
> Likewise, He took the Cup and when He had given thanks, He blessed and sanctified and gave it to His holy disciples, and said: Take, drink of it, all of you. This is My Blood which for you and for many is shed and given for the remission of sins and for eternal life.[11]

3 Divine fire

Another image that emerges in the Liturgy and the writings of the early Syriac Fathers is that of divine fire. Fire is an image of divine action or of the divinity. Thus, Ephrem, in his *Hymns on Faith,* addresses Christ saying:

> See, Fire and Spirit are in the womb of her who bore you,
> Fire and Spirit are within the river in which you were baptized.
> Fire and Spirit are in our baptismal font,
> In the Bread and Cup are fire and Holy Spirit.[12]

As Sebastian Brock remarks, 'The image of divine fire has a double aspect: On the one hand, this fire may consume and burn up (the fate of a number of sinners in the Old Testament), or it may purify and sanctify.'[13] He goes on to say that in the New Testament, the image of divine fire emerges in the story of Pentecost as narrated in the Acts of the Apostles.[14] Early Syriac Fathers also speak of divine fire in two other places, namely, in the womb of the Virgin Mary, and in the River Jordan at the Baptism of Christ as we have already seen in the above hymn by Ephrem.[15]

The presence of fire in Mary's womb and in the River Jordan is comparable to the presence of divine fire in the sacraments of baptism and Eucharist. Thus, Ephrem in his *Hymns on Faith* says:

Fire and Spirit are in our baptismal font,
In the Bread and Cup are fire and Holy Spirit.[16]

The same link between Christ as fire in Mary's womb and Christ as fire in the eucharistic mysteries is brought out in couplets 40 and 41 in the dialogue poem between the angel Gabriel and Mary (Luke 1.26–38) by the use of the phrase, *gmurto*, 'The Burning Coal', derived from the Book of the Prophet Isaiah 6.6.[17] Also, Ephrem, in his *Hymns on Faith*, mentions the presence of the fire that is present in the eucharistic mysteries of the bread and wine saying:

In Your Bread there is hidden the Spirit which is not consumed,
in Your Wine there dwells the Fire that is not drunk:
the spirit in Your Bread, the Fire in Your Wine –
A manifest wonder, that our lips have received.[18]

The term *gmurto*, 'The Burning Coal', is frequently used of the consecrated holy *Qurbono*, the eucharistic elements, as we have it in the following rubric and the prayer said upon receiving the Holy *Qurbono*/Communion:

The celebrant takes the gmurto, the 'Burning Coal' from the paten with the spoon and puts it into the chalice. He now fills the spoon from the chalice and drinks of the blood, saying:

By Your Living and Life-giving Blood which was shed on the Cross, may my offenses be pardoned, and my sins be remitted, O Jesus the Word of God, Who came for our salvation and will come for our resurrection and for the restoration of our kind, forever and ever. Amen.

Also, the celebrant upon administering the Holy Communion to the faithful, says:

The atoning *gmurto*, the 'Burning Coal' of the Body and Blood of Christ our God is given to the faithful for the remission of offenses and for the forgiveness of sins in both worlds forever and ever.[19]

4   Divine love and the image of Christ as the heavenly bridegroom

God's boundless love and the image of Christ as the heavenly bridegroom is a central theme throughout Syriac tradition. The Syriac dialogue poem between Angel Gabriel and the Virgin Mary mentioned above opens with the following words:

O Power of the Father who came down and dwelt,
compelled by His love, in a virgin womb,
grant me utterance that I may speak
of this great deed of Yours which cannot be grasped.[20]

Among the earlier Syriac writers and poets, God's boundless love is expressed through the theme and image of Christ the heavenly bridegroom. Thus, Ephrem in his *Hymns on Faith* addressing Christ exclaims:

The soul is Your bride, the body too is Your bridal chamber,
Your guests are the senses and the thoughts.
And if a single body is a wedding feast for You,
How great is Your banquet with the whole church![21]

Among later Syriac writers, references to God's boundless love are especially noticeable in the writings of East Syriac mystics such as Sohduno (also known as Martyrius) and Isaac of Nineveh (also known as St Isaac the Syrian). For St Isaac, the main purpose of the Incarnation and crucifixion was to express to humanity God's love for humanity:

If zeal had been appropriate for putting humanity right, why did God the Word clothe Himself in the body in order to bring the world back to His Father using gentleness and humility? And why was He stretched out on the Cross for the sake of sinners, handing over His sacred body to suffering on behalf of the world? I myself say that God did all this for no other reason, except to make known to the world the love that He has, His aim being that we, as a result of our greater love arising from an awareness of this, might be captivated by His love when He provided the occasion of this manifestation of the kingdom of heaven's mighty power – which consists in love – by means of the death of His Son.[22]

'This divine outpouring of love', explains Sebastian Brock, 'never imposes itself on humanity, out of respect for the gift to humanity of free will; nevertheless, it seeks a response, and basically the Christian life should be seen as a striving to respond to, and reciprocate, this boundless love.'[23]

In Discourse 43, Isaac of Nineveh describes in vivid terms what happens when God's boundless love is discovered by the Christian faithful. He says:

When we have found love, we eat the heavenly bread and we are sustained without labor and without weariness. Heavenly bread is that which has descended from heaven and which gives the world life: this is the food of angels. The person who has found love eats Christ at all times and becomes immortal from thence onwards. For whoever eats of this bread shall not taste death in eternity. Blessed is the person who has eaten from the bread of love, which is Jesus. Whoever is fed with love is fed with Christ, who is the all-governing God. John is witness, when he says, 'God is love' (1 John 4:16). Thus, whoever lives with love in this creation smells life from God, breathing here the air of the resurrection. Love is the Kingdom of which our Lord spoke when symbolically he promised the disciples they would eat in his Kingdom, 'You shall eat and drink at the table of my Kingdom' (Luke 22:30). What should they eat, if not love? Love is sufficient to feed mankind instead of food and drink. This is the wine that gladdens the heart of humanity (Psalms 104:15). Blessed is the person who has drunk from this wine. This is the wine from which the debauched have drunk – and they became chaste; sinners drank – and they forgot the paths of stumbling; drunkards – and they became 'fasters'; the rich – and they became desirous of poverty; the poor – and they became rich in hope; the sick – and they regained strength; the foolish – and they became wise![24]

The Prayer of Thanksgiving in the Anaphora of Dionysius bar Salibi expresses this very theme also:

O Christ, the true Bread, who came down from heaven and became the imperishable food to us, guard our souls and bodies from the unquenching *Gehenna* and from the worm that never dies that we may offer You praise and thanksgiving and to Your Father and to Your Holy Spirit, now, always and forever.[25]

5 The merciful judge

In the prayer following the anamnesis, in the Anaphora of St James we encounter the image of Christ as a merciful judge. The prayer said by the priest, and to which the gathered congregation responds, reads:

While we remember, O Lord, Your death and Your resurrection on the third day, Your ascension into heaven, Your sitting at the right hand of God the Father and Your second coming whereby You will judge the world in righteousness and reward everyone according to his deeds; on account of this, we offer You this bloodless sacrifice so that You may not deal with us according to our debts, nor reward us according to our sins, but according to Your abundant mercies, blot out the sins of Your servants for Your people and Your inheritance make supplication unto You and through You to Your Father, saying:

(People): *Have mercy upon us, O God, Father Almighty. We glorify You, we bless You, we worship You and we beseech You. O Lord our God have compassion and mercy upon us, O Good One.*[26]

6   Self-emptying and humility

The ultimate expression of God's love is to be found in his 'self-emptying' (Phil. 2.7). God's love seeks to be reciprocated, and if human love is to reflect and imitate divine love, it needs to imitate the divine self-emptying. The term 'self-emptying' (Syriac, *msarqutho*/ܡܣܪܩܘܬܐ) is frequently encountered in writings of Syriac Fathers on the ascetic lifestyle. Thus, for example, Isaac in his ascetical writings says:

> For humility is the robe of divinity: for when God the Word became incarnate, He put on humility and thereby communicated with us by means of our human body. Accordingly, everyone who is truly clothed in humility will resemble Him who descended from the height, hiding the radiance of His greatness and covering up His glory by means of His low estate.[27]

Conclusion

Finally, by way of conclusion, I would like to say that the eucharistic anaphoras, hymns and homilies of the Syriac Fathers of the Oriental Orthodox 'miaphysite' liturgical tradition offer us many images of Christ, notably the heavenly physician, the heavenly bridegroom, the merciful judge, the divine fire and the divine love. These varied images enable us to see and know more vividly and lovingly Christ the Saviour who sanctified us and restored us to communion with himself. As the Syriac Fathers have emphasized in their writings, the aim of the sanctified life is the retrieval of the paradisiacal state, when Adam and Eve were still clad in the 'Robe of Glory' (ܐܣܛܠܐ ܫܘܒܚܐ). As we learn from the biblical account, Adam and Eve, through their disobedience, failed to receive the divinization; this potential for *theosis* was restored for humanity through the coming of Christ. This is expressed most beautifully by the poet-theologian, St Ephrem the Syrian:

> Divinity flew down and descended
> to raise and draw up humanity.
> The Son has made beautiful the servant's deformity,
> and he has become a god, just as he had desired.[28]

Notes

1   Patriarch Ignatius Aphram I Barsoum provides a list of 79 anaphoras. See Ignatius Aphram I Barsoum, *The Scattered Pearls: A History of Syriac Literature and Sciences*, trans. by Matti Moosa, 2nd edn (Piscataway, NJ: Gorgias Press, 2003). In his introduction to the edition of the Anaphoras, A. Reas gives a list of 80. *Anaphorae Syriace*, vol. I–I (Rome, 1939), pp. xxxix–xliii.

2 Archdeacon Murad S. Barsom and Metropolitan Mar Athanasius Y. Samuel, *Anaphoras: The book of the Divine Liturgies according to the rite of the Syrian Orthodox Church of Antioch* (Lodi: The Syrian Orthodox Church, 1991). Syriac text and facing English translation of 13 anaphoras.

3 Baby Varghese, *West Syrian Liturgical Theology* (Aldershot; Burlington, VT: Ashgate, 2004), pp. 47–8. He quotes Irenaeus, *Against the Heresies*, IV, 18, 5, *Sources chrétiennes*.100 (1965), p. 611.

4 Galatians 4.6; Romans 8.16.

5 *The Book of Common Prayer*, trans. By Bede Griffith (Kottayam: St Ephrem Ecumenical Research Institute Publications, 2006), p. 545.

6 Carmel McCarthy, *Saint Ephrem's Commentary on Tatian's Diatessaron*, Journal of Semitic Studies Supplement 2 (Oxford: Oxford University Press, 1993), p. 247.

7 Barsom and Samuel, *Anaphoras*, p. 198.

8 Barsom and Samuel, *Anaphoras*, p. 102.

9 Quoted in Sebastian Brock, *Spirituality in the Syriac Tradition*, 2nd edn, Moran Etho 2 (Kottayam, India: St. Ephrem Ecumenical Research Institute, 2005), p. 42.

10 Brock, *Spirituality in the Syriac Tradition*, p. 42.

11 Barsom and Samuel, *Anaphoras*, p. 102.

12 Quoted in Brock, *Spirituality in the Syriac Tradition*, p. 42.

13 Brock, *Spirituality in the Syriac Tradition*, p. 42.

14 Acts 2.3.

15 Quoted in Brock, *Spirituality in the Syriac Tradition*, p. 43.

16 Quoted in Brock, *Spirituality in the Syriac Tradition*, p. 44.

17 Sebastian Brock, *Treasure-House of Mysteries: Explorations of the Sacred Text through Poetry in the Syriac Tradition*, Popular Patristics Series 45 (Yonkers, NY: St Vladimir's Seminary Press, 2012), p. 141.

18 Sebastian P. Brock and George A. Kiraz, eds, *Ephrem the Syrian: Select Poems*, Eastern Christian Texts vol. 2 (Provo, UT: Brigham Young University Press, 2009), p. 207.

19 Barsom and Samuel, *Anaphoras*, p. 140.

20 Brock, *Treasure-House of Mysteries*, p. 136.

21 Brock and Kiraz, eds, *Ephrem the Syrian*, p. 219.

22 Isaac, Part II, Century IV.78. Quoted in Sebastian P. Brock, *The Wisdom of St. Isaac of Nineveh* (Piscataway, NJ: Gorgias Press, 2006), p. xii.

23 Brock, *Spirituality in the Syriac Tradition*, p. 85.

24 Quoted in Brock, *Spirituality in the Syriac Tradition*, pp. 85–86.

25 Barsom and Samuel, *Anaphoras*, p. 456.

26 Barsom and Samuel, *Anaphoras*, p. 104.

27 Brock, *The Wisdom of St. Isaac of Nineveh*, p. 26.

28 *Hymns on Virginity*, 48: 17–18. Observed by Sebastian Brock in Sebastian Brock, ed. trans., *St. Ephrem the Syrian: Hymns on Paradise* (Crestwood, NY: St Vladimir's Seminary Press, 1990), pp. 72, 73.

18

Christ the Categorical Imperative

OLIVER O'DONOVAN

How does Christ save us? That question can be explored in two directions. It may be asked, first, how his life, death and resurrection are an act of God's redemptive love for mankind, which takes us onto the highroad of soteriology. Second, it may be asked how our lives are reoriented by faith in Christ, to live and act as those whom Christ has saved, and this leads onto the less-travelled road of Christian ethics – or should do so, at least, if that always uncertain discipline can realize itself not merely as a pietist sociology, but as a genuinely evangelical theology. I want to introduce a little-known text of the later twentieth century which seeks to follow the second route. It is called *Nine Propositions on Christian Ethics* and was composed in 1974 by Hans Urs von Balthasar for the International Theological Commission of the Catholic Church, of which he was a member. It is uncharacteristic of Balthasar's authorship, which may explain its comparative neglect even in the heady days of Balthasar-mania. It is so short that it could not be published on its own in the format of his shorter books, but appeared bound together with two papers written by other German-speaking members of the Commission, which breathe an entirely different air to Balthasar's text.[1] It is written as an annotated series of headings, so densely that it sometimes fails to achieve complete sentences. I have often set it for students to read and have become accustomed to the glazed eyes with which they confess they have never before found themselves quite so much out of their depth. Yet I have found it enormously rewarding to wrestle with. The fact that its author never wrote it up into a longer work means that it is largely free of the flannel wrappings of encyclopedic intellectual history, in which it was his habit to conceal, rather than reveal, what he thought. That leaves the structure perfectly clear and the confrontations shockingly sharp.

Nine Propositions on Christian Ethics was produced in a polemic context, which the Commission was proposing to address, though it never finally did. A passionate argument about the shape and purpose of moral theology had broken out in the wake of the unfortunate papal encyclical *Humanae Vitae* (1968), with advocates of what was called 'faith ethics' (broadly supportive of the encyclical, though the disagreements ran deeper than anything in that text) opposed to those who defended an 'autonomous ethics' of human nature. In the very first sentence, Balthasar makes it plain that he aligns himself with the principle of 'faith ethics': 'The Christian who lives by faith is right to base his conduct on his faith.' But the way that claim is developed will have given its adherents a shock. Questions of ecclesiology, he blandly observes, are ignored in his treatment – and though they are in fact not actually ignored, they are certainly denied the commanding position usually assigned them in the Catholic tradition. The focus instead is on Christ, who 'reveals the divine love of the Trinity' and has 'assumed the form and indebtedness of the first Adam, including the limitations, perplexities and decisions of his existence'. The Chalcedonian 'two natures' of the Incarnation are the foundation stone of a Christian ethics, expressing both the saving presence of God and the renewal of human nature in the Second Adam.

The first proposition, entitled 'Christ the concrete norm', presents the central claim of an ethics founded on Christ: the 'concrete', which is to say, the actual event of history, constitutes the 'imperative' or 'norm'. The question bequeathed to Western thought by Kant was whether Christ's life could be more than a supreme exemplification of a moral truth, since the moral truth, Kant thought, is what we must follow, not the event of his life. Balthasar's response first of all identifies the moral force of Christ's life not simply as an instantiation but as a historical achievement: 'As Son of the Father he fulfilled within the world the entire will of God – the whole content of the "Ought"'. The 'fulfilment' of moral truth is meant in the sense of a 'completion' (*Vollendung*). This was a historical fulfilment of a historical purpose. In the second place, Balthasar invokes Christ's representative status to show how this decisive historical realization can also be a form to which our own action and life can be shaped: 'That he has done "for us", that from him, as the concrete norm of all moral conduct, we might win the freedom to perform God's will and to live out our nature as free children of the Father'.

'[T]he whole content of the "Ought"' is the point at which Balthasar joins battle with Kant, the only moral philosopher whom he thinks worth taking seriously, and steals his clothes for Christology. We do not derive what we ought from a formal rule, the famous 'categorical imperative' – 'so act as to will that the maxim of your act be a universal law'. We derive it from what has concretely come to pass in Jesus. Christ, as 'a normative concrete person', is the generative principle and inner formal meaning of all material duties arising from the will of God. To enlist the Kantian motif in Christology serves Balthasar's purpose in two ways, one negative, one positive. Negatively, it allows him to assert, against Kant, that the conceptual key to all our right acting and living is a once-and-for-all historical reality. In place of a logical truth arising from the necessities of practical reason, we have the revealed truth of history. Positively, it appropriates the Kantian conviction that the sphere of action is coherent and unitary: whatever is done well conforms to a universal form. But it is not merely formal, but concrete and personal: 'in him and with him to love his children and to worship in Spirit and in truth'. 'The imperative rests on the indicative', he declares, piercing the great wall of separation between theoretical and practical reason which was the Enlightenment legacy. And with it the opposition of 'heteronomy' and 'autonomy', upheld by the Catholic autonomists, is disposed of once and for all. Ethics cannot and need not entitle Christians to take a holiday from the principle of *Christus solus*. The two natures have secured Christ's representative relation to humanity as a whole, not just as a 'man of Galilee', whom we may admire and imitate just as far as our moral convictions dictate, and not as a commander who chooses in our place. 'Free' (*gratis*) action on God's part reproduces itself in free (*gratis*) action on ours. What sense of *moral obligation* does this leave us with, then? Balthasar's answer closely follows lines made familiar by Barth: obligation is expressed as 'you may', not 'you must'.

If, then, we have taken a universal principle, a 'categorical imperative', and associated it inseparably with a concrete person, we have opened the door to 'an eschatological and unsurpassable', a 'completion' of morality. So Balthasar is now committed to giving an account of how the morality of Christ draws together and gives a decisive form to all other forms of human morality. Throughout this text, Balthasar conducts an ongoing meditation on the Epistle to the Hebrews, which begins, as you may recall, with a contrast between the 'fragmentary' representations of God's word in prophetic history and the decisive address that he makes to us in the Son.

There are two major deposits of these moral 'fragments': the morality of law and promise inherited from the Old Covenant, and the morality of nature derived from the pagan world. The *Nine Propositions* is arranged accordingly: a section on the morality of Christ (Propositions 1–4) leads to one on the morality of the Old Covenant (5–6) and then to elements of pagan morality, which are conscience and nature (7–9). The point in proceeding in this way – 'backwards', as Balthasar puts it – is that ethics must begin with its moral criterion. To do otherwise would be to renounce its practical purpose and settle back into some descriptive anthropology. So Christian ethics begins with Christ and the 'end-time'. Yet the preliminaries are not simply set aside and ignored, but form a benchmark against which Christ can be seen to have fulfilled morality. This is expounded in a careful statement about Jesus' own 'obedience to the Father', which relates itself to the keeping of the law and faith in the promise. For Christian people, too, there are laws to keep and promises to believe, even while the fulfilment of all laws and promises is present in the life bestowed on us in Christ.

But before he makes the move backwards from the Christological centre to the fragments, Balthasar undertakes two worked examples that will demonstrate the evangelical and eschatological force that morality acquires in its completion by Jesus Christ. First, he considers an element in Christian ethics that most invites assimilation to natural law, Jesus' teaching on reciprocity, often called the Golden Rule. Balthasar places the Golden Rule firmly within the context of the Sermon on the Mount, alongside the

Beatitudes, love for the enemy and the command to be as 'perfect' and 'merciful' as the heavenly Father himself. On the face of it, a simple description of the natural conditions of human society, in reality 'it looks beyond basic human sociality and implies a sharing with one another of the divine life', an evangelical summary of the history of salvation, the law and the prophets, which points to a community of fulfilment where Christ himself is shared by all with all.

There can be no departure from Christ at any point; neither personal nor social morality can have a self-authenticating 'natural' standing. The cross is the true shape of ethics, pointing both upwards and outwards. It is not that Christian ethics is *not* 'natural ethics', but that it *completes* natural ethics. The innocence of a purely natural sociality is no longer open to us, for the natural has become a historical moment in the communication of God with humankind. Morality is now unthinkable except as an aspect of God's dialogue with man, which takes a Christological form. This turns the good of human action into a history, an expanding series of circles that successively overcome the divisions immanent in human society.

The second worked example, which concludes the first section of the Propositions, is sin. For sin, too, and not only good, can appear as what it truly is only by the revelation of God in Jesus. It is 'the holiness of the Holy Spirit in Christ and the Church' which 'convicts the world of sin' (John 16.8–11). Before that, what the world knew of wrong was simply *Schuld*, which can be variously translated 'blame' or 'indebtedness'. Balthasar makes no reference at all to the primal sin of Adam and Eve; the first sin, on his account, was the betrayal of Judas, which could occur 'only when the love of God "has gone to the end"', quoting John 13.1. Sin is self-conscious refusal of the concrete norm revealed by Christ, and it implies the Church's constant struggle against 'the vortex of Anti-Christ'.

And so, with the fifth proposition, Balthasar turns to the preparatory elements of morality, and first of all to those within the Old Covenant of God and Israel. The 'moral subject' comes first – identified with Abraham, whose significance Balthasar develops through a profound meditation on the narrative of Genesis placed alongside Hebrews 11. Abraham is the decisive paradigm of a status that is by no means a natural endowment of the human race, for moral agency is 'constituted' by the call of God. The knowledge that this is so is the decisive revelation of biblical ethics, setting it apart from a pagan ethic of values or duties. For Balthasar, this goes together with the revelation of the divine name, YHWH. For the moral agent, too, must have a 'name' – that is what constitutes a series of diverse actions as a personal self-expression. But naming is God's prerogative, and it occurs together with his own self-naming. The moral agent emerges, then, from the mists of mere 'experience' in response to a definite call, addressed to him by name, and so is isolated for the assumption of personal responsibility as an agent. The point of the 'isolation' is not to promote the moral individual at the expense of the community, but it does suggest that true community (as opposed to the mere 'collective', to which Balthasar will return) is in some way dependent upon individuals who know themselves as moral agents summoned by God. Precisely by assuming individual responsibility in answer to the call Abraham becomes the founder of a national community.

Originally, there is a bare call which demands bare obedience. The promise, the rationality of the call, which is hidden in the future, cannot be known until the call is obeyed, and even then its content is 'immeasurable', overspilling the limits of anything that can be imagined. The promise which corresponds to obedience contains the future welfare of the whole human race; yet is focused on a particular 'person', the 'seed' of Abraham, understood Christologically following Galatians 3.16. So Abraham is a universal representative, like Adam and Christ, as is indicated by the 'name' conferred upon him 'that reveals the mission', 'father of many'. Through the promise, bare obedience is bodied out as 'faith', the total assent of mind and body to the purposes of God, launching the history of blessing as a developing and unfolding sphere of grace and normativity. 'Covenant' is the name for this new framework of promise and faithful action, and it lays claim on every dimension of moral agency: not only on the spiritual act of faith itself, but also on 'the flesh and its possibilities'. 'Raised to the level' of belief in resurrection, faith transcends the natural possibilities of physical existence, so that self-protection and the protection of the race can never constitute autonomous foci of moral self-direction.

The giving of the Mosaic law is dependent, for Balthasar as for most twentieth-century exegesis, on the covenant-promise. 'The law "comes afterwards"', he writes, 'and does not make the situation of the promise "void"'. Law in no sense stands against promise, but expounds the ethics of faith, developing what Balthasar calls *Gesinnung*, a term current in German moral philosophy since Kant. Here we have a sharp problem of translation. English versions of German texts variously render *Gesinnung* as 'motive', 'intention' and 'disposition', all unsatisfactorily, or, at best, partially. The best way to grasp this term is as an equivalent of the Greek noun γνώμη, which in Hellenistic Greek means a resolution of principle, a decision that will govern an agent's subsequent intentions and actions. Balthasar refers to the law as revealing God's inner *Gesinnung* – God's foundational purpose – of 'deepening the response evoked by the covenant'. And the effect of this disclosure of divine purpose is to address the inner *Gesinnung* of humankind. God intends, in other words, not merely to get a reaction from us, but to form us as agents with a settled purpose, like himself, capable of sustaining through the vicissitudes of circumstance and intention an overriding purpose that corresponds to his. The Levitical formula, 'You shall be holy, for I am holy', expresses, he believes, this correspondence of *Gesinnung*.

The third major section takes us behind biblical revelation to elementary 'fragments' of pagan morality that were not developed by Israel's revelation. Here Balthasar locates (with an irony that should not be missed) two moral categories of great importance for Catholic theology: conscience and natural law. He also presents his most sustained polemic against modernity, although he is far from seeing that as any kind of simple reversion to the untaught innocence of paganism. The section as a whole, then, is headed 'extra-biblical ethics', and is meant, within the wider purpose of the text, as a critique of misguided Christian attempts to revert to naturalism, as well as of the post-Christian ethics of 'gnosis', a term which he uses to suggest something like our term 'scientism'.

Conscience and nature are the inner and the outer sides of the natural encounter of man with the world. Balthasar will not endorse the high claims sometimes made for conscience as 'the voice of God'. Moral conscience (*Gewissen*) is an aspect of ordinary human self-consciousness (*Selbstbewußtsein*). There is a world, and I dispose myself within it; these two things are given simultaneously in that consciousness to which, as Balthasar puts it, we 'awaken' when fellow humanity 'lovingly addresses' us. Human consciousness as such attests that freedom is not worldless, not solitary, but always embedded in reality and fellowship. To this extent, then, there is a natural recognition of moral light within the human creature: human nature is aware of its own freedom and conscious of being attracted to the unconditioned good. There can be no freedom that is not passive, i.e. receptive to this attraction of the good. That is what permits us to 'moralize' our sensual responses to nature, attaining a degree of conscious self-control which was classically called 'virtue' – the only reference in Balthasar to a category which played so large a part in the ethics of Thomas Aquinas. But virtue is no more than negative self-discipline, falling far short of the positive moral agency conferred on Abraham by the call of God.

Yet this basic orientation is not actual moral knowledge. It is striking how very freely, even wilfully, Balthasar handles Thomas's doctrine of natural law, minimizing his claims for *a priori* moral principles. 'Abstract formulations of the human orientation to the good as a "natural law" . . . are derivative' – in the sense, that is, that they are secondary constructs upon our perception of the anthropological reality, not axioms known *a priori*. Kant's 'categorical imperative' and Thomas' 'natural law' are both included in this judgement. There are, in fact, no *a priori* moral axioms. We can devise moral principles, but we are not born with them; they derive their force from prior convictions and are as true or as false as our convictions may be. Subjective recollections of the good 'must . . . keep their essentially relative character as a sign'. There is danger in 'rigidifying' conscience as a law-like principle, when it is only as good or as bad as the moral knowledge of those who experience it.

It is possible, of course, to add content to natural law from the observed regularities of non-human nature. For there really is a good that belongs to human nature, just as there are goods of other living things. It is partly social, partly individual, partly physical, partly intellectual. And there is scope for ordering moral action in the light of this purely anthropological criterion. But such a normative construct cannot accommodate radical human freedom, and when faced with the historical 'fact' of God's self-unveiling in biblical history, it 'collapses'. The question cannot be suppressed: what claim, after all, does this human nature and its regularities have upon me? At which point there is an eschatological parting of the ways: freedom may be accepted in humility as God's gift, or it may be asserted nihilistically in man's autonomous self-direction. Since Balthasar never admits that these 'law-like regularities' of the natural world attest the act of God in creation, the antithesis he sets up between natural order and historical revelation is very sharply defined.

With no safe space left for nature, we find the light of the Christ-event diffracted even through non-biblical religions. Anonymous Christianity is as real a possibility for Balthasar as it was for Rahner. But there is a difference: it is not an individual and hidden reality, but a perfectly evident one, seen in the influence of Christianity on other traditions of thought. Yet Christianity, confessed and anonymous, is not the only cultural reality. The demonic is also present and especially powerful on the Western ground once occupied by Christianity. With 'the biblical fact' raised to view, man can no longer sink back into naturalism, but is faced with the apocalypse of sin, ever more present. The final proposition, then, takes the description of post-Christian possibilities further.

An ethics shaped by Christ is a 'dialogue of human freedoms', that is to say, a reciprocal relation in which each individual agent's freedom is fulfilled in the freedom of the other or of the whole community. But if gratitude to God is not the primary act of freedom, there is no reason to find the freedom of others welcome, no reason to look for fulfilment in the freedom others enjoy. The agent thus faces the alternative, to enslave or be enslaved. Either I make the other's freedom serve my purposes, or I must suffer it as an imposition on my own freedom. Neither way leads to a 'synthesis' of individual and communal fulfilment. And so post-Christian ethics oscillates between an unfree collectivism and an egocentric liberalism, which accommodates community only through self-interested calculation. Balthasar has in view here the whole modern period of political theory from the seventeenth century on and follows a well-trodden path of criticizing 'contract' theories of society. 'Contract' does not amount to the reciprocity expressed in the Golden Rule; the mutuality it effects is that of hedgehogs making love, a 'calculated' strategy of cooperative self-enhancement. Philosophically, the same reduction of community is reflected in the so-called 'problem of other minds'. Privacy is unbreachable in the modern understanding of the self, so that ethics can have no place for genuine mutual regard.

The condition for a morally authoritative ethic, then, is the self-disclosure of a covenanting God in Christ. Balthasar finally makes this more specific: 'the conquest of death' is the only condition on which human existence can be thought of as at once truly free and truly socialized. It is an eschatological condition: God must be 'all in all'.

What is the special interest and originality of Balthasar's approach? Primarily and essentially it addresses the only question really worth asking about Christian ethics, which is how practical reason can be 'evangelical', shaped by good news. Or we might turn it round: how can a saving history yield a distinctive and authentic practical reason? To this question there has been a variety of answers that share a common approach: a salvific act of God may have *moral effects*, and the moral effects of Christ include the evangelical freedom and joy with which practical reason can be exercised. In Trinitarian terms, we might describe the approach as a moral pneumatology. Saving history having been accomplished, the Son of Man sits at the right hand of Majesty on high and pours forth his Spirit to enable his people to live and act in joyful freedom.

But Balthasar breaks with the underlying conception of Christian practical reason as the moral *effect*. Practical reason, and the ethics which reflects upon it, are themselves historicized. If our life in Christ *is* the gospel, not merely the corollary of the gospel, then a redeemed practical reason, and an ethics that reflects on a redeemed practical reason, must themselves form a saving history. Instead of saving history resetting the conditions of moral possibility, which are then (in the common phrase) 'lived out', saving history has the emergence of practical reason itself as its central narrative, a narrative that finds its concluding event in Christ. As a proposal for understanding Christian ethics, one might claim to trace this back to Barth; but where Barth stopped short, merely gesturing to a variety of possible programmes for Christian ethics, Balthasar develops the proposal by integrating the categories of ethics into Christology. If there is such a thing as a 'categorical imperative', a governing norm that subsumes all norms and maxims, and from which they all derive their moral authority, such a norm cannot be a *principle*, as Kant thought, but can only be a *person*, who emerged on the stage of history.

From the beginning of his first major work, *The Glory of the Lord*, Balthasar had maintained the thesis that the decisive event of saving history had to be a *form of beauty*, a shape given to things by the person of Christ. Now he allows that central Christological form to command our reflections on the life we lead. One's first thought might be that he is learning from Max Scheler's account of how we are transformed by following a moral exemplar. But for Balthasar it is important to say something stronger than that. Christ is not merely a model for us, not even a model whose life inspires not imitation but creative improvisation. He is the achievement of the climax of moral history, in whom, in one sense, 'everything is done already'. Practical reason must participate in the achievement. It may express itself in principles in order to facilitate moral deliberation, but practical reason is not essentially a principle, rather it is a concrete life actually lived and actually shared with disciples. Deliberation, then, is subordinated to the prior act of moral acknowledgement, which is to say, worship. The sequence of theoretical and practical propositions, 'God has acted *this* way, so that we may and must act *that* way', melts into the single proposition, 'God has so acted that acting in that way has come to be a historical reality in Christ'.

Yet the Christological reorientation of practical reason must not sub-
vert either its practical or its rational character. Norms are communicated
within human society through principles and rules. These instruct us in
the practical good in what Balthasar calls 'typical situations of incarnate,
socially conscious mind'. Some of them are widely shared and universal,
others are predicated on the life of the Church, which 'gives instructions'
meant to 'lead believers . . . to claim their true identity in freedom'. And
since these directive formulations, whether commonplace or churchly, are
not self-interpreting, their reasoned understanding and application always
remain something demanded of the agent in deliberation and decision.
Freedom is not freedom *from* ordinary practical consideration. So on the
surface nothing much may seem to have changed. But when it comes to
interpretation and authorization of moral rules, the fact that nothing is
self-evident and nothing rests solely on the posited authority of any institution, not even the Church, is critical. Universal moral meaning can only be
conferred by historical promise, and promise has to be found at the point
of history where it is given. The idea of 'natural law' is ahistorical and
therefore only a fragmentary conceptualization of the good. At each point
the believer may and must hold practical norms up to the authoritative light
shed on them by the narrative of Christ.

And here we can observe how far Balthasar transcended the internal
polemics that rent the Roman Catholic theological world after the Second
Vatican Council and pointed a way out of them. He found himself at one
with the conservative opposition to a Catholic humanism, which employed
the idea of natural law to secure a rapprochement with the modern world
and deny the Church a special competence in moral discussion. But, in the
broader picture, the sharpest edge of his critique fell directly upon poor Paul
VI and the arguments of *Humanae Vitae*, which offered no Christological
reflection at all. That the next major attempt by a pope to give universal
teaching on morality (18 years later, in 1992) presented its moral theory
through an extended expository discussion of Christ's encounter with the
rich young ruler, cannot be accidental.

It is impossible to read Balthasar's text without being struck by the very
strong claims it makes for moral evolution, not only within the bounds of
saving history, but extending it through the Christian mission to the assimilation of the ethics of other religions. Before Barth, Balthasar's major influence was Henri de Lubac, and Lubac was a friend and supporter of Pierre
Teilhard de Chardin. It is a typical mark of that inheritance to replace the
order of creation with quasi-Platonist ascending levels of being: inanimate,
organic, animal and spiritual. Behind it, we may discern a nineteenth-century
tradition (sometimes labelled 'post-millennialist') of understanding history
as the evolving spiritualization of creation, with Christendom as its social
and political embodiment. This gives us a perspective on a matter I find
troubling, the lack of an ethics of creation in Balthasar. Whereas natural
law survives, though in a secondary and derivative position, creation makes

no appearance. One might find this 'Barthian', though Barth, who devoted a whole volume of *Church Dogmatics* to the ethics of creation, was not 'Barthian' at this point. Balthasar is: ethics having become the inner meaning of saving history, Creation, the precondition of history, can no longer be for him the site of a disclosure of the good.

Yet we also find a strong countermovement; Balthasar's account of modernity is anything but progressivist. His apocalyptic account of the emergence of radical evil in the Western world, especially through the contractual or 'aggregative' theory of human society and the deconstructive influence of the human sciences, joins forces with a tradition of Catholic modernity-criticism which had become widely diffused across the philosophical spectrum by the post-Catholic Heidegger. In the modern world, he tells us, there are three alternatives for a post-Christian morality. It may ground itself on law, but apart from history and promise, that leads to pure abstraction. Every 'deontological' ethics, from Kant on, takes this line. The second alternative is the attempt to 'dissolve the law . . . in the flow of promise and hope', overcoming the abstract with the historical, making defiance of the past a fundamental project of human agency. Here belong the familiar teleological theories, the varieties of utilitarianism and post-Marxism, together with which Balthasar includes Freud. But this strategy depends entirely on its own self-generated hope, unrelated to actual history or to credible promise. These two modernist strategies are then combined in what Balthasar sees as a modern and atheistic version of Old Testament ethics, Marxism. Like the faith of ancient Israel, Marxism aims at a reconciliation of individual freedom and historical purposiveness, but cannot, as Israel could, count on the promise of the Spirit to realize the 'uniqueness' of each individual, so that it is condemned to allowing the collective a superior power and right. But this, Balthasar tells us, is what the Church ends up doing when it fails to be true to its vocation, which is to identify with Christ's sacrificial freedom. The Church may end up propounding the ethics of the Antichrist.

And this, perhaps, is what may surprise the unprepared reader most: Balthasar's framing of his critique of modernity with the theme of the Antichrist, accompanied, as in the Apocalypse, by its 'false prophet', the human sciences, 'self-authenticating and without love, claiming to be comprehensive'. The programme of bringing human undertakings, social and spiritual, within a value-free observer's view of the world as an ahistorical system involves, as Balthasar sees it, dissolving the actuality of God's love into a philosophical principle. The critique begins straightforwardly enough with the distinction between descriptive and normative discourse: observation of human life from a scientific distance may give 'valuable . . . insights', but cannot provide a reason *for* doing anything. A human science that accepted its limitations, and offered its observations as a contribution to a preliminary description, would be open to no more damning judgement than that of not answering questions it could not ask. But a deeper level of criticism is intended. Erich Voegelin and Hans Jonas, two philosophers in the Heideggerian school, had already drawn comparisons between modern scientism and ancient 'gnosis', the first heresy the Christian Church had to confront, and had found in the human sciences titanic pretensions to achieving a human self-knowledge by technological self-mastery. The Catholic autonomists, who had nothing but a liberal accommodation in view, offered a comparatively naive and un-titanic version of this heady project. But they sustained their social gospel by falling silent at precisely the decisive point, human mortality. They ignored the significance of the fact that the individual human always dies, which is to make any final reconciliation of the private and the common impossible. 'Life must go on' can only mean that *society* will conquer; *the individual* will die and be of no final account. The resurrection of Christ, Balthasar concludes, is 'the only place where the two lines converge'.

Note

1 Hans Urs von Balthasar, Joseph Ratzinger and Heinz Schürmann, *Prinzipien christlicher Moral* [Eng. *Principles of Christian Morality*] (Einsiedeln: Johannes-Verlag, 1975). There are two English translations, of which that by Graham Harrison (San Francisco: Ignatius Press, 1986) has had wider circulation. Neither seems to me to be wholly successful in capturing the thrust of the argument, so I depend here upon my own re-translation.

Knowing and Loving the Son of Man

Heaven in Ordinary

Because high heaven made itself so low
That I might glimpse it through a stable door,
Or hear it bless me through a hammer blow,
And call me through the voices of the poor,
Unbidden now, its hidden light breaks through
Amidst the clutter of the every day,
Illuminating things I thought I knew,
Whose dark glass brightens, even as I pray.

Then this world's walls no longer stay my eyes,
A veil is lifted likewise from my heart,
The moment holds me in its strange surprise,
The gates of paradise are drawn apart,
I see his tree, with blossom on its bough,
And nothing can be ordinary now.[1]

1 Originally published in Malcolm Guite, *After Prayer* (Norwich: Canterbury Press, 2019).

19

'On Christ, the solid rock, I stand'

ROWAN WILLIAMS

'From the beginning God has been God and God's own image of God.' That, you might say, is one way of rendering the very beginning of John's Gospel, a text to which we have returned again and again, predictably, in this collection of essays. And because God is God, God's own image of God is active and loving and intelligent because that is how God is. 'In the beginning was the Logos, and the Logos was with God, and what the Logos was was *God*'. From the very first verse of St John's Gospel we are alerted to the fact that this text is going to explore that place where the Logos eternally is. At the end of the first of the Pusey House conferences, 'A Transforming Vision' in 2016, and in the book that brought the lectures of that conference together, I reflected a little bit on how the doctrine of the Trinity was in a sense an answer to the question: Where are we? Where do we live, where do we stand, as Christian believers?[1]

And it's the same question, it seems, which we have come back to in this conference. 'Rabbi, where do you live?' the apostles ask Jesus in the first chapter of John. And we already know the answer. We know that the Logos is πρὸς τὸν θεόν, the Logos is eternally in relation to God. We know therefore that the Logos is εἰς τὸν κόλπον τοῦ πατρὸς, in the bosom of the Father. We know therefore that the Word made flesh, Jesus, is the one who lives in that eternal place where God's own image actively reflects back to God God's own superabundant love and glory. Through the Gospel we return more than once to these themes, the language of 'abiding in' that place which is the place of the Logos. It comes back in the Farewell Discourses: the beloved disciple nestling, ἐν τῷ κόλπῳ, in the bosom of Jesus at the Last Supper must be a further echo of the first chapter where the Logos, the Son, is in the bosom of the Father. So, when in chapter 12 Jesus promises that where he is, there his servant will be also, we have already the kernel of all that we can say about Christology. Thinking about Christology is thinking about that eternal place where God's image of God actively and lovingly reflects God – that place where *we* are called to live, where we are called to abide in the eternal abiding that belongs to the Word. But the first chapter of St John's Gospel tells us also that 'in the Logos all things were made', or that 'all things that were made came into being through the Logos', depending where you punctuate the Greek text. The point then is clear. That place where God's image of God actively and lovingly reflects

God is the place in which the world, all that is made, is to be found. There is a world *because* there is a place where God's glory is reflected – eternally, fully, ceaselessly reflected in the everlasting life of the Word, and somewhat more vulnerably and contingently reflected in the life of creation. But that's where creation is: in the Logos.

Why then is this story, the story of the Gospel, to be told? As John tells us, obliquely but vividly, in that first chapter, the world appears to be blind to where it lives. The world has failed to see what it is and where it belongs. The world, the creation, has, you could say, attempted to become something other than itself and so it has failed to be itself. And into that broken creation, that blinded world, the Word enters afresh. The Logos now coincides with something of the world; the Word was made flesh and dwelt among us. And by that coinciding and coming together of the infinite and the finite in Christ, the finite world recovers itself, finds again what it is meant to be, becomes gloriously and completely *creation* instead of trying to be God. It is as if only the Creator can be a perfect creature, and so restore creation to what it truly is and where it belongs. So this opening chapter of John has already told us three things: that God is God and is God's image of God; that all that is in the finite universe belongs in this reality, reflecting that reflection of God's overflowing glory; and that when creation, significantly in this part of it that we are most familiar with, turns away from its place and pretends not to be created but seeks to gain control of itself, then the healing presence of the Word comes to restore it – not to make it more than creation or less than creation, but to make it what it is: God's beloved making.

Within that framework, so much of what we have heard through the contributions to this book falls into place. Think first of all of some of those themes which were so very vividly expounded to us by Johannes Zachhuber. The intellectual problem of how to understand the relation between the individual and the determined process of history has something to do with this issue of the Word becoming flesh, because the 'becoming' flesh of the Logos in our midst is a wholly free and new act, so unexpected that it is unrecognizable to those who might most have been expected to recognize it. Yet at the same time it is an event which has been prepared for through the ages of prayer and reflection, of suffering and witness, exile and return, that have formed the history of Israel. And behind that in turn, it has been prepared for by the entire history of humankind. The Word becomes flesh, but not out of nowhere. The Word, in becoming flesh, takes a flesh that has been shaped by history, shaped by a tradition of speaking and imagining, and shaped in a much more literal sense by actually and physically inhabiting the body of a Jewish woman. In the womb of Mary, the Word first takes flesh, Jewish flesh, a flesh whose history has a particular form, a particular 'music' to it. So we see already, in reflecting on how the Word becomes flesh, how the act of God in our history occupies precisely that delicate, almost imperceptible borderland between process and freedom, between the causal nexus of the world and the unpredictable newness of what God alone can do.

To pursue this a little further: echoes will start in our minds of the way in which the life of Jesus and the record of his acts and sufferings acted as a kind of magnet for all of the images of God and God's action that had been around in the history out of which the incarnate Word comes. Both Tom Wright and John Behr have reminded us in great depth of the sheer range of story, metaphor, ritual, even – in the widest sense – myth, on which people drew to make sense of the Word incarnate. A Galilean artisan becomes someone described in terms of heavenly and angelic mythology, in terms of the ritual of the temple, of royalty and prophecy and so much more. As Tom Wright has reminded us in his chapter, recognizing the significance of these themes is an index of just how far we have come theologically in the last few decades. Like him, I was brought up in a theological milieu in which the default setting appeared to be that the story of Jesus had been variously improved and elaborated by the evangelists in order to make it fit with a set of pre-existing theological and mythological conceptualities. A great deal that we have encountered in these chapters should have made it clear that the truth is almost the exact opposite. A story so extraordinary, whose effects were so unpredictable, left the first believers reaching in every possible direction for every available bundle of the world's images they could lay their hands on. They were not particularly concerned to tie them all together in neat patterns. As has often been said, the writers of the New Testament (not knowing that they were writing 'the New Testament') have left us with what appears in many respects a conceptually chaotic picture. But what lies behind that is precisely a reality that exceeds the available structures and available images, not a reality that is being revised and trimmed in a sort of Procrustean manner to fit a set of pre-existing patterns. That richness of evocation, the density and plurality of resonance that the story of Jesus sets up in the imagination of his own Jewish people, is to be echoed, of course, generation after generation, in culture after culture, as the gospel spreads.

Turn back, then, for a moment to another aspect of this mystery of Incarnation. Jesus is who he is because Israel is what it is; and because Mary is who she is. So his human identity is *dependent* – not, as we have seen, a bolt from the blue, but something that is generated out of the world's processes. And Jesus' own life and ministry reflect a grateful and creative acknowledgement of that dependence without rebellion or resentment. Jesus, as we might put it very simply, does not 'mind' being Jewish, any more than he minds being human. He does not mind being someone who has inherited his identity as part of a tradition. In this respect, of course, as is evident throughout the Fourth Gospel, he shows himself yet again to occupy that almost imperceptible territory between the two options we sometimes think of as exclusive. He neither denies his *dependence* nor denies his *authority* and his freedom. He exercises his sovereign freedom in and out of the human dependence he is part of, the community he belongs to. He is not a solitary, temporary visitor, descended from heaven with lots of good advice and fine teaching, like the saviours of the Gnostic gospels. In Kierkegaard's memorable phrase, once he has decided on Incarnation he doesn't change his mind. He stays faithful to the form of human contingency that he has made his own. As John's Gospel above all shows us, Jesus lives out of and works out of the various dependences of his context and his tradition to do something radically new. And it is through this that we see him restoring the cosmos, the created order, to its proper place. So radical is the distortion of the created order in which we are all implicated that its restoration takes nothing less than Jesus' death. So deep is the wound that the physician dies of it. Only in the acceptance of the ultimate helplessness, the ultimate passivity that is death, does the presence of the Word in our midst bring God's action fully, healingly, into the world.

Moving on from this, the implication drawn out in many of the writers we have been hearing about is that, in some sense, the Word made flesh is the paradigm not only of human existence but of *created* existence. If one of the focal and central functions of creation is, as Robin Ward's French theologians argued, simply the adoration of the Creator, then the incarnate Christ, who as a creature fully and uninterruptedly perceives the glory of the Father, becomes the one who fulfils *creation*'s calling and destiny. Just as he is the one who fulfils the *human* destiny of taking the complex and tangled relations and destinies of human beings and bringing into them healing and reconciliation. Just as, within a more specifically Jewish context, Jesus is the one in whom the law is made not a set of rules or even a set of ideals but – thinking back to Oliver O'Donovan's exposition of Balthasar and 'Christ the concrete norm' – an utterly concrete inspiration, provocation and 'capacitation' of holy and reconciled life. Christ fulfils the human vocation and fulfils it, we believe, at every point in the incarnate life. And here is a very challenging doctrine to reflect on. Jesus is not the Word incarnate only at the 'interesting' or dramatic moments of his life; Jesus is the Word incarnate in the nine months of his habitation in the womb of Mary, back to where it all began. Jesus is the incarnate Word when he is sleeping in the boat on the stormy Sea of Galilee. And Jesus is the Word incarnate on Holy Saturday when he is a dead body in the tomb, an insight which one of the prayers of the Orthodox Liturgy makes very clear. How is this to be understood? Ian McFarland's chapter reflects on all of the complex conceptual tangles around the ideas of hypostasis and nature. Without going too deeply into those waters, we can at least say this: the individual human nature that was Jesus of Nazareth was and is finally what it is and was because of its unity with the second person of the Trinity. It would not *be* at all without that. And yet this union does not interrupt or break or lessen the humanity at all. What that means is that here is a human person, a member of the human race, whose deepest root of existence is divine personhood; and divine personhood is and is not like ours. It is important that it is *not* like ours in the sense that it, unlike us, is wholly open in communion. Divine personhood is not involved in the battles for territory that human persons get trapped in. We all tend to take for granted that for us to be ourselves it is necessary that somebody else be less than ourselves. Our world is routinely that competitive, struggling, mutually destructive environment which is the effect of creation's disorder and dislocation. But the way in which Christ is a person is a way which means that his human identity is, in every encounter and every relation into which it enters, a free embrace of communion, an offer of sharing if we are ready to accept it. Every relationship in which the incarnate Word is involved is charged with immeasurable potential *because of who Jesus is*. There is no limit to the relationships into which Jesus can enter with healing authority, and all of them have this potentially converting and transforming quality because there is in Jesus no self-defensiveness, no pulling back in fear or rivalry from the other, but only the utter self-bestowal and self-sharing that is the divine life. And so we can say that in the womb of Mary, asleep on the ship and, most boldly of all, as a dead body in the tomb, the sustaining, everlasting, personal reality of God the Word reaches out and opens out to whomever is around the promise of reconciliation and healing. This is what it means to believe that the Incarnation is not either an episodic series of events, where (as some careless theologians have implied) the divinity occasionally peeps out through the humanity at the more interesting points, or a single episode where the Word just takes flesh and then does fleshly things. Rather, at every moment in the incarnate life, from Conception to Holy Saturday and beyond, this humanity is soaked through with the hypostatic reality that is the Word of God, and therefore reaches out, opens the door into the divine life. And in the mystery of the resurrection, this divine life, humanly embodied in Jesus, becomes accessible to the entire human world. The apostles and evangelists go out in the rash, sublime confidence that wherever they go Jesus will make transforming sense for whatever human being they encounter. It is that confidence which grounds all our mission – now as then. This is how we attempt to keep our focus clear on the abiding significance of the particular humanity of Jesus. As we have been reminded several times, not least in Professor McFarland's chapter, we have to negotiate again and again the temptation to say, 'Well, we've gone beyond . . .', or 'we've gone past . . .' the stage of thinking about the Galilean artisan. The Galilean artisan has shown us what it is like for the finite and the infinite to coincide. In the ministry of healing and absolution, of prophetic release, of address to prisoners and captives and outsiders, Jesus has embodied what the radical welcome and love of the Trinity mean. We cannot give any shape to talking about the love of God unless we talk of love like that. And this is not just a matter of information, as we shall see in a moment; it is a matter of mapping the world we know we now inhabit, the place where we now live.

So far then, we have reflected on how the Prologue to John's Gospel sets out the broadest possible context of this 'map' of where we are. We have reflected on the way in which Christ incarnate can be seen as the one in whom the Jewish, the human and the created vocations all come together. We have seen something of what it might mean – to pick up a phrase Lydia Schumacher quoted – to say, *Homo omnis creatura*, the human is every creature. Human beings have a unifying, coordinating role in creation; Christ is the one who allows humanity to be what it is so that creation can be what it is. That early Franciscan vision has spoken eloquently to all of us of how all the themes we are considering belong together. But to move on again a little further, what the Word incarnate does in the ministry, the words, works and sufferings of Jesus, is to re-create *bonds* between creatures – what Lewis Ayres identified as the bonds that are both disrupting and unifying at the same time, the bonds that arise out of the deep disruption involved in the newness of Christ. Jesus has reconnected what has been broken; and in the immediate aftermath of the cross and resurrection, the disciples increasingly sense that all the divisions and the tensions belonging to the finite world are resolved and overcome in Jesus – the divisions between Jew and Gentile, and slave and free, and male and female. It is Maximus the Confessor, of course, who builds on this in his work towards the great synthesis centred upon the Logos who overcomes all the distances and differences between us. But more specifically, what Jesus does in reconnecting us to one another and to our created environment is to make a connected, historical, material community. The Church, you could say, does not begin simply at Pentecost. It does not even begin with the issue of blood from Christ's side on the cross, an image that has very properly resonated with many. It does not begin at the Last Supper. The Church begins with the very first moment where the Incarnate is in contact with another human being. The Church's birthday, we could say, is in fact 25 March, the Feast of the Annunciation. At the moment of conception, where the first human and material relationship in which the incarnate Word is involved comes to be, we see that the effect of the incarnate presence is connection, communion. What we are following through in the Gospel narrative and beyond is the gradual consolidation and expansion of that connectedness as the body establishes itself in the world and extends to the ends of creation. The body is the place where the fruition and fulfilment of creation is real. If Christ is the paradigm human and the paradigm creature, then Christ's continuing body on earth, 'Christ existing as community' in Dietrich Bonhoeffer's wonderful phrase, is where creation comes to itself. This sense of the reality of the body of Christ as abidingly Christ's identity in history is, we hardly need say, not easy to believe when we look at the way the Church actually is and behaves. We should have to say that it may be abidingly real, but it is somewhat sporadically *manifest*. Yet to believe in the Church at all is to believe, recalling a phrase that Paul Dominiak quoted from Richard Hooker, that Christ has truly decided *not to be without us* – and that therefore, whatever the appearances and whatever the likelihood, we may say that Christ is faithful in and to this, his body, because it is who and what he is here and now. Andrew Louth has reminded us eloquently of how all of this is in a sense a long gloss on the experience of the Eucharist itself, the Eucharist as the place where Christ is active, where Christ is actually here and now in the world's history, praying his prayer to the Father, offering himself, and *in* himself all humanity and all creation, to the Father. That is what happens at every Eucharist, and that is why at every Eucharist the end of time has indeed come: this is what creation should be, this is what humanity should be. This is where we belong. This is creation restored to its place, where the things of this world take on the quality of transfiguring divine gift, where – instead of relations of possession and manipulation towards the things of this world and to one another – all is gift, all is offering and all is prayer. This is where we learn who we are, and in what relation we stand: what we must realize in ourselves.

We have been brought back repeatedly in these discussions to reflection on Christ's body, and this is utterly right. We have not allowed ourselves in these reflections to think that Christology could ever be a set of speculations about somebody else and something distant. Thinking about Christology is thinking about *ourselves*, thinking about who and where we are. We do Christology because of this sense of *belonging somewhere new*. This is why reflection on the body, its nature and its calling, its worship and adoration, is utterly inseparable from the complexities of working out who Christ is, how we are to make sense of the Chalcedonian definition. And I think that the Fathers of Chalcedon would have been the first to allow that they were not trying to think about somebody else or something else.

Lewis Ayres's chapter poses questions about the place of the theologian, about who knows what in the Church. We know what we know in the Church because of where we stand. If we stand fully, confidently, properly in the place of humility, which is where we *must* stand in the Church, there are things we shall know that we will not otherwise know. And because Augustine has been quite rightly quoted in abundance in this book, I make no apology for turning to Augustine again for inspiration, this time to the Seventh Book of his *Confessions*, to that famous text where Augustine is describing his puzzles about Christology and concludes, 'I was not yet humble enough to know the humble Christ'.[2] He speaks, in one of his most unforgettable images, of how pride had made his face swell so much that his eyes were closed. So, he says, the only answer is to open your eyes to the Christ who is already lying at your feet, who has already been borne down by the weight of the suffering and sinning world; and you must cast yourself down upon him so that 'when He rises you will rise'. That is the knowledge of humility: the stooping to where Christ is. And that is why it is those who cast themselves down, who are cast down and understand what is happening, who know and love the Son of Man most effectively and most truly. Those who stand closest to or those most deeply rooted in the humility of the Word made flesh will know what no one else knows. They are the 'Spirituals', if you want to use such terms; and the saving grace is, of course, that they by definition do not know that they are. This is where the wisdom and insight of the martyr and the contemplative and, of course, the utterly unobtrusive and invisible saint of the Church become the central source of knowledge and illumination.

It is crucial that, as we think about the knowledge and understanding of the incarnate Word, we think – as we all can – of those we have known who would probably not have relished a theological conference very much, but nonetheless know how to 'relish' the Word of God, unobtrusively, in service and love and fidelity. For us who have some claim to intellectual interest, it is essential to learn to say this without even a touch of the patronizing. Tempting to say, 'Of course they know so much more than we do', and not really mean it. But we had better mean it. What you and I do not know we fail to know because, like Augustine, we cannot see properly out of our swollen eyes. We have not yet cast ourselves down. To pick up a question that came up in discussion about the knowledge of those who are 'cast down' – what James Alison calls 'the intelligence of the victim', and what some other theologians speak of in terms of what the poor know – this is something to which the Church continually needs to attend, and to attend not in its own preferred intellectual and conceptual terms, but just to *attend*. Years ago, I heard a rather celebrated theologian saying that we ought to do theology out of the experience of the poor; and someone else pointed out rather sharply that theologians 'borrowing' the experience of the poor in order to do theology was not quite what the 'option for the poor' meant. The poor had little enough already, said this critic; if theologians came and took their experience away as well, this was not particularly good news. This is one aspect of what I mean by the temptation to be patronizing and manipulative in our recognition of what the (apparent) non-theologian knows. We actually do need to listen, to learn and to be aware of the extraordinary intermingling, interfusing, of gifts, visions, charisms and voices in the Church that allows mutual learning genuinely to happen and reminds us all the time that (to return again to some insights in these chapters), the voice of the Word is something more than just the words we utter. Carol Harrison's superb meditation on 'Sound and Silence' brings this very clearly into focus for us. The voice is what we listen for. *Words* we negotiate and worry about, and we who like to think of ourselves as intellectuals make a good deal of them. It is not wicked or time-wasting. But what we have to listen for is the *voice*.

Once again, when we talk about humility as the locus for our thinking and acting, we are brought back to the pervasive sense that we have to learn to be creaturely, to be dependent, to be continually learning and growing *in the body*. Because the whole point of the body – as St Paul puts the image before us – is not that any part of it has arrived at its perfect form, but that we are all together becoming not only the body as a whole but the specific organ that we are – becoming the gift that we are, because of the gift of the other. It is in this becoming what we are because of the becoming of the gift of the other, that the body finds its lived coherence, and we need to 'abide' patiently in daily participation in the common life for that mutuality of learning and growing. One implication of this is that, in Christ, the gift we receive is the fullness of who we are not only as human beings in general but as persons in particular. The gift I receive in the body is the gift of the freedom to be the person in communion God has made me to be. And so when (to take up some thoughts that Andrew Louth sketched out – tantalizingly briefly) we consider that the gift we are receiving is this gift of becoming ourselves in Christ, we realize that the self we are called to love is *the self in Christ*. We learn to love ourselves *in* the community – to love, that is, the self that is freed from fear and rivalry and corruption and deceit. Likewise, to love our neighbours as ourselves in Christ is to love in the other the work of Christ in them. That is not, I hasten to add, to say we 'just' love the work of Christ in us or in them and ignore all the specific features and peculiarities that we have in addition to that. It is to see them with all those features as being worked through by Christ, just as all my own distinctive features are (I pray) being worked through by Christ. I love my neighbour as myself, or try to, because the self I love is a self which I know in all its frailty and sinfulness is being worked with by the Word incarnate and the Holy Spirit to become what it can be. And when I look at my neighbour that is what I strive to see – not the dangerous rival who will infringe on my territory, not the one who will succeed at my expense or at whose expense I must succeed, but the one whose gift to me and to others is steadily being refined by the faithful presence of the incarnate Word. To know the Son of Man and to love the Son of Man in myself and in my neighbour is the expression, the immediate expression, of this reality that is the body.

Recall again the phrase that Paul Dominiak reminded us of from Hooker, about Christ not willing to be without us and about each being 'in the possession' of the other in the relation between Christ and ourselves. It means that what we know in communion is the absolute kenotic love, the absolute self-emptying love that is the Word's eternal characteristic in the divine life. So, when we are called to love in the Church, we are quite simply called to love *whom and what Christ loves*, because the body cannot do either more or less than that. If we are truly his Church, the body of Christ, we love what Christ loves, no more, no less. And we love our neighbour as our self because we see our self as being transfigured in the life of the body by the exchange of gifts, and we know that those gifts are being refined and matured in one another. In his description of different models of salvation in Christ, Bishop Kallistos shows how the focus on kenotic love dissolves many of the conceptual tangles that attend various models and theories of the Atonement, and this is indeed where we finally 'come home', as we might say, back to where we started. God is eternally God and God's own image of God. God's eternal, outpouring, unrestrained love finds its image in the unrestrained outpouring of love. All that God does is this. And God – if I can speak with a touch of theological recklessness – really 'cannot' do anything other. This is God's utter freedom and, as some have said, God's utter poverty paradoxically standing inseparably together. God does not have a set of options from which God can select how to be or what to do. We, who love choices, might be tempted to tut and shake our heads, 'How unfortunate for God. And how very lucky for God that he had the opportunity of becoming incarnate, acquiring all sorts of experiences he wouldn't otherwise have had.' That does seem to me to be the very opposite of theology. Theology rejoices in this divine 'poverty'. It rejoices in the fact that God cannot be other than the God who *is*, who is perfectly imaged in the Word and who pours out the divine life in the Spirit which conforms us to the Word. That is the mystery by which we live in the richness, the simplicity and the infinite wealth of God's being. This defines the place where we take our stand.

At the conference, Bishop Kallistos movingly referred to his nanny's deathbed and the simple words she spoke, 'The blood of Christ cleanses from all sin.' The simplicity of the trust in Christ that we are encouraged to live into is a simplicity that has finally to be captured in the simplest of words. I have been reflecting a good deal here on the 'place' we are called to occupy, that place which is the Word's place in the bosom of the Father, the place where the whole world finds itself naturally and supernaturally, where the whole world is pulled together, remade, re-created. These are enormous subjects to reflect on, which will take us the rest of our lives even to begin to make sense of, or to give thanks for. So I think the best way I can conclude is with two lines, which some of you may conceivably remember from Sunday School, nearly all of them monosyllables. Only three words of more than one syllable here because this, I think, sums up where we are, who we are, how we look, how we see from where we are the love that moves us and defines us:

On Christ, the solid rock, I stand;
All other ground is sinking sand.
All other ground is sinking sand.

Notes

1 See Rowan Williams, 'Conclusion: Knowing and Loving the Triune God', in *A Transforming Vision: Knowing and Love the Triune God* (London: SCM Press, 2018), pp. 232–3.

2 *Confessions* VII.18.

20

The Shape of Hope, a Sermon

ANTHONY BURTON

Evensong at the conclusion of the *Totus Christus* Conference
Pusey House, 11 July 2018

We celebrate this afternoon the Feast of St Benedict of Nursia, 'the Father of Western Monasticism'. This title could be misleading in that Benedict, who was born in the year 480, was in fact a product of the Western monastic tradition, which had been established more than a century earlier – by among others St Martin of Tours, who established Ligugé Abbey about 370, and St Augustine of Hippo, who had established a monastic community in Roman North Africa. The title stuck to Benedict, however, owing to the extensive use of Benedict's *Rule* in the West. More than any other document, his *Rule* served as a bridge from the Eastern monastic tradition to medieval Europe. Its influence is very much with us today.

Henry Chadwick dryly defined a saint as 'a person whose life has been under-researched'. Fortunately for us, St Benedict was blessed with the most distinguished of biographers in the person of St Gregory the Great who was a dutiful researcher, tracking down those of Benedict's friends who survived him 50 years after his death to ascertain the facts. This afternoon I would like us to think about these two saints – Benedict and Gregory – together.

Gregory had no interest in biography as we think of it today. What mattered about a life was its holiness; the true subject of any written life was God. Gregory's biography of Benedict is a collection of stories ('flowers' he called them), evidences of God's work in Benedict's life, colourfully described as a continual contest between good and evil:

- A jealous priest poisons Benedict's bread, but a companionable raven swoops down at the last moment to fly off with the loaf.
- Seditious monks poison their abbot's wine, but when Benedict says grace over the meal, his chalice shatters into pieces, exposing the plot.
- As Benedict has a Temple of Apollo and its grove of sacred trees demolished to build a church on the site, the resident demon appears breathing fire: 'You are Maledict not Benedict', says the demon.

Gregory was much less interested in Benedict's career or posthumous impact than the miracle stories. Why? Gregory doesn't want the reader to think 'what a great man!' but 'what a great God!' And with a God like that you can become a saint too.

To get a sense of the timeline of Benedict's life, we have to sift a bit. The Benedict we know by the accounts of his friends, and as the author of the *Rule*, is the man in his maturity – endlessly charitable, forgiving, sympathetic, balanced, humane, deeply and charismatically holy with a gift for friendship. He seems to have been much like the ideal abbot he describes in the *Rule*: a tender father and a strict teacher (cf. 2, 24), a true educator. Inflexible against vices, the abbot, Benedict writes, is nevertheless called above all to imitate the tenderness of the Good Shepherd (27, 8), to 'serve rather than to rule' (64, 8) in order 'to show them all what is good and holy by his deeds more than by his words'.[1]

Yet the beauty of Benedict's mature personality was hard won, the fruit of much struggle. As a young man he seems to have been a brittle, somewhat priggish character, given to extremes: not the portrait of *stabilitas* he later became. There is a tendency today to confuse holiness with wholeness – but history is full of unbalanced characters whose sanctity was nonetheless beyond dispute. In the history of the Church, not every stylite or hermit was naturally fitted to be a deputy minister. But Benedict inspires us in part because he demonstrably became more Christlike over time.

To begin at the beginning, Benedict was sent by his wealthy family to Rome for his education. He didn't fit in with the other students and reacted against their partying lifestyle. He fled the city for a country village where he met a monk, Romanus of Subiaco, who encouraged him to become a cave-dwelling hermit. (Perhaps Romanus thought Benedict needed to sort himself out.) Benedict then spent three years in his cave, almost entirely alone, brought food by Romanus.

Like Christ in the desert, Benedict is tested in isolation, in prayer, in hardship. He came to understand himself and how he related to other people. By God's grace, Benedict came to master the fundamental temptations common to us all – the temptations to self-centredness, to lust, to anger and revenge.

When the abbot of the local monastery died, the monks begged Benedict to be their abbot, but it was not a success; it was here that his monks attempted to poison him, which Benedict took as a sign to move on. His response to this debacle? Did he retire to his cave? No, he simply took up another ministry. Benedict's organizational gifts came to the fore as he began the work of founding monasteries. He founded 12 of them locally before founding the great monastery of Monte Cassino on a hilltop between Rome and Naples, where he died, in his mid-sixties, of fever.

Allow me to return to the biographer for a moment. It is not difficult to imagine why Gregory, another contemplative called out into the active service of the Church – who had to reconcile a contemplative life with an active one – was attracted to the example of Benedict. I suppose it is never a good time to be pope, but this was Gregory's lot, described by one of his biographers:

On one side the swords of the barbarians hemmed him in, on the other he was exposed to the unscrupulous animosity of Imperial officials. Few sympathized with him, hardly any understood him.

Amid starving people, mutinous soldiers, greedy officials, intriguing bishops, untrustworthy agents, in the ruined capital of a desolated country he stood alone, without support save in his conscience and his God.[2]

How to reconcile an active life with a contemplative one? In this evening's Second Lesson, we have the story of Jesus visiting the home of Martha and Mary. Mary sits at Jesus' feet, listening to him, as Martha is busy in the kitchen preparing dinner. Exasperated, Martha asks Jesus to make Mary get up and help. Jesus replies, 'Martha, Martha, you are anxious and troubled about many things, but one thing is necessary. Mary has chosen the good portion, which will not be taken away from her.' Mary here is sometimes seen as the symbol of the contemplative and Martha of the active life – one good, the other bad – as opposites we must choose between. But this isn't quite right. Jesus' point is about setting priorities, of putting the life of contemplation and prayer first, of ordering the practical to the spiritual rather than the other way around. 'The good portion' is not the only portion. Benedict's *Rule* speaks directly to this. The *Rule* is much more than a handbook of practical community management. It is about an ordered spiritual life, *ora et labora*, in which first things are put first. The *Rule* was written to help its followers grow in holiness.

The fact that the *Rule* never goes out of print shows how profound its impact continues to be, not just within religious communities but among individuals. Benedict is very much with us today. Indeed, since Alasdair MacIntyre coined the phrase, there has been much discussion of 'Benedict options', of how Christian communities might, in the providence of God, play a role in the renewal of Western culture. No doubt that work of renewal will necessarily take many forms – and the conference we now conclude is surely one of them. What a delight it has been these last three days to be part of such a remarkable and diverse gathering – some of us in the autumn of our scholarly and pastoral careers, others just starting out – but each engaged in just such work of renewal.

Benedict and Gregory stand before us still, like signposts to the future, directing our attention up as well as back. They did this by pointing out the strange ways in which entirely separate, parallel universes exist beside one another and yet interact[3] – keeping an eye out, if you like, for the 'flowers'. Despite all they went through, Benedict and Gregory disdained to be discouraged. What was their secret? The Venerable Bede tells us that Gregory, 'amid the incessant battering of worldly cares', strove to be 'fastened, as by the cable of an anchor, to the peaceful shore of prayer'.[4] In the midst of our own busy lives, may we likewise remain anchored to that peaceful shore, as we press forward in the great work of renewal in our own generation.

Notes

1 Benedict XVI, General Audience, Wednesday 9 April 2008, St. Peter's Square, < http://w2.vatican.va/content/benedict-xvi/en/audiences/2008/documents/hf_ben-xvi_aud_20080409.html> [accessed 19 May 2019].

2 F. Homes Dudden, *Gregory the Great: His Place in History and Thought*, vol. 2 (New York: Longmans, Green, and Co., 1905) p. 281, quoted in Robert D. Crouse, 'Feed My Sheep: The Consecration of a Bishop', preached at Sacred Heart Cathedral, St. Luke's Day, 1993, <http://www.stpeter.org/crouse/sermons/occ_consecration.htm> [accessed 19 May 2019].

3 Colin Starnes, *Memoir of Robert Crouse* (unpublished).

4 *Historia ecclesiastica gentis Anglorum*, II, I, quoted in Crouse, 'Feed My Sheep'.

Acknowledgements of Sources

The publisher acknowledges with thanks permission to use material under copyright from the following publications.

'Reason', C. S. Lewis, in Walter Hooper, ed., *The Collected Poems of C. S. Lewis* (Fount, 1994).

'Digging' and 'Bone Dreams', Seamus Heaney, in *Opened Ground* (Faber & Faber, 1998). Reprinted by permission of Faber & Faber Ltd.

The Festal Menaion, trans. by Mother Mary and Archimandrite Kallistos Ware (Faber & Faber, 1969). Reprinted by permission of Faber & Faber Ltd.

'East Coker', T. S. Eliot, in *Four Quartets* (Faber & Faber, 2001). Reprinted by permission of Faber & Faber Ltd.

Index of Biblical References

Index of Names and Subjects